STOCK
TRADER'S
ALMANAC
2012

Jeffrey A. Hirsch & Yale Hirsch

WILEY

John Wiley & Sons, Inc.

www.stocktradersalmanac.com

Published by John Wiley & Sons, Inc., Hoboken, New Jersey
Published simultaneously in Canada

Editor in Chief	Jeffrey A. Hirsch
Editor at Large	Yale Hirsch
Director of Research	Christopher Mistal
Graphic Design	Darlene Dion Design

For general information about our other products and services, please contact our Customer Care Department within the United States at 800-762-2974, outside the United States at 317-572-3993 or fax 317-572-4002.

Wiley also publishes its books in a variety of electronic formats. Some content that appears in print may not be available in electronic books. For more information about Wiley products, visit our Web site at www.wiley.com.

ISBN 13: 978-1-118-04869-6
10 9 8 7 6 5 4 3 2 1

Printed in China

This Forty-Fifth Edition is respectfully dedicated to:

Bill Staton

Investment strategies come and go, but the results of Bill Staton's philosophy, investment methodology, and America's Finest Companies® (AFC) have not wavered. Bill has been through all types of markets over the last four decades. His system was forged at the depths of the stagflation, economic malaise, and market morass of the 1970s—and is rock-solid because of it. Since the early 1990s, Bill has written for our newsletters and, thankfully, continues to do so. It has been a pleasure editing Bill's snappy, sometimes down-home, but always entertaining style. He has taught us some new things, reminded us of and reinforced some old ones, provided some great new quotations and ideas for the *Almanac*, and made us laugh out loud. His Baker's Dozen Guided Portfolio® of 13 of his favorite stocks has gained over 25% annually since inception on June 18, 2000, while the broad market has gone virtually nowhere. His latest book *Double Your Money in America's Finest Companies®: The Unbeatable Power of Rising Dividends* was the first installment in our *Almanac Investor* book series. For 19 years, Staton produced his annual directory of America's Finest Companies®. In *Double Your Money*, Bill Staton's simple, do-it-yourself AFC system is revealed and explained with clear step-by-step instructions. His current database of America's Finest Companies® is now kept proprietary for exclusive use in managing the assets of Staton Financial clients (www.statonfinancial.com).

INTRODUCTION TO THE FORTY-FIFTH EDITION

We are pleased and proud to introduce the Forty-Fifth Edition of the *Stock Trader's Almanac*. The *Almanac* provides you with the necessary tools to invest successfully in the twenty-first century.

J. P. Morgan's classic retort, "Stocks will fluctuate," is often quoted with a wink-of-the-eye implication that the only prediction one can make about the stock market is that it will go up, down, or sideways. Many investors agree that no one ever really knows which way the market will move. Nothing could be further from the truth.

We discovered that while stocks do indeed fluctuate, they do so in well-defined, often predictable patterns. These patterns recur too frequently to be the result of chance or coincidence. How else do we explain that since 1950 all the gains in the market were made during November through April, compared to a loss May through October? (See page 48.)

The *Almanac* is a practical investment tool. It alerts you to those little-known market patterns and tendencies on which shrewd professionals enhance profit potential. You will be able to forecast market trends with accuracy and confidence when you use the *Almanac* to help you understand:

- How our presidential elections affect the economy and the stock market—just as the moon affects the tides. Many investors have made fortunes following the political cycle. You can be sure that money managers who control billions of dollars are also political cycle watchers. Astute people do not ignore a pattern that has been working effectively throughout most of our economic history.

- How the passage of the Twentieth Amendment to the Constitution fathered the January Barometer. This barometer has an outstanding record for predicting the general course of the stock market each year, with only seven major errors since 1950, for a 88.5% accuracy ratio. (See page 16.)

- Why there is a significant market bias at certain times of the day, week, month, and year.

Even if you are an investor who pays scant attention to cycles, indicators, and patterns, your investment survival could hinge on your interpretation of one of the recurring patterns found within these pages. One of the most intriguing and important patterns is the symbiotic relationship between Washington and Wall Street. Aside from the potential profitability in seasonal patterns, there's the pure joy of seeing the market very often do just what you expected.

The *Stock Trader's Almanac* is also an organizer. Its wealth of information is presented on a calendar basis. The *Almanac* puts investing in a business framework and makes investing easier because it:

- Updates investment knowledge and informs you of new techniques and tools.
- Is a monthly reminder and refresher course.
- Alerts you to both seasonal opportunities and dangers.
- Furnishes a historical viewpoint by providing pertinent statistics on past market performance.
- Supplies forms necessary for portfolio planning, record keeping, and tax preparation.

 The WITCH icon signifies THIRD FRIDAY OF THE MONTH on calendar pages and alerts you to extraordinary volatility due to the expiration of equity and index options and index futures contracts. Triple-witching days appear during March, June, September, and December.

 The BULL icon on calendar pages signifies favorable trading days based on the S&P 500 rising 60% or more of the time on a particular trading day during the 21-year period January 1990 to December 2010.

 A BEAR icon on calendar pages signifies unfavorable trading days based on the S&P falling 60% or more of the time for the same 21-year period.

Also, to give you even greater perspective, we have listed next to the date of every day that the market is open the Market Probability numbers for the same 21-year period for the Dow (D), S&P 500 (S) and NASDAQ (N). You will see a "D," "S," and "N" followed by a number signifying the actual Market Probability number for that trading day, based on the recent 21-year period. On pages 121–128 you will find complete Market Probability Calendars, both long-term and 21-year for the Dow, S&P, and NASDAQ, as well as for the Russell 1000 and Russell 2000 indices.

Other seasonalities near the ends, beginnings, and middles of months—options expirations, around holidays, and other significant times—as well as all FOMC Meeting dates are noted for *Almanac* investors' convenience on the weekly planner pages. All other important economic releases are provided in the Strategy Calendar every month in our e-newsletter, *Almanac Investor*, available at our website *www.stocktradersalmanac.com*.

As a reminder to long time *Almanac* readers, the ten years of monthly Daily Dow Point Changes have moved from their respective *Almanac* pages to the Databank section toward the rear of this book. We continue to rely on the clarity of this presentation to observe market tendencies. In response to newsletter subscriber feedback, we include our well-received Monthly Vital Stats on the *Almanac* pages.

The Year in Review on page 6 provides a handy list of major events of the past year that can be helpful when evaluating things that may have moved the market. Over the past few years, our research had been restructured to flow better with the rhythm of the year. This has also allowed us more room for added data. Again, we have included historical data on the Russell 1000 and Russell 2000 indices. The Russell 2K is an excellent proxy for small and mid caps, which we have used over the years, and the Russell 1K provides a broader view of large caps. Annual highs and lows for all five indices covered in the *Almanac* appear on pages 149–151. We've tweaked the Best & Worst section and "Option Trading Codes" appear on page 190.

In order to cram in all the new material, we had to cut some of our Record Keeping section. We have converted many of these paper forms into computer spreadsheets for our own internal use. As a service to our faithful readers, we are making these forms available at our website *www.stocktradersalmanac.com*.

Presidential election year perspectives are summarized on page 24. There have been only two losses in the last seven months of election years since 1950 (page 52). The first five months of election years are better when the incumbent party retains the White House. War can be a major factor in presidential races, but homeland issues dominated elections the last three decades. As was the case in 2009, market bottoms often occur within two years after a change in presidential party. As shown in the table on page 24, there have been only six election year declines greater than 5% since 1896. We discuss how the government manipulates the economy to stay in power on page 34 and the difference in market behavior during incumbent victories and defeats on page 38. "Market Charts of Presidential Election Years" on page 28 provides a view of the last 21 election years at a glance. Second years have been the fourth worst year in the decennial cycle for 130 years, but better when they are also election years since 1932 (pages 26 and 129). A more significant correction in 2011 increases the potential for greater gains in 2012.

Sector seasonalities were revamped last year to include several consistent shorting opportunities, moved to pages 92–96 and expanded to three pages. In response to many reader inquiries about how and what to trade when implementing the Best Months Switching Strategies, we detail some simple techniques, including a sampling of tradable mutual funds and ETFs on page 32. As a follow up to our projection for the Next Super Boom to start in 2017 and carry the Dow up 500% to 38,820 by 2025 that appeared on page 36 of the *2011 Almanac*, we offer our Fifteen Year Projection for the Dow on page 74.

We are constantly searching for new insights and nuances about the stock market and welcome any suggestions from our readers.

Have a healthy and prosperous 2012!

NOTABLE EVENTS

2010

May 14	Space Shuttle Atlantis departs on final mission
May 31	9 Activists killed crashing Gaza blockade
Jun 3	FSA fines JPMorgan $48.2 million
Jun 9	UN Imposes 4th round of sanctions against Iran
Jun 11	2010 FIFA World Cup Begins in South Africa
Jul 15	Goldman Sachs fined $550 million by SEC
Aug 27	Fed Chair Bernanke outlines further quantitative monetary easing (QE2)
Sep 19	Gulf of Mexico oil spill stopped
Sep 30	Federal Budget Deficit $1.3 trillion, 2nd highest
Oct 15	Social Security COLA is zero, 2nd year in-a-row
Nov 2	Republicans take House in midterm election
Nov 3	QE2 officially announced by Fed
Nov 23	North Korea shells South Korean island
Nov 24	Ireland receives €85 billion rescue package
Dec 17	Bush tax cuts extended
Dec 18	Arab Spring begins in Tunisia

2011

Jan 14	Zine El Abidine Ben Ali of Tunisian deposed
Jan 27	Over 16K demonstrate in Sana'a, Yemen
Jan 27	Amidst turmoil, Egyptian stock market closes
Feb 11	Egyptian president Hosni Mubarak ousted
Feb 15	Civil war breaks out in Libya
Mar 11	9.0 earthquake and tsunami strike Japan, causing Fukushima Daiichi nuclear disaster
Mar 14	Saudi Arabia sends troops to Bahrain to quell protests
Mar 17	UN authorizes force to protect Libyan civilians
Mar 23	Egyptian stock market resumes trading, -8.9%
Apr 28	Silver trades at $48.97
Apr 29	Royal Wedding of Prince William and Catherine Middleton
May 1	Osama bin Laden killed
May 2	Gold trades to new all-time high of $1557.10
May 2	Air France Flight 447 flight recorders recovered
May 14	Morganza Spillway opened to control Mississippi flooding, only second time in history
May 16	Federal government reaches debt limit of $14.294 trillion
May 16	Portugal receives €78 billion rescue package
May 19	LinkedIn IPO more than doubles 1st day
May 21	Erupting Iceland volcano threatens EU airspace
May 25	Supreme Court orders California to reduce prison population
May 26	Bosnian Serb Army Commander Ratko Mladic arrested

2012 OUTLOOK

2008's 33.8% Dow loss was the worst election year decline since 1932 at the outset of the Depression and the first double digit election year loss since war-torn 1940. Four other down election years in the 17 since 1940 have suffered relatively mild declines for the Dow: 1948 (-2.1%, Truman upsets Dewey), 1960 (-9.3%, Russia/Cuba/Cold War), 1984 (-3.7%, AT&T breakup/Continental Illinois bailout), 2000 (-6.2%, Tech bubble popped). Over the last thirteen decades, "second" years' small average Dow gain of 1.8% ranks seventh. Election "second" years since 1932 fared well in 1952, 1972 and 1992.

President Obama's first two and a half years were accompanied by dynamic stock market moves and a heated political environment. After a major bear market bottom in his first 100 days the Dow is up 95.7% at the recent high. His low presidential approval ratings have recently been improving, helped by the killing of Osama bin Laden. Republicans have yet to mount a formidable challenger for the 2012 presidential election. The stock market has performed better in election years when strong incumbent presidents were running for reelection.

At press time, the Dow is up 32.3% from its 2010 midterm year low to the 2011 pre-election year high to date, about two-thirds of the average 50% gain since 1914. The bull market is currently under pressure from a slowing economic recovery; financial and debt concerns overseas; economic fallout from the Japanese earthquake, tsunami, and nuclear crisis; geopolitical worries with respect to the Arab Spring and elsewhere; mounting U.S. federal deficits; and the political battles ahead of the election.

The Dow is on the precipice of a substantial correction that in a bad case scenario could bring it back to 10,000 before yearend 2011. A steeper decline in 2011 would increase the prospects for greater gains in 2012. If Obama can lead from the bully pulpit, forcing Republicans to compromise on key issues, and engineer more diplomatic successes, he will be hard to beat in 2012; and the stock market is likely to perform better—as long as the Fed keeps the money flowing and rates low.

— *Jeffrey A. Hirsch, June 1, 2011*

THE 2012 STOCK TRADER'S ALMANAC

CONTENTS

DIRECTORY OF TRADING PATTERNS AND DATABANK

STRATEGY PLANNING AND RECORD SECTION

2012 STRATEGY CALENDAR

(Option expiration dates circled)

	MONDAY	TUESDAY	WEDNESDAY	THURSDAY	FRIDAY	SATURDAY	SUNDAY
JANUARY	26	27	28	29	30	31	1 JANUARY New Year's Day
	2	3	4	5	6	7	8
	9	10	11	12	13	14	15
	16 Martin Luther King Day	17	18	19	(20)	21	22
	23	24	25	26	27	28	29
FEBRUARY	30	31	1 FEBRUARY	2	3	4	5
	6	7	8	9	10	11	12
	13	14 ♥	15	16	(17)	18	19
	20 Presidents' Day	21	22 Ash Wednesday	23	24	25	26
MARCH	27	28	29	1 MARCH	2	3	4
	5	6	7	8	9	10	11 Daylight Saving Time Begins
	12	13	14	15	(16)	17 St. Patrick's Day ♣	18
	19	20	21	22	23	24	25
APRIL	26	27	28	29	30	31	1 APRIL
	2	3	4	5	6 Good Friday	7 Passover	8 Easter
	9	10	11	12	13	14	15
	16 Tax Deadline	17	18	19	(20)	21	22
MAY	23	24	25	26	27	28	29
	30	1 MAY	2	3	4	5	6
	7	8	9	10	11	12	13 Mother's Day
	14	15	16	17	(18)	19	20
	21	22	23	24	25	26	27
JUNE	28 Memorial Day	29	30	31	1 JUNE	2	3
	4	5	6	7	8	9	10
	11	12	13	14	(15)	16	17 Father's Day
	18	19	20	21	22	23	24
	25	26	27	28	29	30	1 JULY

10   *Market closed on shaded weekdays; closes early when half-shaded.*

2012 STRATEGY CALENDAR
(Option expiration dates circled)

MONDAY	TUESDAY	WEDNESDAY	THURSDAY	FRIDAY	SATURDAY	SUNDAY	
2	3	4 *Independence Day*	5	6	7	8	JULY
9	10	11	12	13	14	15	
16	17	18	19	(20)	21	22	
23	24	25	26	27	28	29	
30	31	1 AUGUST	2	3	4	5	
6	7	8	9	10	11	12	AUGUST
13	14	15	16	(17)	18	19	
20	21	22	23	24	25	26	
27	28	29	30	31	1 SEPTEMBER	2	
3 *Labor Day*	4	5	6	7	8	9	SEPTEMBER
10	11	12	13	14	15	16	
17 *Rosh Hashanah*	18	19	20	(21)	22	23	
24	25	26 *Yom Kippur*	27	28	29	30	
1 OCTOBER	2	3	4	5	6	7	OCTOBER
8 *Columbus Day*	9	10	11	12	13	14	
15	16	17	18	(19)	20	21	
22	23	24	25	26	27	28	
29	30	31 🎃	1 NOVEMBER	2	3	4 *Daylight Saving Time Ends*	NOVEMBER
5	6 *Election Day*	7	8	9	10	11 *Veterans' Day*	
12	13	14	15	(16)	17	18	
19	20	21	22 *Thanksgiving*	23	24	25	
26	27	28	29	30	1 DECEMBER	2	
3	4	5	6	7	8	9 *Chanukah*	DECEMBER
10	11	12	13	14	15	16	
17	18	19	20	(21)	22	23	
24	25 *Christmas*	26	27	28	29	30	
31	1 JANUARY *New Year's Day*	2	3	4	5	6	

JANUARY ALMANAC

JANUARY								FEBRUARY					
S	M	T	W	T	F	S		S	M	T	W	T	F	S
1	2	3	4	5	6	7					1	2	3	4
8	9	10	11	12	13	14		5	6	7	8	9	10	11
15	16	17	18	19	20	21		12	13	14	15	16	17	18
22	23	24	25	26	27	28		19	20	21	22	23	24	25
29	30	31						26	27	28	29			

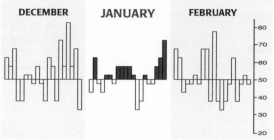

Market Probability Chart above is a graphic representation of the S&P 500 Recent Market Probability Calendar on page 124.

◆ January Barometer predicts year's course with .770 batting average (page 16) ◆ 11 of last 15 presidential election years followed January's direction ◆ Every down January on the S&P since 1950, *without exception*, preceded a new or extended bear market, a flat market, or a 10% correction (page 42) ◆ S&P gains January's first five days preceded full-year gains 86.8% of the time; 13 of last 15 presidential years followed first five day's direction (page 14) ◆ November, December, and January constitute the year's best three-month span, a 4.3% S&P gain (pages 44 and 147) ◆ January NASDAQ up a powerful 2.8% since 1971 (pages 56 and 148) ◆ "January Effect" now starts in mid-December and favors small-cap stocks (pages 104 and 108) ◆ 2009 has the dubious honor of the worst S&P 500 January on record.

January Vital Statistics

	DJIA	S&P 500	NASDAQ	Russell 1K	Russell 2K
Rank	6	5	1	5	4
Up	40	38	27	21	18
Down	22	24	14	12	15
Avg % Change	1.0%	1.1%	2.8%	1.0%	1.7%
Election Year	0.1%	0.2%	2.0%	0.2%	1.7%
Best and Worst January					
	% Change	% Change	% Change	% Change	% Change
Best	1976 14.4	1987 13.2	1975 16.6	1987 12.7	1985 13.1
Worst	2009 −8.8	2009 −8.6	2008 −9.9	2009 −8.3	2009 −11.2
Best and Worst January Weeks					
Best	1/9/76 6.1	1/2/09 6.8	1/12/01 9.1	1/2/09 6.8	1/9/87 7.0
Worst	1/24/03 −5.3	1/28/00 −5.6	1/28/00 −8.2	1/28/00 −5.5	1/4/08 −6.5
Best and Worst January Days					
Best	1/17/91 4.6	1/3/01 5.0	1/3/01 14.2	1/3/01 5.3	1/2/09 5.3
Worst	1/8/88 −6.9	1/8/88 −6.8	1/2/01 −7.2	1/8/88 −6.1	1/20/09 −7.0
First Trading Day of Expiration Week: 1980–2011					
Record (#Up–#Down)	22–10	20–12	19–13	19–13	19–13
Current Streak	U2	U2	U2	U2	D1
Avg % Change	0.14	0.14	0.18	0.12	0.20
Options Expiration Day: 1980–2011					
Record (#Up–#Down)	15–17	16–16	18–14	16–16	17–15
Current Streak	U1	U1	D2	U1	D2
Avg % Change	−0.15	−0.11	−0.16	−0.13	−0.14
Options Expiration Week: 1980–2011					
Record (#Up–#Down)	16–16	13–19	17–15	13–19	16–16
Current Streak	U1	D7	D7	D7	D7
Avg % Change	−0.28	−0.16	0.17	−0.18	0.14
Week After Options Expiration: 1980–2011					
Record (#Up–#Down)	17–15	19–13	17–15	19–13	21–11
Current Streak	D3	D3	D5	D3	U1
Avg % Change	0.001	0.19	0.06	0.16	0.13
First Trading Day Performance					
% of Time Up	58.1	48.4	56.1	42.4	45.5
Avg % Change	0.24	0.13	0.15	0.10	0.01
Last Trading Day Performance					
% of Time Up	59.7	64.5	65.9	63.6	75.8
Avg % Change	0.25	0.28	0.31	0.37	0.29

Dow and S&P 1950–April 2011, NASDAQ 1971–April 2011, Russell 1K and 2K 1979–April 2011.

20th Amendment made "lame ducks" disappear.
Now, "As January goes, so goes the year."

New Year's Day

(Market Closed)

The highest reward for a person's toil is not what they get for it, but what they become by it.
— John Ruskin (English writer)

Small Caps Punished First Trading Day of Year
Russell 2000 Down 14 of Last 22, But Up Last 3

D 66.7
S 42.9
N 61.9

Change is the law of life. And those who look only to the past or present are certain to miss the future.
— John F. Kennedy (35th U.S. president, 1917–1963)

Second Trading Day of the Year, Dow Up 13 of Last 18
Santa Claus Rally Ends (Page 112)

D 61.9
S 61.9
N 71.4

Markets are constantly in a state of uncertainty and flux and money is made by discounting the obvious and betting on the unexpected.
— George Soros (Financier, philanthropist, political activist, author, and philosopher, b. 1930)

D 42.9
S 47.6
N 47.6

In investing, the return you want should depend on whether you want to eat well or sleep well.
— J. Kenfield Morley

D 52.4
S 42.9
N 47.6

In the realm of ideas, everything depends on enthusiasm; in the real world, all rests on perseverance.
— Johann Wolfgang von Goethe (German poet and polymath, 1749–1832)

January Almanac Investor Seasonalities: See Pages 92, 94, and 96

JANUARY'S FIRST FIVE DAYS: AN EARLY WARNING SYSTEM

The last 38 up First Five Days were followed by full-year gains 33 times for an 86.8% accuracy ratio and a 13.9% average gain in all 38 years. The five exceptions include flat 1994 and four related to war. Vietnam military spending delayed start of 1966 bear market. Ceasefire imminence early in 1973 raised stocks temporarily. Saddam Hussein turned 1990 into a bear. The war on terrorism, instability in the Mideast, and corporate malfeasance shaped 2002 into one of the worst years on record. The 23 down First Five Days were followed by 12 up years and 11 down (47.8% accurate) and an average gain of 0.2%.

Bullish four-year-presidential-election-cycle forces have given this indicator a 13–2 record in election years. Two of four down years have been wrong. However, a bear market began in 1956 with concern over Eisenhower's heart condition, the Suez Canal Crisis, and Russia's suppression of the Hungarian Revolution. A mini-crash on the fifth day of 1988 felled the S&P 6.8%.

THE FIRST-FIVE-DAYS-IN-JANUARY INDICATOR

Chronological Data

	Previous Year's Close	January 5th Day	5-Day Change	Year Change
1950	16.76	17.09	2.0%	21.8%
1951	20.41	20.88	2.3	16.5
1952	23.77	23.91	0.6	11.8
1953	26.57	26.33	-0.9	-6.6
1954	24.81	24.93	0.5	45.0
1955	35.98	35.33	-1.8	26.4
1956	45.48	44.51	-2.1	2.6
1957	46.67	46.25	-0.9	-14.3
1958	39.99	40.99	2.5	38.1
1959	55.21	55.40	0.3	8.5
1960	59.89	59.50	-0.7	-3.0
1961	58.11	58.81	1.2	23.1
1962	71.55	69.12	-3.4	-11.8
1963	63.10	64.74	2.6	18.9
1964	75.02	76.00	1.3	13.0
1965	84.75	85.37	0.7	9.1
1966	92.43	93.14	0.8	-13.1
1967	80.33	82.81	3.1	20.1
1968	96.47	96.62	0.2	7.7
1969	103.86	100.80	-2.9	-11.4
1970	92.06	92.68	0.7	0.1
1971	92.15	92.19	0.04	10.8
1972	102.09	103.47	1.4	15.6
1973	118.05	119.85	1.5	-17.4
1974	97.55	96.12	-1.5	-29.7
1975	68.56	70.04	2.2	31.5
1976	90.19	94.58	4.9	19.1
1977	107.46	105.01	-2.3	-11.5
1978	95.10	90.64	-4.7	1.1
1979	96.11	98.80	2.8	12.3
1980	107.94	108.95	0.9	25.8
1981	135.76	133.06	-2.0	-9.7
1982	122.55	119.55	-2.4	14.8
1983	140.64	145.23	3.3	17.3
1984	164.93	168.90	2.4	1.4
1985	167.24	163.99	-1.9	26.3
1986	211.28	207.97	-1.6	14.6
1987	242.17	257.28	6.2	2.0
1988	247.08	243.40	-1.5	12.4
1989	277.72	280.98	1.2	27.3
1990	353.40	353.79	0.1	-6.6
1991	330.22	314.90	-4.6	26.3
1992	417.09	418.10	0.2	4.5
1993	435.71	429.05	-1.5	7.1
1994	466.45	469.90	0.7	-1.5
1995	459.27	460.83	0.3	34.1
1996	615.93	618.46	0.4	20.3
1997	740.74	748.41	1.0	31.0
1998	970.43	956.04	-1.5	26.7
1999	1229.23	1275.09	3.7	19.5
2000	1469.25	1441.46	-1.9	-10.1
2001	1320.28	1295.86	-1.8	-13.0
2002	1148.08	1160.71	1.1	-23.4
2003	879.82	909.93	3.4	26.4
2004	1111.92	1131.91	1.8	9.0
2005	1211.92	1186.19	-2.1	3.0
2006	1248.29	1290.15	3.4	13.6
2007	1418.30	1412.11	-0.4	3.5
2008	1468.36	1390.19	-5.3	-38.5
2009	903.25	909.73	0.7	23.5
2010	1115.10	1144.98	2.7	12.8
2011	1257.64	1271.50	1.1	??

Ranked by Performance

Rank		5-Day Change	Year Change
1	1987	6.2%	2.0
2	1976	4.9	19.1
3	1999	3.7	19.5
4	2003	3.4	26.4
5	2006	3.4	13.6
6	1983	3.3	17.3
7	1967	3.1	20.1
8	1979	2.8	12.3
9	2010	2.7	12.8
10	1963	2.6	18.9
11	1958	2.5	38.1
12	1984	2.4	1.4
13	1951	2.3	16.5
14	1975	2.2	31.5
15	1950	2.0	21.8
16	2004	1.8	9.0
17	1973	1.5	-17.4
18	1972	1.4	15.6
19	1964	1.3	13.0
20	1961	1.2	23.1
21	1989	1.2	27.3
22	2011	1.1	??
23	2002	1.1	-23.4
24	1997	1.0	31.0
25	1980	0.9	25.8
26	1966	0.8	-13.1
27	1994	0.7	-1.5
28	1965	0.7	9.1
29	2009	0.7	23.5
30	1970	0.7	0.1
31	1952	0.6	11.8
32	1954	0.5	45.0
33	1996	0.4	20.3
34	1959	0.3	8.5
35	1995	0.3	34.1
36	1992	0.2	4.5
37	1968	0.2	7.7
38	1990	0.1	-6.6
39	1971	0.04	10.8
40	2007	-0.4	3.5
41	1960	-0.7	-3.0
42	1957	-0.9	-14.3
43	1953	-0.9	-6.6
44	1974	-1.5	-29.7
45	1998	-1.5	26.7
46	1988	-1.5	12.4
47	1993	-1.5	7.1
48	1986	-1.6	14.6
49	2001	-1.8	-13.0
50	1955	-1.8	26.4
51	2000	-1.9	-10.1
52	1985	-1.9	26.3
53	1981	-2.0	-9.7
54	1956	-2.1	2.6
55	2005	-2.1	3.0
56	1977	-2.3	-11.5
57	1982	-2.4	14.8
58	1969	-2.9	-11.4
59	1962	-3.4	-11.8
60	1991	-4.6	26.3
61	1978	-4.7	1.1
62	2008	-5.3	-38.5

Based on S&P 500

14

JANUARY

January's First Five Days Act as an "Early Warning" (Page 14)

MONDAY

D 38.1
S 52.4
N 57.1

9

Whoso would be a man, must be a non-conformist...Nothing is at last sacred but the integrity of your own mind.
— Ralph Waldo Emerson (American author, poet, and philosopher, *Self-Reliance*, 1803–1882)

TUESDAY

D 52.4
S 52.4
N 61.9

10

Let us have the courage to stop borrowing to meet the continuing deficits. Stop the deficits.
— Franklin D. Roosevelt (32nd U.S. president, 1932, 1882–1945)

January Ends "Best Three-Month Span" (Pages 44, 54,147, and 148)

WEDNESDAY

D 47.6
S 47.6
N 47.6

11

If a battered stock refuses to sink any lower no matter how many negative articles appear in the papers, that stock is worth a close look. — James L. Fraser (*Contrary Investor*)

THURSDAY

D 52.4
S 57.1
N 52.4

12

Buy a stock the way you would buy a house. Understand and like it such that you'd be content to own it in the absence of any market. — Warren Buffett (CEO Berkshire Hathaway, investor, and philanthropist, b. 1930)

FRIDAY

D 52.4
S 57.1
N 57.1

13

Market risk tends to be poorly rewarded when market valuations are rich and interest rates are rising.
— John P. Hussman, Ph.D. (Hussman Funds, 5/22/06)

SATURDAY

14

SUNDAY

15

THE INCREDIBLE JANUARY BAROMETER (DEVISED 1972): ONLY SEVEN SIGNIFICANT ERRORS IN 61 YEARS

Devised by Yale Hirsch in 1972, our January Barometer states that as the S&P 500 goes in January, so goes the year. The indicator has registered **only seven major errors since 1950 for an 88.5% accuracy ratio**. Vietnam affected 1966 and 1968; 1982 saw the start of a major bull market in August; two January rate cuts and 9/11 affected 2001; the anticipation of military action in Iraq held down the market in January 2003; 2009 was the beginning of a new bull market following the second worst bear market on record; and the Fed saved 2010 with QE2 (*Almanac Investor* newsletter subscribers receive full analysis of each reading as well as its potential implications for the full year.)

Including the seven flat-year errors (less than +/- 5%) yields a 77.0% accuracy ratio. A full comparison of all monthly barometers for the Dow, S&P, and NASDAQ in our February 17, 2011 Investor Alert at *www.stocktradersalmanac.com* details January's market forecasting prowess. Bear markets began or continued when Januarys suffered a loss *(see page 42)*. Full years followed January's direction in 11 of the last 15 presidential election years. Four of seven down years have been wrong. *See pages 18, 22, and 24 for more January Barometer items.*

AS JANUARY GOES, SO GOES THE YEAR

	Market Performance in January					Ranked by Performance		
	Previous Year's Close	January Close	January Change	Year Change	Rank	Year	January Change	Year Change
1950	16.76	17.05	1.7%	21.8%	1	1987	13.2%	2.0% flat
1951	20.41	21.66	6.1	16.5	2	1975	12.3	31.5
1952	23.77	24.14	1.6	11.8	3	1976	11.8	19.1
1953	26.57	26.38	-0.7	-6.6	4	1967	7.8	20.1
1954	24.81	26.08	5.1	45.0	5	1985	7.4	26.3
1955	35.98	36.63	1.8	26.4	6	1989	7.1	27.3
1956	45.48	43.82	-3.6	2.6 flat	7	1961	6.3	23.1
1957	46.67	44.72	-4.2	-14.3	8	1997	6.1	31.0
1958	39.99	41.70	4.3	38.1	9	1951	6.1	16.5
1959	55.21	55.42	0.4	8.5	10	1980	5.8	25.8
1960	59.89	55.61	-7.1	-3.0 flat	11	1954	5.1	45.0
1961	58.11	61.78	6.3	23.1	12	1963	4.9	18.9
1962	71.55	68.84	-3.8	-11.8	13	1958	4.3	38.1
1963	63.10	66.20	4.9	18.9	14	1991	4.2	26.3
1964	75.02	77.04	2.7	13.0	15	1999	4.1	19.5
1965	84.75	87.56	3.3	9.1	16	1971	4.0	10.8
1966	92.43	92.88	0.5	-13.1 X	17	1988	4.0	12.4
1967	80.33	86.61	7.8	20.1	18	1979	4.0	12.3
1968	96.47	92.24	-4.4	7.7 X	19	2001	3.5	-13.0 X
1969	103.86	103.01	-0.8	-11.4	20	1965	3.3	9.1
1970	92.06	85.02	-7.6	0.1 flat	21	1983	3.3	17.3
1971	92.15	95.88	4.0	10.8	22	1996	3.3	20.3
1972	102.09	103.94	1.8	15.6	23	1994	3.3	-1.5 flat
1973	118.05	116.03	-1.7	-17.4	24	1964	2.7	13.0
1974	97.55	96.57	-1.0	-29.7	25	2006	2.5	13.6
1975	68.56	76.98	12.3	31.5	26	1995	2.4	34.1
1976	90.19	100.86	11.8	19.1	27	2011	2.3	??
1977	107.46	102.03	-5.1	-11.5	28	1972	1.8	15.6
1978	95.10	89.25	-6.2	1.1 flat	29	1955	1.8	26.4
1979	96.11	99.93	4.0	12.3	30	1950	1.7	21.8
1980	107.94	114.16	5.8	25.8	31	2004	1.7	9.0
1981	135.76	129.55	-4.6	-9.7	32	1952	1.6	11.8
1982	122.55	120.40	-1.8	14.8 X	33	2007	1.4	3.5 flat
1983	140.64	145.30	3.3	17.3	34	1998	1.0	26.7
1984	164.93	163.41	-0.9	1.4 flat	35	1993	0.7	7.1
1985	167.24	179.63	7.4	26.3	36	1966	0.5	-13.1 X
1986	211.28	211.78	0.2	14.6	37	1959	0.4	8.5
1987	242.17	274.08	13.2	2.0 flat	38	1986	0.2	14.6
1988	247.08	257.07	4.0	12.4	39	1953	-0.7	-6.6
1989	277.72	297.47	7.1	27.3	40	1969	-0.8	-11.4
1990	353.40	329.08	-6.9	-6.6	41	1984	-0.9	1.4 flat
1991	330.22	343.93	4.2	26.3	42	1974	-1.0	-29.7
1992	417.09	408.79	-2.0	4.5 flat	43	2002	-1.6	-23.4
1993	435.71	438.78	0.7	7.1	44	1973	-1.7	-17.4
1994	466.45	481.61	3.3	-1.5 flat	45	1982	-1.8	14.8 X
1995	459.27	470.42	2.4	34.1	46	1992	-2.0	4.5 flat
1996	615.93	636.02	3.3	20.3	47	2005	-2.5	3.0 flat
1997	740.74	786.16	6.1	31.0	48	2003	-2.7	26.4 X
1998	970.43	980.28	1.0	26.7	49	1956	-3.6	2.6 flat
1999	1229.23	1279.64	4.1	19.5	50	2010	-3.7	12.8 X
2000	1469.25	1394.46	-5.1	-10.1	51	1962	-3.8	-11.8
2001	1320.28	1366.01	3.5	-13.0 X	52	1957	-4.2	-14.3
2002	1148.08	1130.20	-1.6	-23.4	53	1968	-4.4	7.7 X
2003	879.82	855.70	-2.7	26.4 X	54	1981	-4.6	-9.7
2004	1111.92	1131.13	1.7	9.0	55	1977	-5.1	-11.5
2005	1211.92	1181.27	-2.5	3.0 flat	56	2000	-5.1	-10.1
2006	1248.29	1280.08	2.5	13.6	57	2008	-6.1	-38.5
2007	1418.30	1438.24	1.4	3.5 flat	58	1978	-6.2	1.1 flat
2008	1468.36	1378.55	-6.1	-38.5	59	1990	-6.9	-6.6
2009	903.25	825.88	-8.6	23.5 X	60	1960	-7.1	-3.0 flat
2010	1115.10	1073.87	-3.7	12.8 X	61	1970	-7.6	0.1 flat
2011	1257.64	1286.12	2.3	??	62	2009	-8.6	23.5 X

X = 7 major errors *Based on S&P 500*

JANUARY

Martin Luther King Jr. Day (Market Closed)

MONDAY
16

very truth passes through three stages before it is recognized. In the first it is ridiculed; in the second it is opposed; the third it is regarded as self evident. — Arthur Schopenhauer (German philosopher, 1788–1860)

First Trading Day of January Expiration Week, Dow Up 14 of Last 19

TUESDAY
17
D 57.1
S 57.1
N 47.6

is the growth of total government spending as a percentage of gross national product—not the way it is financed— at crowds out the private sector. — Paul Craig Roberts (*Business Week*, 1984)

January Expiration Week Horrible Since 1999, Dow Down Big 9 of Last 13

WEDNESDAY
18
D 57.1
S 57.1
N 66.7

That investors really get paid for is holding dogs. Small stocks tend to have higher average returns than big stocks, and value stocks tend to have higher average returns than growth stocks. - Kenneth R. French (Economist, Dartmouth, NBER, b. 1954)

THURSDAY
19
D 33.3
S 52.4
N 61.9

rawing on my fine command of language, I said nothing. - Robert Benchley (American writer, actor, and humorist, 1889–1945)

January Expiration Day, Dow Down 10 of Last 13 with Big Losses, Off 2.1% in 2010, Off 2.0% in 2006, and 1.3% in 2003

FRIDAY
20
D 33.3
S 33.3
N 33.3

ople with a sense of fulfillment think the world is good, while the frustrated blame the world for their failure. - Eric Hoffer (*The True Believer*, 1951)

SATURDAY
21

SUNDAY
22

JANUARY BAROMETER IN GRAPHIC FORM SINCE 1950

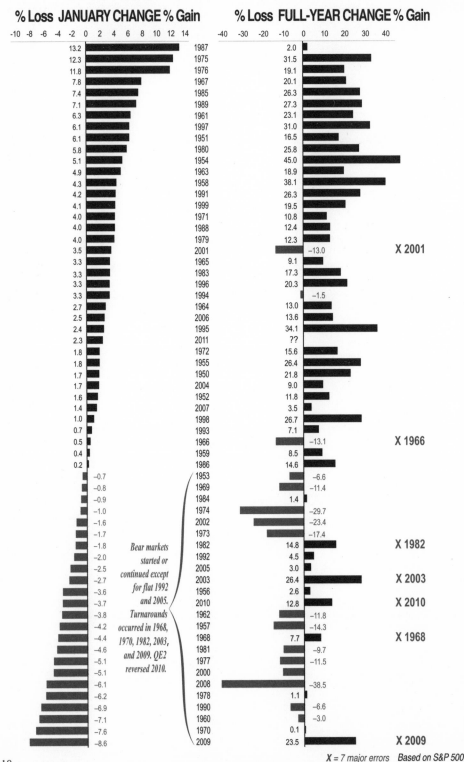

% Loss JANUARY CHANGE % Gain

	Year	
13.2	1987	
12.3	1975	
11.8	1976	
7.8	1967	
7.4	1985	
7.1	1989	
6.3	1961	
6.1	1997	
6.1	1951	
5.8	1980	
5.1	1954	
4.9	1963	
4.3	1958	
4.2	1991	
4.1	1999	
4.0	1971	
4.0	1988	
4.0	1979	
3.5	2001	
3.3	1965	
3.3	1983	
3.3	1996	
3.3	1994	
2.7	1964	
2.5	2006	
2.4	1995	
2.3	2011	
1.8	1972	
1.8	1955	
1.7	1950	
1.7	2004	
1.6	1952	
1.4	2007	
1.0	1998	
0.7	1993	
0.5	1966	
0.4	1959	
0.2	1986	
−0.7	1953	
−0.8	1969	
−0.9	1984	
−1.0	1974	
−1.6	2002	
−1.7	1973	
−1.8	1982	
−2.0	1992	
−2.5	2005	
−2.7	2003	
−3.6	1956	
−3.7	2010	
−3.8	1962	
−4.2	1957	
−4.4	1968	
−4.6	1981	
−5.1	1977	
−5.1	2000	
−6.1	2008	
−6.2	1978	
−6.9	1990	
−7.1	1960	
−7.6	1970	
−8.6	2009	

Bear markets started or continued except for flat 1992 and 2005. Turnarounds occurred in 1968, 1970, 1982, 2003, and 2009. QE2 reversed 2010.

% Loss FULL-YEAR CHANGE % Gain

2.0	
31.5	
19.1	
20.1	
26.3	
27.3	
23.1	
31.0	
16.5	
25.8	
45.0	
18.9	
38.1	
26.3	
19.5	
10.8	
12.4	
12.3	
−13.0	X 2001
9.1	
17.3	
20.3	
−1.5	
13.0	
13.6	
34.1	
??	
15.6	
26.4	
21.8	
9.0	
11.8	
3.5	
26.7	
7.1	
−13.1	X 1966
8.5	
14.6	
−6.6	
−11.4	
1.4	
−29.7	
−23.4	
−17.4	
14.8	X 1982
4.5	
3.0	
26.4	X 2003
2.6	
12.8	X 2010
−11.8	
−14.3	
7.7	X 1968
−9.7	
−11.5	
−38.5	
1.1	
−6.6	
−3.0	
0.1	
23.5	X 2009

X = 7 major errors   Based on S&P 500

JANURY

🐻 MONDAY

D 33.3
S 38.1
N 42.9

23

istory shows that once the United States fully recognizes an economic problem and thereby places all its efforts on solving it,
e problem is about to be solved by natural forces. — James L. Fraser (Contrary Investor)

TUESDAY

D 38.1
S 52.4
N 57.1

24

banking institutions are protected by the taxpayer and they are given free reign to speculate,
may not live long enough to see the crisis, but my soul is going to come back and haunt you.
- Paul A. Volcker (Fed chairman 1979–1987, chairman Economic Recovery Advisory Board, 2/2/2010, b. 1927)

OMC Meeting (2 Days)

WEDNESDAY

D 61.9
S 47.6
N 38.1

25

will never knowingly buy any company that has a real time quote of their stock price in the building lobby.
- Robert Mahan (A trader commenting on Enron)

THURSDAY

D 61.9
S 47.6
N 76.2

26

omen are expected to do twice as much as men in half the time and for no credit. Fortunately, this isn't difficult.
- Charlotte Whitton (Former Ottawa Mayor, feminist, 1896–1975)

FRIDAY

D 57.1
S 57.1
N 66.7

27

anking establishments are more dangerous than standing armies; and that the principle of
ending money to be paid by posterity, under the name of funding, is but swindling futurity on a large scale.
- Thomas Jefferson (3rd U.S. president, 1743–7/4/1826, 1816 letter to John Taylor of Caroline)

SATURDAY

28

February Almanac Investor Seasonalities: See Pages 92, 94, and 96

SUNDAY

29

FEBRUARY ALMANAC

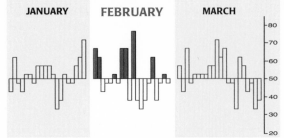

FEBRUARY							MARCH						
S	M	T	W	T	F	S	S	M	T	W	T	F	S
				1	2	3						1	2	3
5	6	7	8	9	10	11	4	5	6	7	8	9	10
12	13	14	15	16	17	18	11	12	13	14	15	16	17
19	20	21	22	23	24	25	18	19	20	21	22	23	24
26	27	28	29				25	26	27	28	29	30	31

Market Probability Chart above is a graphic representation of the S&P 500 Recent Market Probability Calendar on page 124.

◆ February is the weak link in "Best Six Months" (pages 44, 48, and 147) ◆ RECENT RECORD deteriorating: S&P up 5, down 8, average change -2.0% last 13 years ◆ Second best NASDAQ month in presidential election years, average 2.6%, up 6, down 4 (page 157); #9 Dow, up 8, down 7; and #10 S&P (pages 153 and 155), up 8, down 7 ◆ Day before Presidents' Day weekend S&P down 16 of 20, 11 straight 1992–2002; day after dicey, up 10 of 20 (see page 86 and 133) ◆ Many technicians modify market predictions based on January's market.

February Vital Statistics

	DJIA	S&P 500	NASDAQ	Russell 1K	Russell 2K
Rank	9	11	9	11	7
Up	35	33	21	19	18
Down	27	29	20	14	15
Avg % Change	0.005%	−0.2%	0.3%	−0.05%	1.0%
Election Year	−0.3%	−0.2%	2.6%	−0.1%	2.5%
Best and Worst February					
	% Change	% Change	% Change	% Change	% Change
Best	1986 8.8	1986 7.1	2000 19.2	1986 7.2	2000 16.4
Worst	2009 −11.7	2009 −11.0	2001 −22.4	2009 −10.7	2009 −12.3
Best and Worst February Weeks					
Best	2/1/08 4.4	2/6/09 5.2	2/4/00 9.2	2/6/09 5.3	2/1/91 6.6
Worst	2/20/09 −6.2	2/20/09 −6.9	2/9/01 −7.1	2/20/09 −6.9	2/20/09 −8.3
Best and Worst February Days					
Best	2/24/09 3.3	2/24/09 4.0	2/11/99 4.2	2/24/09 4.1	2/24/09 4.5
Worst	2/10/09 −4.6	2/10/09 −4.9	2/16/01 −5.0	2/10/09 −4.8	2/10/09 −4.7
First Trading Day of Expiration Week: 1980–2011					
Record (#Up–#Down)	19–13	22–10	17–15	22–10	18–14
Current Streak	D1	U2	U2	U2	U2
Avg % Change	0.28	0.22	−0.02	0.19	0.003
Options Expiration Day: 1980–2011					
Record (#Up–#Down)	15–17	13–19	13–19	14–18	14–18
Current Streak	U2	U2	U2	U2	U2
Avg % Change	−0.09	−0.16	−0.30	−0.16	−0.11
Options Expiration Week: 1980–2011					
Record (#Up–#Down)	19–13	16–16	16–16	15–17	19–13
Current Streak	U2	U2	U2	U2	U2
Avg % Change	0.32	0.07	−0.10	0.07	0.07
Week After Options Expiration: 1980–2011					
Record (#Up–#Down)	13–9	14–18	17–15	14–18	17–15
Current Streak	D3	D3	D4	D3	D4
Avg % Change	−0.40	−0.30	−0.26	−0.25	−0.15
First Trading Day Performance					
% of Time Up	61.3	61.3	70.7	66.7	66.7
Avg % Change	0.14	0.15	0.35	0.19	0.36
Last Trading Day Performance					
% of Time Up	51.6	58.1	56.1	60.6	60.6
Avg % Change	0.02	0.003	−0.03	−0.03	0.17

Dow and S&P 1950–April 2011, NASDAQ 1971–April 2011, Russell 1K and 2K 1979–April 2011.

Either go short, or stay away the day before Presidents' Day.

JANUARY/FEBRUARY

We always live in an uncertain world. What is certain is that the United States will go forward over time.
— Warren Buffett (CEO Berkshire Hathaway, investor, and philanthropist, CNBC, 9/22/2010, b. 1930)

"January Barometer" 88.5% Accurate (Page 16)
Almanac Investor Subscribers E-mailed Official Results (See Insert)

TUESDAY

D 66.7
S 71.4
N 61.9

31

The government would not look fondly on Caesar's Palace if it opened a table for wagering on corporate failure.
It should not give greater encouragement for Goldman Sachs [et al] to do so.
— Roger Lowenstein (Financial journalist and author, *End of Wall Street,* NY Times OpEd, 4/20/2010, b. 1954)

First Day Trading in February, Dow and S&P Up 8 of Last 9
NASDAQ Up 7 Years in a Row

WEDNESDAY

D 66.7
S 66.7
N 81.0

1

Don't be overly concerned about your heirs. Usually, unearned funds do them more harm than good.
— Gerald M. Loeb (E.F. Hutton, *The Battle for Investment Survival,* predicted 1929 Crash, 1900–1974)

THURSDAY

D 52.4
S 61.9
N 66.7

2

Cooperation is essential to address 21st-century challenges; you can't fire cruise missiles at the global financial crisis.
— Nicholas D. Kristof (*NY Times* columnist, 10/23/2008)

FRIDAY

D 42.9
S 42.9
N 47.6

3

We may face more inflation pressure than currently shows up in formal data.
— William Poole (Economist, president Federal Reserve Bank St. Louis, 1998–2008, June 2006 speech, b. 1937)

SATURDAY

4

SUNDAY

5

HOT JANUARY INDUSTRIES BEAT S&P NEXT 11 MONTHS

The S&P 500 in January tends to predict the market's direction for the year. In turn, Standard & Poor's top 10 industries in January outperform the index over the next 11 months.

Our friend Sam Stovall, chief investment strategist at S&P, has crunched the numbers over the years. He calls it the "January Barometer Portfolio," or JBP. Since 1970, a portfolio of the top 10 S&P industries during January has beaten the S&P 500 itself—and performed even better in years when January was up.

The JBP went on to outperform the S&P 500 during the remaining 11 months of the year 71% of the time, 14.6% to 6.8%, on average. When the S&P 500 is up in January, a top-10 industries portfolio increases the average portfolio gain to 19.4% for the last 11 months of the year vs. 12.2% for the S&P. For more of Sam's Sector Watch, click on "Free Trial" at *http://www.marketscope.com*.

AS JANUARY GOES, SO GOES THE YEAR
FOR TOP-PERFORMING INDUSTRIES
January's Top 10 Industries vs. S&P 500 Next 11 Months

	11 Month % Change		S&P Jan	After S&P Up in January		After S&P Down in January	
	Portfolio	S&P	%	Portfolio	S&P	Portfolio	S&P
1970	−4.7	−0.3	−7.6			−4.7	−0.3
1971	23.5	6.1	4.0	23.5	6.1		
1972	19.7	13.7	1.8	19.7	13.7		
1973	5.2	−20.0	−1.7			5.2	−20.0
1974	−29.2	−30.2	−1.0			−29.2	−30.2
1975	57.3	22.2	12.3	57.3	22.2		
1976	16.3	8.1	11.8	16.3	8.1		
1977	−9.1	−9.6	−5.1			−9.1	−9.6
1978	7.3	6.5	−6.2			7.3	6.5
1979	21.7	8.1	4.0	21.7	8.1		
1980	38.3	20.4	5.8	38.3	20.4		
1981	5.0	−6.9	−4.6			5.0	−6.9
1982	37.2	18.8	−1.8			37.2	18.8
1983	17.2	13.9	3.3	17.2	13.9		
1984	−5.0	−1.1	−0.9			−5.0	−1.1
1985	28.2	20.8	7.4	28.2	20.8		
1986	18.1	19.4	0.2	18.1	19.4		
1987	−1.5	−8.9	13.2	−1.5	−8.9		
1988	18.4	10.4	4.0	18.4	10.4		
1989	16.1	22.1	7.1	16.1	22.1		
1990	−4.4	−3.3	−6.9			−4.4	−3.3
1991	35.7	19.4	4.2	35.7	19.4		
1992	14.6	4.7	−2.0			14.6	4.7
1993	23.7	7.2	0.7	23.7	7.2		
1994	−7.1	−4.6	3.3	−7.1	−4.6		
1995	25.6	30.9	2.4	25.6	30.9		
1996	5.4	16.5	3.3	5.4	16.5		
1997	4.7	23.4	6.1	4.7	23.4		
1998	45.2	25.4	1.0	45.2	25.4		
1999	67.9	14.8	4.1	67.9	14.8		
2000	23.6	−5.3	−5.1			23.6	−5.3
2001	−13.1	−16.0	3.5	−13.1	−16.0		
2002	−16.2	−22.2	−1.6			−16.2	−22.2
2003	69.3	29.9	−2.7			69.3	29.9
2004	9.9	7.1	1.7	9.9	7.1		
2005	20.7	5.7	−2.5			20.7	5.7
2006	−0.3	10.8	2.5	−0.3	10.8		
2007	−5.5	2.1	1.4	−5.5	2.1		
2008	−27.1	−34.5	−6.1			−27.1	−34.5
2009	38.7	35.0	−8.6			38.7	35.0
2010	9.2	17.1	−3.7			9.2	17.1
2011			2.3				
Averages	**14.6%**	**6.8%**		**19.4%**	**12.2%**	**7.9%**	**−0.9%**

22

MONDAY

D 47.6
S 47.6
N 57.1

6

Don't compete. Create. Find out what everyone else is doing and then don't do it.
— Joel Weldon (Motivational speaker)

TUESDAY

D 52.4
S 47.6
N 52.4

7

Bankruptcy was designed to forgive stupidity, not reward criminality.
— William P. Barr (Verizon general counsel, calling for government liquidation of
MCI-WorldCom in Chapter 7, 4/14/2003)

WEDNESDAY

D 42.9
S 52.4
N 57.1

8

The only function of economic forecasting is to make astrology look respectable.
— John Kenneth Galbraith (Canadian/American economist and diplomat, 1908–2006)

Week before February Expiration Week, NASDAQ Down 8 of Last 11,
2010 Up 2.0%, 2011 Up 1.5%

THURSDAY

D 57.1
S 47.6
N 47.6

9

There's no trick to being a humorist when you have the whole government working for you.
— Will Rogers (American humorist and showman, 1879–1935)

FRIDAY

D 57.1
S 66.7
N 52.4

10

We will have to pay more and more attention to what the funds are doing. They are the ones who have been contributing
to the activity, especially in the high-fliers. — Humphrey B. Neill (Investor, analyst, author, *NY Times, 6/11/1966*, 1895–1977)

SATURDAY

11

SUNDAY

12

2012 PRESIDENTIAL ELECTION YEAR PERPECTIVES

ONLY TWO LOSSES IN LAST SEVEN MONTHS OF ELECTION YEARS

Regardless which Party is victorious, the last seven months have seen gains on the S&P in 13 of the 15 presidential election years since 1950. One loss was in 2000 when the election's outcome was delayed for 36 tumultuous days, though the Dow did end higher. Financial crisis and the worst bear market since the Great Depression impacted 2008. *Page 52.*

FIRST FIVE MONTHS BETTER WHEN PARTY RETAINS WHITE HOUSE

Since 1901 there have been 27 presidential elections. During the 16 times the Party in power retained the White House, the Dow was up 1.5% on average for the first five months, compared to a 4.6% loss the 11 times the Party was ousted. Since 1950, retaining the White House 7 times brought an average gain of 1.9%, compared to −0.1% the other 8 times.

WAR CAN BE A MAJOR FACTOR IN PRESIDENTIAL RACES

Democrats used to lose the White House on foreign shores (1920 WW1, 1952 Korea, 1968 Vietnam, 1980 Iran Crisis). Republicans on the other hand lost it here at home (1912 Party split, 1932 Depression, 1960 Economy, 1976 Watergate). Homeland issues dominated elections the last three decades with the Republican loss in 1992 (Economy), the Democratic loss in 2000 (Scandal), and the Republican loss in 2008 (Economy). As we've learned over the years, it all depends on who the candidates are in 2012.

MARKET BOTTOMS TWO YEARS AFTER A PRESIDENTIAL ELECTION

A takeover of the White House by the opposing party in the past 50 years (1960, 1968, 1976, 1980, 1992, 2000, 2008) has resulted in a bottom within two years, except 1994, a flat year. When incumbent parties retained power (1964, 1972, 1984, 1988, 1996, 2004) stocks often bottomed within two years as well, except 1984 (three years, 1987) and 2004 (one year, flat 2005). Whatever the outcome in 2012, we could see a bottom by 2014.

ONLY SIX ELECTION YEAR DECLINES GREATER THAN 5% SINCE 1896

Presidential election years are the second best performing year of the four-year cycle. Incumbent parties lost power in five of those years. Five losses occurred at the end of the second term. FDR defeated Hoover in 1932 and was reelected to an unprecedented third term as WWII ravaged Europe. Election year 2012 marks the end of the incumbent party's first term, improving the prospects for a solid year.

ELECTION YEAR LOSSES OVER 5% SINCE 1896

Year	Party Switch	Average % DJIA Loss*	End of 2nd Term
1920	X	−32.9%	X
1932	X	−23.1%	Market Crash 1st Term
1940	WWII 3rd term	−12.7%	X
1960	X	−9.3%	X
2000	X	−6.2%	X
2008	X	−33.8%	X

MARKET CHARTS OF PRESIDENTIAL ELECTION YEARS

Market behavior last 21 elections including candidates and winners. *Page 28.*

HOW THE GOVERNMENT MANIPULATES THE ECONOMY TO STAY IN POWER

Money faucets get turned on, if possible, in years divisible by "4." *Page 34.*

INCUMBENT VICTORIES VS. INCUMBENT DEFEATS

Markets tend to be stronger when Party in power wins. *Page 38.*

FEBRUARY

MONDAY

D 61.9
S 66.7
N 52.4
13

I'm not nearly so concerned about the return on my capital as I am the return of my capital.
— Will Rogers (American humorist and showman, 1879–1935)

Valentine's Day ♥ **TUESDAY**

D 42.9
S 38.1
N 52.4
14

When they stop joking with you is when they don't give a damn about you.
— Sammy Davis Jr. (American entertainer, 1925–1990)

WEDNESDAY

D 71.4
S 76.2
N 61.9
15

Sight and Sound function differently in the mind, with sound being the surer investment.
WIN THE EARS OF THE PEOPLE, THEIR EYES WILL FOLLOW. — Roy H. Williams (*The Wizard of Ads*)

THURSDAY

D 42.9
S 38.1
N 33.3
16

Companies which do well generally tend to report (their quarterly earnings) earlier than those which do poorly.
— Alan Abelson (Financial journalist and editor, *Barron's*)

  FRIDAY

D 28.6
S 33.3
N 42.9
17

Explosive growth of shadow banking was about the invisible hand having a party, a non-regulated drinking party,
with rating agencies handing out fake IDs. — Paul McCulley (Economist, bond investor, PIMCO, coined "shadow banking"
in 2007, *NY Times*, 4/26/2010, b. 1957)

SATURDAY

18

SUNDAY

19

THE SECOND YEAR OF DECADES

"Second" years suffered sizeable losses in 1932 (as Depression set in), 1962 (Cuban missile crisis) and 2002 (corporate malfeasance, terrorism, Iraq War buildup). Major bottoms occurred in the last four midterm "second" years: 1942, 1962, 1982, and 2002. 2012 is an election year, and election "second" years since 1932 fared well in 1952, 1972, and 1992. *See pages 129–130 for more.*

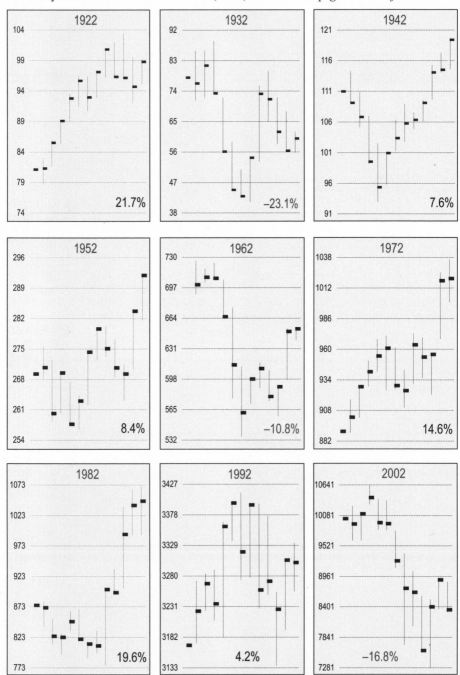

Based on Dow Jones Industrial Average monthly ranges and closing prices.

FEBRUARY

Presidents' Day (Market Closed)

MONDAY

20

I was in search of a one-armed economist so that the guy could never make a statement and then say: "on the other hand."
— Harry S. Truman (33rd U.S. president, 1884–1972)

Day after Presidents Day, S&P Down 7 of Last 11

🐻 TUESDAY

D 42.9
S 38.1
N 38.1

21

It wasn't raining when Noah built the ark.
— Warren Buffett (CEO Berkshire Hathaway, investor, and philanthropist, b. 1930)

Ash Wednesday

WEDNESDAY

D 52.4
S 47.6
N 42.9

22

If you can buy more of your best idea, why put [the money] into your 10th-best idea or your 20th-best idea?
The more positions you have, the more average you are. — Bruce Berkowitz (Fairholme Fund, Barron's, 3/17/08)

End of February, Miserable in Recent Years, (Page 20 and 133)

🐂 THURSDAY

D 52.4
S 61.9
N 61.9

23

I invest in people, not ideas; I want to see fire in the belly and intellect. — Arthur Rock (First venture capitalist)

Week after February Expiration Week, Dow Down 10 of Last 13

🐻 FRIDAY

D 33.3
S 38.1
N 52.4

24

A generation from now, Americans may marvel at the complacency that assumed the dollar's dominance would never end.
— Floyd Norris (Chief financial correspondent, NY Times, 2/2/07)

SATURDAY

25

March Almanac Investor Seasonalities: See Pages 92, 94, and 96

SUNDAY

26

MARCH ALMANAC

MARCH								APRIL					
S	M	T	W	T	F	S		S	M	T	W	T	F	S
					1	2	3		1	2	3	4	5	6	7
4	5	6	7	8	9	10		8	9	10	11	12	13	14
11	12	13	14	15	16	17		15	16	17	18	19	20	21
18	19	20	21	22	23	24		22	23	24	25	26	27	28
25	26	27	28	29	30	31		29	30					

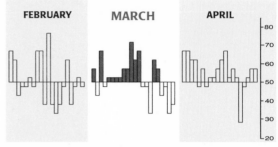

Market Probability Chart above is a graphic representation of the S&P 500 Recent Market Probability Calendar on page 124.

◆ Mid-month strength and late-month weakness are most evident above ◆ RECENT RECORD: S&P 18 up, 10 down, average gain 1.3%, fourth best ◆ Rather turbulent in recent years with wild fluctuations and large gains and losses ◆ March has been taking some mean end-of-quarter hits (page 134), down 1,469 Dow points March 9–22, 2001 ◆ Last three or four days, Dow a net loser 14 out of last 22 years ◆ NASDAQ hard hit in 2001, down 14.5% after 22.4% drop in February ◆ Worst NASDAQ month during presidential election years, average loss 2.2%, up 5, down 5.

March Vital Statistics

	DJIA	S&P 500	NASDAQ	Russell 1K	Russell 2K
Rank	5	4	7	6	6
Up	40	40	26	22	24
Down	22	22	15	11	9
Avg % Change	1.1%	1.1%	0.7%	1.0%	1.2%
Election Year	0.5%	0.7%	−2.2%	−1.1%	−2.6%
Best and Worst March					
	% Change	% Change	% Change	% Change	% Change
Best	2000 7.8	2000 9.7	2009 10.9	2000 8.9	1979 9.7
Worst	1980 −9.0	1980 −10.2	1980 −17.1	1980 −11.5	1980 −18.5
Best and Worst March Weeks					
Best	3/13/09 9.0	3/13/09 10.7	3/13/09 10.6	3/13/09 10.7	3/13/09 12.0
Worst	3/16/01 −7.7	3/6/09 −7.0	3/16/01 −7.9	3/6/09 −7.1	3/6/09 −9.8
Best and Worst March Days					
Best	3/23/09 6.8	3/23/09 7.1	3/10/09 7.1	3/23/09 7.0	3/23/09 8.4
Worst	3/2/09 −4.2	3/2/09 −4.7	3/12/01 −6.3	3/2/09 −4.8	3/27/80 −6.0
First Trading Day of Expiration Week: 1980–2011					
Record (#Up–#Down)	20–12	20–12	14–18	19–13	16–16
Current Streak	D1	D1	D4	D4	D4
Avg % Change	0.13	0.01	−0.37	−0.05	−0.39
Options Expiration Day: 1980–2011					
Record (#Up–#Down)	18–14	19–13	16–16	17–15	15–16
Current Streak	U1	U1	U1	U1	U1
Avg % Change	0.07	0.01	−0.03	0.01	−0.05
Options Expiration Week: 1980–2011					
Record (#Up–#Down)	21–10	20–12	18–14	19–13	16–16
Current Streak	D1	D1	D1	D1	D2
Avg % Change	0.81	0.65	−0.12	0.58	0.05
Week After Options Expiration: 1980–2011					
Record (#Up–#Down)	15–17	12–20	17–15	12–20	17–15
Current Streak	U3	U3	U6	U3	U6
Avg % Change	−0.18	−0.07	0.17	−0.07	0.15
First Trading Day Performance					
% of Time Up	66.1	62.9	61.0	57.6	63.6
Avg % Change	0.15	0.14	0.20	0.09	0.17
Last Trading Day Performance					
% of Time Up	40.3	38.7	65.9	45.5	84.8
Avg % Change	−0.12	−0.02	0.18	0.08	0.40

Dow and S&P 1950–April 2011, NASDAQ 1971–April 2011, Russell 1K and 2K 1979–April 2011.

March has Ides and St. Patrick's Day;
Begins bullishly, then fades away.

MONDAY
D 47.6
S 47.6
N 47.6
27

A person's greatest virtue is his ability to correct his mistakes and continually make a new person of himself.
— Yang-Ming Wang (Chinese philosopher, 1472–1529)

TUESDAY
D 42.9
S 52.4
N 52.4
28

Don't be scared to take big steps—you can't cross a chasm in two small jumps.
— David Lloyd George (British prime minister, 1916–1922)

WEDNESDAY
D 42.9
S 47.6
N 42.9
29

Early in March (1960), Dr. Arthur F. Burns called on me... Burns' conclusion was that unless some decisive action was taken, and taken soon, we were heading for another economic dip, which would hit its low point in October, just before the elections. — Richard M. Nixon (37th U.S. president, Six Crises, 1913–1994)

First Trading Day in March, Dow Down 4 of Last 5, – 4.2% in 2009, 1996–2006 Up 9 of 11

THURSDAY
D 61.9
S 57.1
N 57.1
1

Sell stocks whenever the market is 30% higher over a year ago. — Eugene D. Brody (Oppenheimer Capital)

March Historically Strong Early in the Month (Pages 28 and 134)

FRIDAY
D 52.4
S 42.9
N 38.1
2

The principles of successful stock speculation are based on the supposition that people will continue in the future to make the mistakes that they have made in the past. — Thomas F. Woodlock, (*Wall Street Journal* editor and columnist, quoted in *Reminiscences of a Stock Operator*, 1866–1945)

SATURDAY
3

SUNDAY
4

MARKET CHARTS OF PRESIDENTIAL ELECTION YEARS

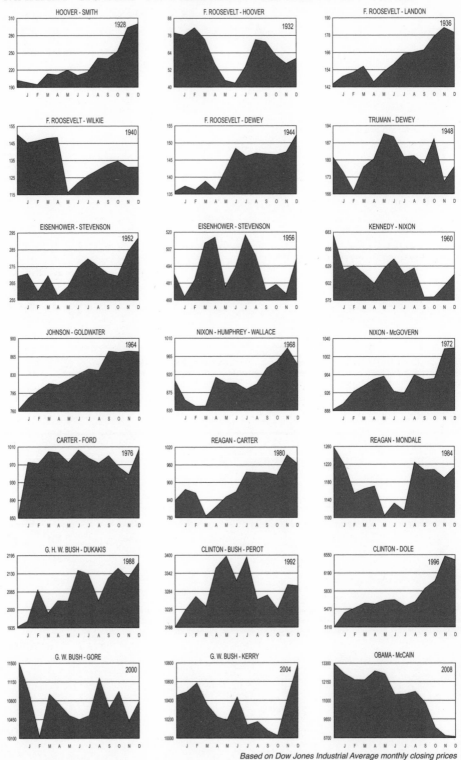

Based on Dow Jones Industrial Average monthly closing prices

MARCH

🐏 MONDAY

D 57.1
S 66.7
N 66.7

5

If the winds of fortune are temporarily blowing against you, remember that you can harness them and make them carry you toward your definite purpose, through the use of your imagination.
— Napoleon Hill (Author, *Think and Grow Rich*, 1883–1970)

TUESDAY

D 47.6
S 47.6
N 47.6

6

Economics is a very difficult subject. I've compared it to trying to learn how to repair a car when the engine is running. — Ben Bernanke (Fed chairman 2006–, June 2004 *Region* interview as Fed governor)

WEDNESDAY

D 57.1
S 52.4
N 52.4

7

Cannot people realize how large an income is thrift?
— Marcus Tullius Cicero (Great Roman orator, politician, 106–43 B.C.)

THURSDAY

D 42.9
S 52.4
N 42.9

8

If a man has no talents, he is unhappy enough; but if he has, envy pursues him in proportion to his ability.
— Leopold Mozart (to his son Wolfgang Amadeus, 1768)

Dow Down 1469 Points March 9–22 in 2001

FRIDAY

D 61.9
S 52.4
N 52.4

9

The most dangerous thing that takes place [in companies] is that success breeds arrogance, and arrogance seems to make people stop listening to their customers and to their employees. And that is the beginning of the end. The challenge is not to be a great company; the challenge is to remain a great company. — George Fisher (Motorola)

SATURDAY

10

Daylight Saving Time Begins

SUNDAY

11

HOW TO TRADE BEST MONTHS SWITCHING STRATEGIES

Our Best Months Switching Strategies found on pages 48, 50, 58, and 60 are simple and reliable with a proven 61-year track record. Thus far we have failed to find a similar trading strategy that even comes close over the past six decades. And to top it off, the strategy has only been improving, since we first discovered it in 1986.

Exogenous factors and cultural shifts must be considered. "Backward" tests that go back to 1925 or even 1896 and conclude that the pattern does not work are best ignored. They do not take into account these factors. Farming made August the best month from 1900–1951. Since 1987 it is the second worst month of the year for the Dow and S&P. Panic caused by financial crisis in 2007–2008 caused every asset class aside from U.S. Treasuries to decline substantially. But the bulk of the major decline in equities in the worst months of 2008 was sidestepped using these strategies.

Our Best Months Switching Strategy will not make you an instant millionaire, as other strategies claim they can do. What it will do is steadily build wealth over time with half the risk (or less) of a "buy and hold" approach.

A sampling of tradable funds for the Best and Worst Months appears in the table below. These are just a starting point and only skim the surface of possible trading vehicles available to take advantage of these strategies. Your specific situation and risk tolerance will dictate a suitable choice. If you are trading in a tax-advantaged account, such as a company sponsored 401(k) or Individual Retirement Account (IRA), your investment options may be limited to what has been selected by your employer or IRA administrator. But if you are a self-directed trader with a brokerage account, then you likely have unlimited choices (perhaps too many).

TRADABLE BEST AND WORST MONTHS SWITCHING STRATEGY FUNDS

Best Months		Worst Months	
Exchange Traded Funds (ETF)		**Exchange Traded Funds (ETF)**	
Symbol	**Name**	**Symbol**	**Name**
DIA	SPDR Dow Jones Industrial Average	SHY	iShares 1–3 Year Treasury Bond
SPY	SPDR S&P 500	IEI	iShares 3–7 Year Treasury Bond
QQQ	PowerShares QQQ	IEF	iShares 7–10 Year Treasury Bond
IWM	iShares Russell 2000	TLT	iShares 20+ Year Treasury Bond
Mutual Funds		**Mutual Funds**	
Symbol	**Name**	**Symbol**	**Name**
VWNDX	Vanguard Windsor Fund	VFSTX	Vanguard Short-Term Investment-Grade Bond Fund
FMAGX	Fidelity Magellan Fund	FBNDX	Fidelity Investment Grade Bond Fund
AMCPX	American Funds AMCAP Fund	ABNDX	American Funds Bond Fund of America
FKCGX	Franklin Flex Cap Growth Fund	FKUSX	Franklin U.S. Government Securities Fund
SECEX	Rydex Large Cap Core Fund	SIUSX	Rydex U.S. Intermediate Bond Fund

Generally speaking, during the Best Months you want to be invested in equities that offer similar exposure to the companies that constitute the Dow, S&P 500, and NASDAQ indices. These would typically be large-cap growth and value stocks as well as technology concerns. Reviewing the holdings of a particular ETF or mutual fund and comparing them to the index members is an excellent way to correlate.

During the Worst Months, switch into Treasury bonds, money market funds, or a bear/short fund. **Federated Prudent Bear** (BEARX) and **Grizzly Short** (GRZZX) worked quite well during the bear market of 2007–2009. Money market funds will be the safest, but are likely to offer the smallest return, while bear/short funds offer potentially greater returns, but more risk. If the market moves sideways or higher during the Worst Months, a bear/short fund is likely to lose money. Treasuries offer a combination of decent returns with limited risk. In the *2012 Commodity Trader's Almanac*, a detailed study of 30-year Treasury bonds covers their seasonal tendency to advance during summer months as well as a correlating ETF option.

Additional Worst Month possibilities include precious metals and the companies that mine them. **SPDR Gold Shares** (GLD), **Market Vectors Gold Miners** (GDX), and **ETF Securities Physical Swiss Gold** (SGOL) are a few well recognized names available from the ETF universe. Gold's seasonal price tendencies are also covered in the *2012 Commodity Trader's Almanac*.

Become an *Almanac Investor*

Almanac Investor subsribers receive specific buy and sell recommendations, based upon the Best Months Switching Strategies, online and via email. Sector Index Seasonalities, found on page 92, are also put into action throughout the year with ETF recommendations. Buy limits, stop losses, and auto-sell price points for the majority of seasonal trades are delivered directly to your inbox. Visit *www.stocktradersalmanac.com,* or see the insert for details and a special offer for new subscribers.

MACD Calculator   January Barometer

- ✓ **Almanac Investor Stock Portfolio Up 37% in 2010**
- ✓ **Portfolio Gain Since Inception 292% (July '01 – Feb '11)**
- ✓ **Called the March 2008 Bear Market**
- ✓ **Called the 2009 Market Rebound**
- ✓ **…And Much More!**

TRY IT FREE for 1 WEEK!
go to **stocktradersalamanc.com/freeweek**

GET THE STA IPHONE APP!

The all new *Stock Trader's Almanac* app gives you on-the-go access to historical market data for every trading day of the year. Get daily market probability percents for the DOW, S&P, NAS, R1K and R2K -- best of all the app shows you what signals to look for "This Week" and links to extended explanations of market timing mechanics, market facts and vital statistics.

Get the app by searching for "Stock Trader's Almanac" in the iTunes App Store today!

Monday before March Triple Witching, Dow Up 17 of Last 24

MONDAY
D 61.9
S 52.4
N 47.6
12

Doubt is the father of invention. — Galileo Galilei (Italian physicist and astronomer, 1564–1642)

FOMC Meeting

TUESDAY
D 42.9
S 57.1
N 61.9
13

A gold mine is a hole in the ground with a liar on top.
— Mark Twain (1835–1910, pen name of Samuel Langhorne Clemens, American novelist and satirist)

WEDNESDAY
D 66.7
S 57.1
N 52.4
14

Genius is the ability to put into effect what is in your mind. — F. Scott Fitzgerald (author, 1896–1940)

Bullish Cluster Highlights March's "Sweet Spot"

THURSDAY
D 66.7
S 71.4
N 47.6
15

At a time of war, we need you to work for peace. At a time of inequality, we need you to work for opportunity.
At a time of so much cynicism and so much doubt, we need you to make us believe again.
— Barack H. Obama (44th U.S. president, Commencement Wesleyan University, 5/28/2008, b. 1961)

March Triple Witching Day, Mixed Last 12 Years
Dow Down 3 of Last 5

FRIDAY
D 61.9
S 61.9
N 66.7
16

Civility is not a sign of weakness, and sincerity is always subject to proof. Let us never negotiate out of fear.
But let us never fear to negotiate.
— John F. Kennedy (35th U.S. president, Inaugural Address, 1/20/1961, 1917–1963)

St. Patrick's Day

SATURDAY
17

SUNDAY
18

HOW THE GOVERNMENT MANIPULATES THE ECONOMY TO STAY IN POWER

Bull markets tend to occur in the third and fourth years of presidential terms, while markets tend to decline in the first and second years. The "making of presidents" is accompanied by an unsubtle manipulation of the economy. Incumbent administrations are duty-bound to retain the reins of power. Subsequently, the "piper must be paid," producing what we have coined the "Post-Presidential Year Syndrome." Most big, bad bear markets began in such years—1929, 1937, 1957, 1969, 1973, 1977 and 1981. Our major wars also began in years following elections—Civil War (1861), WWI (1917), WWII (1941) and Vietnam (1965). Post-election 2001 combined with 2002 for the worst back-to-back years since 1973–74. Plus we had 9/11, the war on terror, and the build-up to confrontation with Iraq.

Some cold hard facts to prove economic manipulation appeared in a book by Edward R. Tufte, *Political Control of the Economy* (Princeton University Press). Stimulative fiscal measures designed to increase per capita disposable income and provide a sense of well-being to the voting public included: increases in federal budget deficits, government spending, and social security benefits; interest rate reductions on government loans; and speed-ups of projected funding.

Federal Spending: During 1962–1973, the average increase was 29% higher in election years than in non-election years.

Social Security: There were nine increases during the 1952–1974 period. Half of the six election-year increases became effective in September, eight weeks before Election Day. The average increase was 100% higher in presidential than in midterm election years. Annual adjustments for inflation have been the norm since then.

Real Disposable Income: Accelerated in all but one election year between 1947 and 1973 (excluding the Eisenhower years). Only one of the remaining odd-numbered years (1973) showed a marked acceleration.

These moves were obviously not coincidences and explain why we tend to have a political (four-year) stock market cycle. Here are more examples of Election Year "generosity":

- Nixon plans to pump about $1 billion a month more than originally planned into spending programs designed to put money into the pockets of millions of currently unhappy voters....Such openhanded spending marks Nixon's conversion from unsuccessful policies of conservatism and gradualism to the activist, pump-priming, Keynesian economic theory. *Time Magazine*, January 31, 1972.

- EPA Administrator Carol M. Browner today announced President Clinton's proposed fiscal year 2001 budget of $7.3 billion for the United States Environmental Protection Agency, the largest increase in the history of the Clinton/Gore Administration in spending for EPA. February 7, 2000.

- Like many of its predecessors, the Bush White House has used the machinery of government to promote the reelection of the president by awarding federal grants to strategically important states. *NY Times*, May 18, 2004.

- Even some conservatives grumble that Bush's tax cuts, expanded drug benefits for seniors, and increased military spending have spurred a dramatic increase in the federal budget deficit, projected to be $477 billion in fiscal 2004, according to the Congressional Budget Office. *TheStreet.com*, July 2, 2004.

The United States does not have an exclusive on electoral spending manipulations:

- An executive increases spending to reward or cultivate loyalty to himself as the party or coalition leader. Evidence from South Korea and Taiwan between the 1970s and 2000 supports the theory. This strategy affects spending outcomes in election years. *Journal of East Asian Studies*, January 2006

As we go to press in 2012, election campaigning has already begun, but a leading Republican challenger has yet to emerge. The Federal Reserve, the White House, and Congress have been priming the pump nonstop since 2008 to keep the U.S. economy solvent, so there is not much that can be done other than additional quantitative easing by the Fed. After two and half rough years and falling approval ratings, Obama turned opinion around by taking out Bin Laden. Republican proposals to reduce entitlement programs and the budget and deficit battles have not gone over well. If Obama has more legislative, political, and diplomatic success and if Republicans continue to fumble, he will be able to campaign from the bully pulpit and be much harder to beat in 2012.

An economist is someone who sees something happen, and then wonders if it would work in theory.
— Ronald Reagan (40th U.S. president, 1911–2004)

Week after Triple Witching, Dow Down 15 of Last 24,   2000 Up 4.9%,
2007 Up 3.1%, 2009 Up 6.8%, 2011 Up 3.1%, Up 6 of Last 8

*If the market does not rally, as it should during bullish seasonal periods, it is a sign that other forces are stronger
and that when the seasonal period ends, those forces will really have their say.*
— Edson Gould (Stock market analyst, *Findings & Forecasts*, 1902–1987)

There are two kinds of people who lose money: those who know nothing and those who know everything.
— Henry Kaufman (German-American economist, b. 1927, to Robert Lenzner in Forbes, 10/19/98, who added,
"With two Nobel Prize winners in the house, Long-Term Capital clearly fits the second case.")

March Historically Weak Later in the Month (Pages 28 and 134)

If a man can see both sides of a problem, you know that none of his money is tied up in it. — Verda Ross

The less a man knows about the past and the present the more insecure must be his judgment of the future.
— Sigmund Freud (Austrian neurologist, psychiatrist, "father of psychoanalysis," 1856–1939)

APRIL ALMANAC

APRIL						
S	M	T	W	T	F	S
1	2	3	4	5	6	7
8	9	10	11	12	13	14
15	16	17	18	19	20	21
22	23	24	25	26	27	28
29	30					

MAY						
S	M	T	W	T	F	S
	1	2	3	4	5	
6	7	8	9	10	11	12
13	14	15	16	17	18	19
20	21	22	23	24	25	26
27	28	29	30	31		

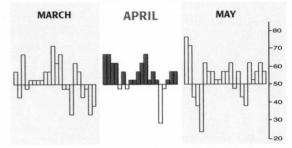

Market Probability Chart above is a graphic representation of the S&P 500 Recent Market Probability Calendar on page 124.

◆ April is still the best Dow month (average 2.0%) since 1950 (page 44) ◆ April 1999 first month ever to gain 1000 Dow points, 856 in 2001, knocked off its high horse in 2002 down 458, 2003 up 488 ◆ Up six straight, average gain 4.2% ◆ Prone to weakness after mid-month tax deadline ◆ Stocks anticipate great first quarter earnings by rising sharply before earnings are reported, rather than after ◆ Rarely a dangerous month, recent exceptions are 2002, 2004, and 2005 ◆ "Best Six Months" of the year end with April (page 48) ◆ Since 1952 election year Aprils have been weaker (Dow 1.0%, S&P 0.8%, NASDAQ -0.1%) ◆ End of April NASDAQ strength (pages 125 and 126).

April Vital Statistics

	DJIA		S&P 500		NASDAQ		Russell 1K		Russell 2K	
Rank	1		2		4		1		2	
Up	40		43		27		22		22	
Down	22		19		14		11		11	
Avg % Change	2.0%		1.5%		1.6%		1.7%		1.9%	
Election Year	1.0%		0.8%		-0.1%		1.1%		0.2%	
Best and Worst April										
	% Change		% Change		% Change		% Change		% Change	
Best	1978	10.6	2009	9.4	2001	15.0	2009	10.0	2009	15.3
Worst	1970	-6.3	1970	-9.0	2000	-15.6	2002	-5.8	2000	-6.1
Best and Worst April Weeks										
Best	4/11/75	5.7	4/20/00	5.8	4/12/01	14.0	4/20/00	5.9	4/3/09	6.3
Worst	4/14/00	-7.3	4/14/00	-10.5	4/14/00	-25.3	4/14/00	-11.2	4/14/00	-16.4
Best and Worst April Days										
Best	4/5/01	4.2	4/5/01	4.4	4/5/01	8.9	4/5/01	4.6	4/9/09	5.9
Worst	4/14/00	-5.7	4/14/00	-5.8	4/14/00	-9.7	4/14/00	-6.0	4/14/00	-7.3
First Trading Day of Expiration Week: 1980–2011										
Record (#Up–#Down)	20–12		19–13		18–14		18–14		13–19	
Current Streak	U2		D1		D1		D1		D1	
Avg % Change	0.24		0.19		0.20		0.18		0.07	
Options Expiration Day: 1980–2011										
Record (#Up–#Down)	22–10		21–11		19–13		21–11		20–12	
Current Streak	U1		U1		U1		U1		U1	
Avg % Change	0.24		0.20		-0.03		0.19		0.20	
Options Expiration Week: 1980–2011										
Record (#Up–#Down)	26–6		23–9		22–10		21–11		24–8	
Current Streak	D1		D2		D1		D2		D1	
Avg % Change	1.17		0.95		1.05		0.92		0.85	
Week After Options Expiration: 1980–2011										
Record (#Up–#Down)	21–11		21–11		23–9		21–11		21–11	
Current Streak	U2		U2		U5		U2		U2	
Avg % Change	0.37		0.32		0.58		0.33		0.79	
First Trading Day Performance										
% of Time Up	59.7		62.9		46.3		60.6		48.5	
Avg % Change	0.17		0.14		-0.14		0.17		-0.10	
Last Trading Day Performance										
% of Time Up	51.6		56.5		68.3		57.6		69.7	
Avg % Change	0.10		0.10		0.20		0.10		0.16	

Dow and S&P 1950–April 2011, NASDAQ 1971–April 2011, Russell 1K and 2K 1979–April 2011.

April "Best Month" for Dow since 1950;
Day-before-Good Friday gains are nifty.

MONDAY
D 57.1
S 57.1
N 61.9
26

With respect to trading Sugar futures, if they give it away for free at restaurants, you probably don't want to be trading it.
— John L. Person (Professional trader, author, speaker, *Commodity Trader's Almanac*, nationalfutures.com, 2/22/2011 TradersExpo, b. 1961)

TUESDAY
D 38.1
S 42.9
N 47.6
27

It is better to be out wishing you were in, than in wishing you were out.
— Albert W. Thomas (Trader, investor, *Over My Shoulder*, mutualfundmagic.com, *If It Doesn't Go Up, Don't Buy It!*, b. 1927)

WEDNESDAY
D 52.4
S 47.6
N 38.1
28

When everybody thinks alike, everyone is likely to be wrong.
— Humphrey B. Neill (Investor, analyst, author, *Art of Contrary Thinking* 1954, 1895–1977)

Start Looking for the Dow and S&P MACD SELL Signal (Pages 48 and 50) **THURSDAY**
Almanac Investor Subscribers E-mailed When It Triggers (See Insert)
D 52.4
S 33.3
N 42.9
29

The power to tax involves the power to destroy.
— John Marshall (Chief justice, U. S. Supreme Court, 1801–1835, opinion, 1819, 1755–1835)

Last Trading Day of March, Dow Down 12 of Last 17 **FRIDAY**
Russell 2000 Up 13 of Last 17
D 33.3
S 38.1
N 57.1
30

The only things that evolve by themselves in an organization are disorder, friction, and malperformance.
— Peter Drucker (Austrian-born pioneer management theorist, 1909–2005)

SATURDAY
31

April Almanac Investor Seasonalities: See Pages 92, 94, and 96

SUNDAY
1

INCUMBENT PARTY WINS AND LOSSES

Since 1944 stocks tend to move up earlier when White House occupants are popular but do even better in November and December when unpopular administrations are ousted.

TREND OF S&P 500 INDEX IN ELECTION YEARS 1944–2008

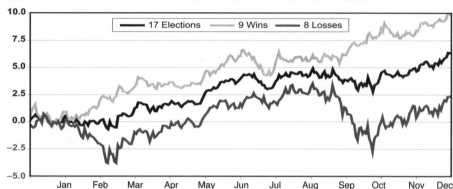

Actual percentage changes reveal that March, June, October, and December are best when incumbents stay in power, while July is worst. January, February, September, and October are the worst when they are removed. Ironically, November is best when incumbents are ousted and second worst when they win.

Other interesting tidbits: there were no major losses in October (1984 off fractionally) and only one in June and December when incumbent parties retained the White House. Republican wins in November resulted in total gains of 23.6% (excluding no-decision 2000). Democratic victories produced total losses of 4.9% in November; however, Democrats "gained" 16.4% in December, the Republicans 7.9%.

MONTHLY % CHANGES IN S&P 500 DURING ELECTION YEARS

Incumbents Win

Year	Jan	Feb	Mar	Apr	May	Jun	Jul	Aug	Sep	Oct	Nov	Dec
1944	1.5	−0.3	1.7	−1.3	4.0	5.1	−2.1	0.9	−0.3	N/C	0.4	3.5
1948	−4.0	−4.7	7.7	2.7	7.8	0.3	−5.3	0.8	−3.0	6.8	−10.8	3.1
1956	−3.6	3.5	6.9	−0.2	−6.6	3.9	5.2	−3.8	−4.5	0.5	−1.1	3.5
1964	2.7	1.0	1.5	0.6	1.1	1.6	1.8	−1.6	2.9	0.8	−0.5	0.4
1972	1.8	2.5	0.6	0.4	1.7	−2.2	0.2	3.4	−0.5	0.9	4.6	1.2
1984	−0.9	−3.9	1.3	0.5	−5.9	1.7	−1.6	10.6	−0.3	−0.01	−1.5	2.2
1988	4.0	4.2	−3.3	0.9	0.3	4.3	−0.5	−3.9	4.0	2.6	−1.9	1.5
1996	3.3	0.7	0.8	1.3	2.3	0.2	−4.6	1.9	5.4	2.6	7.3	−2.2
2004	1.7	1.2	−1.6	−1.7	1.2	1.8	−3.4	0.2	0.9	1.4	3.9	3.2
Totals	**6.5**	**4.2**	**15.6**	**3.3**	**5.9**	**16.7**	**−10.3**	**8.5**	**4.6**	**15.6**	**0.4**	**16.4**
Average	**0.7**	**0.5**	**1.7**	**0.4**	**0.7**	**1.9**	**−1.1**	**0.9**	**0.5**	**1.7**	**0.04**	**1.8**

Incumbents Lose

Year	Jan	Feb	Mar	Apr	May	Jun	Jul	Aug	Sep	Oct	Nov	Dec
1952	1.6	−3.6	4.8	−4.3	2.3	4.6	1.8	−1.5	−2.0	−0.1	4.6	3.5
1960	−7.1	0.9	−1.4	−1.8	2.7	2.0	−2.5	2.6	−6.0	−0.2	4.0	4.6
1968	−4.4	−3.1	0.9	8.2	1.1	0.9	−1.8	1.1	3.9	0.7	4.8	−4.2
1976	11.8	−1.1	3.1	−1.1	−1.4	4.1	−0.8	−0.5	2.3	−2.2	−0.8	5.2
1980	5.8	−0.4	−10.2	4.1	4.7	2.7	6.5	0.6	2.5	1.6	10.2	−3.4
1992	−2.0	1.0	−2.2	2.8	0.1	−1.7	3.9	−2.4	0.9	0.2	3.0	1.0
2000	−5.1	−2.0	9.7	−3.1	−2.2	2.4	−1.6	6.1	−5.3	−0.5	−8.0*	0.4
2008	−6.1	−3.5	−0.6	4.8	1.1	−8.6	−1.0	1.2	−9.1	−16.9	−7.5	0.8
Totals	**−5.5**	**−11.8**	**4.1**	**9.6**	**8.4**	**6.4**	**4.5**	**7.2**	**−12.8**	**−17.4**	**10.3**	**7.9**
Average	**−0.7**	**−1.5**	**0.5**	**1.2**	**1.1**	**0.8**	**0.6**	**0.9**	**−1.6**	**−2.2**	**1.3**	**1.0**

| **17 Elections** | **1.0** | **−7.6** | **19.7** | **12.9** | **14.3** | **23.1** | **−5.8** | **15.7** | **−8.2** | **−1.8** | **10.7** | **24.3** |
| **Average** | **0.1** | **−0.4** | **1.2** | **0.8** | **0.8** | **1.4** | **−0.3** | **0.9** | **−0.5** | **−0.1** | **0.6** | **1.4** |

*Undecided election

APRIL

First Trading Day in April, Dow Up 14 of Last 17

I am not a member of any organized party—I am a Democrat.
— Will Rogers (American humorist and showman, 1879–1935)

April is the Best Month for the Dow, Average 2.0% Gain Since 1950
2nd Best Month for S&P, 4th Best for NASDAQ (Since 1971)

To succeed in the markets, it is essential to make your own decisions. Numerous traders cited listening to others as their worst blunder. — Jack D. Schwager (Investment manager, author, Stock Market Wizards: Interviews with America's Top Stock Traders, b. 1948)

There are very few instances in history when any government has ever paid off debt.
— Walter Wriston (Retired CEO of Citicorp and Citibank)

NASDAQ Up 15 of 17 Day before Good Friday, 11 Straight Since 2001

If you are ready to give up everything else—to study the whole history and background of the market and all the principal companies ... as carefully as a medical student studies anatomy—... and, in addition, you have the cool nerves of a great gambler, the sixth sense of a clairvoyant, and the courage of a lion, you have a ghost of a chance.
— Bernard Baruch (Financier, speculator, statesman, presidential adviser, 1870–1965)

Good Friday (Market Closed)

If I had my life to live over again, I would elect to be a trader of goods rather than a student of science. I think barter is a noble thing.
— Albert Einstein (German/American physicist, 1921 Nobel Prize, 1934, 1879–1955)

Passover

Easter

THE DECEMBER LOW INDICATOR: A USEFUL PROGNOSTICATING TOOL

When the Dow closes below its December closing low in the first quarter, it is frequently an excellent warning sign. Jeffrey Saut, managing director of investment strategy at Raymond James, brought this to our attention a few years ago. The December Low Indicator was originated by Lucien Hooper, a *Forbes* columnist and Wall Street analyst back in the 1970s. Hooper dismissed the importance of January and January's first week as reliable indicators. He noted that the trend could be random or even manipulated during a holiday-shortened week. Instead, said Hooper, "Pay much more attention to the December low. If that low is violated during the first quarter of the New Year, watch out!"

Eighteen of the 32 occurrences were followed by gains for the rest of the year—and 16 full-year gains—after the low for the year was reached. For perspective we've included the January Barometer readings for the selected years. Hooper's "Watch Out" warning was absolutely correct, though. All but two of the instances since 1952 experienced further declines, as the Dow fell an additional 10.9% on average when December's low was breached in Q1.

Only three significant drops occurred (not shown) when December's low was not breached in Q1 (1974, 1981, and 1987). Both indicators were wrong only five times, and nine years ended flat. If the December low is not crossed, turn to our January Barometer for guidance. It has been virtually perfect, right nearly 100% of these times (view the complete results at *www.stocktradersalmanac.com*).

YEARS DOW FELL BELOW DECEMBER LOW IN FIRST QUARTER

Year	Previous Dec Low	Date Crossed	Crossing Price	Subseq. Low	% Change Cross-Low	Rest of Year % Change	Full Year % Change	Jan Bar
1952	262.29	2/19/52	261.37	256.35	−1.9%	11.7%	8.4%	1.6%[2]
1953	281.63	2/11/53	281.57	255.49	−9.3	−0.2	−3.8	−0.7[3]
1956	480.72	1/9/56	479.74	462.35	−3.6	4.1	2.3	−3.6[1,2,3]
1957	480.61	1/18/57	477.46	419.79	−12.1	−8.7	−12.8	−4.2
1960	661.29	1/12/60	660.43	566.05	−14.3	−6.7	−9.3	−7.1
1962	720.10	1/5/62	714.84	535.76	−25.1	−8.8	−10.8	−3.8
1966	939.53	3/1/66	938.19	744.32	−20.7	−16.3	−18.9	0.5[1]
1968	879.16	1/22/68	871.71	825.13	−5.3	8.3	4.3	−4.4[1,2,3]
1969	943.75	1/6/69	936.66	769.93	−17.8	−14.6	−15.2	−0.8
1970	769.93	1/26/70	768.88	631.16	−17.9	9.1	4.8	−7.6[2,3]
1973	1000.00	1/29/73	996.46	788.31	−20.9	−14.6	−16.6	−1.7
1977	946.64	2/7/77	946.31	800.85	−15.4	−12.2	−17.3	−5.1
1978	806.22	1/5/78	804.92	742.12	−7.8	0.01	−3.1	−6.2[3]
1980	819.62	3/10/80	818.94	759.13	−7.3	17.7	14.9	5.8[2]
1982	868.25	1/5/82	865.30	776.92	−10.2	20.9	19.6	−1.8[1,2]
1984	1236.79	1/25/84	1231.89	1086.57	−11.8	−1.6	−3.7	−0.9[3]
1990	2687.93	1/15/90	2669.37	2365.10	−11.4	−1.3	−4.3	−6.9[3]
1991	2565.59	1/7/91	2522.77	2470.30	−2.1	25.6	20.3	4.2[2]
1993	3255.18	1/8/93	3251.67	3241.95	−0.3	15.5	13.7	0.7[2]
1994	3697.08	3/30/94	3626.75	3593.35	−0.9	5.7	2.1	3.3[2,3]
1996	5059.32	1/10/96	5032.94	5032.94	NC	28.1	26.0	3.3[2]
1998	7660.13	1/9/98	7580.42	7539.07	−0.5	21.1	16.1	1.0[2]
2000	10998.39	1/4/00	10997.93	9796.03	−10.9	−1.9	−6.2	−5.1
2001	10318.93	3/12/01	10208.25	8235.81	−19.3	−1.8	−7.1	3.5[1]
2002	9763.96	1/16/02	9712.27	7286.27	−25.0	−14.1	−16.8	−1.6
2003	8303.78	1/24/03	8131.01	7524.06	−7.5	28.6	25.3	−2.7[1,2]
2005	10440.58	1/21/05	10392.99	10012.36	−3.7	3.1	−0.6	−2.5[3]
2006	10717.50	1/20/06	10667.39	10667.39	NC	16.8	16.3	2.5
2007	12194.13	3/2/07	12114.10	12050.41	−0.5	9.5	6.4	1.4[2]
2008	13167.20	1/2/08	13043.96	7552.29	−42.1	−32.7	−33.8	−6.1
2009	8149.09	1/20/09	7949.09	6547.05	−17.6	31.2	18.8	−8.6[1,2]
2010	10285.97	1/22/10	10172.98	9686.48	−4.8	13.8	11.0	−3.7[1,2]
			Average Drop		−10.9%			

[1] January Barometer wrong   [2] December Low Indicator wrong   [3] Year Flat

APRIL

Day after Easter, Worst Post-Holiday, S&P Down 16 of 20 from 1984 to 2003,
But Improving Recently, Up 6 of Last 8, Including 1.5% Gain in 2008

MONDAY

D 42.9
S 47.6
N 38.1

9

Bill Gates' One-Minus Staffing: For every project, figure out the bare minimum of people needed to staff it.
Cut to the absolute muscle and bones, then take out one more. When you understaff, people jump on the loose ball.
You find out who the real performers are. Not so when you're overstaffed. People sit around
waiting for somebody else to do it. — Quoted by Rich Karlgaard (Publisher, *Forbes*, Dec. 25, 2000)

TUESDAY

D 52.4
S 57.1
N 52.4

10

Oil has fostered massive corruption in almost every country that has been "blessed" with it, and the
expectation that oil wealth will transform economies has led to disastrous policy choices.
— Ted Tyson (Chief investment officer, Mastholm Asset Management)

WEDNESDAY

D 47.6
S 47.6
N 47.6

11

Laws are like sausages. It's better not to see them being made.
— Otto von Bismarck (German-Prussian politician, 1st chancellor of Germany, 1815–1898)

THURSDAY

D 66.7
S 52.4
N 61.9

12

When you're one step ahead of the crowd, you're a genius. When you're two steps ahead, you're a crackpot.
— Shlomo Riskin (Rabbi, author, b. 1940)

FRIDAY

D 61.9
S 52.4
N 52.4

13

Life is like riding a bicycle. You don't fall off unless you stop peddling.
— Claude D. Pepper (U.S. senator, Florida, 1936–1951, 1900–1989)

SATURDAY

14

SUNDAY

15

DOWN JANUARYS: A REMARKABLE RECORD

In the first third of the twentieth century, there was no correlation between January markets and the year as a whole (page 24). Then, in 1972 Yale Hirsch discovered that the 1933 "lame duck" Amendment to the Constitution changed the political calendar, and the January Barometer was born. Its record has been quite accurate (page 16).

Down Januarys are harbingers of trouble ahead, in the economic, political, or military arenas. Eisenhower's heart attack in 1955 cast doubt on whether he could run in 1956—a flat year. Two other election years with down Januarys were also flat (1984 and 1992). Twelve bear markets began, and ten continued into second years with poor Januarys. 1968 started down, as we were mired in Vietnam, but Johnson's "bombing halt" changed the climate. Imminent military action in Iraq held January 2003 down before the market triple-bottomed in March. After Baghdad fell, pre-election and recovery forces fueled 2003 into a banner year. 2005 was flat, registering the narrowest Dow trading range on record. 2008 was the worst January on record and preceded the worst bear market since the Great Depression. A negative reading in 2010 preceded a 16% April-July correction, which was quickly reversed by QE2.

Unfortunately, bull and bear markets do not start conveniently at the beginnings and ends of months or years. Though some years ended higher, **every down January since 1950 was followed by a new or continuing bear market, a 10% correction or a flat year. Down Januarys were followed by substantial declines averaging** *minus* **13.9%,** providing excellent buying opportunities later in most years.

FROM DOWN JANUARY S&P CLOSES TO LOW NEXT 11 MONTHS

Year	January Close	% Change	11-Month Low	Date of Low	Jan Close to Low %	% Feb to Dec	Year % Change	
1953	26.38	−0.7%	22.71	14-Sep	−13.9%	−6.0%	−6.6%	bear
1956	43.82	−3.6	44.10	28-May	−0.9	6.5	2.6	FLAT/bear
1957	44.72	−4.2	38.98	22-Oct	−12.8	−10.6	−14.3	Cont. bear
1960	55.61	−7.1	52.30	25-Oct	−6.0	4.5	−3.0	bear
1962	68.84	−3.8	52.32	26-Jun	−24.0	−8.3	−11.8	bear
1968	92.24	−4.4	87.72	5-Mar	−4.9	12.6	7.7	-10%/bear
1969	103.01	−0.8	89.20	17-Dec	−13.4	−10.6	−11.4	Cont. bear
1970	85.02	−7.6	69.20	26-May	−18.6	8.4	0.1	Cont. bear/FLAT
1973	116.03	−1.7	92.16	5-Dec	−20.6	−15.9	−17.4	bear
1974	96.57	−1.0	62.28	3-Oct	−35.5	−29.0	−29.7	Cont. bear
1977	102.03	−5.1	90.71	2-Nov	−11.1	−6.8	−11.5	bear
1978	89.25	−6.2	86.90	6-Mar	−2.6	7.7	1.1	Cont. bear/bear
1981	129.55	−4.6	112.77	25-Sep	−13.0	−5.4	−9.7	bear
1982	120.40	−1.8	102.42	12-Aug	−14.9	16.8	14.8	Cont. bear
1984	163.42	−0.9	147.82	24-Jul	−9.5	2.3	1.4	Cont. bear/FLAT
1990	329.07	−6.9	295.46	11-Oct	−10.2	0.4	−6.6	bear
1992	408.79	−2.0	394.50	8-Apr	−3.5	6.6	4.5	FLAT
2000	1394.46	−5.1	1264.74	20-Dec	−9.3	−5.3	−10.1	bear
2002	1130.20	−1.6	776.76	9-Oct	−31.3	−22.2	−23.4	bear
2003	855.70	−2.7	800.73	11-Mar	−6.4	29.9	26.4	Cont. bear
2005	1181.27	−2.5	1137.50	20-Apr	−3.7	5.7	3.0	FLAT
2008	1378.55	−6.1	752.44	20-Nov	−45.4	−34.5	−38.5	Cont. bear
2009	825.88	−8.6	676.53	9-Mar	−18.1	35.0	23.5	Cont. bear
2010	1073.87	−3.7	1022.58	2-Jul	−4.8	17.1	12.8	-10%/no bear
Totals					−334.4%	−1.1%	−96.2%	
Average					−13.9%	−0.05%	−4.0%	

ncome Tax Deadline, *Generally Bullish, Dow Down Only Five Times Since 1981*
Monday before Expiration, Dow Up 15 of Last 22, Down 4 of Last 7

MONDAY
D 71.4
S 57.1
N 61.9

16

our organization will never get better unless you are willing to admit that there is something wrong with it.
– General Norman Schwartzkof (Retired commander of Allied Forces in 1990–1991 Gulf War)

pril Prone to Weakness after Tax Deadline (Pages 36 and 134)

TUESDAY
D 71.4
S 61.9
N 38.1

17

m a great believer in luck, and I find the harder I work the more I have of it.
– Thomas Jefferson (3rd U.S. president, 1743–7/4/1826)

WEDNESDAY
D 61.9
S 66.7
N 52.4

18

he usual bull market successfully weathers a number of tests until it is considered invulnerable,
hereupon it is ripe for a bust.
– George Soros (Financier, philanthropist, political activist, author, and philosopher, b. 1930)

THURSDAY
D 52.4
S 52.4
N 47.6

19

fake it idiot-proof and someone will make a better idiot. — Bumper sticker

pril Expiration Day, Dow Up 12 of Last 15,
?007 Up 1.2%; 2008 Up 1.8%; 2001, 2005, and 2010 up 1.0%

FRIDAY
D 61.9
S 57.1
N 57.1

20

hree billion new people will be active on the Internet within ten years, as wireless broadband becomes ubiquitous.
– John Mauldin (Millennium Wave Advisors, 2000wave.com, 2/2/07)

SATURDAY

21

SUNDAY

22

TOP PERFORMING MONTHS PAST 61⅓ YEARS: STANDARD & POOR'S 500 AND DOW JONES INDUSTRIALS

Monthly performance of the S&P and the Dow are ranked over the past 61⅓ years. NASDAQ monthly performance is shown on page 56.

April, November, and December still hold the top three positions in both the Dow and the S&P. March has reclaimed the fourth spot on the S&P. Two disastrous Januarys in 2008 and 2009 knocked January into fifth. This, in part, led to our discovery in 1986 of the market's most consistent seasonal pattern. You can divide the year into two sections and have practically all the gains in one six-month section and very little in the other. September is the worst month on both lists. (See "Best Six Months" on page 48.)

MONTHLY % CHANGES (JANUARY 1950 TO APRIL 2011)

	Standard & Poor's 500					Dow Jones Industrials			
Month	Total % Change	Avg. % Change	# Up	# Down	Month	Total % Change	Avg. % Change	# Up	# Down
Jan	65.2%	1.1%	38	24	Jan	63.0%	1.0%	40	22
Feb	−11.5	−0.2	33	29	Feb	0.3	0.005	35	27
Mar	71.1	1.1	40	22	Mar	66.1	1.1	40	22
Apr	95.9	1.5	43	19	Apr	124.2	2.0	40	22
May	15.5	0.3	35	26	May	2.9	0.1	31	30
Jun	−2.7	−0.04	32	29	Jun	−21.7	−0.4	28	33
Jul	59.9	1.0	33	28	Jul	74.3	1.2	38	23
Aug	3.3	0.05	34	27	Aug	−0.4	−0.01	35	26
Sep*	−28.2	−0.5	27	33	Sep	−47.1	−0.8	24	37
Oct	38.4	0.6	36	25	Oct	23.0	0.4	36	25
Nov	93.8	1.5	40	21	Nov	92.5	1.5	40	21
Dec	104.9	1.7	46	15	Dec	104.5	1.7	43	18
% Rank					**% Rank**				
Dec	104.9%	1.7%	46	15	Apr	124.2%	2.0%	40	22
Apr	95.9	1.5	43	19	Dec	104.5	1.7	43	18
Nov	93.8	1.5	40	21	Nov	92.5	1.5	40	21
Mar	71.1	1.1	40	22	Jul	74.3	1.2	38	23
Jan	65.2	1.1	38	24	Mar	66.1	1.1	40	22
Jul	59.9	1.0	33	28	Jan	63.0	1.0	40	22
Oct	38.4	0.6	36	25	Oct	23.0	0.4	36	25
May	15.5	0.3	35	26	May	2.9	0.1	31	30
Aug	3.3	0.05	34	27	Feb	0.3	0.005	35	27
Jun	−2.7	−0.04	32	29	Aug	−0.4	−0.01	35	26
Feb	−11.5	−0.2	33	29	Jun	−21.7	−0.4	28	33
Sep*	−28.2	−0.5	27	33	Sep	−47.1	−0.8	24	37
Totals	505.6%	8.1%			**Totals**	481.6%	7.7%		
Average		0.68%			**Average**		0.65%		

*No change 1979

Anticipators, shifts in cultural behavior, and faster information flow have altered seasonality in recent years. Here is how the months ranked over the past 15⅓ years (184 months), using total percentage gains on the S&P 500: April 38.6, November 28.1, March 25.7, December 23.7, October 18.0, May 8.9, July 0.6, September −0.7, January −4.4, June −6.4, August −14.6, February −17.4.

During the last 15⅓ years, front-runners of our Best Six Months may have helped push October into the number-five spot. May has slipped into the number-six spot. January has declined in seven of the last twelve years. Sizable turnarounds in "bear killing" October were a common occurrence from 1998 to 2007. Recent big Dow losses in the period were: August 1998 (SE Asia crisis), off 15.1%; September 2001 (9/11 attack), off 11.1%; September 2002 (Iraq war drums), off 12.4%; October 2008, off 14.1%; and February 2009 (financial crisis), off 11.7%.

APRIL

April 1999 First Month Ever to Gain 1000 Dow Points

MONDAY
D 57.1
S 52.4
N 52.4
23

If investing is entertaining, if you're having fun, you're probably not making any money. Good investing is boring.
— George Soros (Financier, philanthropist, political activist, author, and philosopher, b. 1930)

TUESDAY
D 42.9
S 28.6
N 47.6
24

Based on my own personal experience—both as an investor in recent years and an expert witness in years past—rarely do more than three or four variables really count. Everything else is noise.
— Martin J. Whitman (Founder, Third Avenue Funds, b. 1924)

FOMC Meeting (2 Days)

WEDNESDAY
D 52.4
S 47.6
N 42.9
25

What's going on... is the end of Silicon Valley as we know it. The next big thing ain't computers... it's biotechnology.
— Larry Ellison (Oracle CEO, quoted in *The Wall Street Journal*, April 8, 2003)

THURSDAY
D 52.4
S 52.4
N 61.9
26

The wisdom of the ages is the fruits of freedom and democracy.
— Lawrence Kudlow (Economist, 24th Annual Paulson SmallCap Conference, Waldorf Astoria NYC, 11/8/01)

FRIDAY
D 61.9
S 57.1
N 66.7
27

Almost any insider purchase is worth investigating for a possible lead to a superior speculation. But very few insider sales justify concern. — William Chidester (*Scientific Investing newsletter*)

SATURDAY
28

May Almanac Investor Seasonalities: See Pages 92, 94, and 96

SUNDAY
29

MAY ALMANAC

MAY							JUNE						
S	M	T	W	T	F	S	S	M	T	W	T	F	S
		1	2	3	4	5							1	2
6	7	8	9	10	11	12	3	4	5	6	7	8	9
13	14	15	16	17	18	19	10	11	12	13	14	15	16
20	21	22	23	24	25	26	17	18	19	20	21	22	23
27	28	29	30	31			24	25	26	27	28	29	30

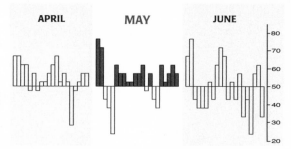

Market Probability Chart above is a graphic representation of the S&P 500 Recent Market Probability Calendar on page 124.

◆ "May/June disaster area" between 1965 and 1984 with S&P down 15 out of 20 Mays ◆ Between 1985 and 1997, May was the best month, with 13 straight gains, gaining 3.3% per year on average, up 7, down 6 since ◆ Worst six months of the year begin with May (page 48) ◆ A $10,000 investment compounded to $609,071 for November to April in 61 years, compared to a $379 loss for May to October ◆ Dow Memorial Day week record: up 12 years in a row (1984–1995), down eight of the last 15 years ◆ Since 1952, presidential election year Mays rank poorly, #10 Dow, #8 S&P, and #6 NASDAQ.

May Vital Statistics

	DJIA		S&P 500		NASDAQ		Russell 1K		Russell 2K	
Rank	8		8		5		4		5	
Up	31		35		24		22		21	
Down	30		26		16		10		11	
Avg % Change	0.05%		0.3%		1.0%		1.2%		1.6%	
Election Year	−0.4%		0.2%		−0.04%		0.2%		0.7%	
Best and Worst May										
	% Change		% Change		% Change		% Change		% Change	
Best	1990	8.3	1990	9.2	1997	11.1	1990	8.9	1997	11.0
Worst	2010	−7.9	1962	−8.6	2000	−11.9	2010	−8.1	2010	−7.7
Best and Worst May Weeks										
Best	5/29/70	5.8	5/2/97	6.2	5/17/02	8.8	5/2/97	6.4	5/14/10	6.3
Worst	5/25/62	−6.0	5/25/62	−6.8	5/7/10	−8.0	5/7/10	−3.9	5/7/10	−8.9
Best and Worst May Days										
Best	5/27/70	5.1	5/27/70	5.0	5/30/00	7.9	5/10/10	4.4	5/10/10	5.6
Worst	5/28/62	−5.7	5/28/62	−6.7	5/23/00	−5.9	5/20/10	−3.9	5/20/10	−5.1
First Trading Day of Expiration Week: 1980–2010										
Record (#Up–#Down)	21–10		21–10		17–14		20–11		16–15	
Current Streak	U1		U1		U1		U1		U1	
Avg % Change	0.23		0.22		0.20		0.19		0.01	
Options Expiration Day: 1980–2010										
Record (#Up–#Down)	14–17		17–14		15–16		17–14		15–16	
Current Streak	U1		U1		U1		U1		U1	
Avg % Change	−0.11		−0.12		−0.12		−0.11		−0.02	
Options Expiration Week: 1980–2010										
Record (#Up–#Down)	17–14		16–15		16–15		15–16		17–14	
Current Streak	D2		D2		D2		D2		D2	
Avg % Change	0.17		0.11		0.30		0.12		−0.04	
Week After Options Expiration: 1980–2010										
Record (#Up–#Down)	17–14		19–12		21–10		19–12		22–9	
Current Streak	D1		U2		U2		U2		U2	
Avg % Change	−0.06		0.06		0.07		0.09		0.18	
First Trading Day Performance										
% of Time Up	59.0		59.0		62.5		56.3		65.6	
Avg % Change	0.22		0.25		0.35		0.29		0.39	
Last Trading Day Performance										
% of Time Up	62.3		63.9		72.5		59.4		71.9	
Avg % Change	0.22		0.30		0.23		0.28		0.39	

Dow and S&P 1950–April 2011, NASDAQ 1971–April 2011, Russell 1K and 2K 1979–April 2011.

May's new pattern, a smile or a frown,
Odd years UP and even years DOWN.

End of "Best Six Months" of the Year (Pages 44, 48, 50, and 147)

MONDAY
D 47.6
S 57.1
N 66.7
30

A cynic is a man who knows the price of everything and the value of nothing.
— Oscar Wilde (Irish-born writer and wit, 1845–1900)

First Trading Day in May, Dow Up 11 of Last 14

TUESDAY
D 76.2
S 76.2
N 76.2
1

"Sell in May and go away." However, no one ever said it was the beginning of the month.
— John L. Person (Professional trader, author, speaker, *Commodity Trader's Almanac*,
nationalfutures.com, 6/19/2009, b. 1961)

WEDNESDAY
D 71.4
S 71.4
N 66.7
2

*The future now belongs to societies that organize themselves for learning. What we know and can do holds
the key to economic progress.* — Ray Marshall (b. 1928) and Marc Tucker (b. 1939)
(*Thinking for a Living: Education and the Wealth of Nations*, 1992)

THURSDAY
D 38.1
S 42.9
N 61.9
3

*There is a vitality, a life force, an energy, a quickening, that is translated through you into action, and because
there is only one of you in all time, this expression is unique. And if you block it, it will never exist through
any other medium and will be lost.* — Martha Graham (American choreographer, dancer, teacher)

FRIDAY
D 47.6
S 38.1
N 52.4
4

*The only way to even begin to manage this new world is by focusing on … nation building—helping
others restructure their economies and put in place decent non-corrupt government.*
— Thomas L. Friedman (*NY Times* Foreign Affairs columnist)

SATURDAY
5

SUNDAY
6

"BEST SIX MONTHS": STILL AN EYE-POPPING STRATEGY

Our Best Six Months Switching Strategy consistently delivers. Investing in the Dow Jones Industrial Average between November 1st and April 30th each year and then switching into fixed income for the other six months has produced reliable returns with reduced risk since 1950.

The chart on page 147 shows November, December, January, March, and April to be the top months since 1950. Add February, and an excellent strategy is born! These six consecutive months gained 13,395.65 Dow points in 61 years, while the remaining May through October months lost 799.44 points. The S&P gained 1332.94 points in the same best six months versus just 12.60 points in the worst six.

Percentage changes are shown along with a compounding $10,000 investment. The November–April $609,071 gain overshadows May–October's $379 loss. (S&P results were $446,635 to $6,544.) Just three November–April losses were double-digit: April 1970 (Cambodian invasion), 1973 (OPEC oil embargo) and 2008 (financial crisis). Similarly, Iraq muted the Best Six and inflated the Worst Six in 2003. When we discovered this strategy in 1986, November–April outperformed May–October by $88,163 to minus $1,522. Results improved substantially these past 25 years, $520,908 to $1,143. A simple timing indicator triples results (page 50).

SIX-MONTH SWITCHING STRATEGY

	DJIA % Change May 1–Oct 31	Investing $10,000	DJIA % Change Nov 1–Apr 30	Investing $10,000
1950	5.0%	$10,500	15.2%	$11,520
1951	1.2	10,626	−1.8	11,313
1952	4.5	11,104	2.1	11,551
1953	0.4	11,148	15.8	13,376
1954	10.3	12,296	20.9	16,172
1955	6.9	13,144	13.5	18,355
1956	−7.0	12,224	3.0	18,906
1957	−10.8	10,904	3.4	19,549
1958	19.2	12,998	14.8	22,442
1959	3.7	13,479	−6.9	20,894
1960	−3.5	13,007	16.9	24,425
1961	3.7	13,488	−5.5	23,082
1962	−11.4	11,950	21.7	28,091
1963	5.2	12,571	7.4	30,170
1964	7.7	13,539	5.6	31,860
1965	4.2	14,108	−2.8	30,968
1966	−13.6	12,189	11.1	34,405
1967	−1.9	11,957	3.7	35,678
1968	4.4	12,483	−0.2	35,607
1969	−9.9	11,247	−14.0	30,622
1970	2.7	11,551	24.6	38,155
1971	−10.9	10,292	13.7	43,382
1972	0.1	10,302	−3.6	41,820
1973	3.8	10,693	−12.5	36,593
1974	−20.5	8,501	23.4	45,156
1975	1.8	8,654	19.2	53,826
1976	−3.2	8,377	−3.9	51,727
1977	−11.7	7,397	2.3	52,917
1978	−5.4	6,998	7.9	57,097
1979	−4.6	6,676	0.2	57,211
1980	13.1	7,551	7.9	61,731
1981	−14.6	6,449	−0.5	61,422
1982	16.9	7,539	23.6	75,918
1983	−0.1	7,531	−4.4	72,578
1984	3.1	7,764	4.2	75,626
1985	9.2	8,478	29.8	98,163
1986	5.3	8,927	21.8	119,563
1987	−12.8	7,784	1.9	121,835
1988	5.7	8,228	12.6	137,186
1989	9.4	9,001	0.4	137,735
1990	−8.1	8,272	18.2	162,803
1991	6.3	8,793	9.4	178,106
1992	−4.0	8,441	6.2	189,149
1993	7.4	9,066	0.03	189,206
1994	6.2	9,628	10.6	209,262
1995	10.0	10,591	17.1	245,046
1996	8.3	11,470	16.2	284,743
1997	6.2	12,181	21.8	346,817
1998	−5.2	11,548	25.6	435,602
1999	−0.5	11,490	0.04	435,776
2000	2.2	11,743	−2.2	426,189
2001	−15.5	9,923	9.6	467,103
2002	−15.6	8,375	1.0	471,774
2003	15.6	9,682	4.3	492,060
2004	−1.9	9,498	1.6	499,933
2005	2.4	9,726	8.9	544,427
2006	6.3	10,339	8.1	588,526
2007	6.6	11,021	−8.0	541,444
2008	−27.3	8,012	−12.4	474,305
2009	18.9	9,526	13.3	537,388
2010	1.0	9,621	15.2	619,071
Average/Gain	**0.4%**	**($379)**	**7.5%**	**$609,071**
# Up/Down	**37/24**		**47/14**	

48

MAY

MONDAY
D 33.3
S 23.8
N 33.3
7

A fanatic is one who can't change his mind and won't change the subject.
— Winston Churchill (British statesman, 1874–1965)

TUESDAY
D 71.4
S 61.9
N 76.2
8

There is no tool to change human nature… people are prone to recurring bouts of optimism and pessimism that manifest themselves from time to time in the buildup or cessation of speculative excesses.
— Alan Greenspan (Fed chairman 1987–2006, July 18, 2001 monetary policy report to the Congress)

WEDNESDAY
D 61.9
S 57.1
N 52.4
9

Man's mind, once stretched by a new idea, never regains its original dimensions.
— Oliver Wendell Holmes (American author, poet, and physician, 1809–1894)

THURSDAY
D 66.7
S 57.1
N 42.9
10

Have not great merchants, great manufacturers, great inventors done more for the world than preachers and philanthropists? Can there be any doubt that cheapening the cost of necessities and conveniences of life is the most powerful agent of civilization and progress? — Charles Elliott Perkins (Railroad magnate, 1888, 1840–1907)

Friday before Mother's Day, Dow Up 11 of Last 17

FRIDAY
D 52.4
S 52.4
N 52.4
11

Companies that announce mass layoffs or a series of firings underperform the stock market over a three-year period.
— Bain & Company (*Smart Money Magazine*, August 2001)

SATURDAY
12

Mother's Day

SUNDAY
13

MACD-TIMING TRIPLES "BEST SIX MONTHS" RESULTS

Using the simple MACD (Moving Average Convergence Divergence) indicator developed by our friend Gerald Appel to better time entries and exits into and out of the Best Six Months (page 48) period nearly triples the results. Several years ago, Sy Harding enhanced our Best Six Months Switching Strategy with MACD triggers, dubbing it the "best mechanical system ever." In 2006, we improved it even more, quadrupling the results with just four trades every four years (page 60).

Our *Almanac Investor Newsletter* (see insert) implements this system with quite a degree of success. Starting October 1, we look to catch the market's first hint of an uptrend after the summer doldrums, and beginning April 1, we prepare to exit these seasonal positions as soon as the market falters.

In up-trending markets, MACD signals get you in earlier and keep you in longer. But if the market is trending down, entries are delayed until the market turns up, and exit points can come a month earlier.

The results from applying the simple MACD signals are astounding. Instead of $10,000 gaining $609,071 over the 61 recent years when invested only during the Best Six Months (page 48), the gain nearly tripled to $1,581,034. The $379 loss during the worst six months expanded to a loss of $6,383.

Impressive results for being invested during only 6.4 months of the year on average! For the rest of the year, consider money markets, bonds, puts, bear funds, covered calls, or credit call spreads. See page 32 for more executable trades employing ETFs and mutual funds.

Updated signals are e-mailed to our *Almanac Investor eNewsletter* subscribers as soon as they are triggered. Visit *www.stocktradersalmanac.com,* or see the insert for details and a special offer for new subscribers.

SIX-MONTH SWITCHING STRATEGY+TIMING

	DJIA % Change May 1–Oct 31*	Investing $10,000	DJIA % Change Nov 1–Apr 30*	Investing $10,000
1950	7.3%	$10,730	13.3%	$11,330
1951	0.1	10,741	1.9	11,545
1952	1.4	10,891	2.1	11,787
1953	0.2	10,913	17.1	13,803
1954	13.5	12,386	16.3	16,053
1955	7.7	13,340	13.1	18,156
1956	−6.8	12,433	2.8	18,664
1957	−12.3	10,904	4.9	19,579
1958	17.3	12,790	16.7	22,849
1959	1.6	12,995	−3.1	22,141
1960	−4.9	12,358	16.9	25,883
1961	2.9	12,716	−1.5	25,495
1962	−15.3	10,770	22.4	31,206
1963	4.3	11,233	9.6	34,202
1964	6.7	11,986	6.2	36,323
1965	2.6	12,298	−2.5	35,415
1966	−16.4	10,281	14.3	40,479
1967	−2.1	10,065	5.5	42,705
1968	3.4	10,407	0.2	42,790
1969	−11.9	9,169	−6.7	39,923
1970	−1.4	9,041	20.8	48,227
1971	−11.0	8,046	15.4	55,654
1972	−0.6	7,998	−1.4	54,875
1973	−11.0	7,118	0.1	54,930
1974	−22.4	5,524	28.2	70,420
1975	0.1	5,530	18.5	83,448
1976	−3.4	5,342	−3.0	80,945
1977	−11.4	4,733	0.5	81,350
1978	−4.5	4,520	9.3	88,916
1979	−5.3	4,280	7.0	95,140
1980	9.3	4,678	4.7	99,612
1981	−14.6	3,995	0.4	100,010
1982	15.5	4,614	23.5	123,512
1983	2.5	4,729	−7.3	114,496
1984	3.3	4,885	3.9	118,961
1985	7.0	5,227	38.1	164,285
1986	−2.8	5,081	28.2	210,613
1987	−14.9	4,324	3.0	216,931
1988	6.1	4,588	11.8	242,529
1989	9.8	5,038	3.3	250,532
1990	−6.7	4,700	15.8	290,116
1991	4.8	4,926	11.3	322,899
1992	−6.2	4,621	6.6	344,210
1993	5.5	4,875	5.6	363,486
1994	3.7	5,055	13.1	411,103
1995	7.2	5,419	16.7	479,757
1996	9.2	5,918	21.9	584,824
1997	3.6	6,131	18.5	693,016
1998	−12.4	5,371	39.9	969,529
1999	−6.4	5,027	5.1	1,018,975
2000	−6.0	4,725	5.4	1,074,000
2001	−17.3	3,908	15.8	1,243,692
2002	−25.2	2,923	6.0	1,318,314
2003	16.4	3,402	7.8	1,421,142
2004	−0.9	3,371	1.8	1,446,723
2005	−0.5	3,354	7.7	1,558,121
2006	4.7	3,512	14.4	1,782,490
2007	5.6	3,709	−12.7	1,556,114
2008	−24.7	2,793	−14.0	1,338,258
2009	23.8	3,458	10.8	1,482,790
2010	4.6	3,617	7.3	1,591,034
Average	**−1.1%**		**9.2%**	
# Up	**32**		**52**	
# Down	**29**		**9**	
61-Year Gain (Loss)		**($6,383)**		**$1,581,034**

*MACD generated entry and exit points (earlier or later) can lengthen or shorten six-month periods.

Monday after Mother's Day, Dow Up 14 of Last 17
Monday before May Expiration, Dow Up 20 of Last 24, Average Gain 0.5%

N 47.0

Towering genius disdains a beaten path. It scorns to tread in the footsteps of any predecessor, however illustrious.
It thirsts for distinction. — Abraham Lincoln (16th U.S. president, 1809–1865)

TUESDAY
D 61.9
S 57.1
N 57.1
15

You know you're right when the other side starts to shout. — I. A. O'Shaughnessy (American oilman, 1885–1973)

WEDNESDAY
D 52.4
S 57.1
N 61.9
16

Great spirits have always encountered violent opposition from mediocre minds.
— Albert Einstein (German/American physicist, 1921 Nobel Prize, 1879–1955)

THURSDAY
D 57.1
S 61.9
N 66.7
17

Entrepreneurs who believe they're in business to vanquish the competition are less successful than
those who believe their goal is to maximize profits or increase their company's value.
— Kaihan Krippendorff (Business consultant, strategist, author, *The Art of the Advantage*,
The Strategic Learning Center, b. 1971)

May Expiration Day, Dow Down 13 of Last 22, Average Loss 0.2%

FRIDAY
D 47.6
S 47.6
N 42.9
18

Capitalism is the legitimate racket of the ruling class. — Al Capone (American gangster, 1899–1947)

SATURDAY
19

SUNDAY
20

NLY TWO LOSSES LAST 7 MONTHS OF ELECTION YEARS

Election years are traditionally up years. Incumbent administrations shamelessly attempt to massage the economy so voters will keep them in power. But, sometimes overpowering events occur, and the market crumbles, usually resulting in a change of political control. The Republicans won in 1920, as the post-war economy contracted and President Wilson ailed. The Democrats came back during the 1932 Depression when the Dow hit its lowest level of the twentieth century. A world at war and the fall of France jolted the market in 1940, but Roosevelt won an unprecedented third term. Cold War confrontations and Truman's historic upset of Dewey held markets down through the end of 1948.

Since 1948, investors have barely been bruised during election years, except for a brief span early in the year—until 2000 and then again in 2008. In both years a bubble burst: technology and internet stocks in 2000 and credit in 2008. Barring another massive regulatory failure, financial crisis, political miscalculation or exogenous event, this is unlikely to occur again in 2012.

The table below presents a very positive picture for the last seven or eight months of election years.

- Since 1952, January through April losses occurred in eight of fifteen election years. Incumbent parties were ousted on six of these eight losses. Ironically, bear markets commenced following four of seven gainers in 1956, 1968, 1973, and 1976.

- Comparing month-end June with month-end April reveals gains in 1952, 1960, 1968, 1988, and 2000 for the sixty-day period, when no sitting President ran for reelection.

- Of the fifteen Julys since 1952, nine were losers (1960, 1968, 1976, 1984, 1988, 1996, 2000, 2004, and 2008). Five were years when, at convention time, no strong incumbent was running for reelection. Note that April through July periods had only six losers, the last four in a row: 1972 by a small margin, 1984 as the market was turning around, 1996 and 2000 as the bubble began to work off its excesses, and 2004 and 2008 as the credit bubble burst.

- For a longer perspective, we extended the table to December. Just three losing eight-month periods in an election year are revealed, and only two losses in the last seven months of all these years.

S&P 500 DURING ELECTION YEARS

Election Year	% Change First 4 Months	April	May	June	July	Dec	% Change Last 8 Months	Last 7 Months
1952*	−1.9%	**23.32**	23.86	24.96	25.40	26.57	13.9%	11.4%
1956	6.4	**48.38**	**45.20**	46.97	49.39	46.67	−3.5	3.3
1960*	−9.2	**54.37**	55.83	56.92	**55.51**	58.11	6.9	4.1
1964	5.9	79.46	80.37	81.69	83.18	84.75	6.7	5.4
1968*	1.2	97.59	98.68	99.58	**97.74**	**103.86**	6.4	5.2
1972	5.5	107.67	109.53	**107.14**	107.39	118.05	9.6	7.8
1976*	12.7	**101.64**	**100.18**	104.28	**103.44**	107.46	5.7	7.3
1980*	−1.5	106.29	111.24	114.24	121.67	**135.76**	27.7	22.0
1984	−3.0	160.05	**150.55**	153.18	**150.66**	167.24	4.5	11.1
1988	5.8	261.33	262.16	273.50	**272.02**	277.72	6.3	5.9
1992*	−0.5	414.95	415.35	**408.14**	424.21	435.71	5.0	4.9
1996	6.2	654.17	669.12	670.63	**639.95**	**740.74**	13.2	10.7
2000**	−1.1	**1452.43**	**1420.60**	1454.60	**1430.83**	1320.28	−9.1	−7.1
2004	−0.4	**1107.30**	1120.68	1140.84	1101.72	1211.92	9.4	8.1
2008**	−5.6	1385.59	1400.38	**1280.00**	**1267.38**	903.25	−34.8	−35.5
Totals	20.5%						67.9%	64.6%
Average	1.4%						4.5%	4.3%

*Incumbents ousted ** Incumbent ousted and undecided election*
Down months are bold

MONDAY

D 57.1
S 57.1
N 71.4

21

The political problem of mankind is to combine three things: economic efficiency, social justice, and individual liberty. — John Maynard Keynes (British economist, 1883–1946)

TUESDAY

D 42.9
S 42.9
N 52.4

22

Those heroes of finance are like beads on a string, when one slips off, the rest follow. — Henrik Ibsen (Norwegian playwright, 1828–1906)

WEDNESDAY

D 38.1
S 38.1
N 47.6

23

Unless you've interpreted changes before they've occurred, you'll be decimated trying to follow them. — Robert J. Nurock (Market strategist, Investor's Analysis, Bob Nurock's Advisory, Wall Street Week panelist 1970–1989)

THURSDAY

D 52.4
S 61.9
N 57.1

24

War is God's way of teaching Americans geography. — Ambrose Bierce (Writer, satirist, Civil War hero, *The Devil's Dictionary*, 1842–1914?)

Friday before Memorial Day Tends to Be Lackluster with Light Trading, Dow Down 7 of Last 11, Average –0.4%

FRIDAY

D 47.6
S 52.4
N 47.6

25

We are all born originals; why is it so many die copies? — Edward Young (English poet, 1683–1765)

SATURDAY

26

June Almanac Investor Seasonalities: See Pages 92, 94, and 96

SUNDAY

27

JUNE ALMANAC

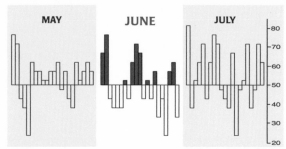

JUNE							JULY						
S	M	T	W	T	F	S	S	M	T	W	T	F	S
					1	2	1	2	3	4	5	6	7
3	4	5	6	7	8	9	8	9	10	11	12	13	14
10	11	12	13	14	15	16	15	16	17	18	19	20	21
17	18	19	20	21	22	23	22	23	24	25	26	27	28
24	25	26	27	28	29	30	29	30	31				

Market Probability Chart above is a graphic representation of the S&P 500 Recent Market Probability Calendar on page 124.

◆ The "summer rally" in most years is the weakest rally of all four seasons (page 70) ◆ Week after June Triple-Witching Day Dow down 18 of last 20 (page 76) ◆ RECENT RECORD: S&P up 10, down 6, average gain 0.8%, ranks sixth ◆ Stronger for NASDAQ, average gain 1.4% last 16 years ◆ Watch out for end-of-quarter "portfolio pumping" on last day of June, Dow down 16 of last 22, NASDAQ down 6 straight ◆ Presidential election year Junes: #2 S&P, #4 NASDAQ, Dow weaker, ranks #5 ◆ June ends NASDAQ's Best Eight Months.

June Vital Statistics

	DJIA		S&P 500		NASDAQ		Russell 1K		Russell 2K	
Rank	11		10		6		10		9	
Up	28		32		23		19		20	
Down	33		29		17		13		12	
Avg % Change	−0.4%		−0.04%		0.8%		0.2%		0.4%	
Election Year	0.7%		1.2%		1.7%		0.5%		1.2%	
Best and Worst June										
	% Change		% Change		% Change		% Change		% Change	
Best	1955	6.2	1955	8.2	2000	16.6	1999	5.1	2000	8.6
Worst	2008	−10.2	2008	−8.6	2002	−9.4	2008	−8.5	2010	−7.9
Best and Worst June Weeks										
Best	6/7/74	6.4	6/2/00	7.2	6/2/00	19.0	6/2/00	8.0	6/2/00	12.2
Worst	6/30/50	−6.8	6/30/50	−7.6	6/15/01	−8.4	6/15/01	−4.2	6/9/06	−4.9
Best and Worst June Days										
Best	6/28/62	3.8	6/28/62	3.4	6/2/00	6.4	6/10/10	3.0	6/2/00	4.2
Worst	6/26/50	−4.7	6/26/50	−5.4	6/29/10	−3.9	6/4/10	−3.5	6/4/10	−5.0
First Trading Day of Expiration Week: 1980–2010										
Record (#Up–#Down)	16–15		18–13		14–17		17–14		12–18	
Current Streak	D3		D2		U1		D2		U1	
Avg % Change	0.01		−0.08		−0.25		−0.09		−0.32	
Options Expiration Day: 1980–2010										
Record (#Up–#Down)	18–13		19–12		18–13		19–12		17–14	
Current Streak	U1		U2		U2		U2		U2	
Avg % Change	−0.09		−0.001		−0.03		−0.04		−0.03	
Options Expiration Week: 1980–2010										
Record (#Up–#Down)	17–14		15–16		13–18		14–17		13–18	
Current Streak	U1		U1		U1		U1		U1	
Avg % Change	−0.12		−0.14		−0.32		−0.19		−0.34	
Week After Options Expiration: 1980–2010										
Record (#Up–#Down)	10–21		16–15		17–14		16–15		14–17	
Current Streak	D12		D8		D1		D6		D1	
Avg % Change	−0.45		−0.17		0.07		−0.14		−0.20	
First Trading Day Performance										
% of Time Up	54.1		52.5		60.0		59.4		65.6	
Avg % Change	0.20		0.18		0.24		0.19		0.31	
Last Trading Day Performance										
% of Time Up	52.5		49.2		65.0		46.9		65.6	
Avg % Change	−0.01		0.04		0.23		−0.09		0.31	

Dow and S&P 1950–April 2011, NASDAQ 1971–April 2011, Russell 1K and 2K 1979–April 2011.

Last Day of June not hot for the Dow;
Down 16 of 22, WOW!

MAY/JUNE

Memorial Day (Market Closed)

MONDAY
28

Friendship renders prosperity more brilliant, while it lightens adversity by sharing it and making its burden common. — Marcus Tullius Cicero (Great Roman orator, politician, 106–43 B.C.)

Day after Memorial Day, Dow Up 17 of Last 25

TUESDAY
D 52.4
S 57.1
N 61.9
29

Real knowledge is to know the extent of one's ignorance. — Confucius (Chinese philosopher, 551–478 B.C.)

Memorial Day Week, Dow Down 8 of Last 15, Up 12 Straight 1984–1995 🐻

WEDNESDAY
D 71.4
S 61.9
N 76.2
30

The average man desires to be told specifically which particular stock to buy or sell. He wants to get something for nothing. He does not wish to work.
— William LeFevre (Senior analyst, Ehrenkrantz King Nussbaum, 1928–1997)

Start Looking for NASDAQ MACD Sell Signal (Page 58)
Almanac Investor Subscribers E-mailed When It Triggers (See Insert)

THURSDAY
D 47.6
S 57.1
N 66.7
31

The authority of a thousand is not worth the humble reasoning of a single individual.
— Galileo Galilei (Italian physicist and astronomer, 1564–1642)

First Trading Day in June, Dow Up 18 of Last 23, 2002 –2.2%, 2008/2010 –1.1% 🐻

FRIDAY
D 76.2
S 66.7
N 66.7
1

Anyone who has achieved excellence knows that it comes as a result of ceaseless concentration.
— Louise Brooks (Actress, 1906–1985)

SATURDAY
2

SUNDAY
3

TOP PERFORMING NASDAQ MONTHS PAST 40⅓ YEARS

NASDAQ stocks continue to run away during three consecutive months, November, December, and January, with an average gain of 6.5% despite the slaughter of November 2000, down 22.9%, December 2000, –4.9%, December 2002, –9.7%, November 2007, –6.9%, January 2008, –9.9%, November 2008, –10.8%, January 2009, –6.4%, and January 2010, –5.4%. Solid gains in November and December 2004 offset January 2005's 5.2% Iraq-turmoil-fueled drop.

You can see the months graphically on page 148. January by itself is impressive, up 2.8% on average. April, May, and June also shine, creating our NASDAQ Best Eight Months strategy. What appears as a Death Valley abyss occurs during NASDAQ's bleakest four months: July, August, September, and October. NASDAQ's Best Eight Months seasonal strategy using MACD timing is displayed on page 58.

MONTHLY % CHANGES (JANUARY 1971 TO APRIL 2011)

NASDAQ Composite*					Dow Jones Industrials				
Month	Total % Change	Avg. % Change	# Up	# Down	Month	Total % Change	Avg. % Change	# Up	# Down
Jan	115.2%	2.8%	27	14	Jan	53.3%	1.3%	26	15
Feb	13.7	0.3	21	20	Feb	5.9	0.1	23	18
Mar	30.6	0.7	26	15	Mar	44.9	1.1	27	14
Apr	64.6	1.6	27	14	Apr	93.2	2.3	25	16
May	38.8	1.0	24	16	May	16.3	0.4	21	19
Jun	30.8	0.8	23	17	Jun	–4.5	–0.1	20	20
Jul	1.4	0.04	20	20	Jul	30.8	0.8	22	18
Aug	9.6	0.2	22	18	Aug	–3.1	–0.1	23	17
Sep	–21.3	–0.5	22	18	Sep	–43.2	–1.1	14	26
Oct	13.7	0.3	21	19	Oct	11.6	0.3	24	16
Nov	65.0	1.6	26	14	Nov	48.5	1.2	26	14
Dec	84.3	2.1	24	16	Dec	68.2	1.7	28	12
%					**%**				
Rank					**Rank**				
Jan	115.2%	2.8%	27	14	Apr	93.2%	2.3%	25	16
Dec	84.3	2.1	24	16	Dec	68.2	1.7	28	12
Nov	65.0	1.6	26	14	Jan	53.3	1.3	26	15
Apr	64.6	1.6	27	14	Nov	48.5	1.2	26	14
May	38.8	1.0	24	16	Mar	44.9	1.1	27	14
Jun	30.8	0.8	23	17	Jul	30.8	0.8	22	18
Mar	30.6	0.7	26	15	May	16.3	0.4	21	19
Feb	13.7	0.3	21	20	Oct	11.6	0.3	24	16
Oct	13.7	0.3	21	19	Feb	5.9	0.1	23	18
Aug	9.6	0.2	22	18	Aug	–3.1	–0.1	23	17
Jul	1.4	0.04	20	20	Jun	–4.5	–0.1	20	20
Sep	–21.3	–0.5	22	18	Sep	–43.2	–1.1	14	26
Totals	**446.4%**	**10.9%**			**Totals**	**321.9%**	**7.9%**		
Average		**0.91%**			**Average**		**0.66%**		

Based on NASDAQ composite; prior to February 5, 1971, based on National Quotation Bureau indices.

For comparison, Dow figures are shown. During this period, NASDAQ averaged a 0.91% gain per month, 38 percent more than the Dow's 0.66% per month. Between January 1971 and January 1982, NASDAQ's composite index doubled in twelve years, while the Dow stayed flat. But while NASDAQ plummeted 77.9% from its 2000 highs to the 2002 bottom, the Dow only lost 37.8%. The Great Recession and bear market of 2007–2009 spread its carnage equally across Dow and NASDAQ. Current bull market gains are more in line (pages 131–132).

JUNE

MONDAY

D 57.1
S 76.2
N 81.0

4

*Individualism, private property, the law of accumulation of wealth, and the law of competition...
are the highest result of human experience, the soil in which society so far has produced the best fruit.*
— Andrew Carnegie (Scottish-born U.S. industrialist, philanthropist, *The Gospel of Wealth*, 1835–1919)

TUESDAY

D 47.6
S 42.9
N 52.4

5

If there's anything duller than being on a board in Corporate America, I haven't found it.
— H. Ross Perot (American businessman, *NY Times*, 10/28/92, 2-time presidential
candidate, 1992 and 1996, b. 1930)

🐻 **WEDNESDAY**

D 47.6
S 38.1
N 47.6

6

Wall Street's graveyards are filled with men who were right too soon.
— William Peter Hamilton (Editor, *Wall Street Journal*, *The Stock Market Barometer*, 1922, 1867–1929)

June Ends NASDAQ's "Best Eight Months" (Pages 56, 58, and 148)

🐻 **THURSDAY**

D 47.6
S 38.1
N 33.3

7

We pay the debts of the last generation by issuing bonds payable by the next generation.
— Laurence J. Peter (Educator, hierarchiologist, formulated Peter Principle, 1919–1990)

🐻 **FRIDAY**

D 47.6
S 38.1
N 28.6

8

*Nothing gives one person so much advantage over another as to remain always cool and unruffled under
all circumstances.* — Thomas Jefferson (3rd U.S. president, 1743–7/4/1826)

SATURDAY

9

SUNDAY

10

GET MORE OUT OF NASDAQ'S "BEST EIGHT MONTHS" WITH MACD TIMING

NASDAQ's amazing eight-month run from November through June is hard to miss on pages 56 and 148. A $10,000 investment in these eight months since 1971 gained $360,184 versus a loss of $2,971 during the void that is the four-month period July–October (as of May 20, 2011).

Using the same MACD timing indicators on the NASDAQ as is done for the Dow (page 50) has enabled us to capture much of October's improved performance, pumping up NASDAQ's results considerably. Over the 40 years since NASDAQ began, the gain on the same $10,000 more than doubles to $840,069, and the loss during the four-month void increases to $6,989. Only four sizeable losses occurred during the favorable period, and the bulk of NASDAQ's bear markets were avoided, including the worst of the 2000–2002 bear. See page 32 for more executable trades employing ETFs and mutual funds.

Updated signals are e-mailed to our monthly newsletter subscribers as soon as they are triggered. Visit *www.stocktradersalmanac.com,* or see insert for details and a special offer for new subscribers.

BEST EIGHT MONTHS STRATEGY + TIMING

MACD Signal Date	Worst 4 Months July 1–Oct 31* NASDAQ	% Change	Investing $10,000	MACD Signal Date	Best 8 Months Nov 1–June 30* NASDAQ	% Change	Investing $10,000
22-Jul-71	109.54	-3.6	$9,640	4-Nov-71	105.56	24.1	$12,410
7-Jun-72	131.00	-1.8	9,466	23-Oct-72	128.66	-22.7	9,593
25-Jun-73	99.43	-7.2	8,784	7-Dec-73	92.32	-20.2	7,655
3-Jul-74	73.66	-23.2	6,746	7-Oct-74	56.57	47.8	11,314
11-Jun-75	83.60	-9.2	6,125	7-Oct-75	75.88	20.8	13,667
22-Jul-76	91.66	-2.4	5,978	19-Oct-76	89.45	13.2	15,471
27-Jul-77	101.25	-4.0	5,739	4-Nov-77	97.21	26.6	19,586
7-Jun-78	123.10	-6.5	5,366	6-Nov-78	115.08	19.1	23,327
3-Jul-79	137.03	-1.1	5,307	30-Oct-79	135.48	15.5	26,943
20-Jun-80	156.51	26.2	6,697	9-Oct-80	197.53	11.2	29,961
4-Jun-81	219.68	-17.6	5,518	1-Oct-81	181.09	-4.0	28,763
7-Jun-82	173.84	12.5	6,208	7-Oct-82	195.59	57.4	45,273
1-Jun-83	307.95	-10.7	5,544	3-Nov-83	274.86	-14.2	38,844
1-Jun-84	235.90	5.0	5,821	15-Oct-84	247.67	17.3	45,564
3-Jun-85	290.59	-3.0	5,646	1-Oct-85	281.77	39.4	63,516
10-Jun-86	392.83	-10.3	5,064	1-Oct-86	352.34	20.5	76,537
30-Jun-87	424.67	-22.7	3,914	2-Nov-87	328.33	20.1	91,921
8-Jul-88	394.33	-6.6	3,656	29-Nov-88	368.15	22.4	112,511
13-Jun-89	450.73	0.7	3,682	9-Nov-89	454.07	1.9	114,649
11-Jun-90	462.79	-23.0	2,835	2-Oct-90	356.39	39.3	159,706
11-Jun-91	496.62	6.4	3,016	1-Oct-91	528.51	7.4	171,524
11-Jun-92	567.68	1.5	3,061	14-Oct-92	576.22	20.5	206,686
7-Jun-93	694.61	9.9	3,364	1-Oct-93	763.23	-4.4	197,592
17-Jun-94	729.35	5.0	3,532	11-Oct-94	765.57	13.5	224,267
1-Jun-95	868.82	17.2	4,140	13-Oct-95	1018.38	21.6	272,709
3-Jun-96	1238.73	1.0	4,181	7-Oct-96	1250.87	10.3	300,798
4-Jun-97	1379.67	24.4	5,201	3-Oct-97	1715.87	1.8	306,212
1-Jun-98	1746.82	-7.8	4,795	15-Oct-98	1611.01	49.7	458,399
1-Jun-99	2412.03	18.5	5,682	6-Oct-99	2857.21	35.7	622,047
29-Jun-00	3877.23	-18.2	4,648	18-Oct-00	3171.56	-32.2	421,748
1-Jun-01	2149.44	-31.1	3,202	1-Oct-01	1480.46	5.5	444,944
3-Jun-02	1562.56	-24.0	2,434	2-Oct-02	1187.30	38.5	616,247
20-Jun-03	1644.72	15.1	2,802	6-Oct-03	1893.46	4.3	642,746
21-Jun-04	1974.38	-1.6	2,757	1-Oct-04	1942.20	6.1	681,954
8-Jun-05	2060.18	1.5	2,798	19-Oct-05	2091.76	6.1	723,553
1-Jun-06	2219.86	3.9	2,907	5-Oct-06	2306.34	9.5	792,291
7-Jun-07	2541.38	7.9	3,137	1-Oct-07	2740.99	-9.1	724,796
2-Jun-08	2491.53	-31.3	2,155	17-Oct-08	1711.29	6.1	769,009
15-Jun-09	1816.38	17.8	2,539	9-Oct-09	2139.28	1.6	781,313
7-Jun-10	2461.19	18.6	3,011	4-Nov-10	2577.34	8.8	850,069
20-May-11	2803.32						

As of 5/20/2011, MACD Sell Signal not triggered at press time.

40-Year Loss ($6,989) **40-Year Gain** $840,069

*MACD-generated entry and exit points (earlier or later) can lengthen or shorten eight-month periods.

JUNE

Monday of Triple Witching Week, Dow Down 9 of Last 14

MONDAY
D 42.9
S 52.4
N 47.6
11

What is conservatism? Is it not adherence to the old and tried, against the new and untried?
— Abraham Lincoln (16th U.S. president, 1809–1865)

TUESDAY
D 47.6
S 42.9
N 42.9
12

When a falling stock becomes a screaming buy because it cannot conceivably drop further, try to buy it 30 percent lower. — Al Rizzo (1986)

Triple Witching Week, Often Up in Bull Markets and Down in Bears (Page 76)  **WEDNESDAY**
D 61.9
S 61.9
N 57.1
13

All free governments are managed by the combined wisdom and folly of the people.
— James A. Garfield (20th U.S. president, 1831–1881)

THURSDAY
D 71.4
S 71.4
N 61.9
14

Anyone who believes that exponential growth can go on forever in a finite world is either a madman or an economist. — Kenneth Ewart Boulding (Economist, activist, poet, scientist, philosopher, cofounder, General Systems Theory, 1910–1993)

June Triple Witching Day, Dow Down 7 of Last 13,
Average Los s 0.5%

FRIDAY
D 57.1
S 66.7
N 66.7
15

In the history of the financial markets, arrogance has destroyed far more capital than stupidity.
— Jason Trennert (Managing Partner, Strategas Research Partners, March 27, 2006)

SATURDAY
16

Father's Day

SUNDAY
17

TRIPLE RETURNS, FEWER TRADES: BEST 6 + 4-YEAR CYCLE

We first introduced this strategy to *Almanac Investor* newsletter subscribers in October 2006. Recurring seasonal stock market patterns and the four-year Presidential Election/Stock Market Cycle (page 130) have been integral to our research since the first Almanac 45 years ago. Yale Hirsch discovered the Best Six Months in 1986 (page 48), and it has been a cornerstone of our seasonal investment analysis and strategies ever since.

Most of the market's gains have occurred during the Best Six Months, and the market generally hits a low point every four years in the first (post-election) or second (midterm) year and exhibits the greatest gains in the third (pre-election) year. This strategy combines the best of these two market phenomena, the Best Six Months and the four-year cycle, timing entries and exits with MACD (pages 50 and 58).

We've gone back to 1949 to include the full four-year cycle that began with post-election year 1949. Only four trades every four years are needed to nearly triple the results of the Best Six Months. Buy and sell during the post-election and mid-term years and then hold from the midterm MACD seasonal buy signal sometime after October 1 until the post-election MACD seasonal sell signal sometime after April 1, approximately 2.5 years: better returns, less effort, lower transaction fees, and fewer taxable events. See page 32 for more executable trades employing ETFs and mutual funds.

BEST SIX MONTHS+TIMING+4-YEAR CYCLE STRATEGY

Year	DJIA % Change May 1–Oct 31*	Investing $10,000	DJIA % Change Nov 1–Apr 30*	Investing $10,000
1949	3.0%	$10,300	17.5%	$11,750
1950	7.3	$11,052	19.7	$14,065
1951		$11,052		$14,065
1952		$11,052		$14,065
1953	0.2	$11,074	17.1	$16,470
1954	13.5	$12,569	35.7	$22,350
1955		$12,569		$22,350
1956		$12,569		$22,350
1957	-12.3	$11,023	4.9	$23,445
1958	17.3	$12,930	27.8	$29,963
1959		$12,930		$29,963
1960		$12,930		$29,963
1961	2.9	$13,305	-1.5	$29,514
1962	-15.3	$11,269	58.5	$46,780
1963		$11,269		$46,780
1964		$11,269		$46,780
1965	2.6	$11,562	-2.5	$45,611
1966	-16.4	$9,666	22.2	$55,737
1967		$9,666		$55,737
1968		$9,666		$55,737
1969	-11.9	$8,516	-6.7	$52,003
1970	-1.4	$8,397	21.5	$63,184
1971		$8,397		$63,184
1972		$8,397		$63,184
1973	-11.0	$7,473	0.1	$63,247
1974	-22.4	$5,799	42.5	$90,127
1975		$5,799		$90,127
1976		$5,799		$90,127
1977	-11.4	$5,138	0.5	$90,578
1978	-4.5	$4,907	26.8	$114,853
1979		$4,907		$114,853
1980		$4,907		$114,853
1981	-14.6	$4,191	0.4	$115,312
1982	15.5	$4,841	25.9	$145,178
1983		$4,841		$145,178
1984		$4,841		$145,178
1985	7.0	$5,180	38.1	$200,491
1986	-2.8	$5,035	33.2	$267,054
1987		$5,035		$267,054
1988		$5,035		$267,054
1989	9.8	$5,528	3.3	$275,867
1990	-6.7	$5,158	35.1	$372,696
1991		$5,158		$372,696
1992		$5,158		$372,696
1993	5.5	$5,442	5.6	$393,455
1994	3.7	$5,643	88.2	$740,482
1995		$5,643		$740,482
1996		$5,643		$740,482
1997	3.6	$5,846	18.5	$877,471
1998	-12.4	$5,121	36.3	$1,195,993
1999		$5,121		$1,195,993
2000		$5,121		$1,195,993
2001	-17.3	$4,235	15.8	$1,384,960
2002	-25.2	$3,168	34.2	$1,858,616
2003		$3,168		$1,858,616
2004		$3,168		$1,858,616
2005	-0.5	$3,152	7.7	$2,001,729
2006	4.7	$3,300	-31.7	$1,367,181
2007		$3,300		$1,367,181
2008		$3,300		$1,367,181
2009	23.8	$4,085	10.8	$1,514,738
2010	4.6	$4,273	9.4**	$1,657,124
Average	**-1.0%**		**9.9%**	
# Up	**16**		**28**	
# Down	**16**		**4**	
62-Year Gain (Loss)		**($5,727)**		**$1,647,124**

*MACD and 2.5-year hold lengthen and shorten six-month periods. ** As of 5/20/2011

FOUR TRADES EVERY FOUR YEARS

Year	Worst Six Months May–Oct	Best Six Months Nov–April
Post-election	Sell	Buy
Midterm	Sell	Buy
Pre-election	Hold	Hold
Election	Hold	Hold

D 47.6
S 42.9
N 38.1

18

The fireworks begin today. Each diploma is a lighted match. Each one of you is a fuse.
— Edward Koch (NYC Mayor, Commencement Address, 1983)

Week after June Triple Witching, Dow Down 12 in a Row and 19 of Last 21 Average Loss Since 1990, 1.3%

TUESDAY

D 52.4
S 52.4
N 52.4

19

A.I. (artificial intelligence) is the science of how to get machines to do the things they do in the movies.
— Professor Astro Teller (Carnegie Mellon University)

FOMC Meeting (2 Days)

WEDNESDAY

D 42.9
S 42.9
N 42.9

20

Your emotions are often a reverse indicator of what you ought to be doing.
— John F. Hindelong (Dillon, Reed)

THURSDAY

D 42.9
S 57.1
N 42.9

21

Never overpay for a stock. More money is lost than in any other way by projecting above-average growth and paying an extra multiple for it. — Charles Neuhauser (Bear Stearns)

FRIDAY

D 33.3
S 33.3
N 23.8

22

In democracies, nothing is more great or brilliant than commerce; it attracts the attention of the public and fills the imagination of the multitude; all passions of energy are directed towards it.
— Alexis de Tocqueville (Author, *Democracy in America* 1840, 1805–1859)

SATURDAY

23

SUNDAY

24

JULY ALMANAC

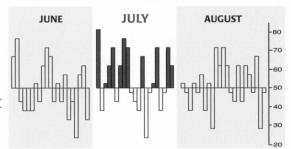

Market Probability Chart above is a graphic representation of the S&P 500 Recent Market Probability Calendar on page 124.

◆ July is the best month of the third quarter, except for NASDAQ (page 64) ◆ Start of second half brings an inflow of retirement funds ◆ First trading day Dow up 18 of last 22 ◆ Graph above shows strength in the beginning and end of July ◆ Huge gain in July usually provides better buying opportunity over next four months ◆ Start of NASDAQ's worst four months of the year (page 58) ◆ Presidential election Julys are ranked #7 Dow (up 7, down 8), #9 S&P (up 6, down 9), and #10 NASDAQ (up 4, down 6).

July Vital Statistics

	DJIA	S&P 500	NASDAQ	Russell 1K	Russell 2K
Rank	4	6	11	7	11
Up	38	33	20	14	16
Down	23	28	20	18	16
Avg % Change	1.2%	1.0%	0.04%	0.6%	−0.4%
Election Year	0.3%	0.1%	−1.5%	−0.5%	−0.9%
Best and Worst July					
	% Change	% Change	% Change	% Change	% Change
Best	1989 9.0	1989 8.8	1997 10.5	1989 8.2	1980 11.0
Worst	1969 −6.6	2002 −7.9	2002 −9.2	2002 −7.5	2002 −15.2
Best and Worst July Weeks					
Best	7/17/09 7.3	7/17/09 7.0	7/17/09 7.4	7/17/09 7.0	7/17/09 8.0
Worst	7/19/02 −7.7	7/19/02 −8.0	7/28/00 −10.5	7/19/02 −7.4	7/2/10 −7.2
Best and Worst July Days					
Best	7/24/02 6.4	7/24/02 5.7	7/29/02 5.8	7/24/02 5.6	7/29/02 4.9
Worst	7/19/02 −4.6	7/19/02 −3.8	7/28/00 −4.7	7/19/02 −3.6	7/23/02 −4.1
First Trading Day of Expiration Week: 1980–2010					
Record (#Up–#Down)	119–12	20–11	21–10	19–12	17–14
Current Streak	U2	U2	U2	D1	D1
Avg % Change	0.13	0.07	0.07	0.04	−0.04
Options Expiration Day: 1980–2010					
Record (#Up–#Down)	14–15	15–16	13–18	15–16	11–20
Current Streak	D1	D2	D1	D2	D5
Avg % Change	−0.28	−0.35	−0.53	−0.37	−0.55
Options Expiration Week: 1980–2010					
Record (#Up–#Down)	19–12	16–15	16–15	16–15	17–14
Current Streak	D1	D1	D1	D1	D1
Avg % Change	0.46	0.12	0.03	0.06	−0.07
Week After Options Expiration: 1980–2010					
Record (#Up–#Down)	15–16	14–17	12–19	14–17	11–20
Current Streak	U2	U2	U3	U2	U3
Avg % Change	−0.08	−0.28	−0.61	−0.29	−0.41
First Trading Day Performance					
% of Time Up	63.9	68.9	57.5	68.8	59.4
Avg % Change	0.24	0.22	0.03	0.25	−0.05
Last Trading Day Performance					
% of Time Up	54.1	65.6	52.5	62.5	68.8
Avg % Change	0.08	0.12	0.02	0.06	0.05

Dow and S&P 1950–April 2011, NASDAQ 1971–April 2011, Russell 1K and 2K 1979–April 2011.

When Dow and S&P in July are inferior, NASDAQ days tend to be even drearier.

JUNE/JULY

008 Second Worst June Ever, Dow –10.2%, S&P –8.6%,
nly 1930 Was Worse, NASDAQ –9.1%, June 2002 –9.4%

MONDAY

D 42.9
S 42.9
N 42.9

25

market is the combined behavior of thousands of people responding to information, misinformation, and whim.
— Kenneth Chang (*NY Times* journalist)

🐻 **TUESDAY**

D 33.3
S 23.8
N 33.3

26

ad an unshakable faith. I had it in my head that if I had to, I'd crawl over broken glass.
I live in a tent—it was gonna happen. And I think when you have that kind of steely determination…
ople get out of the way. — Rick Newcombe (Syndicator, *Investor's Business Daily*)

WEDNESDAY

D 52.4
S 57.1
N 61.9

27

llbacks near the 30-week moving average are often good times to take action.
— Michael L. Burke (*Investors Intelligence*)

🐻 **THURSDAY**

D 52.4
S 61.9
N 71.4

28

good new chairman of the Federal Reserve Bank is worth a $10 billion tax cut.
— Paul H. Douglas (U.S. senator, Illinois 1949–1967, 1892–1976)

ast Day of Q2 Bearish for Dow, Down 15 of Last 20
ut Bullish for NASDAQ, Up 12 of 19, Although Down 6 straight

🐻 **FRIDAY**

D 28.6
S 33.3
N 61.9

29

osperity is a great teacher; adversity a greater. — William Hazlitt (English essayist, 1778–1830)

SATURDAY

30

ly Almanac Investor Seasonalities: See Pages 92, 94, and 96

SUNDAY

1

FIRST MONTH OF QUARTERS IS THE MOST BULLISH

We have observed over the years that the investment calendar reflects the annual, semiannual, and quarterly operations of institutions during January, April, and July. The opening month of the first three quarters produces the greatest gains in the Dow Jones Industrials and the S&P 500. NASDAQ's record differs slightly.

The fourth quarter had behaved quite differently, since it is affected by year-end portfolio adjustments and presidential and congressional elections in even-numbered years. Since 1991, major turnarounds have helped October join the ranks of bullish first months of quarters. October transformed into a bear-killing-turnaround month, posting some mighty gains in eight of the last 13 years, 2008 sharply reversed this trend. (See pages 152–160.)

After experiencing the most powerful bull market of all time during the 1990s, followed by the ferocious bear market early in the millennium, we divided the monthly average percentage changes into two groups: before 1991 and after. Comparing the month-by-month quarterly behavior of the three major U.S. averages in the table, you'll see that first months of the first three quarters perform best overall. Nasty sell-offs in April 2000, 2002, 2004, and 2005, and July 2000–2002 and 2004, hit the NASDAQ hardest. The bear market of October 2007–March 2009, which more than cut the markets in half, took a toll on every first month except April. October 2008 was the worst month in a decade. January was also a difficult month in 2008, 2009, and 2010. (See pages 152–160.)

Between 1950 and 1990, the S&P 500 gained 1.3% (Dow, 1.4%) on average in first months of the first three quarters. Second months barely eked out any gain, while third months, thanks to March, moved up 0.23% (Dow, 0.07%) on average. NASDAQ's first month of the first three quarters averages 1.67% from 1971–1990, with July being a negative drag.

DOW JONES INDUSTRIALS, S&P 500, AND NASDAQ
AVERAGE MONTHLY % CHANGES BY QUARTER

	DJIA 1950–1990			S&P 500 1950–1990			NASDAQ 1971–1990		
	1st Mo	2nd Mo	3rd Mo	1st Mo	2nd Mo	3rd Mo	1st Mo	2nd Mo	3rd Mo
1Q	1.5%	−0.01%	1.0%	1.5%	−0.1%	1.1%	3.8%	1.2%	0.9%
2Q	1.6	−0.4	0.1	1.3	−0.1	0.3	1.7	0.8	1.1
3Q	1.1	0.3	−0.9	1.1	0.3	−0.7	−0.5	0.1	−1.6
Tot	4.2%	−0.1%	0.2%	3.9%	0.1%	0.7%	5.0%	2.1%	0.4%
Avg	1.40%	−0.04%	0.07%	1.30%	0.03%	0.23%	1.67%	0.70%	0.13%
4Q	−0.1%	1.4%	1.7%	0.4%	1.7%	1.6%	−1.4%	1.6%	1.4%
	DJIA 1991–April 2011			S&P 500 1991–April 2011			NASDAQ 1991–April 2011		
1Q	0.1%	0.03%	1.1%	0.2%	−0.4%	1.2%	1.9%	−0.5%	0.6%
2Q	2.7	1.0	−1.2	2.0	1.0	−0.7	1.5	1.1	0.5
3Q	1.5	−0.6	−0.6	0.7	−0.4	−0.1	0.6	0.4	0.5
Tot	4.3%	0.4%	−0.7%	2.9%	0.2%	0.4%	4.0%	1.0%	1.6%
Avg	1.43%	0.14%	−0.23%	0.97%	0.07%	0.14%	1.33%	0.33%	0.53%
4Q	1.4%	1.7%	1.8%	1.1%	1.3%	2.0%	2.0%	1.7%	2.8%
	DJIA 1950–April 2011			S&P 500 1950–April 2011			NASDAQ 1971–April 2011		
1Q	1.0%	0.005%	1.1%	1.1%	−0.2%	1.1%	2.8%	0.3%	0.7%
2Q	2.0	0.05	−0.4	1.5	0.3	−0.04	1.6	1.0	0.8
3Q	1.2	−0.01	−0.8	1.0	0.1	−0.5	0.04	0.2	−0.5
Tot	4.2%	0.05%	−0.1%	3.6%	0.2%	0.6%	4.4%	1.5%	1.0%
Avg	1.40%	0.02%	−0.03%	1.20%	0.07%	0.19%	1.48%	0.51%	0.33%
4Q	0.4%	1.5%	1.7%	0.6%	1.5%	1.7%	0.3%	1.6%	2.1%

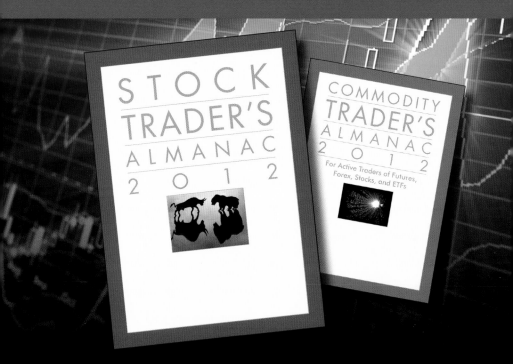

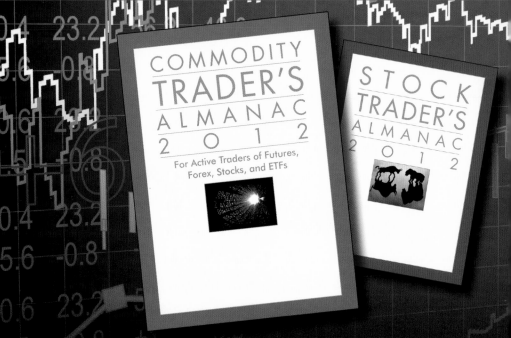

JULY

First Trading Day in July, Dow Up 18 of Last 22

MONDAY

D 81.0
S 81.0
N 66.7

2

I would rather be positioned as a petrified bull rather than a penniless bear.
— John L. Person (Professional trader, author, speaker, *Commodity Trader's Almanac*,
nationalfutures.com, 11/3/2010, b. 1961)

(Shortened Trading Day)

TUESDAY

D 42.9
S 38.1
N 33.3

3

The universal line of distinction between the strong and the weak is that one persists, while the other hesitates, falters, trifles, and at last, collapses or caves in. — Edwin Percy Whipple (American essayist, 1819–1886)

Independence Day
(Market Closed)

WEDNESDAY

4

So at last I was going to America! Really, really going, at last! The boundaries burst. The arch of heaven soared!
A million suns shone out for every star. The winds rushed in from outer space, roaring in my ears, "America! America!"
— Mary Antin (1881–1949, Immigrant writer, *The Promised Land*, 1912)

Market Subject to Elevated Volatility after July 4th

THURSDAY

D 47.6
S 52.4
N 38.1

5

Some men see things as they are and say "why?" I dream things that never were and say "why not?"
— George Bernard Shaw (Irish dramatist, 1856–1950)

July Begins NASDAQ's "Worst Four Months" (Pages 56, 58, and 148)

FRIDAY

D 57.1
S 61.9
N 57.1

6

Bad days are good days in disguise. — Christopher Reeves (Actor, on Johnson & Johnson commercial)

SATURDAY

7

SUNDAY

8

2010 DAILY DOW POINT CHANGES
(DOW JONES INDUSTRIAL AVERAGE)

Week #		Monday**	Tuesday	Wednesday	Thursday	Friday**	Weekly Dow Close	Net Point Change
						2009 Close	10428.05	
1	J	155.91	−11.94	1.66	33.18	11.33	10618.19	190.14
2	A	45.80	−36.73	53.51	29.78	−100.90	10609.65	−8.54
3	N	Holiday	115.78	−122.28	−213.27	−216.90	10172.98	−436.67
4		23.88	−2.57	41.87	−115.70	−53.13	10067.33	−105.65
5	F	118.20	111.32	−26.30	−268.37	10.05	10012.23	−55.10
6	E	−103.84	150.25	−20.26	105.81	−45.05	10099.14	86.91
7	B	Holiday	169.67	40.43	83.66	9.45	10402.35	303.21
8		−18.97	−100.97	91.75	−53.13	4.23	10325.26	−77.09
9		78.53	2.19	−9.22	47.38	122.06	10566.20	240.94
10	M	−13.68	11.86	2.95	44.51	12.85	10624.69	58.49
11	A	17.46	43.83	47.69	45.50	−37.19	10741.98	117.29
12	R	43.91	102.94	−52.68	5.06	9.15	10850.36	108.38
13		45.50	11.56	−50.79	70.44	Holiday	10927.07	76.71
14		46.48	−3.56	−72.47	29.55	70.28	10997.35	70.28
15	A	8.62	13.45	103.69	21.46	−125.91	11018.66	21.31
16	P	73.39	25.01	7.86	9.37	69.99	11204.28	185.62
17	R	0.75	−213.04	53.28	122.05	−158.71	11008.61	−195.67
18		143.22	−225.06	−58.65	−347.80	−139.89	10380.43	−628.18
19	M	404.71	−36.88	148.65	−113.96	−162.79	10620.16	239.73
20	A	5.67	−114.88	−66.58	−376.36	125.38	10193.39	−426.77
21	Y	−126.82	−22.82	−69.30	284.54	−122.36	10136.63	−56.76
22		Holiday	−112.61	225.52	5.74	−323.31	9931.97	−204.66
23	J	−115.48	123.49	−40.73	273.28	38.54	10211.07	279.10
24	U	−20.18	213.88	4.69	24.71	16.47	10450.64	239.57
25	N	−8.23	−148.89	4.92	−145.64	−8.99	10143.81	−306.83
26		−5.29	−268.22	−96.28	−41.49	−46.05	9686.48	−457.33
27		Holiday	57.14	274.66	120.71	59.04	10198.03	511.55
28	J	18.24	146.75	3.70	−7.41	−261.41	10097.90	−100.13
29	U	56.53	75.53	−109.43	201.77	102.32	10424.62	326.72
30	L	100.81	12.26	−39.81	−30.72	−1.22	10465.94	41.32
31		208.44	−38.00	44.05	−5.45	−21.42	10653.56	187.62
32	A	45.19	−54.50	−265.42	−58.88	−16.80	10303.15	−350.41
33	U	−1.14	103.84	9.69	−144.33	−57.59	10213.62	−89.53
34	G	−39.21	−133.96	19.61	−74.25	164.84	10150.65	−62.97
35		−140.92	4.99	254.75	50.63	157.83	10477.93	327.28
36		Holiday	−137.24	46.32	28.23	47.53	10462.77	−15.16
37	S	81.36	−17.64	46.24	22.10	13.02	10607.85	145.08
38	E	145.77	7.41	−21.72	−76.89	197.84	10860.26	252.41
39	P	−48.22	46.10	−22.86	−47.23	41.63	10829.68	−30.58
40		−78.41	193.45	22.93	−19.07	57.90	11006.48	176.80
41	O	3.86	10.06	75.68	−1.51	−31.79	11062.78	56.30
42	C	80.91	−165.07	129.35	38.60	−14.01	11132.56	69.78
43	T	31.49	5.41	−43.18	−12.33	4.54	11118.49	−14.07
44		6.13	64.10	26.41	219.71	9.24	11444.08	325.59
45	N	−37.24	−60.09	10.29	−73.94	−90.52	11192.58	−251.50
46	O	9.39	−178.47	−15.62	173.35	22.32	11203.55	10.97
47	V	−24.97	−142.21	150.91	Holiday	−95.28*	11092.00	−111.55
48		−39.51	−46.47	249.76	106.63	19.68	11382.09	290.09
49		−19.90	−3.03	13.32	−2.42	40.26	11410.32	28.23
50	D	18.24	47.98	−19.07	41.78	−7.34	11491.91	81.59
51	E	−13.78	55.03	26.33	14.00	Holiday	11573.49	81.58
52	C	−18.46	20.51	9.84	−15.67	7.80	11577.51	4.02
TOTALS		1236.88	−421.80	1019.66	−76.73	−608.55		1149.46

Bold Color: Down Friday, Down Monday   ** Shortened trading day: Nov 26*

** Monday denotes first trading day of week, Friday denotes last trading day of week.

JULY

MONDAY

D 71.4
S 71.4
N 76.2

9

*When a company reports higher earnings for its first quarter (over its previous year's first quarter),
chances are almost five to one it will also have increased earnings in its second quarter.*
— Niederhoffer, Cross & Zeckhauser

TUESDAY

D 47.6
S 42.9
N 61.9

10

Every great advance in natural knowledge has involved the absolute rejection of authority.
— Thomas H. Huxley (British scientist and humanist, defender of Darwinism, 1825–1895)

July is the Best Performing Dow and S&P Month of the Third Quarter **WEDNESDAY**

D 66.7
S 61.9
N 71.4

11

Choose a job you love, and you will never have to work a day in your life.
— Confucius (Chinese philosopher, 551–478 B.C.)

THURSDAY

D 66.7
S 76.2
N 76.2

12

*Why is it right-wing [conservatives] always stand shoulder to shoulder in solidarity, while liberals always
fall out among themselves?* — Yevgeny Yevtushenko (Russian poet, Babi Yar,
quoted in London Observer December 15, 1991, b. 1933)

FRIDAY

D 66.7
S 71.4
N 76.2

13

*There are ways for the individual investor to make money in the securities markets. Buying value and
holding long term while collecting dividends has been proven over and over again.*
— Robert M. Sharp (Author, The Lore and Legends of Wall Street)

SATURDAY

14

SUNDAY

15

DON'T SELL STOCKS ON MONDAY OR FRIDAY

Since 1989, Monday*, Tuesday, and Wednesday have been the most consistently bullish days of the week for the Dow; Thursday and Friday* the most bearish, as traders have become reluctant to stay long going into the weekend. Since 1989, Mondays, Tuesdays, and Wednesdays gained 13107.91 Dow points, while Thursday and Friday combined for a total loss of 3050.57 points. Also broken out are the last ten and a third years to illustrate Monday's and Friday's poor performance in bear market years 2001–2002 and 2008–2009. During uncertain market times, traders often sell before the weekend and are reluctant to jump in on Monday. See pages 66, 78, and 141–144 for more.

ANNUAL DOW POINT CHANGES FOR DAYS OF THE WEEK SINCE 1953

Year	Monday*	Tuesday	Wednesday	Thursday	Friday*	Year's DJIA Closing	Year's Point Change
1953	-36.16	-7.93	19.63	5.76	7.70	280.90	-11.00
1954	15.68	3.27	24.31	33.96	46.27	404.39	123.49
1955	-48.36	26.38	46.03	-0.66	60.62	488.40	84.01
1956	-27.15	-9.36	-15.41	8.43	64.56	499.47	11.07
1957	-109.50	-7.71	64.12	3.32	-14.01	435.69	-63.78
1958	17.50	23.59	29.10	22.67	55.10	583.65	147.96
1959	-44.48	29.04	4.11	13.60	93.44	679.36	95.71
1960	-111.04	-3.75	-5.62	6.74	50.20	615.89	-63.47
1961	-23.65	10.18	87.51	-5.96	47.17	731.14	115.25
1962	-101.60	26.19	9.97	-7.70	-5.90	652.10	-79.04
1963	-8.88	47.12	16.23	22.39	33.99	762.95	110.85
1964	-0.29	-17.94	39.84	5.52	84.05	874.13	111.18
1965	-73.23	39.65	57.03	3.20	68.48	969.26	95.13
1966	-153.24	-27.73	56.13	-46.19	-12.54	785.69	-183.57
1967	-68.65	31.50	25.42	92.25	38.90	905.11	119.42
1968†	-6.41	34.94	25.16	-72.06	44.19	943.75	38.64
1969	-164.17	-36.70	18.33	23.79	15.36	800.36	-143.39
1970	-100.05	-46.09	116.07	-3.48	72.11	838.92	38.56
1971	-2.99	9.56	13.66	8.04	23.01	890.20	51.28
1972	-87.40	-1.23	65.24	8.46	144.75	1020.02	129.82
1973	-174.11	10.52	-5.94	36.67	-36.30	850.86	-169.16
1974	-149.37	47.51	-20.31	-13.70	-98.75	616.24	-234.62
1975	39.46	-109.62	56.93	124.00	125.40	852.41	236.17
1976	70.72	71.76	50.88	-33.70	-7.42	1004.65	152.24
1977	-65.15	-44.89	-79.61	-5.62	21.79	831.17	-173.48
1978	-31.29	-70.84	71.33	-64.67	69.31	805.01	-26.16
1979	-32.52	9.52	-18.84	75.18	0.39	838.74	33.73
1980	-86.51	135.13	137.67	-122.00	60.96	963.99	125.25
1981	-45.68	-49.51	-13.95	-14.67	34.82	875.00	-88.99
1982	5.71	86.20	28.37	-1.47	52.73	1046.54	171.54
1983	30.51	-30.92	149.68	61.16	1.67	1258.64	212.10
1984	-73.80	78.02	-139.24	92.79	-4.84	1211.57	-47.07
1985	80.36	52.70	51.26	46.32	104.46	1546.67	335.10
1986	-39.94	97.63	178.65	29.31	83.63	1895.95	349.28
1987	-559.15	235.83	392.03	139.73	-165.56	1938.83	42.88
1988	268.12	166.44	-60.48	-230.84	86.50	2168.57	229.74
1989	-53.31	143.33	233.25	90.25	171.11	2753.20	584.63
SubTotal	*-1937.20*	*941.79*	*1708.54*	*330.82*	*1417.35*		*2461.30*
1990	219.90	-25.22	47.96	-352.55	-9.63	2633.66	-119.54
1991	191.13	47.97	174.53	254.79	-133.25	3168.83	535.17
1992	237.80	-49.67	3.12	108.74	-167.71	3301.11	132.28
1993	322.82	-37.03	243.87	4.97	-81.65	3754.09	452.98
1994	206.41	-95.33	29.98	-168.87	108.16	3834.44	80.35
1995	262.97	210.06	357.02	140.07	312.56	5117.12	1282.68
1996	626.41	155.55	-34.24	268.52	314.91	6448.27	1331.15
1997	1136.04	1989.17	-590.17	-949.80	-125.26	7908.25	1459.98
1998	649.10	679.95	591.63	-1579.43	931.93	9181.43	1273.18
1999	980.49	-1587.23	826.68	735.94	1359.81	11497.12	2315.69
2000	2265.45	306.47	-1978.34	238.21	-1542.06	10786.85	-710.27
SubTotal	*7098.52*	*1594.69*	*-327.96*	*-1299.41*	*967.81*		*8033.65*
2001	-389.33	336.86	-396.53	976.41	-1292.76	10021.50	-765.35
2002	-1404.94	-823.76	1443.69	-428.12	-466.74	8341.63	-1679.87
2003	978.87	482.11	-425.46	566.22	510.55	10453.92	2112.29
2004	201.12	523.28	358.76	-409.72	-344.35	10783.01	329.09
2005	316.23	-305.62	27.67	-128.75	24.96	10717.50	-65.51
2006	95.74	573.98	1283.87	193.34	-401.28	12463.15	1745.65
2007	278.23	-157.93	1316.74	-766.63	131.26	13264.82	801.67
2008	-1387.20	1704.51	-3073.72	-940.88	-791.14	8776.39	-4488.43
2009	-45.22	161.76	617.56	932.68	-15.12	10428.05	1651.66
2010	1236.88	-421.80	1019.66	-76.73	-608.55	11577.51	1149.46
2011‡	147.46	168.24	300.95	202.28	414.10		
Subtotal	*27.84*	*2241.63*	*2473.19*	*120.10*	*-2839.07*		*790.66*
Totals	*5189.16*	*4778.11*	*3853.77*	*-848.49*	*-453.91*		*11285.61*

* On Monday holidays, the following Tuesday is included in the Monday figure.
** On Friday holidays, the preceding Thursday is included in the Friday figure.
†Most Wednesdays closed last 7 months of 1968. ‡Partial year through April 29, 2011.

Monday before July Expiration, Dow Up 7 of Last 8

MONDAY

D 52.4
S 47.6
N 61.9

16

Corporate guidance has become something of an art. The CFO has refined and perfected his art, gracefully leading on the bulls with the calculating grace and cunning of a great matador.
— Joe Kalinowski (I/B/E/S)

TUESDAY

D 52.4
S 42.9
N 47.6

17

Those companies that the market expects will have the best futures, as measured by the price/earnings ratios they are accorded, have consistently done worst subsequently.
— David Dreman (Dreman Value Management, author, *Forbes* columnist, b. 1936)

WEDNESDAY

D 42.9
S 38.1
N 42.9

18

It was never my thinking that made the big money for me. It was always my sitting. Got that? My sitting tight!
— Jesse Livermore (Early 20th century stock trader and speculator, *How to Trade in Stocks*, 1877–1940)

THURSDAY

D 66.7
S 66.7
N 61.9

19

Never tell people how to do things. Tell them what to do and they will surprise you with their ingenuity.
— General George S. Patton Jr. (U.S. Army field commander WWII, 1885–1945)

July Expiration Day, Dow Down 7 of Last 11, – 4.6% in 2002 and –2.5% in 2010

FRIDAY

D 28.6
S 23.8
N 28.6

20

The world has changed! You can't be an 800-pound gorilla; you need to be an economic gazelle. You've got to be able to change directions quickly. — Mark Breier (*The 10-Second Internet Manager*)

SATURDAY

21

SUNDAY

22

A RALLY FOR ALL SEASONS

Most years, especially when the market sells off during the first half, prospects for the perennial summer rally become the buzz on the street. Parameters for this "rally" were defined by the late Ralph Rotnem as the lowest close in the Dow Jones Industrials in May or June to the highest close in July, August, or September. Such a big deal is made of the summer rally that one might get the impression the market puts on its best performance in the summertime. Nothing could be further from the truth! Not only does the market "rally" in every season of the year, but it does so with more gusto in the winter, spring, and fall than in the summer.

Winters in 48 years averaged a 13.0% gain, as measured from the low in November or December to the first quarter closing high. Spring rose 11.6% followed by fall with 10.9%. Last and least was the average 9.3% summer rally. Even 2009's impressive 19.7% summer rally was outmatched by spring. Nevertheless, no matter how thick the gloom or grim the outlook, don't despair! There's always a rally for all seasons, statistically.

SEASONAL GAINS IN DOW JONES INDUSTRIALS

	WINTER RALLY Nov/Dec Low to Q1 High	SPRING RALLY Feb/Mar Low to Q2 High	SUMMER RALLY May/Jun Low to Q3 High	FALL RALLY Aug/Sep Low to Q4 High
1964	15.3%	6.2%	9.4%	8.3%
1965	5.7	6.6	11.6	10.3
1966	5.9	4.8	3.5	7.0
1967	11.6	8.7	11.2	4.4
1968	7.0	11.5	5.2	13.3
1969	0.9	7.7	1.9	6.7
1970	5.4	6.2	22.5	19.0
1971	21.6	9.4	5.5	7.4
1972	19.1	7.7	5.2	11.4
1973	8.6	4.8	9.7	15.9
1974	13.1	8.2	1.4	11.0
1975	36.2	24.2	8.2	8.7
1976	23.3	6.4	5.9	4.6
1977	8.2	3.1	2.8	2.1
1978	2.1	16.8	11.8	5.2
1979	11.0	8.9	8.9	6.1
1980	13.5	16.8	21.0	8.5
1981	11.8	9.9	0.4	8.3
1982	4.6	9.3	18.5	37.8
1983	15.7	17.8	6.3	10.7
1984	5.9	4.6	14.1	9.7
1985	11.7	7.1	9.5	19.7
1986	31.1	18.8	9.2	11.4
1987	30.6	13.6	22.9	5.9
1988	18.1	13.5	11.2	9.8
1989	15.1	12.9	16.1	5.7
1990	8.8	14.5	12.4	8.6
1991	21.8	11.2	6.6	9.3
1992	14.9	6.4	3.7	3.3
1993	8.9	7.7	6.3	7.3
1994	9.7	5.2	9.1	5.0
1995	13.6	19.3	11.3	13.9
1996	19.2	7.5	8.7	17.3
1997	17.7	18.4	18.4	7.3
1998	20.3	13.6	8.2	24.3
1999	15.1	21.6	8.2	12.6
2000	10.8	15.2	9.8	3.5
2001	6.4	20.8	1.7	23.1
2002	14.8	7.9	2.8	17.6
2003	6.5	23.9	14.3	15.7
2004	11.6	5.2	4.4	10.6
2005	9.0	2.1	5.6	5.3
2006	8.8	8.3	9.5	13.0
2007	6.7	13.5	6.6	10.3
2008	2.5	11.2	3.8	4.5
2009	19.6	34.4	19.7	15.5
2010	11.6	13.1	11.1	16.0
2011	12.6	10.3*		
Totals	**624.0%**	**556.8%**	**436.1%**	**512.9%**
Average	**13.0%**	**11.6%**	**9.3%**	**10.9%**

As of 5/20/2011.

D 42.9
S 47.6
N 47.6
23

To an imagination of any scope the most far-reaching form of power is not money, it is the command of ideas.
— Oliver Wendell Holmes Jr. (*The Mind and Faith of Justice Holmes*, edited by Max Lerner)

Week after July Expiration Prone to Wild Swings, Dow Mixed Last 14 years
1998 −4.3%, 2002 +3.1%, 2006 +3.2%, 2007 −4.2%, 2009 +4.0%, 2010 +3 .2

TUESDAY
D 57.1
S 52.4
N 47.6
24

I'm not better than the next trader, just quicker at admitting my mistakes and moving on to the next opportunity.
— George Soros (Financier, philanthropist, political activist, author, and philosopher, b. 1930)

WEDNESDAY
D 71.4
S 71.4
N 76.2
25

A good trader has to have three things: a chronic inability to accept things at face value, to feel continuously unsettled, and to have humility. — Michael Steinhardt (Financier, philanthropist, political activist, chairman, WisdomTree Investments, b. 1940)

Beware the "Summer Rally" Hype
Historically the Weakest Rally of All Seasons (Page 70)

THURSDAY
D 38.1
S 38.1
N 52.4
26

You win some, you lose some. And then there's that little-known third category.
— Albert Gore (U.S. vice president 1993–2000, former 2000 presidential candidate, quoted at the 2004 DNC)

FRIDAY
D 42.9
S 47.6
N 47.6
27

Inflation is the modern way that governments default on their debt.
— Mike Epstein (MTA, MIT/Sloan Lab for Financial Engineering)

SATURDAY
28

August Almanac Investor Seasonalities: See Pages 92, 94, and 96

SUNDAY
29

AUGUST ALMANAC

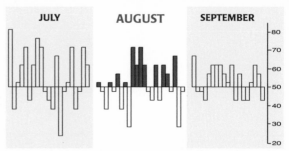

Market Probability Chart above is a graphic representation of the S&P 500 Recent Market Probability Calendar on page 124.

◆ Harvesting made August the best stock market month 1901–1951 ◆ Now about 2% farm, August is the worst Dow, S&P, and NASDAQ (2000 up 11.7%, 2001 down 10.9) month since 1987 ◆ Shortest bear in history (45 days), caused by turmoil in Russia, currency crisis, and hedge fund debacle, ended here in 1998, 1344.22-point drop in the Dow, second worst behind October 2008, off 15.1% ◆ Saddam Hussein triggered a 10.0% slide in 1990 ◆ Best Dow gains: 1982 (11.5%) and 1984 (9.8%), as bear markets ended ◆ Next to last day, S&P was up only twice in last 15 years ◆ Presidential election year boosts Augusts' rankings: #1 NASDAQ, #4 Dow and S&P.

August Vital Statistics

	DJIA	S&P 500	NASDAQ	Russell 1K	Russell 2K
Rank	10	9	10	8	8
Up	35	34	22	21	19
Down	26	27	18	11	13
Avg % Change	–0.01%	0.05%	0.2%	0.5%	0.6%
Election Year	0.8%	0.9%	2.7%	2.2%	3.5%
Best and Worst August					
	% Change	% Change	% Change	% Change	% Change
Best	1982 11.5	1982 11.6	2000 11.7	1982 11.3	1984 11.5
Worst	1998 –15.1	1998 –14.6	1998 –19.9	1998 –15.1	1998 –19.5
Best and Worst August Weeks					
Best	8/20/82 10.3	8/20/82 8.8	8/3/84 7.4	8/20/82 8.5	8/3/84 7.0
Worst	8/23/74 –6.1	8/16/74 –6.4	8/28/98 –8.8	8/28/98 –5.4	8/28/98 –9.4
Best and Worst August Days					
Best	8/17/82 4.9	8/17/82 4.8	8/14/02 5.1	8/17/82 4.4	8/6/02 3.7
Worst	8/31/98 –6.4	8/31/98 –6.8	8/31/98 –8.6	8/31/98 –6.7	8/31/98 –5.7
First Trading Day of Expiration Week: 1980–2010					
Record (#Up–#Down)	20–11	23–8	22–9	23–8	19–12
Current Streak	D2	U1	U1	U1	U1
Avg % Change	0.25	0.24	0.26	0.21	0.16
Options Expiration Day: 1980–2010					
Record (#Up–#Down)	17–14	18–13	18–13	18–13	20–11
Current Streak	D1	D1	U2	D1	D1
Avg % Change	–0.01	0.05	–0.04	0.05	0.16
Options Expiration Week: 1980–2010					
Record (#Up–#Down)	16–15	19–12	18–13	19–12	20–11
Current Streak	D1	D1	U3	D1	U3
Avg % Change	0.38	0.59	0.79	0.62	0.87
Week After Options Expiration: 1980–2010					
Record (#Up–#Down)	19–12	20–11	19–12	20–11	19–12
Current Streak	D1	D1	D1	D1	U1
Avg % Change	0.17	0.17	0.27	0.16	–0.15
First Trading Day Performance					
% of Time Up	49.2	52.5	55.0	50.0	53.1
Avg % Change	0.03	0.06	–0.07	0.12	0.06
Last Trading Day Performance					
% of Time Up	60.7	63.9	67.5	59.4	75.0
Avg % Change	0.13	0.13	0.05	–0.06	0.09

Dow and S&P 1950–April 2011, NASDAQ 1971–April 2011, Russell 1K and 2K 1979–April 2011.

August's a good month to go on vacation;
Trading stocks will likely lead to frustration.

MONDAY

D 66.7
S 71.4
N 66.7

30

Even being right 3 or 4 times out of 10 should yield a person a fortune, if he has the sense to cut his losses quickly on the ventures where he has been wrong.
— Bernard Baruch (Financier, speculator, statesman, presidential adviser, 1870–1965)

Last Trading Day in July, NASDAQ Down 5 of Last 6
FOMC Meeting

TUESDAY

D 47.6
S 61.9
N 47.6

31

I've learned that only through focus can you do world-class things, no matter how capable you are.
— William H. Gates (Microsoft founder, *Fortune*, July 8, 2002)

First Trading Day in August, Dow Down 9 of Last 14, But Up 3 of Last 4
Russell 2000 Up 6 of Last 7

WEDNESDAY

D 42.9
S 52.4
N 57.1

1

If I owe a million dollars, I am lost. But if I owe $50 billion the bankers are lost. — Celso Ming (Brazilian journalist)

THURSDAY

D 52.4
S 47.6
N 42.9

2

The soul is dyed the color of its thoughts. Think only on those things that are in line with your principles and can bear the light of day. The content of your character is your choice. Day by day, what you do is who you become. — Heraclitus (Greek philosopher, 535–475 B.C.)

First Nine Trading Days of August Are Historically Weak (Pages 72 and 124)

FRIDAY

D 38.1
S 38.1
N 33.3

3

There is a perfect inverse correlation between inflation rates and price/earnings ratios...When inflation has been very high... P/E has been [low].
— Liz Ann Sonders (Chief investment strategist, Charles Schwab, June 2006)

SATURDAY

4

SUNDAY

5

FIFTEEN YEAR PROJECTION

Channeling our inner George Lindsay (page 114), the chart below visually portrays my long-term forecast, which projects a continuing sideways market through the year 2017 or 2018, with the Dow remaining in a range of roughly 7,000 to 14,000 before it takes off and completes a 500% move from the intraday low of 6470 on March 6, 2009 to 38,820 by the year 2025. I first revealed this forecast to newsletter subscribers (see insert) on May 13, 2010, again on page 36 of the *Stock Trader's Almanac 2011,* and in full detail, in my new book, *Super Boom* (page 114).

The calculus behind this forecast includes the disengagement of the U.S. military from entrenched overseas wars in Iraq and Afghanistan. Rising inflation from massive government spending and easy monetary policy over the next 5–10 years will begin to taper off as the stock market begins to inflate 6-fold. And finally, technological innovations from alternative energy, biotechnology or other yet-to-be-discovered fields will enable a cultural paradigm shift across the planet that will fuel exponential growth, as the automobile, television, microprocessor, Internet, and cell phone have done in the past. To wit: War and Peace + Inflation + Secular Bull Market + Enabling Technology = 500% Super Boom Move.

In order to create this chart, I relied on the market's behavior and global economic trends during the last three major boom and bust cycles of the twentieth century, revolving around the three major wars (WWI, WWII, and Vietnam) as well as the monthly, seasonal, annual, and 4-year cycle trends during the flat-bust periods and the rising-boom periods.

The Dow is expected to test 10,000 later in 2011. Then, after stalling near the 14,000-resistance level in 2012–2013, Dow 8,000 is likely to come under fire in 2013–2014 as we withdraw from Afghanistan. Resistance will likely be met in 2015–2017 near 13,000–14,000. Another test of the 8,000-support level in 2017–2018 is expected as inflation begins to level off and the next Super Boom commences. By 2020, we should be testing 15,000, and after a brief pullback, be on our way to 25,000 in 2022. A bear market in midterm 2022 should be followed by a three-to-four-year tear toward Dow 40,000.

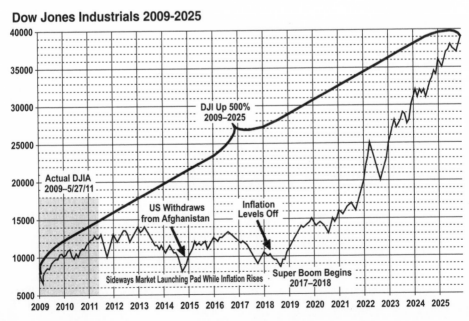

Dow Jones Industrials 2009-2025

AUGUST

e average man is always waiting for something to happen to him instead of setting to work to make things happen.
r one person who dreams of making 50,000 pounds, a hundred people dream of being left 50,000 pounds.
A. A. Milne (British author, *Winnie-the-Pooh*, 1882–1956)

gust Worst Dow and S&P Month 1988–2005—Up 4 of Last 5
rvesting Made August Best Dow Month 1901–1951

TUESDAY

D 47.6
S 47.6
N 47.6

7

ien a country lives on borrowed time, borrowed money, and borrowed energy, it is just begging the markets to
cipline it in their own way at their own time. Usually the markets do it in an orderly way—
ept when they don't. — Thomas L. Friedman (*NY Times* Foreign Affairs columnist, 2/24/05)

WEDNESDAY

D 47.6
S 57.1
N 42.9

8

l great truths begin as blasphemies. — George Bernard Shaw (Irish dramatist, 1856–1950)

THURSDAY

D 42.9
S 38.1
N 38.1

9

day's generation of young people holds more power than any generation before it to make a positive
pact on the world. — William J. Clinton (42nd U.S. president, Clinton Global Initiative, b. 1946)

FRIDAY

D 52.4
S 52.4
N 47.6

10

ar markets don't act like a medicine ball rolling down a smooth hill. Instead, they behave like a basketball
uncing down a rock-strewn mountainside; there's lots of movement up and sideways before the bottom
reached. — Daniel Turov (*Turov on Timing, Barron's,* May 21, 2001, b. 1947)

SATURDAY

11

SUNDAY

12

AURA OF THE TRIPLE WITCH—4TH QUARTER MOST BULLISH: DOWN WEEKS TRIGGER MORE WEAKNESS WEEK AFTER

Options expire the third Friday of every month, but in March, June, September, and December, a powerful coven gathers. Since the S&P index futures began trading on April 21, 1982, stock options, index options, as well as index futures all expire at the same time four times each year—known as Triple Witching. Traders have long sought to understand and master the magic of this quarterly phenomenon.

The market for single-stock and ETF futures continues to grow. However, their impact on the market has thus far been subdued. As their availability continues to expand, trading volumes and market influence are also likely to broaden. Until such time, we do not believe the term "quadruple witching" is applicable just yet.

We have analyzed what the market does prior, during, and following Triple Witching expirations in search of consistent trading patterns. Here are some of our findings of how the Dow Jones Industrials perform around Triple-Witching Week (TWW).

- TWWs became more bullish since 1990, except in the second quarter.
- Following weeks became more bearish. Since Q1 2000, only 16 of 44 were up, and 7 occurred in December, 6 in March, 3 in September, none in June.
- TWWs have tended to be down in flat periods and dramatically so during bear markets.
- DOWN WEEKS TEND TO FOLLOW DOWN TWWs is a most interesting pattern. Since 1991, of 28 down TWWs, 21 following weeks were also down. This is surprising, inasmuch as the previous decade had an exactly opposite pattern: There were 13 down TWWs then, but 12 up weeks followed them.
- TWWs in the second and third quarter (Worst Six Months May through October) are much weaker, and the weeks following, horrendous. But in the first and fourth quarter (Best Six Months period November through April), only the week after Q1 expiration is negative.

Throughout the *Almanac* you will also see notations on the performance of Mondays and Fridays of TWW, as we place considerable significance on the beginnings and ends of weeks (pages 66, 68, 78, and 141–144).

TRIPLE WITCHING WEEK AND WEEK AFTER DOW POINT CHANGES

	Expiration Week Q1	Week After	Expiration Week Q2	Week After	Expiration Week Q3	Week After	Expiration Week Q4	Week After
1991	-6.93	-89.36	-34.98	-58.81	33.54	-13.19	20.12	167.04
1992	40.48	-44.95	-69.01	-2.94	21.35	-76.73	9.19	12.97
1993	43.76	-31.60	-10.24	-3.88	-8.38	-70.14	10.90	6.15
1994	32.95	-120.92	3.33	-139.84	58.54	-101.60	116.08	26.24
1995	38.04	65.02	86.80	75.05	96.85	-33.42	19.87	-78.76
1996	114.52	51.67	55.78	-50.60	49.94	-15.54	179.53	76.51
1997	-130.67	-64.20	14.47	-108.79	174.30	4.91	-82.01	-76.98
1998	303.91	-110.35	-122.07	231.67	100.16	133.11	81.87	314.36
1999	27.20	-81.31	365.05	-303.00	-224.80	-524.30	32.73	148.33
2000	666.41	517.49	-164.76	-44.55	-293.65	-79.63	-277.95	200.60
2001	-821.21	-318.63	-353.36	-19.05	-1369.70	611.75	224.19	101.65
2002	34.74	-179.56	-220.42	-10.53	-326.67	-284.57	77.61	-207.54
2003	662.26	-376.20	83.63	-211.70	173.27	-331.74	236.06	46.45
2004	-53.48	26.37	6.31	-44.57	-28.61	-237.22	106.70	177.20
2005	-144.69	-186.80	110.44	-325.23	-36.62	-222.35	97.01	7.68
2006	203.31	0.32	122.63	-25.46	168.66	-52.67	138.03	-102.30
2007	-165.91	370.60	215.09	-279.22	377.67	75.44	110.80	-84.78
2008	410.23	-144.92	-464.66	-496.18	-33.55	-245.31	-50.57	-63.56
2009	54.40	497.80	-259.53	-101.34	214.79	-155.01	-142.61	191.24
2010	117.29	108.38	239.57	-306.83	145.08	252.41	81.59	81.58
2011	-185.88	362.07						
Up	14	9	11	2	12	5	16	14
Down	7	12	9	18	8	15	4	6

AUGUST

D 28.6
S 28.6
N 42.9

13

When investment decisions need to consider the speed of light, something is seriously wrong.
— Frank M. Bifulco (Senior Portfolio Manager, Alcott Capital Management,
Barron's Letters to the Editor, 5/24/2010)

🐻 TUESDAY

D 66.7
S 71.4
N 71.4

14

Since 1950, the S&P 500 has achieved total returns averaging just 3.50% annually during periods when the
S&P 500 price/peak earnings ratio was above 15 and both 3-month T-bill yields and 10-year Treasury yields
were above their levels of 6 months earlier. — John P. Hussman, Ph.D. (Hussman Funds, 5/22/06)

Mid-August Stronger Than Beginning and End

🐻 WEDNESDAY

D 47.6
S 61.9
N 61.9

15

The "canonical" market bottom typically features below-average valuations, falling interest rates,
new lows in some major indices on diminished trading volume...and finally, a quick high-volume
reversal in breadth... — John P. Hussman, Ph.D. (Hussman Funds, 5/22/06)

🐻 THURSDAY

D 61.9
S 71.4
N 66.7

16

It isn't the incompetent who destroy an organization. It is those who have achieved something and want to rest upon
their achievements who are forever clogging things up. — Charles E. Sorenson (Danish-American engineer, officer,
director of Ford Motor Co. 1907–1950, helped develop 1st auto assembly line, 1881–1968)

August Expiration Day Bullish Lately, Dow Up 7 in a Row 2003–2009
Up 156 Points (1.7%) in 2009

🐻🦃 FRIDAY

D 57.1
S 61.9
N 61.9

17

Nothing is more uncertain than the favor of the crowd.
— Marcus Tullius Cicero (Great Roman orator, politician, 106–43 B.C.)

SATURDAY

18

SUNDAY

19

TAKE ADVANTAGE OF DOWN FRIDAY/ DOWN MONDAY WARNING

Fridays and Mondays are the most important days of the week. Friday is the day for squaring positions—trimming longs or covering shorts before taking off for the weekend. Traders want to limit their exposure (particularly to stocks that are not acting well) since there could be unfavorable developments before trading resumes two or more days later.

Monday is important because the market then has the chance to reflect any weekend news, plus what traders think after digesting the previous week's action and the many Monday morning research and strategy comments.

For over 30 years, a down Friday followed by down Monday has frequently corresponded to important market inflection points that exhibit a clearly negative bias, often coinciding with market tops and, on a few climactic occasions, such as in October 2002 and March 2009, near major market bottoms.

One simple way to get a quick reading on which way the market may be heading is to keep track of the performance of the Dow Jones Industrial Average on Fridays and the following Mondays. Since 1995, there have been 165 occurrences of Down Friday/Down Monday (DF/DM), with 46 falling in the bear market years of 2001, 2002, and 2008, producing an average decline of 14.1%.

To illustrate how Down Friday/Down Monday can telegraph market inflection points we created the chart below of the

DOWN FRIDAY/DOWN MONDAYS

Year	Total Number Down Friday/ Down Monday	Subsequent Average % Dow Loss*	Average Number of Days it took
1995	8	−1.2%	18
1996	9	−3.0%	28
1997	6	−5.1%	45
1998	9	−6.4%	47
1999	9	−6.4%	39
2000	11	−6.6%	32
2001	13	−13.5%	53
2002	18	−11.9%	54
2003	9	−3.0%	17
2004	9	−3.7%	51
2005	10	−3.0%	37
2006	11	−2.0%	14
2007	8	−6.0%	33
2008	15	−17.0%	53
2009	10	−8.7%	15
2010	7	−3.1%	10
2011**	3	−2.4%	23
Average	**10**	**−6.1%**	**33**

*Over next 3 months; **Ending May 20, 2011*

Dow Jones Industrials from November 2009 to May 20, 2011 with arrows pointing to occurrences of DF/DM. Use DF/DM as a warning to examine market conditions carefully. The unprecedented 31-week streak without a DF/DM that began in October 2009 came to an end on June 1, 2010. Subsequent DF/DM's have preceded short-lived and relatively mild pullbacks, typical during bull markets.

DOW JONES INDUSTRIALS (November 2009 to May 20, 2011)

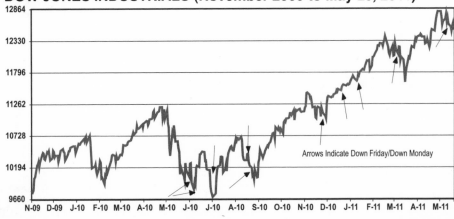

Arrows Indicate Down Friday/Down Monday

MONDAY

D 52.4
S 47.6
N 42.9

20

The symbol of all relationships among such men, the moral symbol of respect for human beings, is the trader. — Ayn Rand (Russian-born American novelist and philosopher, from Galt's Speech, *Atlas Shrugged*, 1957, 1905–1982)

TUESDAY

D 38.1
S 42.9
N 33.3

21

When everyone starts downgrading a stock, it's usually time to buy. — Meryl Witmer (General partner, Eagle Capital Partners, *Barron's*, 1/29/07)

WEDNESDAY

D 61.9
S 61.9
N 81.0

22

If you spend more than 14 minutes a year worrying about the market, you've wasted 12 minutes. — Peter Lynch (Fidelity Investments, *One Up On Wall Street*, b. 1944)

End of August Stronger Last 8 Years

THURSDAY

D 42.9
S 42.9
N 47.6

23

Over the last 25 years, computer processing capacity has risen more than a millionfold, while communication capacity has risen over a thousandfold. — Richard Worzel (Futurist, *Facing the Future*, b. 1950)

FRIDAY

D 57.1
S 61.9
N 47.6

24

History must repeat itself because we pay such little attention to it the first time. — Blackie Sherrod (Sportswriter, b. 1919)

SATURDAY

25

SUNDAY

26

SEPTEMBER ALMANAC

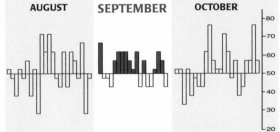

SEPTEMBER							OCTOBER						
S	M	T	W	T	F	S	S	M	T	W	T	F	S
						1			1	2	3	4	5	6
2	3	4	5	6	7	8	7	8	9	10	11	12	13
9	10	11	12	13	14	15	14	15	16	17	18	19	20
16	17	18	19	20	21	22	21	22	23	24	25	26	27
23	24	25	26	27	28	29	28	29	30	31			
30													

Market Probability Chart above is a graphic representation of the S&P 500 Recent Market Probability Calendar on page 124.

◆ Start of business year, end of vacations, and back to school made September a leading barometer month in first 60 years of 20th century; now portfolio managers back after Labor Day tend to clean house ◆ Biggest % loser on the S&P, Dow, and NASDAQ (pages 44 and 56) ◆ Streak of four great Dow Septembers averaging 4.2% gains ended in 1999 with six losers in a row averaging −5.9% (see page 152), up three straight 2005–2007, down 6% in 2008 ◆ Day after Labor Day, Dow up 13 of last 17 ◆ S&P opened strong 12 of last 16 years but tends to close weak due to end-of-quarter mutual fund portfolio restructuring; last trading day, S&P down 12 of past 18 ◆ September Triple-Witching Week can be dangerous, week after is pitiful (see page 76).

September Vital Statistics

	DJIA	S&P 500	NASDAQ	Russell 1K	Russell 2K
Rank	12	12	12	12	10
Up	24	27	22	16	18
Down	37	33	18	16	14
Avg % Change	−0.8%	−0.5%	−0.5%	−0.6%	−0.2%
Election Year	−0.6%	−0.3%	−0.4%	−0.1%	0.4%
Best and Worst September					
	% Change	% Change	% Change	% Change	% Change
Best	2010 7.7	2010 8.8	1998 13.0	2010 9.0	2010 12.3
Worst	2002 −12.4	1974 −11.9	2001 −17.0	2002 −10.9	2001 −13.6
Best and Worst September Weeks					
Best	9/28/01 7.4	9/28/01 7.8	9/20/74 5.7	9/28/01 7.6	9/28/01 6.9
Worst	9/21/01 −14.3	9/21/01 −11.6	9/21/01 −16.1	9/21/01 −11.7	9/21/01 −14.0
Best and Worst September Days					
Best	9/8/98 5.0	9/30/08 5.4	9/8/98 6.0	9/30/08 5.3	9/18/08 7.0
Worst	9/17/01 −7.1	9/29/08 −8.8	9/29/08 −9.1	9/29/08 −8.7	9/29/08 −6.7
First Trading Day of Expiration Week: 1980–2010					
Record (#Up–#Down)	20–11	17–14	12–19	17–14	12–19
Current Streak	U2	U2	U2	U2	U2
Avg % Change	−0.13	−0.17	−0.38	−0.19	−0.25
Options Expiration Day: 1980–2010					
Record (#Up–#Down)	16–15	18–13	21–10	18–13	21–10
Current Streak	U7	U7	U7	U7	U6
Avg % Change	0.03	0.17	0.17	0.15	0.21
Options Expiration Week: 1980–2010					
Record (#Up–#Down)	16–15	18–13	17–14	18–13	16–15
Current Streak	U2	U5	U5	U5	U5
Avg % Change	−0.46	−0.20	−0.20	−0.21	−0.05
Week After Options Expiration: 1980–2010					
Record (#Up–#Down)	12–19	10–21	14–17	10–20	11–20
Current Streak	U1	U1	U1	U1	U1
Avg % Change	−0.54	−0.56	−0.71	−0.56	−1.11
First Trading Day Performance					
% of Time Up	62.3	63.9	55.0	53.1	50.0
Avg % Change	0.06	0.04	0.02	0.02	0.09
Last Trading Day Performance					
% of Time Up	39.3	42.6	50.0	50.0	65.6
Avg % Change	−0.10	−0.04	0.03	0.09	0.39

Dow and S&P 1950–April 2011, NASDAQ 1971–April 2011, Russell 1K and 2K 1979–April 2011.

September is when leaves and stocks tend to fall;
On Wall Street it's the worst month of all.

MONDAY

D 57.1
S 57.1
N 57.1

27

Stocks are super-attractive when the Fed is loosening and interest rates are falling. In sum: Don't fight the Fed!
— Martin Zweig (Fund manager, *Winning on Wall Street*)

TUESDAY

D 42.9
S 47.6
N 42.9

28

The big guys are the status quo, not the innovators. — Kenneth L. Fisher (*Forbes* columnist)

🐂 WEDNESDAY

D 66.7
S 66.7
N 71.4

29

To achieve satisfactory investment results is easier than most people realize. The typical individual investor has a great advantage over the large institutions. — Benjamin Graham (Economist, investor, *Securities Analysis* 1934, *The Intelligent Investor* 1949, 1894–1976)

August's Next-to-Last Trading Day, S&P Up Only Twice in Last 15 Years 🐻 THURSDAY

D 28.6
S 28.6
N 57.1

30

Financial markets will find and exploit hidden flaws, particularly in untested new innovations—and do so at a time that will inflict the most damage to the most people. — Raymond F. DeVoe Jr. (Market strategist, Jesup & Lamont, *The DeVoe Report*, 3/30/07)

FRIDAY

D 47.6
S 47.6
N 52.4

31

Foolish consistency is the hobgoblin of little minds.
— Ralph Waldo Emerson (American author, poet and philosopher, *Self-Reliance*, 1803–1882)

SATURDAY

1

September Almanac Investor Seasonalities: See Pages 92, 94, and 96

SUNDAY

2

A CORRECTION FOR ALL SEASONS

While there's a rally for every season (page 70), almost always there's a decline or correction, too. Fortunately, corrections tend to be smaller than rallies, and that's what gives the stock market its long-term upward bias. In each season the average bounce outdoes the average setback. On average, the net gain between the rally and the correction is smallest in summer and fall.

The summer setback tends to be slightly outdone by the average correction in the fall. Tax selling and portfolio cleaning are the usual explanations—individuals sell to register a tax loss and institutions like to get rid of their losers before preparing year-end statements. The October jinx also plays a major part. Since 1964, there have been 17 fall declines of over 10%, and in 10 of them (1966, 1974, 1978, 1979, 1987, 1990, 1997, 2000, 2002, and 2008) much damage was done in October, where so many bear markets end. Recent October lows were also seen in 1998, 1999, 2004, and 2005. Most often, it has paid to buy after fourth quarter or late third quarter "waterfall declines" for a rally that may continue into January or even beyond. Anticipation of war in Iraq put the market down in 2003 Q1. Quick success rallied stocks through Q3. Financial crisis affected the pattern in 2008–2009, producing the worst winter decline since 1932. Easy monetary policy and strong corporate earnings spared 2011 Q1 from a seasonal slump.

SEASONAL CORRECTIONS IN DOW JONES INDUSTRIALS

	WINTER SLUMP Nov/Dec High to Q1 Low	SPRING SLUMP Feb/Mar High to Q2 Low	SUMMER SLUMP May/Jun High to Q3 Low	FALL SLUMP Aug/Sep High to Q4 Low
1964	−0.1%	−2.4%	−1.0%	−2.1%
1965	−2.5	−7.3	−8.3	−0.9
1966	−6.0	−13.2	−17.7	−12.7
1967	−4.2	−3.9	−5.5	−9.9
1968	−8.8	−0.3	−5.5	+0.4
1969	−8.7	−8.7	−17.2	−8.1
1970	−13.8	−20.2	−8.8	−2.5
1971	−1.4	−4.8	−10.7	−13.4
1972	−0.5	−2.6	−6.3	−5.3
1973	−11.0	−12.8	−10.9	−17.3
1974	−15.3	−10.8	−29.8	−27.6
1975	−6.3	−5.5	−9.9	−6.7
1976	−0.2	−5.1	−4.7	−8.9
1977	−8.5	−7.2	−11.5	−10.2
1978	−12.3	−4.0	−7.0	−13.5
1979	−2.5	−5.8	−3.7	−10.9
1980	−10.0	−16.0	−1.7	−6.8
1981	−6.9	−5.1	−18.6	−12.9
1982	−10.9	−7.5	−10.6	−3.3
1983	−4.1	−2.8	−6.8	−3.6
1984	−11.9	−10.5	−8.4	−6.2
1985	−4.8	−4.4	−2.8	−2.3
1986	−3.3	−4.7	−7.3	−7.6
1987	−1.4	−6.6	−1.7	−36.1
1988	−6.7	−7.0	−7.6	−4.5
1989	−1.7	−2.4	−3.1	−6.6
1990	−7.9	−4.0	−17.3	−18.4
1991	−6.3	−3.6	−4.5	−6.3
1992	+0.1	−3.3	−5.4	−7.6
1993	−2.7	−3.1	−3.0	−2.0
1994	−4.4	−9.6	−4.4	−7.1
1995	−0.8	−0.1	−0.2	−2.0
1996	−3.5	−4.6	−7.5	+0.2
1997	−1.8	−9.8	−2.2	−13.3
1998	−7.0	−3.1	−18.2	−13.1
1999	−2.7	−1.7	−8.0	−11.5
2000	−14.8	−7.4	−4.1	−11.8
2001	−14.5	−13.6	−27.4	−16.2
2002	−5.1	−14.2	−26.7	−19.5
2003	−15.8	−5.3	−3.1	−2.1
2004	−3.9	−7.7	−6.3	−5.7
2005	−4.5	−8.5	−3.3	−4.5
2006	−2.4	−5.4	−7.8	−0.4
2007	−3.7	−3.2	−6.1	−8.4
2008	−14.5	−11.0	−20.6	−35.9
2009	−32.0	−6.3	−7.4	−3.5
2010	−6.1	−10.4	−13.1	−1.0
2011	+0.2	−1.5*		
Totals	**−317.9%**	**−319.0%**	**−423.7%**	**−429.5%**
Average	**−6.6%**	**−6.6%**	**−9.0%**	**−9.1%**

As of 5/20/2011.

SEPTEMBER

Labor Day (Market Closed)

Take care of your employees and they'll take care of your customers.
— John W. Marriott (Founder Marriott International, 1900–1985)

First Trading Day in September, S&P Up 12 of Last 16
Day after Labor Day, Dow Up 13 of Last 17, 1997 Up 3.4%, 1998 Up 5.0%

TUESDAY

D 57.1
S 66.7
N 61.9

4

Our firm conviction is that, sooner or later, capitalism will give way to socialism ... We will bury you.
— Nikita Khrushchev (Soviet leader 1953–1964, 1894–1971)

WEDNESDAY

D 61.9
S 47.6
N 61.9

5

If you can ever buy with a P/E equivalent to growth, that's a good starting point.
— Alan Lowenstein (Co-Portfolio manager, John Hancock Technology Fund, *TheStreet.com*, 3/12/2001)

THURSDAY

D 52.4
S 47.6
N 52.4

6

We are nowhere near a capitulation point because it's at that point where it's despair, not hope, that reigns supreme, and there was scant evidence of any despair at any of the meetings I gave.
— David Rosenberg (Economist, Merrill Lynch, *Barron's*, 4/21/2008)

FRIDAY

D 38.1
S 42.9
N 52.4

7

You have to keep digging, keep asking questions, because otherwise you'll be seduced or brainwashed into the idea that it's somehow a great privilege, an honor, to report the lies they've been feeding you.
— David Halberstam (American writer, war reporter, 1964 Pulitzer Prize, 1934–2007)

SATURDAY

8

SUNDAY

9

FIRST-TRADING-DAY-OF-THE-MONTH PHENOMENON: DOW GAINS MORE ONE DAY THAN ALL OTHER DAYS

Over the last 14 years the Dow Jones Industrial Average has gained more points on the first trading days of all months than all other days combined. While the Dow has gained 4889.62 points between September 2, 1997 (7622.42) and May 20, 2011 (12512.04), it is incredible that 5912.80 points were gained on the first trading days of these 165 months. The remaining 3288 trading days combined lost 1023.18 points during the period. This averages out to gains of 35.84 points on first days, in contrast to a loss of 0.31 points on all others.

Note September 1997 through October 2000 racked up a total gain of 2632.39 Dow points on the first trading days of these 38 months (winners except for seven occasions). But between November 2000 and September 2002, when the 2000–2002 bear markets did the bulk of their damage, frightened investors switched from pouring money into the market on that day to pulling it out, fourteen months out of twenty-three, netting a 404.80 Dow point loss. The 2007–2009 bear market lopped off 964.14 Dow points on first days in 17 months, November 2007–March 2009. Since the March 2009 bottom, 20 of 26 first days have produced solid gains.

First days of March have performed worst. Triple digit declines in 2009 and 2011 have resulted in the only net loss. Impressive first-day strength in August and December 2010 has returned these months to net gainers. In rising market trends, first days perform much better, as institutions are likely anticipating strong performance at each month's outset. S&P 500 first days track the Dow's pattern closely, but NASDAQ first days are not as strong, with weakness in April, August, and October.

DOW POINTS GAINED FIRST DAY OF MONTH
SEPTEMBER 1997 TO MAY 20, 2011

	Jan	Feb	Mar	Apr	May	Jun	Jul	Aug	Sep	Oct	Nov	Dec	Totals
1997									257.36	70.24	232.31	189.98	749.89
1998	56.79	201.28	4.73	68.51	83.70	22.42	96.65	−96.55	288.36	−210.09	114.05	16.99	646.84
1999	2.84	−13.13	18.20	46.35	225.65	36.52	95.62	−9.19	108.60	−63.95	−81.35	120.58	486.74
2000	−139.61	100.52	9.62	300.01	77.87	129.87	112.78	84.97	23.68	49.21	−71.67	−40.95	636.30
2001	−140.70	96.27	−45.14	−100.85	163.37	78.47	91.32	−12.80	47.74	−10.73	188.76	−87.60	268.11
2002	51.90	−12.74	262.73	−41.24	113.41	−215.46	−133.47	−229.97	−355.45	346.86	120.61	−33.52	−126.34
2003	265.89	56.01	−53.22	77.73	−25.84	47.55	55.51	−79.83	107.45	194.14	57.34	116.59	819.32
2004	−44.07	11.11	94.22	15.63	88.43	14.20	−101.32	39.45	−5.46	112.38	26.92	162.20	413.69
2005	−53.58	62.00	63.77	−99.46	59.19	82.39	28.47	−17.76	−21.97	−33.22	−33.30	106.70	143.23
2006	129.91	89.09	60.12	35.62	−23.85	91.97	77.80	−59.95	83.00	−8.72	−49.71	−27.80	397.48
2007	11.37	51.99	−34.29	27.95	73.23	40.47	126.81	150.38	91.12	191.92	−362.14	−57.15	311.66
2008	−220.86	92.83	−7.49	391.47	189.87	−134.50	32.25	−51.70	−26.63	−19.59	−5.18	−679.95	−439.48
2009	258.30	−64.03	−299.64	152.68	44.29	221.11	57.06	114.95	−185.68	−203.00	76.71	126.74	299.49
2010	155.91	118.20	78.53	70.44	143.22	−112.61	−41.49	208.44	254.75	41.63	6.13	249.76	1172.91
2011	93.24	148.23	−162.32	56.99	−3.18								132.96
Totals	427.33	937.63	−10.18	1001.83	1209.36	302.40	497.99	40.44	666.87	457.08	219.48	162.57	5912.80

SUMMARY FIRST DAYS VS. OTHER DAYS OF MONTH

	# of Days	Total Points Gained	Average Daily Point Gain
First days	165	5912.80	35.84
Other days	3288	−1023.18	−0.31

SEPTEMBER

MONDAY
D 61.9
S 57.1
N 66.7
10

The first human who hurled an insult instead of a stone was the founder of civilization.
— Sigmund Freud (Austrian neurologist, psychiatrist, "father of psychoanalysis," 1856–1939)

2001 4-Day Market Closing, Longest Since
9-Day Banking Moratorium in March 1933

TUESDAY
D 52.4
S 61.9
N 61.9
11

"In Memory"

It is totally unproductive to think the world has been unfair to you. Every tough stretch is an opportunity.
— Charlie Munger (Vice-chairman, Berkshire Hathaway, 2007 Wesco Annual Meeting, b. 1924)

FOMC Meeting

WEDNESDAY
D 61.9
S 61.9
N 57.1
12

Experience is helpful, but it is judgment that matters. — General Colin Powell (Chairman Joint
Chiefs, 1989–93, Secretary of State, 2001–05, *NY Times*, 10/22/2008, b. 1937)

THURSDAY
D 66.7
S 61.9
N 66.7
13

Self-discipline is a form of freedom. Freedom from laziness and lethargy, freedom from expectations
and demands of others, freedom from weakness and fear—and doubt.
— Harvey A. Dorfman (Sports psychologist, *The Mental ABC's of Pitching*, b. 1935)

FRIDAY
D 47.6
S 57.1
N 71.4
14

[A contrarian's opportunity] If everybody is thinking alike, then somebody isn't thinking.
— General George S. Patton Jr. (U.S. Army field commander WWII, 1885–1945)

SATURDAY
15

SUNDAY
16

MARKET BEHAVIOR THREE DAYS BEFORE AND THREE DAYS AFTER HOLIDAYS

The *Stock Trader's Almanac* has tracked holiday seasonality annually since the first edition in 1968. Stocks used to rise on the day before holidays and sell off the day after, but nowadays, each holiday moves to its own rhythm. Eight holidays are separated into seven groups. Average percentage changes for the Dow, S&P 500, NASDAQ, and Russell 2000 are shown.

The Dow and S&P consist of blue chips and the largest cap stocks, whereas NASDAQ and the Russell 2000 would be more representative of smaller-cap stocks. This is evident on the last day of the year with NASDAQ and the Russell 2000 having a field day, while their larger brethren in the Dow and S&P are showing losses on average.

Thanks to the Santa Claus Rally, the three days before and after New Year's Day and Christmas are best. NASDAQ and the Russell 2000 average gains of 1.4% to 1.8% over the six-day spans. However, trading around the first day of the year has been mixed. Traders have been selling more the first trading day of the year recently, pushing gains and losses into the New Year.

Bullishness before Labor Day and after Memorial Day is affected by strength the first day of September and June. The second worst day after a holiday is the day after Easter. Surprisingly, the following day is one of the best second days after a holiday, right up there with the second day after New Year's Day.

Presidents' Day is the least bullish of all the holidays, bearish the day before and three days after. NASDAQ has dropped 17 of the last 22 days before Presidents' Day (Dow, 16 of 22; S&P, 17 of 22; Russell 2000, 12 of 22).

HOLIDAYS: 3 DAYS BEFORE, 3 DAYS AFTER (Average % Change 1980 to April 2011)

	−3	−2	−1	Mixed	+1	+2	+3
S&P 500	0.06	0.27	−0.13	**New Year's**	0.16	0.38	0.04
DJIA	0.02	0.20	−0.20	**Day**	0.29	0.38	0.18
NASDAQ	0.15	0.32	0.19	*1/1/12 (Closed 1/2)*	0.14	0.71	0.20
Russell 2K	0.15	0.43	0.48		−0.01	0.27	0.13
S&P 500	0.39	−0.02	−0.26	Negative Before and After	−0.27	−0.02	−0.14
DJIA	0.40	−0.01	−0.19	**Presidents'**	−0.16	−0.08	−0.18
NASDAQ	0.59	0.23	−0.40	**Day**	−0.64	−0.01	−0.09
Russell 2K	0.47	0.09	−0.12	*2/20/12*	−0.49	−0.10	−0.10
S&P 500	0.21	−0.03	0.42	**Positive Before and**	−0.21	0.37	0.12
DJIA	0.18	−0.06	0.32	**Negative After**	−0.14	0.36	0.12
NASDAQ	0.46	0.29	0.52	**Good Friday**	−0.33	0.39	0.23
Russell 2K	0.24	0.15	0.56	*4/6/12*	−0.29	0.29	0.15
S&P 500	0.03	0.05	−0.02	**Positive After**	0.29	0.25	0.27
DJIA	0.001	0.003	−0.07	**Memorial**	0.37	0.25	0.18
NASDAQ	0.08	0.24	0.001	**Day**	0.19	0.08	0.52
Russell 2K	−0.09	0.29	0.07	*5/28/12*	0.18	0.21	0.44
S&P 500	0.01	0.05	−0.01	**Negative After**	−0.15	0.07	0.03
DJIA	−0.01	0.04	−0.004	**Independence**	−0.09	0.09	0.02
NASDAQ	0.15	0.06	−0.03	**Day**	−0.19	−0.06	0.18
Russell 2K	0.14	−0.05	−0.13	*7/4/12*	−0.25	0.01	−0.02
S&P 500	0.16	−0.18	0.26	**Positive Day**	0.07	0.003	−0.12
DJIA	0.13	−0.25	0.25	**Before**	0.13	0.08	−0.22
NASDAQ	0.39	0.06	0.28	**Labor Day**	−0.06	−0.15	0.03
Russell 2K	0.56	0.15	0.26	*9/3/12*	0.01	0.02	0.04
S&P 500	0.15	0.02	0.35	**Positive Before**	0.19	−0.54	0.33
DJIA	0.17	0.03	0.35	**and After**	0.14	−0.47	0.36
NASDAQ	0.06	−0.26	0.50	**Thanksgiving**	0.48	−0.57	0.14
Russell 2K	0.15	−0.11	0.48	*11/22/12*	0.38	−0.65	0.30
S&P 500	0.16	0.19	0.22	**Christmas**	0.16	0.04	0.34
DJIA	0.25	0.24	0.28	*12/25/12*	0.20	0.04	0.29
NASDAQ	−0.09	0.45	0.44		0.12	0.10	0.40
Russell 2K	0.18	0.37	0.39		0.22	0.13	0.53

SEPTEMBER

Rosh Hashanah
Monday before September Triple Witching, Russell 2000 Down 8 of Last 12

D 52.4
S 52.4
N 33.3
17

Averaging down in a bear market is tantamount to taking a seat on the down escalator at Macy's.
— Richard Russell (Dow Theory Letters, 1984)

TUESDAY
D 52.4
S 61.9
N 61.9
18

One determined person can make a significant difference; a small group of determined people can change the course of history. — Sonia Johnson (Author, lecturer)

Expiration Week 2001, Dow Lost 1370 Points (14.3%)
2nd Worst Weekly Point Loss Ever, 5th Worst Week Overall

WEDNESDAY
D 33.3
S 42.9
N 52.4
19

Beware of inside information... all inside information.
— Jesse Livermore (Early twentieth century stock trader and speculator, How to Trade in Stocks, 1877–1940)

THURSDAY
D 52.4
S 57.1
N 66.7
20

If there is something you really want to do, make your plan and do it. Otherwise, you'll just regret it forever.
— Richard Rocco (PostNet franchisee, Entrepreneur Magazine, 12/2006, b. 1946)

September Triple Witching, Dow Up 7 Straight and 8 of Last 9

FRIDAY
D 42.9
S 42.9
N 42.9
21

The heights by great men reached and kept, were not attained by sudden flight, but they, while their companions slept, were toiling upward in the night. — Henry Wadsworth Longfellow (American poet and educator, 1743–1826)

SATURDAY
22

SUNDAY
23

MARKET GAINS MORE ON SUPER-8 DAYS EACH MONTH THAN ON ALL 13 REMAINING DAYS COMBINED

For many years, the last day plus the first four days were the best days of the month. The market currently exhibits greater bullish bias from the last three trading days of the previous month through the first two days of the current month, and now shows significant bullishness during the middle three trading days, 9 to 11, due to 401(k) cash inflows (see pages 145 and 146). This pattern was not as pronounced during the boom years of the 1990s, with market strength all month long. It returned in 2000 with monthly bullishness at the ends, beginnings and middles of months versus weakness during the rest of the month. "Super Eight" performance in 2009 was severely lacking. However, in 2010 strength returned to give the period an advantage over all other days.

SUPER-8 DAYS* DOW % CHANGES VS. REST OF MONTH

	Super-8 Days	Rest of Month	Super-8 Days	Rest of Month	Super-8 Days	Rest of Month
	2003		**2004**		**2005**	
Jan	1.00%	−4.86%	3.79%	−1.02%	−1.96%	−1.35%
Feb	2.71	−4.82	−1.20	0.83	1.76	−0.07
Mar	5.22	−0.90	−1.64	−1.69	0.31	−2.05
Apr	2.87	−1.91	3.20	−0.60	−4.62	1.46
May	3.17	2.46	−2.92	−0.51	0.57	2.43
Jun	3.09	−0.38	1.15	1.36	1.43	−3.00
Jul	1.18	1.64	−1.91	−0.88	0.96	1.83
Aug	−0.74	1.55	0.51	0.40	1.36	−3.07
Sep	3.58	−3.47	0.47	−2.26	0.90	−0.31
Oct	2.87	1.41	0.85	−1.82	1.14	−2.18
Nov	−0.47	0.48	3.08	3.20	1.67	3.89
Dec	2.10	3.70	2.03	1.13	0.57	−1.96
Totals	**26.58%**	**−5.10%**	**7.41%**	**−1.86%**	**4.09%**	**−4.37%**
Average	**2.22%**	**−0.43%**	**0.62%**	**−0.16%**	**0.34%**	**−0.36%**
	2006		**2007**		**2008**	
Jan	−0.03%	0.34%	0.68%	−0.04%	−4.76%	−4.11%
Feb	1.67	0.71	3.02	−1.72	1.83	0.65
Mar	0.81	−0.03	−5.51	3.64	−4.85	2.92
Apr	1.69	−0.53	2.66	2.82	−0.27	4.09
May	−0.66	0.08	2.21	0.95	2.19	−4.81
Jun	2.39	−4.87	3.84	−5.00	0.37	−6.30
Jul	1.65	0.07	2.59	−1.47	−3.80	−1.99
Aug	1.83	0.41	−2.94	−0.26	1.53	1.06
Sep	1.13	1.64	4.36	1.18	−2.23	−1.19
Oct	1.58	2.59	1.28	−1.05	−3.39	−13.70
Nov	−0.01	−0.31	−0.59	−5.63	6.07	−11.90
Dec	2.40	−0.05	−0.04	4.62	−2.54	3.49
Totals	**14.45%**	**0.04%**	**11.56%**	**−1.96%**	**−9.85%**	**−31.79%**
Average	**1.20%**	**0.003%**	**0.96%**	**−0.16%**	**−0.82%**	**−2.65%**
	2009		**2010**		**2011**	
Jan	3.16%	−6.92%	0.66%	−3.92%	1.70%	1.80%
Feb	−6.05	−4.39	3.31	−2.38	0.45	0.57
Mar	−4.37	12.84	1.91	3.51	−1.40	2.21
Apr	1.52	−0.24	1.13	0.18	2.30	0.95
May	2.64	2.98	−3.08	−5.75		
Jun	1.71	−1.64	4.33	−3.26		
Jul	2.30	5.03	−7.07	11.34		
Aug	0.04	4.91	0.20	−5.49		
Sep	−0.81	2.21	3.83	4.22		
Oct	−0.05	2.40	−0.18	3.47		
Nov	0.00	5.57	−1.20	1.37		
Dec	0.62	0.46	1.98	1.45		
Totals	**0.71%**	**23.21%**	**5.82%**	**4.74%**	**3.05%**	**5.53%**
Average	**0.06%**	**1.93%**	**0.49%**	**0.40%**	**0.76%**	**1.38%**

	Super-8 Days*		Rest of Month (13 Days)	
100	Net % Changes	63.82%	Net % Changes	−11.55%
Month	Average Period	0.64%	Average Period	−0.12%
Totals	Average Day	0.08%	Average Day	−0.01%

* Super-8 Days = Last 3 + First 2 + Middle 3

SEPTEMBER

Week after September Triple Witching, Dow Down 16 of Last 21,
Average Loss Since 1990, 0.9%

MONDAY

D 47.6
S 42.9
N 42.9

24

History is replete with episodes in which the real patriots were the ones who defied their governments.
— Jim Rogers (Financier, *Adventure Capitalist*, b. 1942)

End of September Prone to Weakness
From End-of-Q3 Institutional Portfolio Restructuring

TUESDAY

D 57.1
S 52.4
N 52.4

25

In this age of instant information, investors can experience both fear and greed at the exact same moment.
— Sam Stovall (Chief investment strategist, Standard & Poor's, October 2003)

Yom Kippur

WEDNESDAY

D 57.1
S 61.9
N 42.9

26

Being uneducated is sometimes beneficial. Then you don't know what can't be done. — Michael Ott (Venture capitalist)

THURSDAY

D 52.4
S 57.1
N 47.6

27

Every man who knows how to read has it in his power to magnify himself, to multiply the ways in which
he exists, to make his life full, significant, and interesting.
— Aldous Huxley (English author, *Brave New World*, 1894–1963)

Last Day of Q3, Dow Down 10 of Last 14, Massive 4.7% Rally in 2008

FRIDAY

D 42.9
S 42.9
N 42.9

28

The four most expensive words in the English language, "This time it's different."
— Sir John Templeton (Founder Templeton Funds, philanthropist, 1912–2008)

SATURDAY

29

October Almanac Investor Seasonalities: See Pages 92, 94, and 96

SUNDAY

30

OCTOBER ALMANAC

OCTOBER							NOVEMBER					
S	M	T	W	T	F	S	S	M	T	W	T	F	S
		1	2	3	4	5	6					1	2	3
7	8	9	10	11	12	13	4	5	6	7	8	9	10
14	15	16	17	18	19	20	11	12	13	14	15	16	17
21	22	23	24	25	26	27	18	19	20	21	22	23	24
28	29	30	31				25	26	27	28	29	30

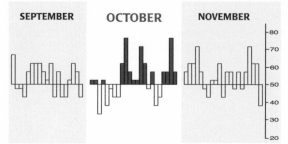

Market Probability Chart above is a graphic representation of the S&P 500 Recent Market Probability Calendar on page 124.

◆ Known as the jinx month because of crashes in 1929, 1987, the 554-point drop on October 27, 1997, back-to-back massacres in 1978 and 1979, Friday the 13th in 1989, and the meltdown in 2008 ◆ Yet October is a "bear killer" and turned the tide in 11 post-WWII bear markets: 1946, 1957, 1960, 1962, 1966, 1974, 1987, 1990, 1998, 2001, and 2002 ◆ First October Dow top in 2007, 20-year 1987 crash anniversary −2.6% ◆ Worst Six Months of the year ends with October (page 48) ◆ No longer worst month (pages 44 and 58) ◆ Best Dow, S&P, and NASDAQ month from 1993 to 2007 ◆ Presidential election year Octobers since 1952, Dow and S&P rank last, NASDAQ #11 ◆ October is a great time to buy ◆ Big October gains five years 1999–2003 after atrocious Septembers ◆ Can get into Best Six Months earlier using MACD (page 50).

October Vital Statistics

	DJIA	S&P 500	NASDAQ	Russell 1K	Russell 2K
Rank	7	7	8	9	12
Up	36	36	21	20	17
Down	25	25	19	12	15
Avg % Change	0.4%	0.6%	0.3%	0.5%	−1.0%
Election Year	−0.7%	−0.6%	−1.9%	−1.4%	−2.7%
Best and Worst October					
	% Change	% Change	% Change	% Change	% Change
Best	1982 10.7	1974 16.3	1974 17.2	1982 11.3	1982 14.1
Worst	1987 −23.2	1987 −21.8	1987 −27.2	1987 −21.9	1987 −30.8
Best and Worst October Weeks					
Best	10/11/74 12.6	10/11/74 14.1	10/31/08 10.9	10/31/08 10.8	10/31/08 14.1
Worst	10/10/08 −18.2	10/10/08 −18.2	10/23/87 −19.2	10/10/08 −18.2	10/23/87 −20.4
Best and Worst October Days					
Best	10/13/08 11.1	10/13/08 11.6	10/13/08 11.8	10/13/08 11.7	10/13/08 9.3
Worst	10/19/87 −22.6	10/19/87 −20.5	10/19/87 −11.4	10/19/87 −19.0	10/19/87 −12.5
First Trading Day of Expiration Week: 1980–2010					
Record (#Up–#Down)	26–5	24–7	22–9	25–6	24–7
Current Streak	U3	U3	U1	U3	D2
Avg % Change	0.92	0.88	0.71	0.86	0.55
Options Expiration Day: 1980–2010					
Record (#Up–#Down)	13–18	15–16	16–15	15–16	13–18
Current Streak	D6	U1	U1	U1	D5
Avg % Change	−0.27	−0.34	−0.19	−0.32	−0.25
Options Expiration Week: 1980–2010					
Record (#Up–#Down)	21–10	21–10	18–13	21–10	19–12
Current Streak	U3	U3	U3	U3	U3
Avg % Change	0.63	0.65	0.77	0.63	0.31
Week After Options Expiration: 1980–2010					
Record (#Up–#Down)	13–18	12–19	15–16	12–19	13–18
Current Streak	U1	U1	U1	U1	U1
Avg % Change	−0.62	−0.66	−0.74	−0.69	−0.96
First Trading Day Performance					
% of Time Up	49.2	49.2	50.0	53.1	50.0
Avg % Change	0.11	0.10	−0.08	0.35	−0.12
Last Trading Day Performance					
% of Time Up	55.7	55.7	70.0	65.6	75.0
Avg % Change	0.11	0.19	0.59	0.45	0.73

Dow and S&P 1950–April 2011, NASDAQ 1971–April 2011, Russell 1K and 2K 1979–April 2011.

October has killed many a bear;
Buy techs and small caps and soon wear a grin ear to ear.

OCTOBER

First Trading Day in October, Dow Down 4 of Last 6
Off 2.1% in 2009

MONDAY

D 57.1
S 52.4
N 47.6

1

The market can stay irrational longer than you can stay solvent.
— John Maynard Keynes (British economist, 1883–1946)

TUESDAY

D 42.9
S 52.4
N 52.4

2

I have seen it repeatedly throughout the world: politicians get a country in trouble but swear
everything is okay in the face of overwhelming evidence to the contrary.
— Jim Rogers (Financier, *Adventure Capitalist*, b. 1942)

Start Looking for MACD BUY Signals (Pages 50 and 58)
Almanac Investor Subscribers E-mailed When It Triggers (See Insert)

WEDNESDAY

D 38.1
S 33.3
N 42.9

3

My best shorts come from research reports where there are recommendations to buy stocks on weakness;
also, where a brokerage firm changes its recommendation from a buy to a hold.
— Marc Howard (Hedge fund manager, *New York Magazine*, 1976, b. 1941)

THURSDAY

D 61.9
S 52.4
N 57.1

4

Executives owe it to the organization and to their fellow workers not to tolerate nonperforming
individuals in important jobs.
— Peter Drucker (Austria-born pioneer management theorist, 1909–2005)

FRIDAY

D 33.3
S 38.1
N 47.6

5

It is a funny thing about life; if you refuse to accept anything but the best, you very often get it.
— W. Somerset Maugham (English playwright and novelist, 1874–1965)

SATURDAY

6

SUNDAY

7

SECTOR SEASONALITY: SELECTED PERCENTAGE PLAYS

Sector seasonality was featured in the first 1968 *Almanac*. A Merrill Lynch study showed that buying seven sectors around September or October and selling in the first few months of 1954–1964 tripled the gains of holding them for 10 years. Over the years we have honed this strategy significantly and now devote a large portion of our time and resources to investing and trading during positive and negative seasonal periods for different sectors with Exchange Traded Funds (ETFs).

Updated seasonalities appear in the table below. We specify whether the seasonality starts or finishes in the beginning third (B), middle third (M), or last third (E) of the month. These selected percentage plays are geared to take advantage of the bulk of seasonal sector strength or weakness.

By design, entry points are in advance of the major seasonal moves, providing traders ample opportunity to accumulate positions at favorable prices. Conversely, exit points have been selected to capture the majority of the move.

From the major seasonalities in the table below, we created the Sector Index Seasonality Strategy Calendar on pages 94 and 96. Note the concentration of bullish sector seasonalities during the Best Six Months, November to April, and bearish sector seasonalities during the Worst Six Months, May to October.

Almanac Investor newsletter subscribers receive specific entry and exit points for highly correlated ETFs and detailed analysis in our monthly ETF Lab. Visit *www.stocktradersalmanac.com,* or see the insert for additional details and a special offer for new subscribers. Top 300 ETFs appear on pages 188–189.

SECTOR INDEX SEASONALITY TABLE

			Seasonality					Average % Return[†]		
Ticker	Sector Index	Type	Start		Finish			15-Year	10-Year	5-Year
XCI	Computer Tech	Short	January	B	March	B		−8.1	−10.2	−10.4
IIX	Internet	Short	January	B	February	E		−10.2	−10.0	−5.8
XNG	Natural Gas	Long	February	E	June	B		19.2	14.4	18.3
RXP	Healthcare Prod	Long	March	M	June	M		6.5	6.3	4.0
RXH	Healthcare Prov	Long	March	M	June	M		15.7	16.7	18.7
MSH	High-Tech	Long	March	M	July	B		11.8	9.1	10.1
XCI	Computer Tech	Long	April	M	July	M		12.4	5.7	4.6
IIX	Internet	Long	April	M	July	B		12.6	6.6	2.9
CYC	Cyclical	Short	May	M	October	E		−7.6	−5.7	−6.1
XAU	Gold & Silver	Short	May	M	June	E		−9.1	−7.1	−10.1
S5MATR*	Materials	Short	May	M	October	M		−8.5	−6.3	−5.6
BKX	Banking	Short	June	B	July	B		−5.9	−7.7	−11.0
XNG	Natural Gas	Short	June	M	July	M		−8.8	−10.0	−8.4
XAU	Gold & Silver	Long	July	E	December	E		14.2	21.0	12.5
DJT	Transports	Short	July	M	October	M		−7.5	−5.3	−3.6
UTY	Utilities	Long	July	E	January	B		9.2	7.8	3.9
BTK	Biotech	Long	August	B	March	B		29.4	10.9	7.8
RXP	Healthcare Prod	Long	August	B	February	B		11.3	8.1	5.4
MSH	High-Tech	Long	August	M	January	M		18.5	13.3	7.1
IIX	Internet	Long	August	B	January	B		28.0	19.7	11.4
SOX	Semiconductor	Short	August	M	October	E		−12.0	−10.3	−10.2
CMR	Consumer	Long	September	E	June	B		12.0	7.8	3.2
RXH	Healthcare Prov	Short	September	M	November	B		−7.1	−8.4	−10.6
XOI	Oil	Short	September	B	November	E		−3.9	−5.2	−5.2
BKX	Banking	Long	October	B	June	B		12.9	6.1	−3.8
XBD	Broker/Dealer	Long	October	B	June	E		29.9	10.8	2.3
XCI	Computer Tech	Long	October	B	January	B		18.3	16.7	8.8
CYC	Cyclical	Long	October	B	May	M		19.4	19.0	16.1
RXH	Healthcare Prov	Long	October	E	January	M		12.1	10.0	10.4
S5MATR*	Materials	Long	October	M	May	M		16.9	18.2	16.4
DRG	Pharmaceutical	Long	October	M	January	B		7.3	5.8	5.4
RMZ	Real Estate	Long	October	E	July	B		14.1	14.0	4.7
SOX	Semiconductor	Long	October	E	December	B		18.9	15.6	7.2
XTC	Telecom	Long	October	M	December	E		11.9	10.6	4.8
DJT	Transports	Long	October	B	May	B		20.1	18.1	15.1
XOI	Oil	Long	December	M	July	B		13.2	12.7	7.3

[†]*Average % return based on full seasonality completion through April 2011.*
* *S5MATR available @ bloomberg.com.*

OCTOBER

olumbus Day (Bond Market Closed)

MONDAY

D 47.6
S 47.6
N 61.9

8

on't be the last bear or last bull standing, let history guide you, be contrary to the crowd, and *the tape tell you when to act.* — Jeffrey A. Hirsch (Editor, *Stock Trader's Almanac*, b. 1966)

TUESDAY

D 47.6
S 42.9
N 52.4

9

is the mark of many famous people that they cannot part with their brightest hour. Lillian Hellman, (Playwright, *The Children's Hour and Little Foxes*, 1905–1984)

ow Lost 1874 Points (18.2%) on the Week Ending 10/10/08 *Vorst Dow Week in the History of Wall Street*

WEDNESDAY

D 38.1
S 42.9
N 57.1

10

x words that spell business success: create concept, communicate concept, sustain momentum. Yale Hirsch (Creator of *Stock Trader's Almanac*, b. 1923)

October Ends Dow and S&P "Worst Six Months" (Pages 44, 48, 50, and 147) *nd NASDAQ "Worst Four Months" (Pages 54, 58, and 148)*

THURSDAY

D 61.9
S 61.9
N 71.4

11

here is nothing like a ticker tape except a woman—nothing that promises, hour after hour, day after day, such *dden developments; nothing that disappoints so often or occasionally fulfils with such unbelievable,* *ssionate magnificence.* — Walter K. Gutman (Financial analyst, described as the "Proust of Wall Street" *New Yorker, You Only Have to Get Rich Once, 1961, The Gutman Letter, 1903–1986)*

FRIDAY

D 76.2
S 76.2
N 71.4

12

hen I talk to a company that tells me the last analyst showed up three years ago, I can hardly contain my *thusiasm.* — Peter Lynch (Fidelity Investments, *One Up On Wall Street*, b. 1944)

SATURDAY

13

SUNDAY

14

Sector Index Seasonality Strategy Calendar*

* Graphic representation of the Sector Index Seasonality Percentage Plays on page 92.
L = Long Trade, S = Short Trade, → = Start of Trade

94

(continued on page 96)

OCTOBER

Monday before October Expiration, Dow Up 25 of 31

MONDAY
D 57.1
S 57.1
N 57.1
15

I'm very big on having clarified principles. I don't believe in being reactive. You can't do that in the markets effectively. I can't. I need perspective. I need a game plan.
— Ray Dalio (Money manager, founder, Bridgewater Associates, *Fortune*, 3/16/2009, b. 1949)

TUESDAY
D 47.6
S 52.4
N 42.9
16

I've never been poor, only broke. Being poor is a frame of mind. Being broke is only a temporary situation.
— Mike Todd (Movie Producer, 1903–1958)

WEDNESDAY
D 47.6
S 52.4
N 42.9
17

Analysts are supposed to be critics of corporations. They often end up being public relations spokesmen for them. — Ralph Wanger (Chief investment officer, Acorn Fund)

THURSDAY
D 66.7
S 71.4
N 76.2
18

Ideas are easy; it's execution that's hard. — Jeff Bezos (Amazon.com)

October Expiration Day, Dow Down 6 Straight and 7 of Last 8
Crash of October 19, 1987, Dow down 22.6% in One Day

FRIDAY
D 52.4
S 61.9
N 52.4
19

No other country can substitute for the U.S. The U.S. is still No. 1 in military, No. 1 in economy, No. 1 in promoting human rights and No. 1 in idealism. Only the U.S. can lead the world. No other country can.
— Senior Korean official (to Thomas L. Friedman, *NY Times* Foreign Affairs columnist, 2/25/2009)

SATURDAY
20

SUNDAY
21

(continued from page 94)

Sector Index Seasonality Strategy Calendar*

* Graphic representation of the Sector Index Seasonality Percentage Plays on page 92.
L = Long Trade, S = Short Trade, ➔ = Start of Trade

96

OCTOBER

In my experience, selling a put is much safer than buying a stock.
— Kyle Rosen (Boston Capital Mgmt., *Barron's*, 8/23/04)

One only gets to the top rung on the ladder by steadily climbing up one at a time, and suddenly all sorts of powers, all sorts of abilities, which you thought never belonged to you—suddenly become within your own possibility.... — Margaret Thatcher (British, prime minister, 1979–1990, b. 1925)

FOMC Meeting (2 Days)

By the law of nature the father continues master of his child no longer than the child stands in need of his assistance; after that term they become equal, and then the son entirely independent of the father, owes him no obedience, but only respect.
— Jean-Jacques Rousseau (Swiss philosopher, *The Social Contract*, 1712–1778)

Late October is Time to Buy Depressed Stocks
Especially Techs and Small Caps

Writing a book is an adventure. To begin with it is a toy, an amusement; then it is a mistress, and then a master, and then a tyrant. — Winston Churchill (British statesman, 1874–1965)

Every age has a blind eye and sees nothing wrong in practices and institutions, which its successors view with just horror. — Sir Richard Livingston (*On Education*)

NOVEMBER ALMANAC

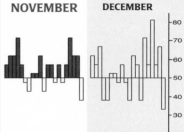

NOVEMBER

S	M	T	W	T	F	S
				1	2	3
4	5	6	7	8	9	10
11	12	13	14	15	16	17
18	19	20	21	22	23	24
25	26	27	28	29	30	

DECEMBER

S	M	T	W	T	F	S
						1
2	3	4	5	6	7	8
9	10	11	12	13	14	15
16	17	18	19	20	21	22
23	24	25	26	27	28	29
30	31					

Market Probability Chart above is a graphic representation of the S&P 500 Recent Market Probability Calendar on page 124.

◆ #2 S&P month and #3 on Dow since 1950, #3 on NASDAQ since 1971 (pages 44 and 56) ◆ Start of the "Best Six Months" of the year (page 48), NASDAQ's Best Eight Months and Best Three (pages 147 and 148) ◆ Simple timing indicator almost triples "Best Six Months" strategy (page 50), doubles NASDAQ's Best Eight (page 58) ◆ Day before and after Thanksgiving Day combined, only 12 losses in 59 years (page 102) ◆ Week before Thanksgiving, Dow up 15 of last 18 ◆ Presidential election year Novembers rank #1 Dow and S&P, #9 NASDAQ.

November Vital Statistics

	DJIA	S&P 500	NASDAQ	Russell 1K	Russell 2K
Rank	3	3	3	3	3
Up	40	40	26	23	21
Down	21	21	14	9	11
Avg % Change	1.5%	1.5%	1.6%	1.7%	1.9%
Election Year	1.6%	1.4%	-0.8%	0.5%	-0.2%
Best and Worst November					
	% Change	% Change	% Change	% Change	% Change
Best	1962 10.1	1980 10.2	2001 14.2	1980 10.1	2002 8.8
Worst	1973 -14.0	1973 -11.4	2000 -22.9	2000 -9.3	2008 -12.0
Best and Worst November Weeks					
Best	11/28/08 9.7	11/28/08 12.0	11/28/08 10.9	11/28/08 12.5	11/28/08 16.4
Worst	11/21/08 -5.3	11/21/08 -8.4	11/10/00 -12.2	11/21/08 -8.8	11/21/08 -11.0
Best and Worst November Days					
Best	11/13/08 6.7	11/13/08 6.9	11/13/08 6.5	11/13/08 7.0	11/13/08 8.5
Worst	11/20/08 -5.6	11/20/08 -6.7	11/19/08 -6.5	11/20/08 -6.9	11/19/08 -7.9
First Trading Day of Expiration Week: 1980–2010					
Record (#Up–#Down)	16–15	13–18	12–19	14–17	14–17
Current Streak	U2	D1	D1	D1	U2
Avg % Change	-0.04	-0.07	-0.14	-0.08	-0.06
Options Expiration Day: 1980–2010					
Record (#Up–#Down)	19–12	18–13	16–15	18–13	14–16
Current Streak	U1	U1	U1	U1	U1
Avg % Change	0.22	0.15	0.02	0.14	0.09
Options Expiration Week: 1980–2010					
Record (#Up–#Down)	21–10	19–12	16–15	18–13	16–15
Current Streak	U2	U1	D3	U1	U1
Avg % Change	0.38	0.11	0.06	0.08	-0.21
Week After Options Expiration: 1980–2010					
Record (#Up–#Down)	18–13	19–12	20–11	19–12	18–13
Current Streak	D2	D1	U1	D2	U1
Avg % Change	0.81	0.78	0.87	0.78	0.94
First Trading Day Performance					
% of Time Up	63.9	63.9	65.0	71.9	65.6
Avg % Change	0.31	0.33	0.34	0.47	0.30
Last Trading Day Performance					
% of Time Up	54.1	54.1	65.0	46.9	71.9
Avg % Change	0.04	0.08	-0.19	-0.10	0.05

Dow and S&P 1950–April 2011, NASDAQ 1971–April 2011, Russell 1K and 2K 1979–April 2011.

Astute investors always smile and remember,
When stocks seasonally start soaring, and salute November.

OCTOBER/NOVEMBER

*83rd Anniversary of 1929 Crash, Dow Down 23.0% in Two Days,
October 28 and 29*

MONDAY

D 61.9
S 57.1
N 57.1

29

All there is to investing is picking good stocks at good times and staying with them as long as they remain good companies. — Warren Buffett (CEO, Berkshire Hathaway, investor and philanthropist, b. 1930)

TUESDAY

D 66.7
S 76.2
N 71.4

30

A "tired businessman" is one whose business is usually not a successful one.
— Joseph R. Grundy (U.S. senator, Pennsylvania, 1929–1930, businessman, 1863–1961)

Halloween

WEDNESDAY

D 52.4
S 57.1
N 76.2

31

There is no great mystery to satisfying your customers. Build them a quality product and treat them with respect. It's that simple. — Lee Iacocca (American industrialist, Former Chrysler CEO, b. 1924)

First Trading Day in November, Dow Down 4 of Last 6

THURSDAY

D 57.1
S 57.1
N 66.7

1

I have noticed over the years the difficulty some people have in cutting losses, admitting an error, and moving on. I am rather frequently—and on occasion, quite spectacularly—wrong. However, if we expect to be wrong, then there should be no ego tied up in admitting the error, honoring the stop loss, selling the loser—and preserving your capital.
— Barry L. Ritholtz (CEO, Fusion IQ, *Bailout Nation*, The Big Picture blog, 8/12/2010, b. 1961)

*November Begins Dow and S&P "Best Six Months" (Pages 44, 48, 50, 147)
And NASDAQ "Best Eight Months" (Pages 54, 58, and 148)*

FRIDAY

D 52.4
S 61.9
N 61.9

2

Everything possible today was at one time impossible. Everything impossible today may at some time in the future be possible. — Edward Lindaman (Apollo space project, president, Whitworth College, 1920–1982)

November Almanac Investor Seasonalities: See Pages 92, 94, and 96

SATURDAY

3

Daylight Saving Time Ends

SUNDAY

4

FOURTH QUARTER MARKET MAGIC

Examining market performance on a quarterly basis reveals several intriguing and helpful patterns. Fourth-quarter market gains have been magical, providing the greatest and most consistent gains over the years. First-quarter performance runs a respectable second. This should not be surprising, as cash inflows, trading volume, and buying bias are generally elevated during these two quarters.

Positive market psychology hits a fever pitch, as the holiday season approaches, and does not begin to wane until spring. Professionals drive the market higher, as they make portfolio adjustments to maximize year-end numbers. Bonuses are paid and invested around the turn of the year.

The market's sweet spot of the four-year cycle begins in the fourth quarter of the midterm year. The best two-quarter span runs from the fourth quarter of the midterm year through the first quarter of the pre-election year, averaging 15.3% for the Dow, 16.0% for the S&P 500, and an amazing 23.3% for NASDAQ.

Quarterly strength fades in the latter half of the pre-election year, but stays impressively positive through the election year. Losses dominate the first and third quarter of post-election years and the first and second quarters of midterm years. Once again, the global financial crisis trumped seasonality, hammering the fourth quarter of 2008 onto the list of 10 worst quarters of all time (see page 168).

QUARTERLY % CHANGES

	Q1	Q2	Q3	Q4	Year	Q2–Q3	Q4–Q1
Dow Jones Industrials (1949 to March 2011)							
Average	2.0%	1.8%	0.5%	3.7%	8.2%	2.3%	6.1%
Post-Election	−1.1%	1.6%	0.2%	3.4%	4.4%	1.8%	5.2%
Midterm	1.5%	−1.8%	−0.5%	7.3%	6.7%	−2.2%	15.3%
Pre-Election	7.5%	5.6%	2.5%	1.6%	17.7%	7.5%	1.9%
Election	0.3%	1.2%	0.4%	2.3%	4.6%	1.6%	1.2%
S&P 500 (1949 to March 2011)							
Average	2.0%	1.7%	0.8%	4.0%	8.8%	2.5%	6.3%
Post-Election	−1.2%	2.2%	0.4%	3.1%	4.8%	2.7%	4.3%
Midterm	1.0%	−2.8%	0.1%	8.0%	6.4%	−2.7%	16.0%
Pre-Election	7.5%	5.6%	2.1%	2.5%	18.3%	7.2%	3.1%
Election	0.7%	2.1%	0.6%	2.1%	6.1%	2.6%	1.0%
NASDAQ Composite (1971 to March 2011)							
Average	4.0%	3.4%	−0.04%	4.4%	12.3%	3.6%	8.6%
Post-Election	−3.3%	6.8%	1.3%	4.2%	8.4%	8.1%	6.3%
Midterm	2.1%	−3.4%	−5.2%	8.9%	1.7%	−8.1%	23.3%
Pre-Election	13.8%	8.9%	3.1%	4.9%	34.2%	12.1%	7.8%
Election	2.5%	1.3%	0.6%	−0.6%	4.8%	2.4%	−3.1%

NOVEMBER

Government is like fire—useful when used legitimately, but dangerous when not.
— David Brooks (*NY Times columnist*, 10/5/07)

Election Day

A president is elected and tries to get rid of the dirty stuff in the economy as quickly as possible, so that by the time the next election comes around, he looks like a hero. The stock market is reacting to what the politicians are doing. — Yale Hirsch (Creator of *Stock Trader's Almanac*, *NY Times*, 10/10/2010, b. 1923)

During the first period of a man's life, the greatest danger is not to take the risk.
— Soren Kierkegaard (*Danish philosopher*, 1813–1855)

If you torture the data long enough, it will confess to anything.
— Darrell Huff (*How to Lie With Statistics*, 1954)

Today's Ponzi-style acute fragility and speculative dynamics dictate that he who panics first panics best.
— Doug Noland (Prudent Bear Funds, *Credit Bubble Bulletin*, 10/26/07)

Veterans' Day

TRADING THE THANKSGIVING MARKET

For 35 years, the "holiday spirit" gave the Wednesday before Thanksgiving and the Friday after a great track record, except for two occasions. Publishing it in the 1987 *Almanac* was the "kiss of death." Wednesday, Friday, and Monday were all crushed, down 6.6% over the three days in 1987. Since 1988, Wednesday–Friday gained 14 of 23 times, with a total Dow point-gain of 713.14 versus Monday's total Dow point-loss of 910.30, down nine of 13 since 1998. The best strategy appears to be coming into the week long and exiting into strength Friday. Dubai's debt crisis cancelled Black Friday on Wall Street in 2009.

DOW JONES INDUSTRIALS BEFORE AND AFTER THANKSGIVING

	Tuesday Before	Wednesday Before		Friday After	Total Gain Dow Points	Dow Close	Next Monday
1956	-4.49	-2.16		4.65	2.49	472.56	-2.27
1957	-9.04	10.69		3.84	14.53	449.87	-2.96
1958	-4.37	8.63		8.31	16.94	557.46	2.61
1959	2.94	1.41		1.42	2.83	652.52	6.66
1960	-3.44	1.37		4.00	5.37	606.47	-1.04
1961	-0.77	1.10		2.18	3.28	732.60	-0.61
1962	6.73	4.31		7.62	11.93	644.87	-2.81
1963	32.03	-2.52		9.52	7.00	750.52	1.39
1964	-1.68	-5.21		-0.28	-5.49	882.12	-6.69
1965	2.56	N/C		-0.78	-0.78	948.16	-1.23
1966	-3.18	1.84	**T**	6.52	8.36	803.34	-2.18
1967	13.17	3.07		3.58	6.65	877.60	4.51
1968	8.14	-3.17	**H**	8.76	5.59	985.08	-1.74
1969	-5.61	3.23		1.78	5.01	812.30	-7.26
1970	5.21	1.98	**A**	6.64	8.62	781.35	12.74
1971	-5.18	0.66		17.96	18.62	816.59	13.14
1972	8.21	7.29		4.67	11.96	1025.21	-7.45
1973	-17.76	10.08	**N**	-0.98	9.10	854.00	-29.05
1974	5.32	2.03		-0.63	1.40	618.66	-15.64
1975	9.76	3.15	**K**	2.12	5.27	860.67	-4.33
1976	-6.57	1.66		5.66	7.32	956.62	-6.57
1977	6.41	0.78	**S**	1.12	1.90	844.42	-4.85
1978	-1.56	2.95		3.12	6.07	810.12	3.72
1979	-6.05	-1.80	**G**	4.35	2.55	811.77	16.98
1980	3.93	7.00		3.66	10.66	993.34	-23.89
1981	18.45	7.90	**I**	7.80	15.70	885.94	3.04
1982	-9.01	9.01		7.36	16.37	1007.36	-4.51
1983	7.01	-0.20		1.83	1.63	1277.44	-7.62
1984	9.83	6.40	**V**	18.78	25.18	1220.30	-7.95
1985	0.12	18.92		-3.56	15.36	1472.13	-14.22
1986	6.05	4.64	**I**	-2.53	2.11	1914.23	-1.55
1987	40.45	-16.58		-36.47	-53.05	1910.48	-76.93
1988	11.73	14.58	**N**	-17.60	-3.02	2074.68	6.76
1989	7.25	17.49		18.77	36.26	2675.55	19.42
1990	-35.15	9.16	**G**	-12.13	-2.97	2527.23	5.94
1991	14.08	-16.10		-5.36	-21.46	2894.68	40.70
1992	25.66	17.56		15.94	33.50	3282.20	22.96
1993	3.92	13.41		-3.63	9.78	3683.95	-6.15
1994	-91.52	-3.36		33.64	30.28	3708.27	31.29
1995	40.46	18.06	**D**	7.23*	25.29	5048.84	22.04
1996	-19.38	-29.07		22.36*	-6.71	6521.70	N/C
1997	41.03	-14.17	**A**	28.35*	14.18	7823.13	189.98
1998	-73.12	13.13		18.80*	31.93	9333.08	-216.53
1999	-93.89	12.54	**Y**	-19.26*	-6.72	10988.91	-40.99
2000	31.85	-95.18		70.91*	-24.27	10470.23	75.84
2001	-75.08	-66.70		125.03*	58.33	9959.71	23.04
2002	-172.98	255.26		-35.59*	219.67	8896.09	-33.52
2003	16.15	15.63		2.89*	18.52	9782.46	116.59
2004	3.18	27.71		1.92*	29.63	10522.23	-46.33
2005	51.15	44.66		15.53*	60.19	10931.62	-40.90
2006	5.05	5.36		-46.78*	-41.42	12280.17	-158.46
2007	51.70	-211.10		181.84*	-29.26	12980.88	-237.44
2008	36.08	247.14		102.43*	349.57	8829.04	-679.95
2009	-17.24	30.69		-154.48*	-123.79	10309.92	34.92
2010	-142.21	150.91		-95.28*	55.63	11092.00	-39.51

Shortened trading day

102

NOVEMBER

Monday before November Expiration, Dow Down 7 of Last 12
Dow Hit Big in 2008, Down 224 Points (2.6%)

MONDAY
D 57.1
S 52.4
N 57.1
12

It isn't as important to buy as cheap as possible as it is to buy at the right time.
— Jesse Livermore (Early twentieth century stock trader and speculator, *How to Trade in Stocks*, 1877–1940)

TUESDAY
D 57.1
S 52.4
N 61.9
13

A senior European diplomat said he was convinced that the choice of starting a war this spring was made for political as well as military reasons. [The President] clearly does not want to have a war raging on the eve of his presumed reelection campaign. — Reported by Steven R. Weisman (*NY Times*, 3/14/03)

Week before Thanksgiving, Dow Up 15 of Last 18,
2003 –1.4%, 2004 – 0.8%, 2008 – 5.3%

WEDNESDAY
D 66.7
S 61.9
N 61.9
14

I never buy at the bottom and I always sell too soon.
— Baron Nathan Rothschild's success formula (London Financier, 1777–1836)

THURSDAY
D 52.4
S 42.9
N 38.1
15

There is a habitual nature to society and human activity. People's behavior and what they do with their money and time bears upon economics and the stock market.
— Jeffrey A. Hirsch (Editor, *Stock Trader's Almanac*, b. 1966)

November Expiration Day, Dow Up 7 of Last 9
Dow Surged in 2008, Up 494 Points (6.5%)

FRIDAY
D 47.6
S 57.1
N 47.6
16

We can guarantee cash benefits as far out and at whatever size you like, but we cannot guarantee their purchasing power. — Alan Greenspan (Fed chairman, 1987–2006, on funding Social Security to Senate Banking Committee, 2/15/05)

SATURDAY
17

SUNDAY
18

MOST OF THE SO-CALLED "JANUARY EFFECT" TAKES PLACE IN THE LAST HALF OF DECEMBER

Over the years we reported annually on the fascinating January Effect, showing that small-cap stocks handily outperformed large-cap stocks during January 40 out of 43 years between 1953 and 1995. Readers saw that "Cats and Dogs" on average quadrupled the returns of blue chips in this period. Then, the January Effect disappeared over the next four years.

Looking at the graph on page 108, comparing the Russell 1000 index of large-capitalization stocks to the Russell 2000 smaller-capitalization stocks, shows small-cap stocks beginning to outperform the blue chips in mid-December. Narrowing the comparison down to half-month segments was an inspiration and proved to be quite revealing, as you can see in the table below.

24-YEAR AVERAGE RATES OF RETURN (DEC 1987 TO FEB 2011)

From mid-Dec*	Russell 1000 Change	Russell 1000 Annualized	Russell 2000 Change	Russell 2000 Annualized
12/15–12/31	1.8%	50.5%	3.5%	119.9%
12/15–01/15	2.0	25.5	3.8	53.3
12/15–01/31	2.2	19.4	3.9	36.5
12/15–02/15	2.9	18.7	5.4	37.1
12/15–02/28	2.1	11.0	5.1	28.5
end-Dec*				
12/31–01/15	0.2	4.3	0.3	6.5
12/31–01/31	0.4	4.9	0.4	4.9
12/31–02/15	1.1	9.0	1.8	15.1
12/31–02/28	0.3	1.9	1.6	10.5

32-YEAR AVERAGE RATES OF RETURN (DEC 1979 TO FEB 2011)

From mid-Dec*	Russell 1000 Change	Russell 1000 Annualized	Russell 2000 Change	Russell 2000 Annualized
12/15–12/31	1.6%	43.9%	3.0%	96.8%
12/15–01/15	2.2	28.3	4.2	60.2
12/15–01/31	2.5	22.2	4.5	43.0
12/15–02/15	3.2	20.8	5.9	41.1
12/15–02/28	2.6	13.5	5.8	32.1
end-Dec*				
12/31–01/15	0.6	13.4	1.2	28.5
12/31–01/31	0.9	11.4	1.4	18.2
12/31–02/15	1.6	13.3	2.8	24.3
12/31–02/28	1.1	7.0	2.7	17.8

* Mid-month dates are the 11th trading day of the month; month-end dates are monthly closes.

Small-cap strength in the last half of December became even more magnified after the 1987 market crash. Note the dramatic shift in gains in the last half of December during the 24-year period starting in 1987, versus the 32 years from 1979 to 2011. With all the beaten-down small stocks being dumped for tax loss purposes, it generally pays to get a head start on the January Effect in mid-December. You don't have to wait until December either; the small-cap sector often begins to turn around toward the end of October and November.

NOVEMBER

People do not change when you tell them they should; they change when they tell themselves they must.
— Michael Mandelbaum (Johns Hopkins foreign policy specialist, *NY Times*, 6/24/2009, b. 1946)

Trading Thanksgiving Market: Long into Weakness Prior,
Exit into Strength After (Page 102)

TUESDAY
D 47.6
S 47.6
N 57.1
20

Learn from the mistakes of others; you can't live long enough to make them all yourself.
— Eleanor Roosevelt (First Lady, 1884–1962)

WEDNESDAY
D 61.9
S 57.1
N 57.1
21

When new money is created on a grand scale, it must go somewhere and have some major consequences. One of these will be greatly increased volatility and instability in the economy and financial system.
— J. Anthony Boeckh, Ph.D (Chairman, Bank Credit Analyst 1968–2002, *The Great Reflation, Boeckh Investment Letter*)

Thanksgiving (Market Closed)

THURSDAY
22

I went to a restaurant that serves "breakfast at any time." So I ordered French toast during the Renaissance.
— Steven Wright (Comedian, b. 1955)

(Shortened Trading Day)

FRIDAY
D 57.1
S 47.6
N 61.9
23

A weak currency is the sign of a weak economy, and a weak economy leads to a weak nation.
— H. Ross Perot (American businessman, *The Dollar Crisis*, 2-time 3rd-party presidential candidate 1992 and 1996, b. 1930)

SATURDAY
24

SUNDAY
25

DECEMBER ALMANAC

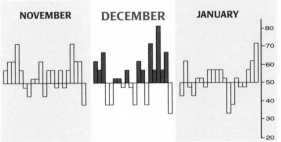

Market Probability Chart above is a graphic representation of the S&P 500 Recent Market Probability Calendar on page 124.

◆ #1 S&P (+1.7%) and #2 Dow (+1.7%) month since 1950 (page 44), #2 NASDAQ (2.1%) since 1971 ◆ 2002 worst December since 1931, down over 6% Dow and S&P, –9.7% on NASDAQ (pages 152, 155, and 157) ◆ "Free lunch" served on Wall Street before Christmas (page 110) ◆ Small caps start to outperform larger caps near middle of month (pages 104 and 108) ◆ "Santa Claus Rally" visible in graph above and on page 112 ◆ In 1998 was part of best fourth quarter since 1928 (page 167) ◆ Fourth-quarter expiration week most bullish triple witching week, Dow up 16 of last 20 (page 76) ◆ In presidential election years, Decembers rankings slip: #3 S&P, # 5 NASDAQ, still #2 Dow month.

December Vital Statistics

	DJIA	S&P 500	NASDAQ	Russell 1K	Russell 2K
Rank	2	1	2	2	1
Up	43	46	24	25	25
Down	18	15	16	7	7
Avg % Change	1.7%	1.7%	2.1%	1.7%	2.9%
Election Year	1.4%	1.2%	1.5%	0.7%	3.0%
Best and Worst December					
	% Change	% Change	% Change	% Change	% Change
Best	1991 9.5	1991 11.2	1999 22.0	1991 11.2	1999 11.2
Worst	2002 –6.2	2002 –6.0	2002 –9.7	2002 –5.8	2002 –5.7
Best and Worst December Weeks					
Best	12/18/87 5.8	12/18/87 5.9	12/8/00 10.3	12/18/87 6.0	12/18/87 7.7
Worst	12/4/87 –7.5	12/6/74 –7.1	12/15/00 –9.1	12/4/87 –7.0	12/12/80 – 6.5
Best and Worst December Days					
Best	12/16/08 4.2	12/16/08 5.1	12/5/00 10.5	12/16/08 5.2	12/16/08 6.7
Worst	12/1/08 –7.7	12/1/08 –8.9	12/1/08 –9.0	12/1/08 –9.1	12/1/08 –11.9
First Trading Day of Expiration Week: 1980–2010					
Record (#Up–#Down)	18–13	19–12	13–18	19–12	14–17
Current Streak	U2	U2	D1	D1	D1
Avg % Change	0.20	0.16	–0.06	0.12	–0.17
Options Expiration Day: 1980–2010					
Record (#Up–#Down)	21–10	23–8	22–9	23–8	20–11
Current Streak	D1	U5	U5	U5	U4
Avg % Change	0.39	0.43	0.38	0.41	0.43
Options Expiration Week: 1980–2010					
Record (#Up–#Down)	24–7	23–8	18–13	22–9	16–15
Current Streak	U1	U1	U5	U1	U5
Avg % Change	0.76	0.28	0.23	0.71	0.56
Week After Options Expiration: 1980–2010					
Record (#Up–#Down)	21–9	18–13	19–12	18–13	21–10
Current Streak	U2	U2	U2	U2	U2
Avg % Change	0.70	0.41	0.65	0.44	0.78
First Trading Day Performance					
% of Time Up	49.2	52.5	62.5	56.3	56.3
Avg % Change	–0.05	–0.02	0.17	–0.03	–0.05
Last Trading Day Performance					
% of Time Up	54.1	62.3	75.0	53.1	71.9
Avg % Change	0.08	0.11	0.35	–0.08	0.48

Dow and S&P 1950–April 2011, NASDAQ 1971–April 2011, Russell 1K and 2K 1979–April 2011.

*If Santa Claus should fail to call,
Bears may come to Broad and Wall.*

NOVEMBER/DECEMBER

MONDAY
D 61.9
S 57.1
N 52.4
26

The monuments of wit survive the monuments of power.
— Francis Bacon (English philosopher, essayist, statesman, 1561–1626)

TUESDAY
D 71.4
S 71.4
N 61.9
27

Whatever method you use to pick stocks…, your ultimate success or failure will depend on your ability to ignore the worries of the world long enough to allow your investments to succeed. It isn't the head but the stomach that determines the fate of the stockpicker.
— Peter Lynch (Fidelity Investments, Beating the Street, 1994)

WEDNESDAY
D 57.1
S 61.9
N 57.1
28

Today we deal with 65,000 more pieces of information each day than did our ancestors 100 years ago.
— Dr. Jean Houston (A founder of the Human Potential Movement, b. 1937)

THURSDAY
D 47.6
S 61.9
N 71.4
29

The stock market is that creation of man which humbles him the most. — Anonymous

*Last Trading Day of November, S&P Down 9 of Last 13
Average Loss 0.4%*

FRIDAY
D 52.4
S 38.1
N 52.4
30

A government which robs Peter to pay Paul can always depend on the support of Paul.
— George Bernard Shaw (Irish dramatist, 1856–1950)

SATURDAY
1

December Almanac Investor Seasonalities: See Pages 92, 94, and 96

SUNDAY
2

JANUARY EFFECT NOW STARTS IN MID-DECEMBER

Small-cap stocks tend to outperform big caps in January. Known as the "January Effect," the tendency is clearly revealed by the graph below. Thirty-three years of daily data for the Russell 2000 index of smaller companies are divided by the Russell 1000 index of largest companies, and then compressed into a single year to show an idealized yearly pattern. When the graph is descending, big blue chips are outperforming smaller companies; when the graph is rising, smaller companies are moving up faster than their larger brethren.

In a typical year, the smaller fry stay on the sidelines while the big boys are on the field. Then, around late October, small stocks begin to wake up, and in mid-December, they take off. Anticipated year-end dividends, payouts, and bonuses could be a factor. Other major moves are quite evident just before Labor Day—possibly because individual investors are back from vacations—and off the low points in late October and November. Small caps hold the lead through the beginning of May.

RUSSELL 2000/RUSSELL 1000 ONE-YEAR SEASONAL PATTERN

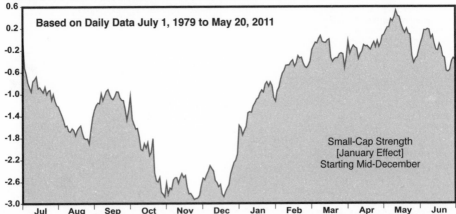

The bottom graph shows the actual ratio of the Russell 2000 divided by the Russell 1000 from 1979. Smaller companies had the upper hand for five years into 1983, as the last major bear trend wound to a close and the nascent bull market logged its first year. After falling behind for about eight years, they came back after the Persian Gulf War bottom in 1990, moving up until 1994, when big caps ruled the latter stages of the millennial bull. For six years, the picture was bleak for small fry, as the blue chips and tech stocks moved to stratospheric PE ratios. Small caps spiked in late 1999 and early 2000 and reached a peak in early 2006, as the four-year-old bull entered its final year. Note how the small-cap advantage has waned during major bull moves and intensified during weak market times. Look for a clear move lower to confirm a major bull move is in place.

RUSSELL 2000/RUSSELL 1000 (1979 TO APRIL 2011)

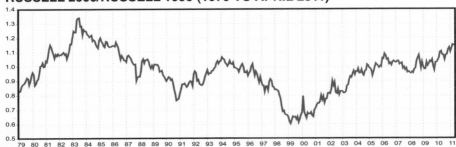

DECEMBER

First Trading Day in December, NASDAQ Up 18 of 24
Down Three Straight 2006–2008

MONDAY
D 57.1
S 61.9
N 71.4

3

Age is a question of mind over matter. If you don't mind, it doesn't matter.
— Leroy Robert "Satchel" Paige (Negro League and Hall of Fame pitcher, 1906–1982)

TUESDAY
D 52.4
S 57.1
N 66.7

4

*Politics ought to be the part-time profession of every citizen who would protect the rights and privileges
of free people and who would preserve what is good and fruitful in our national heritage.*
— Dwight D. Eisenhower (34th U.S. president, 1890–1969)

WEDNESDAY
D 61.9
S 66.7
N 66.7

5

When an old man dies, a library burns down. — African proverb

THURSDAY
D 52.4
S 38.1
N 57.1

6

*Let me end my talk by abusing slightly my status as an official representative of the Federal Reserve.
I would like to say to Milton [Friedman]: regarding the Great Depression, you're right; we did it.
We're very sorry. But thanks to you, we won't do it again.*
— Ben Bernanke (Fed chairman 2006–, 11/8/02 speech as Fed governor)

FRIDAY
D 38.1
S 38.1
N 38.1

7

That's the American way. If little kids don't aspire to make money like I did, what the hell good is this country?
— Lee Iacocca (American industrialist, former Chrysler CEO, b. 1924)

SATURDAY

8

Chanukah

SUNDAY

9

WALL STREET'S ONLY "FREE LUNCH" SERVED BEFORE CHRISTMAS

Investors tend to get rid of their losers near year-end for tax purposes, often hammering these stocks down to bargain levels. Over the years, the *Almanac* has shown that NYSE stocks selling at their lows on December 15 will usually outperform the market by February 15 in the following year. Preferred stocks, closed-end funds, splits, and new issues are eliminated. When there are a huge number of new lows, stocks down the most are selected, even though there are usually good reasons why some stocks have been battered.

BARGAIN STOCKS VS. THE MARKET*

Short Span* Late Dec–Jan/Feb	New Lows Late Dec	% Change Jan/Feb	% Change NYSE Composite	Bargain Stocks Advantage
1974–75	112	48.9%	22.1%	26.8%
1975–76	21	34.9	14.9	20.0
1976–77	2	1.3	−3.3	4.6
1977–78	15	2.8	−4.5	7.3
1978–79	43	11.8	3.9	7.9
1979–80	5	9.3	6.1	3.2
1980–81	14	7.1	−2.0	9.1
1981–82	21	−2.6	−7.4	4.8
1982–83	4	33.0	9.7	23.3
1983–84	13	−3.2	−3.8	0.6
1984–85	32	19.0	12.1	6.9
1985–86	4	−22.5	3.9	−26.4
1986–87	22	9.3	12.5	−3.2
1987–88	23	13.2	6.8	6.4
1988–89	14	30.0	6.4	23.6
1989–90	25	−3.1	−4.8	1.7
1990–91	18	18.8	12.6	6.2
1991–92	23	51.1	7.7	43.4
1992–93	9	8.7	0.6	8.1
1993–94	10	−1.4	2.0	−3.4
1994–95	25	14.6	5.7	8.9
1995–96	5	−11.3	4.5	−15.8
1996–97	16	13.9	11.2	2.7
1997–98	29	9.9	5.7	4.2
1998–99	40	−2.8	4.3	−7.1
1999–00	26	8.9	−5.4	14.3
2000–01	51	44.4	0.1	44.3
2001–02	12	31.4	−2.3	33.7
2002–03	33	28.7	3.9	24.8
2003–04	15	16.7	2.3	14.4
2004–05	36	6.8	−2.8	9.6
2005–06	71	12.0	2.6	9.4
2006–07	43	5.1	−0.5	5.6
2007–08	71	−3.2	−9.4	6.2
2008–09	88	11.4	−2.4	13.8
2009–10	25	1.8	−3.0	4.8
2010–11	20	8.3%	3.4%	4.9%
37-Year Totals		**463.0%**	**113.4%**	**349.6%**
Average		**12.5%**	**3.1%**	**9.4%**

Dec 15 to Feb 15 (1974–1999), Dec 1999–2010 based on actual newsletter advice.

In response to changing market conditions, we tweaked the strategy the last 12 years, adding selections from NASDAQ, AMEX, and the OTC Bulletin Board and selling in mid-January some years. We e-mail the list of stocks to our *Almanac Investor* newsletter subscribers. Visit *www.stocktradersalmanac.com,* or see the insert for additional details and a special offer for new subscribers.

We have come to the conclusion that the most prudent course of action is to compile our list from the stocks making new lows on Triple-Witching Friday before Christmas, capitalizing on the Santa Claus Rally (page 112). This also gives us the weekend to evaluate the issues in greater depth and weed out any glaringly problematic stocks. Subscribers will receive the list of stocks selected from the new lows made on December 16, 2011 and December 21, 2012 via e-mail.

This "Free Lunch" strategy is only an extremely short-term strategy reserved for the nimblest traders. It has performed better after market corrections and when there are more new lows to choose from. The object is to buy bargain stocks near their 52-week lows and sell any quick, generous gains, as these issues can often be real dogs.

DECEMBER

Selling a soybean contract short is worth two years at the Harvard Business School.
— Robert Stovall (Managing director, Wood Asset Management, b. 1926)

FOMC Meeting

TUESDAY

D 52.4
S 52.4
N 47.6

11

Benjamin Graham was correct in suggesting that while the stock market in the short run may be a voting mechanism, in the long run it is a weighing mechanism. True value will win out in the end.
— Burton G. Malkiel (Economist, April 2003 Princeton Paper, *A Random Walk Down Wall Street*, b. 1932)

Small Cap Strength Starts in Mid-December (Page 104)

WEDNESDAY

D 57.1
S 47.6
N 47.6

12

Those that forget the past are condemned to repeat its mistakes, and those that misstate the past should be condemned. — Eugene D. Cohen (Letter to the Editor, *Financial Times*, 10/30/06)

THURSDAY

D 52.4
S 57.1
N 52.4

13

I'd be a bum on the street with a tin cup, if the markets were always efficient.
— Warren Buffett (CEO Berkshire Hathaway, investor, and philanthropist, b. 1930)

FRIDAY

D 52.4
S 47.6
N 42.9

14

The more feted by the media, the worse a pundit's accuracy. — Sharon Begley (Senior editor, *Newsweek*, 2/23/2009, referencing Philip E. Tetlock's 2005 *Expert Political Judgment*)

SATURDAY

15

SUNDAY

16

IF SANTA CLAUS SHOULD FAIL TO CALL, BEARS MAY COME TO BROAD AND WALL

Santa Claus tends to come to Wall Street nearly every year, bringing a short, sweet, respectable rally within the last five days of the year and the first two in January. This has been good for an average 1.6% gain since 1969 (1.5% since 1950). Santa's failure to show tends to precede bear markets, or times stocks could be purchased later in the year at much lower prices. We discovered this phenomenon in 1972.

DAILY % CHANGE IN S&P 500 AT YEAR END

	Trading Days Before Year End					First Days in January			Rally %
	6	5	4	3	2	1	1	2	3	Change
1969	−0.4	1.1	0.8	−0.7	0.4	0.5	1.0	0.5	−0.7	3.6
1970	0.1	0.6	0.5	1.1	0.2	−0.1	−1.1	0.7	0.6	1.9
1971	−0.4	0.2	1.0	0.3	−0.4	0.3	−0.4	0.4	1.0	1.3
1972	−0.3	−0.7	0.6	0.4	0.5	1.0	0.9	0.4	−0.1	3.1
1973	−1.1	−0.7	3.1	2.1	−0.2	0.01	0.1	2.2	−0.9	6.7
1974	−1.4	1.4	0.8	−0.4	0.03	2.1	2.4	0.7	0.5	7.2
1975	0.7	0.8	0.9	−0.1	−0.4	0.5	0.8	1.8	1.0	4.3
1976	0.1	1.2	0.7	−0.4	0.5	0.5	−0.4	−1.2	−0.9	0.8
1977	0.8	0.9	0.0	0.1	0.2	0.2	−1.3	−0.3	−0.8	−0.3
1978	0.03	1.7	1.3	−0.9	−0.4	−0.2	0.6	1.1	0.8	3.3
1979	−0.6	0.1	0.1	0.2	−0.1	0.1	−2.0	−0.5	1.2	−2.2
1980	−0.4	0.4	0.5	−1.1	0.2	0.3	0.4	1.2	0.1	2.0
1981	−0.5	0.2	−0.2	−0.5	0.5	0.2	0.2	−2.2	−0.7	−1.8
1982	0.6	1.8	−1.0	0.3	−0.7	0.2	−1.6	2.2	0.4	1.2
1983	−0.2	−0.03	0.9	0.3	−0.2	0.05	−0.5	1.7	1.2	2.1
1984	−0.5	0.8	−0.2	−0.4	0.3	0.6	−1.1	−0.5	−0.5	−0.6
1985	−1.1	−0.7	0.2	0.9	0.5	0.3	−0.8	0.6	−0.1	1.1
1986	−1.0	0.2	0.1	−0.9	−0.5	−0.5	1.8	2.3	0.2	2.4
1987	1.3	−0.5	−2.6	−0.4	1.3	−0.3	3.6	1.1	0.1	2.2
1988	−0.2	0.3	−0.4	0.1	0.8	−0.6	−0.9	1.5	0.2	0.9
1989	0.6	0.8	−0.2	0.6	0.5	0.8	1.8	−0.3	−0.9	4.1
1990	0.5	−0.6	0.3	−0.8	0.1	0.5	−1.1	−1.4	−0.3	−3.0
1991	2.5	0.6	1.4	0.4	2.1	0.5	0.04	0.5	−0.3	5.7
1992	−0.3	0.2	−0.1	−0.3	0.2	−0.7	−0.1	−0.2	0.04	−1.1
1993	0.01	0.7	0.1	−0.1	−0.4	−0.5	−0.2	0.3	0.1	−0.1
1994	0.01	0.2	0.4	−0.3	0.1	−0.4	−0.03	0.3	−0.1	0.2
1995	0.8	0.2	0.4	0.04	−0.1	0.3	0.8	0.1	−0.6	1.8
1996	−0.3	0.5	0.6	0.1	−0.4	−1.7	−0.5	1.5	−0.1	0.1
1997	−1.5	−0.7	0.4	1.8	1.8	−0.04	0.5	0.2	−1.1	4.0
1998	2.1	−0.2	−0.1	1.3	−0.8	−0.2	−0.1	1.4	2.2	1.3
1999	1.6	−0.1	0.04	0.4	0.1	0.3	−1.0	−3.8	0.2	−4.0
2000	0.8	2.4	0.7	1.0	0.4	−1.0	−2.8	5.0	−1.1	5.7
2001	0.4	−0.02	0.4	0.7	0.3	−1.1	0.6	0.9	0.6	1.8
2002	0.2	−0.5	−0.3	−1.6	0.5	0.05	3.3	−0.05	2.2	1.2
2003	0.3	−0.2	0.2	1.2	0.01	0.2	−0.3	1.2	0.1	2.4
2004	0.1	−0.4	0.7	−0.01	0.01	−0.1	−0.8	−1.2	−0.4	−1.8
2005	0.4	0.04	−1.0	0.1	−0.3	−0.5	1.6	0.4	0.002	0.4
2006	−0.4	−0.5	0.4	0.7	−0.1	−0.5	−0.1	0.1	−0.6	0.003
2007	1.7	0.8	0.1	−1.4	0.1	−0.7	−1.4	0.0	−2.5	−2.5
2008	−1.0	0.6	0.5	−0.4	2.4	1.4	3.2	−0.5	0.8	7.4
2009	0.2	0.5	0.1	−0.1	0.02	−1.0	1.6	0.3	0.05	1.4
2010	−0.2	0.1	0.1	0.1	−0.2	−0.02	1.1	−0.1	0.5	1.1
Avg	0.10	0.32	0.29	0.08	0.21	0.02	0.19	0.44	0.03	1.6

The couplet above was certainly on the mark in 1999, as the period suffered a horrendous 4.0% loss. On January 14, 2000, the Dow started its 33-month 37.8% slide to the October 2002 midterm election year bottom. NASDAQ cracked eight weeks later, falling 37.3% in 10 weeks, eventually dropping 77.9% by October 2002. Saddam Hussein cancelled Christmas by invading Kuwait in 1990. Energy prices and Middle East terror woes may have grounded Santa in 2004. In 2007, the third worst reading since 1950 was recorded, as subprime mortgages and their derivatives led to a full-blown financial crisis and the second worst bear market in history.

DECEMBER

Monday before December Triple Witching, S&P Up 8 of Last 11

MONDAY
D 42.9
S 38.1
N 42.9
17

The only title in our democracy superior to that of president is the title of citizen.
— Louis D. Brandeis (U.S. Supreme Court justice 1916–1939, 1856–1941)

TUESDAY
D 61.9
S 61.9
N 52.4
18

Another factor contributing to productivity is technology, particularly the rapid introduction of new microcomputers based on single-chip circuits.... The results over the next decade will be a second industrial revolution. — Yale Hirsch (Creator of *Stock Trader's Almanac, Smart Money Newsletter* 9/22/1976, b. 1923)

December Triple Witching Week, S&P Up 22 of Last 27
2009 Broke 8-Year Bull Run

WEDNESDAY
D 47.6
S 57.1
N 47.6
19

But how do we know when irrational exuberance has unduly escalated asset values, which then become subject to unexpected and prolonged contractions, as they have in Japan over the past decade?
— Alan Greenspan (Fed chairman 1987–2006, 12/5/96 speech to American Enterprise Institute, b. 1926)

THURSDAY
D 47.6
S 38.1
N 52.4
20

First-rate people hire first-rate people; second-rate people hire third-rate people.
— Leo Rosten (American author, 1908–1997)

December Triple Witching, S&P Up 21 of 29, Average Gain 0.4%
Watch for the Santa Claus Rally (Page 112)

 **FRIDAY**
D 71.4
S 71.4
N 76.2
21

A man will fight harder for his interests than his rights.
— Napoleon Bonaparte (Emperor of France 1804–1815, 1769–1821)

SATURDAY
22

The Only FREE LUNCH on Wall Street is Served (Page 110)
Almanac Investors E-mailed Alert before the Open, Monday (See Insert)

SUNDAY
23

BEST INVESTMENT BOOK OF THE YEAR

George Lindsay and the Art of Technical Analysis: Trading Systems of a Market Master

By Ed Carlson

The late, great technician, George Lindsay, has been an integral part of the market research and analysis at the Hirsch Organization from the beginning over 45 years ago to this day (page 74). Lindsay was a brilliant market prognosticator who made numerous bold and uncannily accurate predictions. He was an intense student of history, market cycles, and repetitive price patterns. From memory, George could reproduce a chart of stock market prices for every one of the previous 160 years prior to his death in 1987.

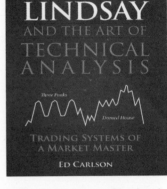

George Lindsay's Opinion was a highly respected newsletter that predicted the course of the stock market for the calendar year month-by-month. We first published George's work in 1968 in our first *Stock Trader's Almanac*. His forecast for 1968 was a bull's-eye. The following year, we presented his groundbreaking "Three Peaks and a Domed House" pattern for identifying market tops that he would become famous for.

George's most impressive forecast was made in July 1969. Appearing in our *1970 Stock Trader's Almanac*, it showed the Dow gaining virtually no ground over the next twelve years. As the years unfolded, the Dow spent most of its time in the 800–1000 range, in line with George's forecast. In October 1981 on *Wall Street Week* with Louis Rukeyser, he called the 1982 bottom within weeks and seven Dow points. Then for his last hoorah, in July 1987 he called the August 1987 top.

Finally, after all these years, in *George Lindsay and the Art of Technical Analysis*, Ed Carlson has illuminated the life, times, and iconic work of the master technician. After a succinct and interesting personal history, Carlson decodes and clearly explains Lindsay's, patterns methods, techniques, and timing models with copious visual aids in such a manner that every analyst, investor, and trader can apply them with ease.

Financial Times Press, $34.99. *http://georgelindsay.com/*. **2012 Best Investment Book of the Year.**

YEAR'S TOP INVESTMENT BOOKS

Super Boom: Why the Dow Jones Will Hit 38,820 and How You Can Profit From It, Jeffrey A. Hirsch, Wiley, $24.95. Detailed analysis of *2011 Almanac* forecast, including prospects for several more years of sideways markets (see page 74) before next 500% move to Dow 38,820 by 2025. How to invest now and for the boom. Debunks previous erroneous forecasts and permabears. Doug Kass says, "Jeff's rationale for another super boom is well articulated in his own unique set of facts, figures, and dissection of history. To every serious investor I say, 'Read *Super Boom* or perish!' "

Probable Outcomes: Secular Stock Market Insights, Ed Easterling, Cypress House, $39.95. Lends support to our *Super Boom* forecast. Brilliant graphics and analysis to guide your investment decisions regardless of your outlook for the market, economy, and inflation.

The Little Book of Sideways Markets: How to Make Money in Markets that Go Nowhere, Vitaliy N. Katsenelson, Wiley, $19.95. Renowned value investor shows you how to survive the next several years of sideways markets.

(continued on page 116)

DECEMBER

(Shortened Trading Day)
Last Trading Day before Christmas, Dow Up Last 4 Years

D 52.4
S 57.1
N 61.9

MONDAY
24

The worst mistake investors make is taking their profits too soon, and their losses too long.
— Michael Price (Mutual Shares Fund)

Christmas Day (Market Closed)

TUESDAY
25

You are your own Promised Land, your own new frontier.
— Julia Margaret Cameron (Nineteenth century English photographer)

WEDNESDAY

D 90.5
S 81.0
N 71.4

26

We were fairly arrogant, until we realized the Japanese were selling quality products for what it cost us to make them. — Paul A. Allaire (Former chairman of Xerox)

THURSDAY

D 57.1
S 57.1
N 57.1

27

As for it being different this time, it is different every time. The question is in what way, and to what extent.
— Tom McClellan (*The McClellan Market Report*)

FRIDAY

D 47.6
S 66.7
N 57.1

28

The mind is not a vessel to be filled but a fire to be kindled.
— Plutarch (Greek biographer and philosopher, *Parallel Lives*, 46–120 A.D.)

SATURDAY
29

January Almanac Investor Seasonalities: See Pages 92, 94, and 96

SUNDAY
30

YEAR'S TOP INVESTMENT BOOKS

(continued from page 114)

The Great Super Cycle: Profit from the Coming Inflation Tidal Wave and Dollar Devaluation, David Skarica, Wiley, $27.95. It is not the end of the world. Ride the economic cycle with Skarica's recommendations to profit from the coming inflation.

The Next Great Bull Market: How To Pick Winning Stocks and Sectors in the New Global Economy, Matthew McCall, Wiley, $39.95. Man after our own heart. More great ideas for investing in the next *Super Boom*, including themes on investing with the Obama administration.

Survive The Great Inflation: How to Protect Your Family, Your Future and Your Fortune from the Worst Fed Regime Ever, Michael Murphy, Next Paradigm Press, $27.95. Inflation is coming. 40-year investment veteran Murphy shares where to put your money.

Inflated: How Money and Debt Built the American Dream, R. Christopher Whalen, Wiley, $34.95. A frank assessment of America's historic addiction to debt and inflation, but in the end, he believes Americans will once again muster the courage to pull up their boot straps and make the hard choices for economic prosperity.

The Globalization Paradox: Democracy and the Future of the World Economy, Dani Rodrik, W. W. Norton, $26.95. Harvard professor examines economic history since the seventeenth century and prescribes his recipe for sustainable globalization.

Endgame: The End of the Debt SuperCycle and How It Changes Everything, John Maudlin and Jonathan Tepper, Wiley, $27.95. Aside from worst-case scenarios, depicts 5–6 years of pain before the healing from the debt crisis begins, plus where future investment opportunities lie.

All About Market Indicators, Michael Sincere, Wiley, $22.00. Quick, handy guide on how to use market indicators, timing strategies, sentiment, fundamentals, technicals, and cycles and which work and why.

Finding #1 Stocks: Screening, Backtesting and Time-Proven Strategies, Kevin Matras, Wiley, $49.95. We've successfully used Zacks for years as a stock screening tool. This is a great, commonsense guide for everyday investors.

Trading with Ichimoku Clouds: The Essential Guide to Ichimoku Kinko Hyo Technical Analysis, Manesh Patel, Wiley, $70.00. Next evolution of candlestick method. John Person says, "An inside look into a trading system that can be applied to all markets—stocks, futures, and especially Forex. Excellent work!"

The ART of Trading: Combining the Science of Technical Analysis with the Art of Reality-Based Trading, Bennett A. McDowell, Wiley, $70.00. Free DVD and 1-month trial. ART® (Applied Reality Trading®) system determines position size, stop losses, entries, and exits. ART Profile determines best style for you.

One Good Trade: Inside the Highly Competitive World of Proprietary Trading, Mike Bellafiore, Wiley, $60.00. Inner workings of proprietary trading show how to identify good trades, take profits at right time, and limit losses.

Debunkery: Learn It, Do It, and Profit from It—Seeing Through Wall Street's Money-Killing Myths, Ken Fisher, Wiley, $27.95. Another classic from the legendary investor. Only beef is he goes back too far to 1925 to disprove January Barometer and Sell in May. January Barometer starts in 1938 after 20th Amendment, and summer was strong before 1950 when most of Americans farmed.

If It Doesn't Go Up, Don't Buy It: Never Lose Money in the Stock Market Again, 3rd Edition, Al Thomas, Williamsburg Investment Company, $29.95. Unwittingly omitted first and second additions. Simple, no-nonsense method for buying mutual funds and ETFs that go up and making money when market goes down.

Lessons from the Financial Crisis: Causes, Consequences, and Our Economic Future, Robert Kolb, Wiley, $95.00. 78 articles from leading minds in finance, government, and academia dig deep into the core of the 2007–2009 crisis, the long term implications, and the real solutions to shore up system for future stability and growth.

DECEMBER/JANUARY 2013

Last Trading Day of the Year, NASDAQ Down 10 of last 11
NASDAQ Was Up 29 Years in a Row 1971–1999

🐻 **MONDAY**

D 42.9
S 33.3
N 52.4

31

We're not believers that the government is bigger than the business cycle.
— David Rosenberg (Economist, Merrill Lynch, Barron's, 4/21/2008)

New Year's Day (Market Closed)

TUESDAY

1

I measure what's going on, and I adapt to it. I try to get my ego out of the way. The market is smarter than I am so I bend. — Martin Zweig (Fund manager, Winning on Wall Street)

Small Caps Punished First Trading Day of Year
Russell 2000 Down 14 of Last 22, But Up Last 3

WEDNESDAY

D 66.7
S 42.9
N 61.9

2

Q. What kind of grad students do you take? A. I never take a straight-A student. A real scientist tends to be critical, and somewhere along the line, they had to rebel against their teachers.
— Lynn Margulis, (U. Mass science professor, The Scientist, 6/30/03)

Second Trading Day of the Year, Dow Up 13 of Last 18
Santa Claus Rally Ends (Page 112)

🐂 **THURSDAY**

D 61.9
S 61.9
N 71.4

3

One of the more prolonged and extreme periods favoring large-cap stocks was 1994–1999. The tide turned in 2000. A cycle has begun of investors favoring small-cap stocks, which is likely to continue through the next several years. — Jim Oberweis (The Oberweis Report, February 2001)

FRIDAY

D 42.9
S 47.6
N 47.6

4

There is no one who can replace America. Without American leadership, there is no leadership. That puts a tremendous burden on the American people to do something positive. You can't be tempted by the usual nationalism. — Lee Hong-koo (South Korean prime minister 1994–1995 and ambassador to U.S. 1998–2000, NY Times, 2/25/2009)

SATURDAY

5

SUNDAY

6

2013 STRATEGY CALENDAR

(Option expiration dates circled)

	MONDAY	TUESDAY	WEDNESDAY	THURSDAY	FRIDAY	SATURDAY	SUNDAY
JANUARY	31	1 JANUARY New Year's Day	2	3	4	5	6
	7	8	9	10	11	12	13
	14	15	16	17	(18)	19	20
	21 Martin Luther King Day	22	23	24	25	26	27
FEBRUARY	28	29	30	31	1 FEBRUARY	2	3
	4	5	6	7	8	9	10
	11	12	13 Ash Wednesday	14 ♥	(15)	16	17
	18 Presidents' Day	19	20	21	22	23	24
MARCH	25	26	27	28	1 MARCH	2	3
	4	5	6	7	8	9	10 Daylight Saving Time Begins
	11	12	13	14	(15)	16	17 St. Patrick's Day ♣
	18	19	20	21	22	23	24
	25	26 Passover	27	28	29 Good Friday	30	31 Easter
APRIL	1 APRIL	2	3	4	5	6	7
	8	9	10	11	12	13	14
	15 Tax Deadline	16	17	18	(19)	20	21
	22	23	24	25	26	27	28
MAY	29	30	1 MAY	2	3	4	5
	6	7	8	9	10	11	12 Mother's Day
	13	14	15	16	(17)	18	19
	20	21	22	23	24	25	26
JUNE	27 Memorial Day	28	29	30	31	1 JUNE	2
	3	4	5	6	7	8	9
	10	11	12	13	14	15	16 Father's Day
	17	18	19	20	(21)	22	23
	24	25	26	27	28	29	30

Market closed on shaded weekdays; closes early when half-shaded.

118

2013 STRATEGY CALENDAR

(Option expiration dates circled)

MONDAY	TUESDAY	WEDNESDAY	THURSDAY	FRIDAY	SATURDAY	SUNDAY
1 JULY	2	3	4 Independence Day	5	6	7
8	9	10	11	12	13	14
15	16	17	18	(19)	20	21
22	23	24	25	26	27	28
29	30	31	1 AUGUST	2	3	4
5	6	7	8	9	10	11
12	13	14	15	(16)	17	18
19	20	21	22	23	24	25
26	27	28	29	30	31	1 SEPTEMBER
2 Labor Day	3	4	5 Rosh Hashanah	6	7	8
9	10	11	12	13	14 Yom Kippur	15
16	17	18	19	(20)	21	22
23	24	25	26	27	28	29
30	1 OCTOBER	2	3	4	5	6
7	8	9	10	11	12	13
14 Columbus Day	15	16	17	(18)	19	20
21	22	23	24	25	26	27
28	29	30	31	1 NOVEMBER	2	3 Daylight Saving Time Ends
4	5 Election Day	6	7	8	9	10
11 Veterans' Day	12	13	14	(15)	16	17
18	19	20	21	22	23	24
25	26	27	28 Thanksgiving Chanukah	29	30	1 DECEMBER
2	3	4	5	6	7	8
9	10	11	12	13	14	15
16	17	18	19	(20)	21	22
23	24	25 Christmas	26	27	28	29
30	31	1 JANUARY New Year's Day	2	3	4	5

JULY · AUGUST · SEPTEMBER · OCTOBER · NOVEMBER · DECEMBER

DIRECTORY OF TRADING PATTERNS AND DATABANK

CONTENTS

DOW JONES INDUSTRIALS MARKET PROBABILITY CALENDAR 2012
THE % CHANCE OF THE MARKET RISING ON ANY TRADING DAY OF THE YEAR*
(Based on the number of times the DJIA rose on a particular trading day during January 1954 to December 2010.)

Date	Jan	Feb	Mar	Apr	May	Jun	Jul	Aug	Sep	Oct	Nov	Dec
1	S	57.9	64.9	S	57.9	57.9	S	45.6	S	47.4	61.4	S
2	H	54.4	63.2	59.6	64.9	S	63.2	47.4	S	57.9	50.9	S
3	56.1	36.8	S	59.6	50.9	S	59.6	49.1	H	50.9	S	47.4
4	71.9	S	S	56.1	50.9	54.4	H	S	59.6	61.4	S	54.4
5	49.1	S	59.6	57.9	S	52.6	59.6	S	57.9	45.6	66.7	63.2
6	57.9	54.4	49.1	H	S	57.9	56.1	50.9	59.6	S	59.6	57.9
7	S	47.4	45.6	S	43.9	50.9	S	54.4	43.9	S	47.4	45.6
8	S	40.4	52.6	S	50.9	45.6	S	45.6	S	50.9	59.6	S
9	47.4	45.6	59.6	54.4	49.1	S	64.9	47.4	S	43.9	50.9	S
10	49.1	63.2	S	59.6	52.6	S	56.1	49.1	49.1	38.6	S	45.6
11	47.4	S	S	61.4	45.6	36.8	52.6	S	43.9	54.4	S	54.4
12	47.4	S	54.4	64.9	S	57.9	40.4	S	56.1	57.9	59.6	59.6
13	57.9	43.9	54.4	54.4	S	59.6	64.9	43.9	59.6	S	47.4	45.6
14	S	49.1	52.6	S	54.4	57.9	S	63.2	45.6	S	50.9	54.4
15	S	56.1	59.6	S	56.1	50.9	S	57.9	S	52.6	56.1	S
16	H	38.6	63.2	70.2	45.6	S	49.1	52.6	S	49.1	49.1	S
17	54.4	47.4	S	64.9	52.6	S	45.6	47.4	52.6	42.1	S	43.9
18	59.6	S	S	57.9	43.9	47.4	49.1	S	52.6	61.4	S	57.9
19	38.6	S	57.9	56.1	S	49.1	50.9	S	38.6	50.9	50.9	49.1
20	35.1	H	52.6	54.4	S	43.9	42.1	56.1	49.1	S	50.9	52.6
21	S	49.1	40.4	S	47.4	47.4	S	43.9	47.4	S	59.6	50.9
22	S	56.1	50.9	S	42.1	40.4	S	59.6	S	47.4	H	S
23	40.4	35.1	36.8	52.6	35.1	S	47.4	47.4	S	42.1	66.7	S
24	47.4	45.6	S	52.6	50.9	S	49.1	52.6	50.9	45.6	S	59.6
25	57.9	S	S	56.1	43.9	38.6	61.4	S	54.4	28.1	S	H
26	57.9	S	47.4	52.6	S	45.6	50.9	S	52.6	54.4	59.6	73.7
27	50.9	59.6	47.4	47.4	S	43.9	45.6	50.9	49.1	S	64.9	50.9
28	S	45.6	54.4	S	H	54.4	S	45.6	40.4	S	57.9	56.1
29	S	52.6	42.1	S	45.6	50.9	S	57.9	S	52.6	50.9	S
30	59.6		42.1	50.9	56.1	S	63.2	40.4	S	59.6	50.9	S
31	59.6		S		59.6		52.6	61.4		56.1		54.4

*See new trends developing on pages 68, 88, 141–146.

RECENT DOW JONES INDUSTRIALS MARKET PROBABILITY CALENDAR 2012

THE % CHANCE OF THE MARKET RISING ON ANY TRADING DAY OF THE YEAR*

(Based on the number of times the DJIA rose on a particular trading day during January 1990 to December 2010.**)

Date	Jan	Feb	Mar	Apr	May	Jun	Jul	Aug	Sep	Oct	Nov	Dec
1	S	66.7	61.9	S	76.2	76.2	S	42.9	S	57.1	57.1	S
2	H	52.4	52.4	71.4	71.4	S	81.0	52.4	S	42.9	52.4	S
3	66.7	42.9	S	66.7	38.1	S	42.9	38.1	H	38.1	S	57.1
4	61.9	S	S	52.4	47.6	57.1	H	S	57.1	61.9	S	52.4
5	42.9	S	57.1	66.7	S	47.6	47.6	S	61.9	33.3	61.9	61.9
6	52.4	47.6	47.6	H	S	47.6	57.1	47.6	52.4	S	71.4	52.4
7	S	52.4	57.1	S	33.3	47.6	S	47.6	38.1	S	57.1	38.1
8	S	42.9	42.9	S	71.4	47.6	S	47.6	S	47.6	52.4	S
9	38.1	57.1	61.9	42.9	61.9	S	71.4	42.9	S	47.6	38.1	S
10	52.4	57.1	S	52.4	66.7	S	47.6	52.4	61.9	38.1	S	52.4
11	47.6	S	S	47.6	52.4	42.9	66.7	S	52.4	61.9	S	52.4
12	52.4	S	61.9	66.7	S	47.6	66.7	S	61.9	76.2	57.1	57.1
13	52.4	61.9	42.9	61.9	S	61.9	66.7	28.6	66.7	S	57.1	52.4
14	S	42.9	66.7	S	57.1	71.4	S	66.7	47.6	S	66.7	52.4
15	S	71.4	66.7	S	61.9	57.1	S	47.6	S	57.1	52.4	S
16	H	42.9	61.9	71.4	52.4	S	52.4	61.9	S	47.6	47.6	S
17	57.1	28.6	S	71.4	57.1	S	52.4	57.1	52.4	47.6	S	42.9
18	57.1	S	S	61.9	47.6	47.6	42.9	S	52.4	66.7	S	61.9
19	33.3	S	57.1	52.4	S	52.4	66.7	S	33.3	52.4	52.4	47.6
20	33.3	H	61.9	61.9	S	42.9	28.6	52.4	52.4	S	47.6	47.6
21	S	42.9	38.1	S	57.1	42.9	S	38.1	42.9	S	61.9	71.4
22	S	52.4	42.9	S	42.9	33.3	S	61.9	S	38.1	H	S
23	33.3	52.4	38.1	57.1	38.1	S	42.9	42.9	S	52.4	57.1	S
24	38.1	33.3	S	42.9	52.4	S	57.1	57.1	47.6	42.9	S	52.4
25	61.9	S	S	52.4	47.6	42.9	71.4	S	57.1	38.1	S	H
26	61.9	S	57.1	52.4	S	33.3	38.1	S	57.1	52.4	61.9	90.5
27	57.1	47.6	38.1	61.9	S	52.4	42.9	57.1	52.4	S	71.4	57.1
28	S	42.9	52.4	S	H	52.4	S	42.9	42.9	S	57.1	47.6
29	S	42.9	52.4	S	52.4	28.6	S	66.7	S	61.9	47.6	S
30	57.1		33.3	47.6	71.4	S	66.7	28.6	S	66.7	52.4	S
31	66.7		S		47.6		47.6	47.6		52.4		42.9

*See new trends developing on pages 68, 88, 141–146. ** Based on most recent 21-year period.

S&P 500 MARKET PROBABILITY CALENDAR 2012

THE % CHANCE OF THE MARKET RISING ON ANY TRADING DAY OF THE YEAR*

(Based on the number of times the S&P 500 rose on a particular trading day during January 1954 to December 2010.)

Date	Jan	Feb	Mar	Apr	May	Jun	Jul	Aug	Sep	Oct	Nov	Dec
1	S	59.6	61.4	S	57.9	56.1	S	49.1	S	47.4	61.4	S
2	H	57.9	57.9	64.9	70.2	S	68.4	45.6	S	64.9	57.9	S
3	47.4	45.6	S	59.6	56.1	S	56.1	49.1	H	52.6	S	49.1
4	71.9	S	S	57.9	45.6	63.2	H	S	63.2	61.4	S	54.4
5	52.6	S	63.2	54.4	S	52.6	54.4	S	54.4	49.1	68.4	61.4
6	52.6	49.1	47.4	H	S	56.1	59.6	50.9	59.6	S	56.1	56.1
7	S	50.9	47.4	S	40.4	45.6	S	56.1	43.9	S	47.4	40.4
8	S	42.1	56.1	S	50.9	43.9	S	45.6	S	49.1	57.9	S
9	45.6	40.4	59.6	56.1	49.1	S	63.2	52.6	S	40.4	57.9	S
10	50.9	63.2	S	61.4	52.6	S	56.1	47.4	50.9	43.9	S	50.9
11	50.9	S	S	63.2	43.9	42.1	52.6	S	52.6	52.6	S	56.1
12	54.4	S	50.9	56.1	S	57.9	49.1	S	56.1	52.6	57.9	50.9
13	61.4	50.9	61.4	49.1	S	63.2	70.2	45.6	63.2	S	47.4	50.9
14	S	43.9	47.4	S	50.9	57.9	S	64.9	50.9	S	50.9	47.4
15	S	56.1	61.4	S	56.1	57.9	S	63.2	S	52.6	47.4	S
16	H	35.1	63.2	61.4	50.9	S	54.4	56.1	S	52.6	50.9	S
17	61.4	50.9	S	63.2	54.4	S	42.1	54.4	52.6	40.4	S	43.9
18	54.4	S	S	61.4	40.4	43.9	43.9	S	54.4	66.7	S	57.9
19	50.9	S	57.9	52.6	S	54.4	50.9	S	45.6	50.9	54.4	45.6
20	43.9	H	49.1	54.4	S	40.4	40.4	52.6	54.4	S	54.4	45.6
21	S	42.1	45.6	S	45.6	52.6	S	45.6	50.9	S	57.9	47.4
22	S	49.1	43.9	S	49.1	42.1	S	61.4	S	49.1	H	S
23	43.9	40.4	52.6	45.6	43.9	S	47.4	45.6	S	42.1	63.2	S
24	61.4	38.6	S	45.6	52.6	S	45.6	50.9	49.1	40.4	S	61.4
25	52.6	S	S	56.1	49.1	38.6	59.6	S	50.9	33.3	S	H
26	52.6	S	42.1	47.4	S	38.6	50.9	S	59.6	59.6	59.6	73.7
27	47.4	56.1	49.1	43.9	S	49.1	49.1	49.1	49.1	S	68.4	54.4
28	S	49.1	54.4	S	H	57.9	S	45.6	43.9	S	59.6	64.9
29	S	59.6	36.8	S	47.4	49.1	S	57.9	S	56.1	56.1	S
30	63.2		40.4	57.9	56.1	S	64.9	43.9	S	61.4	50.9	S
31	64.9		S		61.4		64.9	64.9		56.1		63.2

*See new trends developing on pages 68, 88, 141–146.

RECENT S&P 500 MARKET PROBABILITY CALENDAR 2012

THE % CHANCE OF THE MARKET RISING ON ANY TRADING DAY OF THE YEAR*

(Based on the number of times the S&P 500 rose on a particular trading day during January 1990 to December 2010.**)

Date	Jan	Feb	Mar	Apr	May	Jun	Jul	Aug	Sep	Oct	Nov	Dec
1	S	66.7	57.1	S	76.2	66.7	S	52.4	S	52.4	57.1	S
2	H	61.9	42.9	66.7	71.4	S	81.0	47.6	S	52.4	61.9	S
3	42.9	42.9	S	66.7	42.9	S	38.1	38.1	H	33.3	S	61.9
4	61.9	S	S	61.9	38.1	76.2	H	S	66.7	52.4	S	57.1
5	47.6	S	66.7	61.9	S	42.9	52.4	S	47.6	38.1	61.9	66.7
6	42.9	47.6	47.6	H	S	38.1	61.9	52.4	47.6	S	71.4	38.1
7	S	47.6	52.4	S	23.8	38.1	S	47.6	42.9	S	57.1	38.1
8	S	52.4	52.4	S	61.9	38.1	S	57.1	S	47.6	47.6	S
9	52.4	47.6	52.4	47.6	57.1	S	71.4	38.1	S	42.9	42.9	S
10	52.4	66.7	S	57.1	57.1	S	42.9	52.4	57.1	42.9	S	52.4
11	47.6	S	S	47.6	52.4	52.4	61.9	S	61.9	61.9	S	52.4
12	57.1	S	52.4	52.4	S	42.9	76.2	S	61.9	76.2	52.4	47.6
13	57.1	66.7	57.1	52.4	S	61.9	71.4	28.6	61.9	S	52.4	57.1
14	S	38.1	57.1	S	52.4	71.4	S	71.4	57.1	S	61.9	47.6
15	S	76.2	71.4	S	57.1	66.7	S	61.9	S	57.1	42.9	S
16	H	38.1	61.9	57.1	57.1	S	47.6	71.4	S	52.4	57.1	S
17	57.1	33.3	S	61.9	61.9	S	42.9	61.9	52.4	52.4	S	38.1
18	57.1	S	S	66.7	47.6	42.9	38.1	S	61.9	71.4	S	61.9
19	52.4	S	66.7	52.4	S	52.4	66.7	S	42.9	61.9	57.1	57.1
20	33.3	H	47.6	57.1	S	42.9	23.8	47.6	57.1	S	47.6	38.1
21	S	38.1	47.6	S	57.1	57.1	S	42.9	42.9	S	57.1	71.4
22	S	47.6	33.3	S	42.9	33.3	S	61.9	S	47.6	H	S
23	38.1	61.9	61.9	52.4	38.1	S	47.6	42.9	S	57.1	47.6	S
24	52.4	38.1	S	28.6	61.9	S	52.4	61.9	42.9	38.1	S	57.1
25	47.6	S	S	47.6	52.4	42.9	71.4	S	52.4	42.9	S	H
26	47.6	S	57.1	52.4	S	23.8	38.1	S	61.9	57.1	57.1	81.0
27	57.1	47.6	42.9	57.1	S	57.1	47.6	57.1	57.1	S	71.4	57.1
28	S	52.4	47.6	S	H	61.9	S	47.6	42.9	S	61.9	66.7
29	S	47.6	33.3	S	57.1	33.3	S	66.7	S	57.1	61.9	S
30	61.9		38.1	57.1	61.9	S	71.4	28.6	S	76.2	38.1	S
31	71.4		S		57.1		61.9	47.6		57.1		33.3

*See new trends developing on pages 68, 88, 141–146. ** Based on most recent 21-year period.

NASDAQ COMPOSITE MARKET PROBABILITY CALENDAR 2012

THE % CHANCE OF THE MARKET RISING ON ANY TRADING DAY OF THE YEAR*

(Based on the number of times the NASDAQ rose on a particular trading day during January 1972 to December 2010.)

Date	Jan	Feb	Mar	Apr	May	Jun	Jul	Aug	Sep	Oct	Nov	Dec
1	S	69.2	61.5	S	64.1	59.0	S	53.8	S	48.7	66.7	S
2	H	69.2	53.8	43.6	71.8	S	56.4	43.6	S	59.0	56.4	S
3	53.8	53.8	S	64.1	61.5	S	46.2	48.7	H	53.8	S	61.5
4	74.4	S	S	66.7	56.4	74.4	H	S	53.8	61.5	S	64.1
5	56.4	S	66.7	51.3	S	56.4	41.0	S	61.5	61.5	69.2	64.1
6	61.5	64.1	53.8	H	S	59.0	51.3	59.0	59.0	S	59.0	61.5
7	S	56.4	51.3	S	51.3	48.7	S	56.4	53.8	S	51.3	41.0
8	S	48.7	53.8	S	64.1	43.6	S	41.0	S	61.5	53.8	S
9	53.8	48.7	56.4	48.7	53.8	S	64.1	51.3	S	51.3	56.4	S
10	59.0	64.1	S	61.5	41.0	S	64.1	48.7	56.4	48.7	S	53.8
11	53.8	S	S	61.5	53.8	43.6	61.5	S	51.3	76.9	S	46.2
12	59.0	S	53.8	64.1	S	53.8	71.8	S	51.3	64.1	64.1	46.2
13	66.7	56.4	69.2	51.3	S	64.1	74.4	51.3	61.5	S	53.8	43.6
14	S	59.0	51.3	S	56.4	66.7	S	59.0	61.5	S	53.8	43.6
15	S	61.5	51.3	S	59.0	59.0	S	56.4	S	53.8	41.0	S
16	H	46.2	64.1	61.5	56.4	S	66.7	51.3	S	48.7	46.2	S
17	64.1	56.4	S	51.3	51.3	S	48.7	61.5	35.9	38.5	S	41.0
18	66.7	S	S	61.5	41.0	43.6	53.8	S	51.3	74.4	S	56.4
19	61.5	S	59.0	56.4	S	53.8	56.4	S	51.3	46.2	53.8	48.7
20	41.0	H	61.5	56.4	S	46.2	41.0	53.8	66.7	S	56.4	51.3
21	S	38.5	41.0	S	48.7	48.7	S	35.9	53.8	S	53.8	66.7
22	S	41.0	59.0	S	48.7	43.6	S	71.8	S	61.5	H	S
23	46.2	48.7	56.4	53.8	48.7	S	51.3	51.3	S	46.2	69.2	S
24	56.4	53.8	S	48.7	56.4	S	51.3	48.7	51.3	38.5	S	69.2
25	43.6	S	S	43.6	53.8	46.2	61.5	S	46.2	33.3	S	H
26	66.7	S	46.2	69.2	S	43.6	48.7	S	48.7	46.2	59.0	71.8
27	64.1	59.0	46.2	61.5	S	59.0	46.2	53.8	48.7	S	59.0	51.3
28	S	51.3	51.3	S	H	66.7	S	51.3	48.7	S	64.1	66.7
29	S	53.8	51.3	S	59.0	64.1	S	61.5	S	56.4	64.1	S
30	56.4		64.1	69.2	56.4	S	56.4	61.5	S	61.5	64.1	S
31	64.1		S		71.8		53.8	69.2		69.2		74.4

See new trends developing on pages 68, 88, 141–146.
Based on NASDAQ composite; prior to February 5, 1971, based on National Quotation Bureau indices.

RECENT NASDAQ COMPOSITE MARKET PROBABILITY CALENDAR 2012

THE % CHANCE OF THE MARKET RISING ON ANY TRADING DAY OF THE YEAR*

(Based on the number of times the NASDAQ rose on a particular trading day during January 1990 to December 2010.**)

Date	Jan	Feb	Mar	Apr	May	Jun	Jul	Aug	Sep	Oct	Nov	Dec
1	S	81.0	57.1	S	76.2	66.7	S	57.1	S	47.6	66.7	S
2	H	66.7	38.1	52.4	66.7	S	66.7	42.9	S	52.4	61.9	S
3	61.9	47.6	S	61.9	61.9	S	33.3	33.3	H	42.9	S	71.4
4	71.4	S	S	71.4	52.4	81.0	H	S	61.9	57.1	S	66.7
5	47.6	S	66.7	52.4	S	52.4	38.1	S	61.9	47.6	76.2	66.7
6	47.6	57.1	47.6	H	S	47.6	57.1	52.4	52.4	S	66.7	57.1
7	S	52.4	52.4	S	33.3	33.3	S	47.6	52.4	S	61.9	38.1
8	S	57.1	42.9	S	76.2	28.6	S	42.9	S	61.9	57.1	S
9	57.1	47.6	52.4	38.1	52.4	S	76.2	38.1	S	52.4	47.6	S
10	61.9	52.4	S	52.4	42.9	S	61.9	47.6	66.7	57.1	S	52.4
11	47.6	S	S	47.6	52.4	47.6	71.4	S	61.9	71.4	S	47.6
12	52.4	S	47.6	61.9	S	42.9	76.2	S	57.1	71.4	57.1	47.6
13	57.1	52.4	61.9	52.4	S	57.1	76.2	42.9	66.7	S	61.9	52.4
14	S	52.4	52.4	S	47.6	61.9	S	71.4	71.4	S	61.9	42.9
15	S	61.9	47.6	S	57.1	66.7	S	61.9	S	57.1	38.1	S
16	H	33.3	66.7	61.9	61.9	S	61.9	66.7	S	42.9	47.6	S
17	47.6	42.9	S	38.1	66.7	S	47.6	61.9	33.3	42.9	S	42.9
18	66.7	S	S	52.4	42.9	38.1	42.9	S	61.9	76.2	S	52.4
19	61.9	S	61.9	47.6	S	52.4	61.9	S	52.4	52.4	52.4	47.6
20	33.3	H	61.9	57.1	S	42.9	28.6	42.9	66.7	S	57.1	52.4
21	S	38.1	28.6	S	71.4	42.9	S	33.3	42.9	S	57.1	76.2
22	S	42.9	52.4	S	52.4	23.8	S	81.0	S	52.4	H	S
23	42.9	61.9	57.1	52.4	47.6	S	47.6	47.6	S	52.4	61.9	S
24	57.1	52.4	S	47.6	57.1	S	47.6	47.6	42.9	33.3	S	61.9
25	38.1	S	S	42.9	47.6	42.9	76.2	S	52.4	33.3	S	H
26	76.2	S	61.9	61.9	S	33.3	52.4	S	42.9	47.6	52.4	71.4
27	66.7	47.6	47.6	66.7	S	61.9	47.6	57.1	47.6	S	61.9	57.1
28	S	52.4	38.1	S	H	71.4	S	42.9	42.9	S	57.1	57.1
29	S	42.9	42.9	S	61.9	61.9	S	71.4	S	57.1	71.4	S
30	52.4		57.1	66.7	76.2	S	66.7	57.1	S	71.4	52.4	S
31	61.9		S		66.7		47.6	52.4		76.2		52.4

*See new trends developing on page 68, 88, 141–146.   ** Based on most recent 21-year period.

RUSSELL 1000 INDEX MARKET PROBABILITY CALENDAR 2012

THE % CHANCE OF THE MARKET RISING ON ANY TRADING DAY OF THE YEAR*

(Based on the number of times the Russell 1000 rose on a particular trading day during January 1980 to December 2010.)

Date	Jan	Feb	Mar	Apr	May	Jun	Jul	Aug	Sep	Oct	Nov	Dec
1	S	64.5	58.1	S	58.1	58.1	S	48.4	S	54.8	71.0	S
2	H	61.3	45.2	61.3	67.7	S	71.0	41.9	S	54.8	58.1	S
3	38.7	54.8	S	61.3	54.8	S	41.9	48.4	H	48.4	S	58.1
4	64.5	S	S	54.8	41.9	64.5	H	S	54.8	58.1	S	54.8
5	58.1	S	61.3	54.8	S	48.4	41.9	S	51.6	45.2	61.3	61.3
6	54.8	48.4	41.9	H	S	54.8	58.1	48.4	51.6	S	61.3	38.7
7	S	61.3	41.9	S	35.5	32.3	S	54.8	35.5	S	48.4	38.7
8	S	45.2	54.8	S	54.8	41.9	S	54.8	S	54.8	51.6	S
9	51.6	38.7	54.8	51.6	58.1	S	61.3	45.2	S	38.7	45.2	S
10	61.3	67.7	S	67.7	51.6	S	51.6	48.4	51.6	38.7	S	48.4
11	51.6	S	S	54.8	54.8	41.9	61.3	S	58.1	67.7	S	54.8
12	54.8	S	48.4	54.8	S	51.6	67.7	S	58.1	67.7	58.1	45.2
13	61.3	61.3	58.1	45.2	S	61.3	80.6	38.7	64.5	S	58.1	48.4
14	S	41.9	48.4	S	54.8	61.3	S	61.3	58.1	S	54.8	45.2
15	S	67.7	58.1	S	58.1	61.3	S	61.3	S	61.3	45.2	S
16	H	32.3	61.3	58.1	58.1	S	48.4	64.5	S	48.4	48.4	S
17	67.7	41.9	S	67.7	54.8	S	51.6	64.5	51.6	38.7	S	48.4
18	67.7	S	S	61.3	48.4	45.2	45.2	S	48.4	74.2	S	61.3
19	41.9	S	58.1	48.4	S	61.3	61.3	S	41.9	54.8	64.5	51.6
20	29.0	H	48.4	51.6	S	35.5	35.5	64.5	51.6	S	51.6	41.9
21	S	38.7	45.2	S	48.4	54.8	S	48.4	41.9	S	54.8	58.1
22	S	45.2	45.2	S	48.4	38.7	S	71.0	S	54.8	H	S
23	41.9	45.2	48.4	54.8	41.9	S	48.4	48.4	S	48.4	61.3	S
24	51.6	45.2	S	41.9	61.3	S	38.7	54.8	41.9	32.3	S	61.3
25	48.4	S	S	51.6	61.3	38.7	77.4	S	48.4	35.5	S	H
26	64.5	S	51.6	54.8	S	35.5	51.6	S	67.7	54.8	61.3	71.0
27	61.3	58.1	38.7	51.6	S	48.4	45.2	45.2	54.8	S	71.0	61.3
28	S	54.8	48.4	S	H	58.1	S	54.8	51.6	S	71.0	67.7
29	S	58.1	41.9	S	58.1	45.2	S	54.8	S	51.6	61.3	S
30	61.3		48.4	58.1	54.8	S	67.7	45.2	S	67.7	48.4	S
31	64.5		S		58.1		61.3	58.1		67.7		51.6

* See new trends developing on pages 68, 88, 141–146.

RUSSELL 2000 INDEX MARKET PROBABILITY CALENDAR 2012

THE % CHANCE OF THE MARKET RISING ON ANY TRADING DAY OF THE YEAR*

(Based on the number of times the Russell 2000 rose on a particular trading day during January 1980 to December 2010.)

Date	Jan	Feb	Mar	Apr	May	Jun	Jul	Aug	Sep	Oct	Nov	Dec
1	S	67.7	64.5	S	64.5	64.5	S	51.6	S	51.6	64.5	S
2	H	64.5	58.1	48.4	64.5	S	61.3	48.4	S	45.2	71.0	S
3	41.9	51.6	S	61.3	64.5	S	48.4	45.2	H	48.4	S	58.1
4	67.7	S	S	48.4	61.3	74.2	H	S	51.6	67.7	S	61.3
5	58.1	S	64.5	51.6	S	51.6	38.7	S	64.5	45.2	67.7	67.7
6	64.5	67.7	58.1	H	S	54.8	51.6	48.4	54.8	S	61.3	61.3
7	S	67.7	61.3	S	48.4	51.6	S	48.4	61.3	S	58.1	41.9
8	S	58.1	48.4	S	54.8	32.3	S	45.2	S	48.4	51.6	S
9	61.3	45.2	54.8	45.2	61.3	S	54.8	54.8	S	48.4	48.4	S
10	61.3	71.0	S	61.3	48.4	S	61.3	51.6	54.8	54.8	S	58.1
11	51.6	S	S	61.3	58.1	48.4	54.8	S	61.3	71.0	S	45.2
12	67.7	S	41.9	64.5	S	54.8	64.5	S	58.1	61.3	71.0	51.6
13	67.7	58.1	58.1	48.4	S	61.3	64.5	45.2	64.5	S	51.6	38.7
14	S	64.5	54.8	S	51.6	67.7	S	74.2	54.8	S	54.8	45.2
15	S	58.1	48.4	S	48.4	58.1	S	61.3	S	61.3	45.2	S
16	H	48.4	61.3	54.8	58.1	S	54.8	64.5	S	38.7	19.4	S
17	64.5	41.9	S	61.3	51.6	S	51.6	61.3	32.3	45.2	S	32.3
18	74.2	S	S	58.1	51.6	45.2	48.4	S	48.4	71.0	S	58.1
19	74.2	S	67.7	48.4	S	38.7	51.6	S	41.9	58.1	61.3	61.3
20	29.0	H	54.8	58.1	S	38.7	35.5	51.6	45.2	S	45.2	58.1
21	S	35.5	48.4	S	51.6	45.2	S	48.4	48.4	S	35.5	67.7
22	S	35.5	61.3	S	48.4	41.9	S	74.2	S	54.8	H	S
23	48.4	51.6	48.4	51.6	51.6	S	41.9	45.2	S	48.4	61.3	S
24	54.8	61.3	S	51.6	58.1	S	48.4	58.1	45.2	38.7	S	77.4
25	41.9	S	S	58.1	51.6	45.2	64.5	S	32.3	38.7	S	H
26	67.7	S	51.6	64.5	S	45.2	64.5	S	54.8	38.7	58.1	67.7
27	61.3	58.1	45.2	58.1	S	54.8	45.2	54.8	58.1	S	64.5	58.1
28	S	64.5	51.6	S	H	71.0	S	58.1	67.7	S	61.3	64.5
29	S	61.3	48.4	S	71.0	64.5	S	61.3	S	51.6	67.7	S
30	58.1		83.9	71.0	67.7	S	58.1	61.3	S	61.3	71.0	S
31	77.4		S		74.2		67.7	74.2		77.4		71.0

* See new trends developing on pages 68, 88, 141–146.

DECENNIAL CYCLE: A MARKET PHENOMENON

By arranging each year's market gain or loss so the first and succeeding years of each decade fall into the same column, certain interesting patterns emerge—strong fifth and eighth years; weak first, seventh, and zero years.

This fascinating phenomenon was first presented by Edgar Lawrence Smith in *Common Stocks and Business Cycles* (William-Frederick Press, 1959). Anthony Gaubis co-pioneered the decennial pattern with Smith.

When Smith first cut graphs of market prices into 10-year segments and placed them above one another, he observed that each decade tended to have three bull market cycles and that the longest and strongest bull markets seem to favor the middle years of a decade.

Don't place too much emphasis on the decennial cycle nowadays, other than the extraordinary fifth and zero years, as the stock market is more influenced by the quadrennial presidential election cycle, shown on page 130. Also, the last half-century, which has been the most prosperous in U.S. history, has distributed the returns among most years of the decade. Interestingly, NASDAQ suffered its worst bear market ever in a zero year.

Second years have the fourth worst record within the Decennial Cycle. However, 2012 is a presidential election year, which has the second best record of the 4-year presidential election cycle. The last three presidential election years since the Depression that were also second years have produced an average gain of 9.1%. As historical patterns reassert themselves, the probability of a positive 2012 is increasing (see pages 24, 26, 28, 34, 38, 52, and 130).

THE 10-YEAR STOCK MARKET CYCLE
Annual % Change in Dow Jones Industrial Average
Year of Decade

DECADES	1st	2nd	3rd	4th	5th	6th	7th	8th	9th	10th
1881–1890	3.0%	-2.9%	-8.5%	-18.8%	20.1%	12.4%	-8.4%	4.8%	5.5%	-14.1%
1891–1900	17.6	-6.6	-24.6	-0.6	2.3	-1.7	21.3	22.5	9.2	7.0
1901–1910	-8.7	-0.4	-23.6	41.7	38.2	-1.9	-37.7	46.6	15.0	-17.9
1911–1920	0.4	7.6	-10.3	-5.4	81.7	-4.2	-21.7	10.5	30.5	-32.9
1921–1930	12.7	21.7	-3.3	26.2	30.0	0.3	28.8	48.2	-17.2	-33.8
1931–1940	-52.7	-23.1	66.7	4.1	38.5	24.8	-32.8	28.1	-2.9	-12.7
1941–1950	-15.4	7.6	13.8	12.1	26.6	-8.1	2.2	-2.1	12.9	17.6
1951–1960	14.4	8.4	-3.8	44.0	20.8	2.3	-12.8	34.0	16.4	-9.3
1961–1970	18.7	-10.8	17.0	14.6	10.9	-18.9	15.2	4.3	-15.2	4.8
1971–1980	6.1	14.6	-16.6	-27.6	38.3	17.9	-17.3	-3.1	4.2	14.9
1981–1990	-9.2	19.6	20.3	-3.7	27.7	22.6	2.3	11.8	27.0	-4.3
1991–2000	20.3	4.2	13.7	2.1	33.5	26.0	22.6	16.1	25.2	-6.2
2001–2010	-7.1	-16.8	25.3	3.1	-0.6	16.3	6.4	-33.8	18.8	11.0
Total % Change	**0.1%**	**23.1%**	**66.1%**	**91.8%**	**368.0%**	**87.3%**	**-31.9%**	**187.9%**	**129.4%**	**-75.9%**
Avg % Change	**0.01%**	**1.8%**	**5.1%**	**7.1%**	**28.3%**	**6.8%**	**-2.5%**	**14.5%**	**10.0%**	**-5.8%**
Up Years	8	7	6	8	12	8	7	10	10	5
Down Years	5	6	7	5	1	5	6	3	3	8

Based on annual close; Cowles indices 1881–1885; 12 Mixed Stocks, 10 Rails, 2 Inds 1886–1889;
20 Mixed Stocks, 18 Rails, 2 Inds 1890–1896; Railroad average 1897 (First industrial average published May 26, 1896).

PRESIDENTIAL ELECTION/STOCK MARKET CYCLE: THE 178-YEAR SAGA CONTINUES

It is no mere coincidence that the last two years (pre-election year and election year) of the 44 administrations since 1833 produced a total net market gain of 718.5%, dwarfing the 273.1% gain of the first two years of these administrations.

Presidential elections every four years have a profound impact on the economy and the stock market. Wars, recessions, and bear markets tend to start or occur in the first half of the term; prosperous times and bull markets, in the latter half. After nine straight annual Dow gains during the millennial bull, the four-year election cycle reasserted its overarching domination of market behavior the last 11 years. However, 2008 was the worst presidential election year on record.

STOCK MARKET ACTION SINCE 1833
Annual % Change In Dow Jones Industrial Average[1]

4-Year Cycle Beginning	Elected President	Post-Election Year	Mid-Term Year	Pre-Election Year	Election Year
1833	Jackson (D)	−0.9	13.0	3.1	−11.7
1837	Van Buren (D)	−11.5	1.6	−12.3	5.5
1841*	W.H. Harrison (W)**	−13.3	−18.1	45.0	15.5
1845*	Polk (D)	8.1	−14.5	1.2	−3.6
1849*	Taylor (W)	N/C	18.7	−3.2	19.6
1853*	Pierce (D)	−12.7	−30.2	1.5	4.4
1857	Buchanan (D)	−31.0	14.3	−10.7	14.0
1861*	Lincoln (R)	−1.8	55.4	38.0	6.4
1865	Lincoln (R)**	−8.5	3.6	1.6	10.8
1869	Grant (R)	1.7	5.6	7.3	6.8
1873	Grant (R)	−12.7	2.8	−4.1	−17.9
1877	Hayes (R)	−9.4	6.1	43.0	18.7
1881	Garfield (R)**	3.0	−2.9	−8.5	−18.8
1885*	Cleveland (D)	20.1	12.4	−8.4	4.8
1889*	B. Harrison (R)	5.5	−14.1	17.6	−6.6
1893*	Cleveland (D)	−24.6	−0.6	2.3	−1.7
1897*	McKinley (R)	21.3	22.5	9.2	7.0
1901	McKinley (R)**	−8.7	−0.4	−23.6	41.7
1905	T. Roosevelt (R)	38.2	−1.9	−37.7	46.6
1909	Taft (R)	15.0	−17.9	0.4	7.6
1913*	Wilson (D)	−10.3	−5.4	81.7	−4.2
1917	Wilson (D)	−21.7	10.5	30.5	−32.9
1921*	Harding (R)**	12.7	21.7	−3.3	26.2
1925	Coolidge (R)	30.0	0.3	28.8	48.2
1929	Hoover (R)	−17.2	−33.8	−52.7	−23.1
1933*	F. Roosevelt (D)	66.7	4.1	38.5	24.8
1937	F. Roosevelt (D)	−32.8	28.1	−2.9	−12.7
1941	F. Roosevelt (D)	−15.4	7.6	13.8	12.1
1945	F. Roosevelt (D)**	26.6	−8.1	2.2	−2.1
1949	Truman (D)	12.9	17.6	14.4	8.4
1953*	Eisenhower (R)	−3.8	44.0	20.8	2.3
1957	Eisenhower (R)	−12.8	34.0	16.4	−9.3
1961*	Kennedy (D)**	18.7	−10.8	17.0	14.6
1965	Johnson (D)	10.9	−18.9	15.2	4.3
1969*	Nixon (R)	−15.2	4.8	6.1	14.6
1973	Nixon (R)***	−16.6	−27.6	38.3	17.9
1977*	Carter (D)	−17.3	−3.1	4.2	14.9
1981*	Reagan (R)	−9.2	19.6	20.3	−3.7
1985	Reagan (R)	27.7	22.6	2.3	11.8
1989	G. H. W. Bush (R)	27.0	−4.3	20.3	4.2
1993*	Clinton (D)	13.7	2.1	33.5	26.0
1997	Clinton (D)	22.6	16.1	25.2	−6.2
2001*	G. W. Bush (R)	−7.1	−16.8	25.3	3.1
2005	G. W. Bush (R)	−0.6	16.3	6.4	−33.8
2009*	Obama (D)	18.8	11.0		
Total % Gain		**86.1%**	**187.0%**	**464.0%**	**254.5%**
Average % Gain		**2.0%**	**4.2%**	**10.5%**	**5.8%**
# Up		20	27	33	29
# Down		24	18	11	15

*Party in power ousted   **Death in office   ***Resigned   D–Democrat, W–Whig, R–Republican
[1] Based on annual close; Prior to 1886 based on Cowles and other indices; 12 Mixed Stocks, 10 Rails, 2 Inds 1886–1889; 20 Mixed Stocks, 18 Rails, 2 Inds 1890–1896; Railroad average 1897 (First industrial average published May 26, 1896).

DOW JONES INDUSTRIALS BULL AND BEAR MARKETS SINCE 1900

Bear markets begin at the end of one bull market and end at the start of the next bull market (7/17/90 to 10/11/90 as an example). The high at Dow 3978.36 on 1/31/94, was followed by a 9.7 percent correction. A 10.3 percent correction occurred between the 5/22/96 closing high of 5778 and the intraday low on 7/16/96. The longest bull market on record ended on 7/17/98, and the shortest bear market on record ended on 8/31/98, when the new bull market began. The greatest bull super cycle in history that began 8/12/82 ended in 2000 after the Dow gained 1409% and NASDAQ climbed 3072%. The Dow gained only 497% in the eight-year super bull from 1921 to the top in 1929. NASDAQ suffered its worst loss ever from the 2000 top to the 2002 bottom, down 77.9%, nearly as much as the 89.2% drop in the Dow from the 1929 top to the 1932 bottom. The third longest Dow bull since 1900 that began 10/9/02 ended on its fifth anniversary. The ensuing bear market was the second worst bear market since 1900, slashing the Dow 53.8%. At press time, the current bull market was under pressure, as European debt contagion and geopolitical and economic slowdown fears threaten to end this above average bull. (See page 132 for S&P 500 and NASDAQ bulls and bears.)

DOW JONES INDUSTRIALS BULL AND BEAR MARKETS SINCE 1900

— Beginning —		— Ending —		Bull		Bear	
Date	DJIA	Date	DJIA	% Gain	Days	% Change	Days
9/24/00	38.80	6/17/01	57.33	47.8%	266	−46.1%	875
11/9/03	30.88	1/19/06	75.45	144.3	802	−48.5	665
11/15/07	38.83	11/19/09	73.64	89.6	735	−27.4	675
9/25/11	53.43	9/30/12	68.97	29.1	371	−24.1	668
7/30/14	52.32	11/21/16	110.15	110.5	845	−40.1	393
12/19/17	65.95	11/3/19	119.62	81.4	684	−46.6	660
8/24/21	63.90	3/20/23	105.38	64.9	573	−18.6	221
10/27/23	85.76	9/3/29	381.17	344.5	2138	−47.9	71
11/13/29	198.69	4/17/30	294.07	48.0	155	−86.0	813
7/8/32	41.22	9/7/32	79.93	93.9	61	−37.2	173
2/27/33	50.16	2/5/34	110.74	120.8	343	−22.8	171
7/26/34	85.51	3/10/37	194.40	127.3	958	−49.1	386
3/31/38	98.95	11/12/38	158.41	60.1	226	−23.3	147
4/8/39	121.44	9/12/39	155.92	28.4	157	−40.4	959
4/28/42	92.92	5/29/46	212.50	128.7	1492	−23.2	353
5/17/47	163.21	6/15/48	193.16	18.4	395	−16.3	363
6/13/49	161.60	1/5/53	293.79	81.8	1302	−13.0	252
9/14/53	255.49	4/6/56	521.05	103.9	935	−19.4	564
10/22/57	419.79	1/5/60	685.47	63.3	805	−17.4	294
10/25/60	566.05	12/13/61	734.91	29.8	414	−27.1	195
6/26/62	535.76	2/9/66	995.15	85.7	1324	−25.2	240
10/7/66	744.32	12/3/68	985.21	32.4	788	−35.9	539
5/26/70	631.16	4/28/71	950.82	50.6	337	−16.1	209
11/23/71	797.97	1/11/73	1051.70	31.8	415	−45.1	694
12/6/74	577.60	9/21/76	1014.79	75.7	655	−26.9	525
2/28/78	742.12	9/8/78	907.74	22.3	192	−16.4	591
4/21/80	759.13	4/27/81	1024.05	34.9	371	−24.1	472
8/12/82	776.92	11/29/83	1287.20	65.7	474	−15.6	238
7/24/84	1086.57	8/25/87	2722.42	150.6	1127	−36.1	55
10/19/87	1738.74	7/17/90	2999.75	72.5	1002	−21.2	86
10/11/90	2365.10	7/17/98	9337.97	294.8	2836	−19.3	45
8/31/98	7539.07	1/14/00	11722.98	55.5	501	−29.7	616
9/21/01	8235.81	3/19/02	10635.25	29.1	179	−31.5	204
10/9/02	7286.27	10/9/07	14164.53	94.4	1826	−53.8	517
3/9/09	6547.05	4/29/11	12810.54	95.7*	781*	*At Press Time–not in averages	
		Average		**85.7%**	**755**	**− 31.5%**	**410**

Based on Dow Jones industrial average.   *1900–2000 Data: Ned Davis Research*
The NYSE was closed from 7/31/1914 to 12/11/1914 due to World War I.
DJIA figures were then adjusted back to reflect the composition change from 12 to 20 stocks in September 1916.

STANDARD & POOR'S 500 BULL & BEAR MARKETS SINCE 1929 NASDAQ COMPOSITE SINCE 1971

A constant debate of the definition and timing of bull and bear markets permeates Wall Street like the bell that signals the open and close of every trading day. We have relied on the Ned Davis Research parameters for years to track bulls and bears on the Dow (see page 131). Standard & Poor's 500 index has been a stalwart indicator for decades and at times marched to a different beat than the Dow. With the increasing prominence of NASDAQ as a benchmark, we felt the time had come to add bull and bear data on the other two main stock averages to the *Almanac*. We conferred with Sam Stovall, chief investment strategist at Standard & Poor's, and correlated the moves of the S&P 500 and NASDAQ to the bull and bear dates on page 131 to compile the data below on bull and bear markets for the S&P 500 and NASDAQ. Many dates line up for the three indices, but you will notice quite a lag or lead on several occasions, including NASDAQ's independent cadence from 1975 to 1980.

STANDARD & POOR'S 500 BULL AND BEAR MARKETS

— Beginning —		— Ending —		Bull		Bear	
Date	S&P 500	Date	S&P 500	% Gain	Days	% Change	Days
11/13/29	17.66	4/10/30	25.92	46.8%	148	−83.0%	783
6/1/32	4.40	9/7/32	9.31	111.6	98	−40.6	173
2/27/33	5.53	2/6/34	11.82	113.7	344	−31.8	401
3/14/35	8.06	3/6/37	18.68	131.8	723	−49.0	390
3/31/38	8.50	11/9/38	13.79	62.2	223	−26.2	150
4/8/39	10.18	10/25/39	13.21	29.8	200	−43.5	916
4/28/42	7.47	5/29/46	19.25	157.7	1492	−28.8	353
5/17/47	13.71	6/15/48	17.06	24.4	395	−20.6	363
6/13/49	13.55	1/5/53	26.66	96.8	1302	−14.8	252
9/14/53	22.71	8/2/56	49.74	119.0	1053	−21.6	446
10/22/57	38.98	8/3/59	60.71	55.7	650	−13.9	449
10/25/60	52.30	12/12/61	72.64	38.9	413	−28.0	196
6/26/62	52.32	2/9/66	94.06	79.8	1324	−22.2	240
10/7/66	73.20	11/29/68	108.37	48.0	784	−36.1	543
5/26/70	69.29	4/28/71	104.77	51.2	337	−13.9	209
11/23/71	90.16	1/11/73	120.24	33.4	415	−48.2	630
10/3/74	62.28	9/21/76	107.83	73.1	719	−19.4	531
3/6/78	86.90	9/12/78	106.99	23.1	190	−8.2	562
3/27/80	98.22	11/28/80	140.52	43.1	246	−27.1	622
8/12/82	102.42	10/10/83	172.65	68.6	424	−14.4	288
7/24/84	147.82	8/25/87	336.77	127.8	1127	−33.5	101
12/4/87	223.92	7/16/90	368.95	64.8	955	−19.9	87
10/11/90	295.46	7/17/98	1186.75	301.7	2836	−19.3	45
8/31/98	957.28	3/24/00	1527.46	59.6	571	−36.8	546
9/21/01	965.80	1/4/02	1172.51	21.4	105	−33.8	278
10/9/02	776.76	10/9/07	1565.15	101.5	1826	−56.8	517
3/9/09	676.53	4/29/11	1363.61	101.6*	781*	*At Press Time–not in averages	
			Average	80.2%	727	−30.6%	387

NASDAQ COMPOSITE BULL AND BEAR MARKETS

— Beginning —		— Ending —		Bull		Bear	
Date	NASDAQ	Date	NASDAQ	% Gain	Days	% Change	Days
11/23/71	100.31	1/11/73	136.84	36.4%	415	−59.9%	630
10/3/74	54.87	7/15/75	88.00	60.4	285	−16.2	63
9/16/75	73.78	9/13/78	139.25	88.7	1093	−20.4	62
11/14/78	110.88	2/8/80	165.25	49.0	451	−24.9	48
3/27/80	124.09	5/29/81	223.47	80.1	428	−28.8	441
8/13/82	159.14	6/24/83	328.91	106.7	315	−31.5	397
7/25/84	225.30	8/26/87	455.26	102.1	1127	−35.9	63
10/28/87	291.88	10/9/89	485.73	66.4	712	−33.0	372
10/16/90	325.44	7/20/98	2014.25	518.9	2834	−29.5	80
10/8/98	1419.12	3/10/00	5048.62	255.8	519	−71.8	560
9/21/01	1423.19	1/4/02	2059.38	44.7	105	−45.9	278
10/9/02	1114.11	10/31/07	2859.12	156.6	1848	−55.6	495
3/9/09	1268.64	4/29/11	2873.54	126.5*	781*	*At Press Time– not in averages	
			Average	130.5%	844	−37.8%	291

JANUARY DAILY POINT CHANGES DOW JONES INDUSTRIALS

Previous Month	2002	2003	2004	2005	2006	2007	2008	2009	2010	2011
Close	10021.50	8341.63	10453.92	10783.01	10717.50	12463.15	13264.82	8776.39	10428.05	11577.51
1	H	H	H	S	S	H	H	H	H	S
2	51.90	265.89	-44.07	S	H	H*	-220.86	258.30	S	S
3	98.74	-5.83	S	-53.58	129.91	11.37	12.76	S	S	93.24
4	87.60	S	S	-98.65	32.74	6.17	-256.54	S	155.91	20.43
5	S	S	134.22	-32.95	2.00	-82.68	S	-81.80	-11.94	31.71
6	S	171.88	-5.41	25.05	77.16	S	S	62.21	1.66	-25.58
7	-62.69	-32.98	-9.63	-18.92	S	S	27.31	-245.40	33.18	-22.55
8	-46.50	-145.28	63.41	S	S	25.48	-238.42	-27.24	11.33	S
9	-56.46	180.87	-133.55	S	52.59	-6.89	146.24	-143.28	S	S
10	-26.23	8.71	S	17.07	-0.32	25.56	117.78	S	S	-37.31
11	-80.33	S	S	-64.81	31.86	72.82	-246.79	S	45.80	34.43
12	S	S	26.29	61.56	-81.08	41.10	S	-125.21	-36.73	83.56
13	S	1.09	-58.00	-111.95	-2.49	S	S	-25.41	53.51	-23.54
14	-96.11	56.64	111.19	52.17	S	S	171.85	-248.42	29.78	55.48
15	32.73	-119.44	15.48	S	S	H	-277.04	12.35	-100.90	S
16	-211.88	-25.31	46.66	S	H	26.51	-34.95	68.73	S	S
17	137.77	-111.13	S	H	-63.55	-5.44	-306.95	S	S	H
18	-78.19	S	S	70.79	-41.46	-9.22	-59.91	S	H	50.55
19	S	S	H	-88.82	25.85	-2.40	S	H	115.78	-12.64
20	S	H	-71.85	-68.50	-213.32	S	S	-332.13	-122.28	-2.49
21	H	-143.84	94.96	-78.48	S	S	H	279.01	-213.27	49.04
22	-58.05	-124.17	-0.44	S	S	-88.37	-128.11	-105.30	-216.90	S
23	17.16	50.74	-54.89	S	21.38	56.64	298.98	-45.24	S	S
24	65.11	-238.46	S	-24.38	23.45	87.97	108.44	S	S	108.68
25	44.01	S	S	92.95	-2.48	-119.21	-171.44	S	23.88	-3.33
26	S	S	134.22	37.03	99.73	-15.54	S	38.47	-2.57	8.25
27	S	-141.45	-92.59	-31.19	97.74	S	S	58.70	41.87	4.39
28	25.67	99.28	-141.55	-40.20	S	S	176.72	200.72	-115.70	-166.13
29	-247.51	21.87	41.92	S	S	3.76	96.41	-226.44	-53.13	S
30	144.62	-165.58	-22.22	S	-7.29	32.53	-37.47	-148.15	S	S
31	157.14	108.68	S	62.74	-35.06	98.38	207.53	S	S	68.23
Close	9920.00	8053.81	10488.07	10489.94	10864.86	12621.69	12650.36	8000.86	10067.33	11891.93
Change	-101.50	-287.82	34.15	-293.07	147.36	158.54	-614.46	-775.53	-360.72	314.42

* Ford funeral

FEBRUARY DAILY POINT CHANGES DOW JONES INDUSTRIALS

Previous Month	2002	2003	2004	2005	2006	2007	2008	2009	2010	2011
Close	9920.00	8053.81	10488.07	10489.94	10864.86	12621.69	12650.36	8000.86	10067.33	11891.93
1	-12.74	S	S	62.00	89.09	51.99	92.83	S	118.20	148.23
2	S	S	11.11	44.85	-101.97	-20.19	S	-64.03	111.32	1.81
3	S	56.01	6.00	-3.69	-58.36	S	S	141.53	-26.30	20.29
4	-220.17	-96.53	-34.44	123.03	S	S	-108.03	-121.70	-268.37	29.89
5	-1.66	-28.11	24.81	S	S	8.25	-370.03	106.41	10.05	S
6	-32.04	-55.88	97.48	S	4.65	4.57	-65.03	217.52	S	S
7	-27.95	-65.07	S	-0.37	-48.51	0.56	46.90	S	S	69.48
8	118.80	S	S	8.87	108.86	-29.24	-64.87	S	-103.84	71.52
9	S	S	-14.00	-60.52	24.73	-56.80	S	-9.72	150.25	6.74
10	S	55.88	34.82	85.50	35.70	S	S	-381.99	-20.26	-10.60
11	140.54	-77.00	123.85	46.40	S	S	57.88	50.65	105.81	43.97
12	-21.04	-84.94	-43.63	S	S	-28.28	133.40	-6.77	-45.05	S
13	125.93	-8.30	-66.22	S	-26.73	102.30	178.83	-82.35	S	S
14	12.32	158.93	S	-4.88	136.07	87.01	-175.26	S	S	-5.07
15	-98.95	S	S	46.19	30.58	23.15	-28.77	S	H	-41.55
16	S	S	H	-2.44	61.71	2.56	S	H	169.67	61.53
17	S	H	87.03	-80.62	-5.36	S	H	-297.81	40.43	29.97
18	H	132.35	-42.89	30.96	S	S	H	3.03	83.66	73.11
19	-157.90	-40.55	-7.26	S	S	H	-10.99	-89.68	9.45	S
20	196.03	-85.64	-45.70	S	H	19.07	90.04	-100.28	S	S
21	-106.49	103.15	S	H	-46.26	-48.23	-142.96	S	S	H
22	133.47	S	S	-174.02	68.11	-52.39	96.72	S	-18.97	-178.46
23	S	S	-9.41	62.59	-67.95	-38.54	S	-250.89	-100.97	-107.01
24	S	-159.87	-43.25	75.00	-7.37	S	S	236.16	91.75	-37.28
25	177.56	51.26	35.25	92.81	S	S	189.20	-80.05	-53.13	61.95
26	-30.45	-102.52	-21.48	S	S	-15.22	114.70	-88.81	4.23	S
27	12.32	78.01	3.78	S	35.70	-416.02	9.36	-119.15	S	S
28	-21.45	6.09	S	-75.37	-104.14	52.39	-112.10	S	S	95.89
29	—	—	S	—	—	—	-315.79	—	—	—
Close	10106.13	7891.08	10583.92	10766.23	10993.41	12268.63	12266.39	7062.93	10325.26	12226.34
Change	186.13	-162.73	95.85	276.29	128.55	-353.06	-383.97	-937.93	257.93	334.41

133

MARCH DAILY POINT CHANGES DOW JONES INDUSTRIALS

Previous Month	2002	2003	2004	2005	2006	2007	2008	2009	2010	2011
Close	10495.28	10106.13	7891.08	10583.92	10766.23	10993.41	12268.63	12266.39	7062.93	10325.26
1	262.73	S	94.22	63.77	60.12	-34.29	S	S	78.53	-168.32
2	S	S	-86.66	-18.03	-28.02	-120.24	S	-299.64	2.19	8.78
3	S	-53.22	1.63	21.06	-3.92	S	-7.49	-37.27	-9.22	191.40
4	217.96	-132.99	-5.11	107.52	S	S	-45.10	149.82	47.38	-88.32
5	-153.41	70.73	7.55	S	S	-63.69	41.19	-281.40	122.06	S
6	140.88	-101.61	S	S	-63.00	157.18	-214.60	32.50	S	S
7	-48.92	66.04	S	-3.69	22.10	-15.14	-146.70	S	S	-79.85
8	47.12	S	-66.07	-24.24	25.05	68.25	S	S	-13.68	124.35
9	S	S	-72.52	-107.00	-33.46	15.62	S	-79.89	11.86	-1.29
10	S	-171.85	-160.07	45.89	104.06	S	-153.54	379.44	2.95	-228.48
11	38.75	-44.12	-168.51	-77.15	S	S	416.66	3.91	44.51	59.79
12	21.11	28.01	111.70	S	S	42.30	-46.57	239.66	12.85	S
13	-130.50	269.68	S	S	-0.32	-242.66	35.50	53.92	S	S
14	15.29	37.96	S	30.15	75.32	57.44	-194.65	S	S	-51.24
15	90.09	S	-137.19	-59.41	58.43	26.28	S	S	17.46	-137.74
16	S	S	81.78	-112.03	43.47	-49.27	S	-7.01	43.83	-242.12
17	S	282.21	115.63	-6.72	26.41	S	21.16	178.73	47.69	161.29
18	-29.48	52.31	-4.52	3.32	S	S	420.41	90.88	45.50	83.93
19	57.50	71.22	-109.18	S	S	115.76	-293.00	-85.78	-37.19	S
20	-133.68	21.15	S	S	-5.12	61.93	261.66	-122.42	S	S
21	-21.73	235.37	S	-64.28	-39.06	159.42	H	S	S	178.01
22	-52.17	S	-121.85	-94.88	81.96	13.62	S	S	43.91	-17.90
23	S	S	-1.11	-14.49	-47.14	19.87	S	497.48	102.94	67.39
24	S	-307.29	-15.41	-13.15	9.68	S	187.32	-115.89	-52.68	84.54
25	-146.00	65.55	170.59	H	S	S	-16.04	89.84	5.06	50.03
26	71.69	-50.35	-5.85	S	S	-11.94	-109.74	174.75	9.15	S
27	73.55	-28.43	S	S	-29.86	-71.78	-120.40	-148.38	S	S
28	-22.97	-55.68	S	42.78	-95.57	-96.93	-86.06	S	S	-22.71
29	H	S	116.66	-79.95	61.16	48.39	S	S	45.50	81.13
30	S	S	52.07	135.23	-65.00	5.60	S	-254.16	11.56	71.60
31	S	-153.64	-24.00	-37.17	-41.38	S	46.49	86.90	-50.79	-30.88
Close	10403.94	7992.13	10357.70	10503.76	11109.32	12354.35	12262.89	7608.92	10856.63	12319.73
Change	297.81	101.05	-226.22	-262.47	115.91	85.72	-3.50	545.99	531.37	93.39

APRIL DAILY POINT CHANGES DOW JONES INDUSTRIALS

Previous Month	2002	2003	2004	2005	2006	2007	2008	2009	2010	2011
Close	10403.94	7992.13	10357.70	10503.76	11109.32	12354.35	12262.89	7608.92	10856.63	12319.73
1	-41.24	77.73	15.63	-99.46	S	S	391.47	152.68	70.44	56.99
2	-48.99	215.20	97.26	S	S	27.95	-48.53	216.48	H	S
3	-115.42	-44.68	S	S	35.62	128.00	20.20	39.51	S	S
4	36.88	36.77	S	16.84	58.91	19.75	-16.61	S	S	23.31
5	36.47	S	87.78	37.32	35.70	30.15	S	S	46.48	-6.13
6	S	S	12.44	27.56	-23.05	H	S	-41.74	-3.56	32.85
7	S	23.26	-90.66	60.30	-96.46	S	3.01	-186.29	-72.47	-17.26
8	-22.56	-1.49	-38.12	-84.98	S	S	-35.99	47.55	29.55	-29.44
9	-40.41	-100.98	H	S	S	8.94	-49.18	246.27	70.28	S
10	173.06	23.39	S	S	21.29	4.71	54.72	H	S	S
11	-205.65	-17.92	S	-12.78	-51.70	-89.23	-256.56	S	S	1.06
12	14.74	S	73.53	59.41	40.34	68.34	S	S	8.62	-117.53
13	S	S	-134.28	-104.04	7.68	59.17	S	-25.57	13.45	7.41
14	S	147.69	-3.33	-125.18	H	S	-23.36	-137.63	103.69	14.16
15	-97.15	51.26	19.51	-191.24	S	S	60.41	109.44	21.46	56.68
16	207.65	-144.75	54.51	S	S	108.33	256.80	95.81	-125.91	S
17	-80.54	80.04	S	S	-63.87	52.58	1.22	5.90	S	S
18	-15.50	H	S	-16.26	194.99	30.80	228.87	S	S	-140.24
19	51.83	S	-14.12	56.16	10.00	4.79	S	S	73.39	65.16
20	S	S	-123.35	-115.05	64.12	153.35	S	-289.60	25.01	186.79
21	S	-8.75	2.77	206.24	4.56	S	-24.34	127.83	7.86	52.45
22	-120.68	156.09	143.93	-60.89	S	S	-104.79	-82.99	9.37	H
23	-47.19	30.67	11.64	S	S	-42.58	42.99	70.49	69.99	S
24	-58.81	-75.62	S	S	-11.13	34.54	85.73	119.23	S	S
25	4.63	-133.69	S	84.76	-53.07	135.95	42.91	S	S	-26.11
26	-124.34	S	-28.11	-91.34	71.24	15.61	S	S	0.75	115.49
27	S	S	33.43	47.67	28.02	15.44	S	-51.29	-213.04	95.59
28	S	165.26	-135.56	-128.43	-15.37	S	-20.11	-8.05	53.28	72.35
29	-90.85	31.38	-70.33	122.14	S	S	-39.81	168.78	122.05	47.23
30	126.35	-22.90	-46.70	S	S	-58.03	-11.81	-17.61	-158.71	S
Close	9946.22	8480.09	10225.57	10192.51	11367.14	13062.91	12820.13	8168.12	11008.61	12810.54
Change	-457.72	487.96	-132.13	-311.25	257.82	708.56	557.24	559.20	151.98	490.81

MAY DAILY POINT CHANGES DOW JONES INDUSTRIALS

Previous Month Close	2001	2002	2003	2004	2005	2006	2007	2008	2009	2010
Close	10734.97	9946.22	8480.09	10225.57	10192.51	11367.14	13062.91	12820.13	8168.12	11008.61
1	163.37	113.41	-25.84	S	S	-23.85	73.23	189.87	44.29	S
2	-21.66	32.24	128.43	S	59.19	73.16	75.74	48.20	S	S
3	-80.03	-85.24	S	88.43	5.25	-16.17	29.50	S	S	143.22
4	154.59	S	S	3.20	127.69	38.58	23.24	S	214.33	-225.06
5	S	S	-51.11	-6.25	-44.26	138.88	S	-88.66	-16.09	-58.65
6	S	-198.59	56.79	-69.69	5.02	S	S	51.29	101.63	-347.80
7	-16.07	28.51	-27.73	-123.92	S	S	48.35	-206.48	-102.43	-139.89
8	-51.66	305.28	-69.41	S	S	6.80	-3.90	52.43	164.80	S
9	-16.53	-104.41	113.38	S	38.94	55.23	53.80	-120.90	S	S
10	43.46	-97.50	S	-127.32	-103.23	2.88	-147.74	S	S	404.71
11	-89.13	S	S	29.45	19.14	-141.92	111.09	S	-155.88	-36.88
12	S	S	122.13	25.69	-110.77	-119.74	S	130.43	50.34	148.65
13	S	169.74	-47.48	-34.42	-49.36	S	S	-44.13	-184.22	-113.96
14	56.02	188.48	-31.43	2.13	S	S	20.56	66.20	46.43	-162.79
15	-4.36	-54.46	65.32	S	S	47.78	37.06	94.28	-62.68	S
16	342.95	45.53	-34.17	S	112.17	-8.88	103.69	-5.86	S	S
17	32.66	63.87	S	-105.96	79.59	-214.28	-10.81	S	S	5.67
18	53.16	S	S	61.60	132.57	-77.32	79.81	S	235.44	-114.88
19	S	S	-185.58	-30.80	28.74	15.77	S	41.36	-29.23	-66.58
20	S	-123.58	-2.03	-0.07	-21.28	S	S	-199.48	-52.81	-376.36
21	36.18	-123.79	25.07	29.10	S	S	-13.65	-227.49	-129.91	125.38
22	-80.68	52.17	77.59	S	S	-18.73	-2.93	24.43	-14.81	S
23	-151.73	58.20	7.36	S	51.65	-26.98	-14.30	-145.99	S	S
24	16.91	-111.82	S	-8.31	-19.88	18.97	-84.52	S	S	-126.82
25	-117.05	S	S	159.19	-45.88	93.73	66.15	S	S	-22.82
26	S	S	H	-7.73	79.80	67.56	S	S	196.17	-69.30
27	S	H	179.97	95.31	4.95	S	S	68.72	-173.47	284.54
28	H	-122.68	11.77	-16.75	S	S	H	45.68	103.78	-122.36
29	33.77	-58.54	-81.94	S	S	H	14.06	52.19	96.53	S
30	-166.50	-11.35	139.08	S	H	-184.18	111.74	-7.90	S	S
31	39.30	13.56	S	H	-75.07	73.88	-5.44	S	S	H
Close	10911.94	9925.25	8850.26	10188.45	10467.48	11168.31	13627.64	12638.32	8500.33	10136.63
Change	176.97	-20.97	370.17	-37.12	274.97	-198.83	564.73	-181.81	332.21	-871.98

JUNE DAILY POINT CHANGES DOW JONES INDUSTRIALS

Previous Month Close	2001	2002	2003	2004	2005	2006	2007	2008	2009	2010
Close	10911.94	9925.25	8850.26	10188.45	10467.48	11168.31	13627.64	12638.32	8500.33	10136.63
1	78.47	S	S	14.20	82.39	91.97	40.47	S	221.11	-112.61
2	S	S	47.55	60.32	3.62	-12.41	S	-134.50	19.43	225.52
3	S	-215.46	25.14	-67.06	-92.52	S	S	-100.97	-65.59	5.74
4	71.11	-21.95	116.03	46.91	S	S	8.21	-12.37	74.96	-323.31
5	114.32	108.96	2.32	S	S	-199.15	-80.86	213.97	12.89	S
6	-105.60	-172.16	21.49	S	6.06	-46.58	-129.79	-394.64	S	S
7	20.50	-34.97	S	148.26	16.04	-71.24	-198.94	S	S	-115.48
8	-113.74	S	S	41.44	-6.21	7.92	157.66	S	1.36	123.49
9	S	S	-82.79	-64.08	26.16	-46.90	S	70.51	-1.43	-40.73
10	S	55.73	74.89	41.66	9.61	S	S	9.44	-24.04	273.28
11	-54.91	-128.14	128.33	H*	S	S	0.57	-205.99	31.90	38.54
12	26.29	100.45	13.33	S	S	-99.34	-129.95	57.81	28.34	S
13	-76.76	-114.91	-79.43	S	9.93	-86.44	187.34	165.77	S	S
14	-181.49	-28.59	S	-75.37	25.01	110.78	71.37	S	S	-20.18
15	-66.49	S	S	45.70	18.80	198.27	85.76	S	-187.13	213.88
16	S	S	201.84	-0.85	12.28	-0.64	S	S	-107.46	4.69
17	S	213.21	4.06	-2.06	44.42	S	S	-108.78	-7.49	24.71
18	21.74	18.70	-29.22	38.89	S	S	-26.50	-131.24	58.42	16.47
19	-48.71	-144.55	-114.27	S	S	-72.44	22.44	34.03	-15.87	S
20	50.66	-129.80	21.22	S	-13.96	32.73	-146.00	-220.40	S	S
21	68.10	-177.98	S	-44.94	-9.44	104.62	56.42	S	S	-8.23
22	-110.84	S	S	23.60	-11.74	-60.35	-185.58	S	-200.72	-148.89
23	S	S	-127.80	84.50	-166.49	-30.02	S	-0.33	-16.10	4.92
24	S	28.03	36.90	-35.76	-123.60	S	S	-34.93	-23.05	-145.64
25	-100.37	-155.00	-98.32	-71.97	S	S	-8.21	4.40	172.54	-8.99
26	-31.74	-6.71	67.51	S	S	56.19	-14.39	-358.41	-34.01	S
27	-37.64	149.81	-89.99	S	-7.06	-120.54	90.07	-106.91	S	S
28	131.37	-26.66	S	-14.75	114.85	48.82	-5.45	S	S	-5.29
29	-63.81	S	S	56.34	-31.15	217.24	-13.66	S	90.99	-268.22
30	S	S	-3.61	22.05	-99.51	-40.58	S	3.50	-82.38	-96.28
Close	10502.40	9243.26	8985.44	10435.48	10274.97	11150.22	13408.62	11350.01	8447.00	9774.02
Change	-409.54	-681.99	135.18	247.03	-192.51	-18.09	-219.02	-1288.31	-53.33	-362.61

*Reagan funeral

JULY DAILY POINT CHANGES DOW JONES INDUSTRIALS

	2001	2002	2003	2004	2005	2006	2007	2008	2009	2010
Previous Month Close	10502.40	9243.26	8985.44	10435.48	10274.97	11150.22	13408.62	11350.01	8447.00	9774.02
1	S	-133.47	55.51	-101.32	28.47	S	S	32.25	57.06	-41.49
2	91.32	-102.04	101.89	-51.33	S	S	126.81	-166.75	-223.32	-46.05
3	-22.61*	47.22	-72.63*	S	S	77.80*	41.87*	73.03*	H	S
4	H	H	H	S	H	H	H	H	S	H
5	-91.25	324.53*	S	H	68.36	-76.20	-11.46	S	S	H
6	-227.18	S	S	-63.49	-101.12	73.48	45.84	S	44.13	57.14
7	S	S	146.58	20.95	31.61	-134.63	S	-56.58	-161.27	274.66
8	S	-104.60	6.30	-68.73	146.85	S	S	152.25	14.81	120.71
9	46.72	-178.81	-66.88	41.66	S	S	38.29	-236.77	4.76	59.04
10	-123.76	-282.59	-120.17	S	S	12.88	-148.27	81.58	-36.65	S
11	65.38	-11.97	83.55	S	70.58	31.22	76.17	-128.48	S	S
12	237.97	-117.00	S	25.00	-5.83	-121.59	283.86	S	S	18.24
13	60.07	S	S	9.37	43.50	-166.89	45.52	S	185.16	146.75
14	S	S	57.56	-38.79	71.50	-106.94	S	-45.35	27.81	3.70
15	S	-45.34	-48.18	-45.64	11.94	S	S	-92.65	256.72	-7.41
16	-66.94	-166.08	-34.38	-23.38	S	S	43.73	276.74	95.61	-261.41
17	134.27	69.37	-43.77	S	S	8.01	20.57	207.38	32.12	S
18	-36.56	-132.99	137.33	S	-65.84	51.87	-53.33	49.91	S	S
19	40.17	-390.23	S	-45.72	71.57	212.19	82.19	S	S	56.53
20	-33.35	S	S	55.01	42.59	-83.32	-149.33	S	104.21	75.53
21	S	S	-91.46	-102.94	-61.38	-59.72	S	-29.23	67.79	-109.43
22	S	-234.68	61.76	4.20	23.41	S	S	135.16	-34.68	201.77
23	-152.23	-82.24	35.79	-88.11	S	S	92.34	29.88	188.03	102.32
24	-183.30	488.95	-81.73	S	S	182.67	-226.47	-283.10	23.95	S
25	164.55	-4.98	172.06	S	-54.70	52.66	68.12	21.41	S	S
26	49.96	78.08	S	-0.30	-16.71	-1.20	-311.50	S	S	100.81
27	-38.96	S	S	123.22	57.32	-2.08	-208.10	S	15.27	12.26
28	S	S	-18.06	31.93	68.46	119.27	S	-239.61	-11.79	-39.81
29	S	447.49	-62.05	12.17	-64.64	S	S	266.48	-26.00	-30.72
30	-14.95	-31.85	-4.41	10.47	S	S	92.84	186.13	83.74	-1.22
31	121.09	56.56	33.75	S	S	-34.02	-146.32	-205.67	17.15	S
Close	10522.81	8736.59	9233.80	10139.71	10640.91	11185.68	13211.99	11378.02	9171.61	10465.94
Change	20.41	-506.67	248.36	-295.77	365.94	35.46	-196.63	28.01	724.61	691.92

* Shortened trading day

AUGUST DAILY POINT CHANGES DOW JONES INDUSTRIALS

	2001	2002	2003	2004	2005	2006	2007	2008	2009	2010
Previous Month Close	10522.81	8736.59	9233.80	10139.71	10640.91	11185.68	13211.99	11378.02	9171.61	10465.94
1	-12.80	-229.97	-79.83	S	-17.76	-59.95	150.38	-51.70	S	S
2	41.17	-193.49	S	39.45	60.59	74.20	100.96	S	S	208.44
3	-38.40	S	S	-58.92	13.85	42.66	-281.42	S	114.95	-38.00
4	S	S	32.07	6.27	-87.49	-2.24	S	-42.17	33.63	44.05
5	S	-269.50	-149.72	-163.48	-52.07	S	S	331.62	-39.22	-5.45
6	-111.47	230.46	25.42	-147.70	S	S	286.87	40.30	-24.71	-21.42
7	57.43	182.06	64.71	S	S	-20.97	35.52	-224.64	113.81	S
8	-165.24	255.87	64.64	S	-21.10	-45.79	153.56	302.89	S	S
9	5.06	33.43	S	-0.67	78.74	-97.41	-387.18	S	S	45.19
10	117.69	S	S	130.01	-21.26	48.19	-31.14	S	-32.12	-54.50
11	S	S	26.26	-6.35	91.48	-36.34	S	48.03	-96.50	-265.42
12	S	-56.56	92.71	-123.73	-85.58	S	S	-139.88	120.16	-58.88
13	-0.34	-206.50	-38.30	10.76	S	S	-3.01	-109.51	36.58	-16.80
14	-3.74	260.92	38.80	S	S	9.84	-207.61	82.97	-76.79	S
15	-66.22	74.83	11.13	S	34.07	132.39	-167.45	43.97	S	S
16	46.57	-40.08	S	129.20	-120.93	96.86	-15.69	S	S	-1.14
17	-151.74	S	S	18.28	37.26	7.84	233.30	S	-186.06	103.84
18	S	S	90.76	110.32	4.22	46.51	S	-180.51	82.60	9.69
19	S	212.73	16.45	-42.33	4.30	S	S	-130.84	61.22	-144.33
20	79.29	-118.72	-31.39	69.32	S	S	42.27	68.88	70.89	-57.59
21	-145.93	85.16	26.17	S	S	-36.42	-30.49	12.78	155.91	S
22	102.76	96.41	-74.81	S	10.66	-5.21	145.27	197.85	S	S
23	-47.75	-180.68	S	-37.09	-50.31	-41.94	-0.25	S	S	-39.21
24	194.02	S	S	25.58	-84.71	6.56	142.99	S	3.32	-133.96
25	S	S	-31.23	83.11	15.76	-20.41	S	-241.81	30.01	19.61
26	S	46.05	22.81	-8.33	-53.34	S	S	26.62	4.23	-74.25
27	-40.82	-94.60	-6.66	21.60	S	S	-56.74	89.64	37.11	164.84
28	-160.32	-130.32	40.42	S	S	67.96	-280.28	212.67	-36.43	S
29	-131.13	-23.10	41.61	S	65.76	17.93	247.44	-171.63	S	S
30	-171.32	-7.49	S	-72.49	-50.23	12.97	-50.56	S	S	-140.92
31	30.17	S	S	51.40	68.78	-1.76	119.01	S	-47.92	4.99
Close	9949.75	8663.50	9415.82	10173.92	10481.60	11381.15	13357.74	11543.55	9496.28	10014.72
Change	-573.06	-73.09	182.02	34.21	-159.31	195.47	145.75	165.53	324.67	-451.22

SEPTEMBER DAILY POINT CHANGES DOW JONES INDUSTRIALS

Previous Month Close	2001	2002	2003	2004	2005	2006	2007	2008	2009	2010
	9949.75	8663.50	9415.82	10173.92	10481.60	11381.15	13357.74	11543.55	9496.28	10014.72
1	S	S	H	-5.46	-21.97	83.00	S	H	-185.68	254.75
2	S	H	107.45	121.82	-12.26	S	S	-26.63	-29.93	50.63
3	H	-355.45	45.19	-30.08	S	S	H	15.96	63.94	157.83
4	47.74	117.07	19.44	S	S	H	91.12	-344.65	96.66	S
5	35.78	-141.42	-84.56	S	H	5.13	-143.39	32.73	S	S
6	-192.43	143.50	S	H	141.87	-63.08	57.88	S	S	H
7	-234.99	S	S	82.59	44.26	-74.76	-249.97	S	H	-137.24
8	S	S	82.95	-29.43	-37.57	60.67	S	289.78	56.07	46.32
9	S	92.18	-79.09	-24.26	82.63	S	S	-280.01	49.88	28.23
10	-0.34	83.23	-86.74	23.97	S	S	14.47	38.19	80.26	47.53
11	Closed*	-21.44	39.30	S	S	4.73	180.54	164.79	-22.07	S
12	Closed*	-201.76	11.79	S	4.38	101.25	-16.74	-11.72	S	S
13	Closed*	-66.72	S	1.69	-85.50	45.23	133.23	S	S	81.36
14	Closed*	S	S	3.40	-52.54	-15.93	17.64	S	21.39	-17.64
15	S	S	-22.74	-86.80	13.85	33.38	S	-504.48	56.61	46.24
16	S	67.49	118.53	13.13	83.19	S	S	141.51	108.30	22.10
17	-684.81	-172.63	-21.69	39.97	S	S	-39.10	-449.36	-7.79	13.02
18	-17.30	-35.10	113.48	S	S	-5.77	335.97	410.03	36.28	S
19	-144.27	-230.06	-14.31	S	-84.31	-14.09	76.17	368.75	S	S
20	-382.92	43.63	S	-79.57	-76.11	72.28	-48.86	S	S	145.77
21	-140.40	S	S	40.04	-103.49	-79.96	53.49	S	-41.34	7.41
22	S	S	-109.41	-135.75	44.02	-25.13	S	-372.75	51.01	-21.72
23	S	-113.87	40.63	-70.28	-2.46	S	S	-161.52	-81.32	-76.89
24	368.05	-189.02	-150.53	8.34	S	S	-61.13	-29.00	-41.11	197.84
25	56.11	158.69	-81.55	S	S	67.71	19.59	196.89	-42.25	S
26	-92.58	155.30	-30.88	S	24.04	93.58	99.50	121.07	S	S
27	114.03	-295.67	S	-58.70	12.58	19.85	34.79	S	S	-48.22
28	166.14	S	S	88.86	16.88	29.21	-17.31	S	124.17	46.10
29	S	S	67.16	58.84	79.69	-39.38	S	-777.68	-47.16	-22.86
30	S	-109.52	-105.18	-55.97	15.92	S	S	485.21	-29.92	-47.23
Close	8847.56	7591.93	9275.06	10080.27	10568.70	11679.07	13895.63	10850.66	9712.28	10788.05
Change	-1102.19	-1071.57	-140.76	-93.65	87.10	297.92	537.89	-692.89	216.00	773.33

* Market closed for four days following 9/11 terrorist attacks

OCTOBER DAILY POINT CHANGES DOW JONES INDUSTRIALS

Previous Month Close	2001	2002	2003	2004	2005	2006	2007	2008	2009	2010
	8847.56	7591.93	9275.06	10080.27	10568.70	11679.07	13895.63	10850.66	9712.28	10788.05
1	-10.73	346.86	194.14	112.38	S	S	191.92	-19.59	-203.00	41.63
2	113.76	-183.18	18.60	S	S	-8.72	-40.24	-348.22	-21.61	S
3	173.19	-38.42	84.51	S	-33.22	56.99	-79.26	-157.47	S	S
4	-62.90	-188.79	S	23.89	-94.37	123.27	6.26	S	S	-78.41
5	58.89	S	S	-38.86	-123.75	16.08	91.70	S	112.08	193.45
6	S	S	22.67	62.24	-30.26	-16.48	S	-369.88	131.50	22.93
7	S	-105.56	59.63	-114.52	5.21	S	S	-508.39	-5.67	-19.07
8	-51.83	78.65	-23.71	-70.20	S	S	-22.28	-189.01	61.29	57.90
9	-15.50	-215.22	49.11	S	S	7.60	120.80	-678.91	78.07	S
10	188.42	247.68	-5.33	S	-53.55	9.36	-85.84	-128.00	S	S
11	169.59	316.34	S	26.77	14.41	-15.04	-63.57	S	S	3.86
12	-66.29	S	S	-4.79	-36.26	95.57	77.96	S	20.86	10.06
13	S	S	89.70	-74.85	-0.32	12.81	S	936.42	-14.74	75.68
14	S	27.11	48.60	-107.88	70.75	S	S	-76.62	144.80	-1.51
15	3.46	378.28	-9.93	38.93	S	S	-108.28	-733.08	47.08	-31.79
16	36.61	-219.65	-11.33	S	S	20.09	-71.86	401.35	-67.03	S
17	-151.26	239.01	-69.93	S	60.76	-30.58	-20.40	-127.04	S	S
18	-69.75	47.36	S	22.94	-62.84	42.66	-3.58	S	S	80.91
19	40.89	S	S	-58.70	128.87	19.05	-366.94	S	96.28	-165.07
20	S	S	56.15	-10.69	-133.03	-9.36	S	413.21	-50.71	129.35
21	S	215.84	-30.30	-21.17	-65.88	S	S	-231.77	-92.12	38.60
22	172.92	-88.08	-149.40	-107.95	S	S	44.95	-514.45	131.95	-14.01
23	-36.95	44.11	14.89	S	S	114.54	109.26	172.04	-109.13	S
24	5.54	-176.93	-30.67	S	169.78	10.97	-0.98	-312.30	S	S
25	117.28	126.65	S	-7.82	-7.13	6.80	-3.33	S	S	31.49
26	82.27	S	S	138.49	-32.89	28.98	134.78	S	-104.22	5.41
27	S	S	25.70	113.55	-115.03	-73.40	S	-203.18	14.21	-43.18
28	S	-75.95	140.15	2.51	172.82	S	S	889.35	-119.48	-12.33
29	-275.67	0.90	26.22	22.93	S	S	63.56	-74.16	199.89	4.54
30	-147.52	58.47	12.08	S	S	-3.76	-77.79	189.73	-249.85	S
31	-46.84	-30.38	14.51	S	37.30	-5.77	137.54	144.32	S	S
Close	9075.14	8397.03	9801.12	10027.47	10440.07	12080.73	13930.01	9325.01	9712.73	11118.49
Change	227.58	805.10	526.06	-52.80	-128.63	401.66	34.38	-1525.65	0.45	330.44

NOVEMBER DAILY POINT CHANGES DOW JONES INDUSTRIALS

	2001	2002	2003	2004	2005	2006	2007	2008	2009	2010
Previous Month Close	9075.14	8397.03	9801.12	10027.47	10440.07	12080.73	13930.01	9325.01	9712.73	11118.49
1	188.76	120.61	S	26.92	-33.30	-49.71	-362.14	S	S	6.13
2	59.64	S	S	-18.66	65.96	-12.48	27.23	S	76.71	64.10
3	S	S	57.34	101.32	49.86	-32.50	S	-5.18	-17.53	26.41
4	S	53.96	-19.63	177.71	8.17	S	S	305.45	30.23	219.71
5	117.49	106.67	-18.00	72.78	S	S	-51.70	-486.01	203.82	9.24
6	150.09	92.74	36.14	S	S	119.51	117.54	-443.48	17.46	S
7	-36.75	-184.77	-47.18	S	55.47	51.22	-360.92	248.02	S	S
8	33.15	-49.11	S	3.77	-46.51	19.77	-33.73	S	S	-37.24
9	20.48	S	S	-4.94	6.49	-73.24	-223.55	S	203.52	-60.09
10	S	S	-53.26	-0.89	93.89	5.13	S	-73.27	20.03	10.29
11	S	-178.18	-18.74	84.36	45.94	S	S	-176.58	44.29	-73.94
12	-53.63	27.05	111.04	69.17	S	S	-55.19	-411.30	-93.79	-90.52
13	196.58	12.49	-10.89	S	S	23.45	319.54	552.59	73.00	S
14	72.66	143.64	-69.26	S	11.13	86.13	-76.08	-337.94	S	S
15	48.78	36.96	S	11.23	-10.73	33.70	-120.96	S	S	9.39
16	-5.40	S	S	-62.59	-11.68	54.11	66.74	S	136.49	-178.47
17	S	S	-57.85	61.92	45.46	36.74	S	-223.73	30.46	-15.62
18	S	-92.52	-86.67	22.98	46.11	S	S	151.17	-11.11	173.35
19	109.47	-11.79	66.30	-115.64	S	S	-218.35	-427.47	-93.87	22.32
20	-75.08	148.23	-71.04	S	S	-26.02	51.70	-444.99	-14.28	S
21	-66.70	222.14	9.11	S	53.95	5.05	-211.10	494.13	S	S
22	H	-40.31	S	32.51	51.15	5.36	H	S	S	-24.97
23	125.03*	S	S	3.18	44.66	H	181.84*	S	132.79	-142.21
24	S	S	119.26	27.71	H	-46.78*	S	396.97	-17.24	150.91
25	S	44.56	16.15	H	15.53*	S	S	36.08	30.69	H
26	23.04	-172.98	15.63	1.92*	S	S	-237.44	247.14	H	-95.28*
27	-110.15	255.26	H	S	S	-158.46	215.00	H	-154.48*	S
28	-160.74	H	2.89*	S	-40.90	14.74	331.01	102.43*	S	S
29	117.56	-35.59*	S	-46.33	-2.56	90.28	22.28	S	S	-39.51
30	22.14	S	S	-47.88	-82.29	-4.80	59.99	S	34.92	-46.47
Close	9851.56	8896.09	9782.46	10428.02	10805.87	12221.93	13371.72	8829.04	10344.84	11006.02
Change	776.42	499.06	-18.66	400.55	365.80	141.20	-558.29	-495.97	632.11	-112.47

Shortened trading day

DECEMBER DAILY POINT CHANGES DOW JONES INDUSTRIALS

	2001	2002	2003	2004	2005	2006	2007	2008	2009	2010
Previous Month Close	9851.56	8896.09	9782.46	10428.02	10805.87	12221.93	13371.72	8829.04	10344.84	11006.02
1	S	S	116.59	162.20	106.70	-27.80	S	-679.95	126.74	249.76
2	S	-33.52	-45.41	-5.10	-35.06	S	S	270.00	-18.90	106.63
3	-87.60	-119.64	19.78	7.09	S	S	-57.15	172.60	-86.53	19.68
4	129.88	-5.08	57.40	S	S	89.72	-65.84	-215.45	22.75	S
5	220.45	-114.57	-68.14	S	-42.50	47.75	196.23	259.18	S	S
6	-15.15	22.49	S	-45.15	21.85	-22.35	174.93	S	S	-19.90
7	-49.68	S	S	-106.48	-45.95	-30.84	5.69	S	1.21	-3.03
8	S	S	102.59	53.65	-55.79	29.08	S	298.76	-104.14	13.32
9	S	-172.36	-41.85	58.59	23.46	S	S	-242.85	51.08	-2.42
10	-128.01	100.85	-1.56	-9.60	S	S	101.45	70.09	68.78	40.26
11	-33.08	14.88	86.30	S	S	20.99	-294.26	-196.33	65.67	S
12	6.44	-50.74	34.00	S	-10.81	-12.90	41.13	64.59	S	S
13	-128.36	-104.69	S	95.10	55.95	1.92	44.06	S	S	18.24
14	44.70	S	S	38.13	59.79	99.26	-178.11	S	29.55	47.98
15	S	S	-19.34	15.00	-1.84	28.76	S	-65.15	-49.05	-19.07
16	S	193.69	106.74	14.19	-6.08	S	S	359.61	-10.88	41.78
17	80.82	-92.01	15.70	-55.72	S	S	-172.65	-99.80	-132.86	-7.34
18	106.42	-88.04	102.82	S	S	-4.25	65.27	-219.35	20.63	S
19	72.10	-82.55	30.14	S	-39.06	30.05	-25.20	-25.88	S	S
20	-85.31	146.52	S	11.68	-30.98	-7.45	38.37	S	S	-13.78
21	50.16	S	59.78	97.83	28.18	-42.62	205.01	S	85.25	55.03
22	S	-18.03	3.26	56.46	55.71	-78.03	S	-59.34	50.79	26.33
23	S	S	S	11.23	-6.17	S	S	-100.28	1.51	14.00
24	N/C*	-45.18*	-36.07*	H	S	S	98.68*	48.99*	53.66*	H
25	H	H	H	S	S	H	H	H	H	H
26	52.80	-15.50	19.48*	S	H	64.41	2.36	47.07	S	H
27	43.17	-128.83	S	-50.99	-105.50	102.94	-192.08	S	S	-18.46
28	5.68	S	S	78.41	18.49	-9.05	6.26	S	26.98	20.51
29	S	S	125.33	-25.35	-11.44	-38.37	S	-31.62	-1.67	9.84
30	S	29.07	-24.96	-28.89	-67.32	S	S	184.46	3.10	-15.67
31	-115.49*	8.78*	28.88*	-17.29*	S	S	-101.05*	108.00*	-120.46*	7.80*
Close	10021.50	8341.63	10453.92	10783.01	10717.50	12463.15	13264.82	8776.39	10428.05	11577.51
Change	169.94	-554.46	671.46	354.99	-88.37	241.22	-106.90	-52.65	83.21	571.49

Shortened trading day

138

A TYPICAL DAY IN THE MARKET

Half-hourly data became available for the Dow Jones Industrial Average starting in January 1987. The NYSE switched 10:00 a.m. openings to 9:30 a.m. in October 1985. Below is the comparison between half-hourly performance from January1987 to April 29, 2011, and hourly performance from November 1963 to June 1985. Stronger openings and closings in a more bullish climate are evident. Morning and afternoon weaknesses appear an hour earlier.

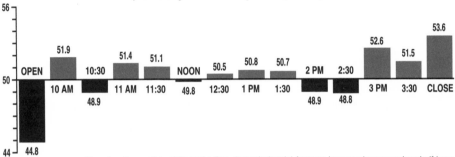

MARKET % PERFORMANCE EACH HALF-HOUR OF THE DAY
(January 1987 to April 29, 2011)

Based on the number of times the Dow Jones Industrial Average increased over previous half-hour.

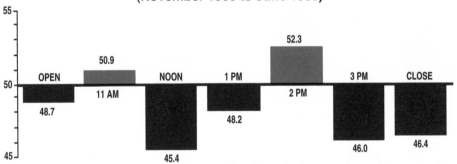

MARKET % PERFORMANCE EACH HOUR OF THE DAY
(November 1963 to June 1985)

Based on the number of times the Dow Jones Industrial Average increased over previous hour.

On the next page, half-hourly movements since January 1987 are separated by day of the week. From 1953 to 1989, Monday was the worst day of the week, especially during long bear markets, but times changed. Monday reversed positions and became the best day of the week and on the plus side eleven years in a row from 1990 to 2000.

During the last eleven years (2001–April 29, 2011) Friday is the sole net loser. Tuesday and Wednesday are solid gainers, Wednesday the best (page 68). On all days stocks do tend to firm up near the close with weakness early morning and from 2 to 2:30 frequently.

THROUGH THE WEEK ON A HALF-HOURLY BASIS

From the chart showing the percentage of times the Dow Jones Industrial Average rose over the preceding half-hour (January 1987 to April 29, 2011*), the typical week unfolds.

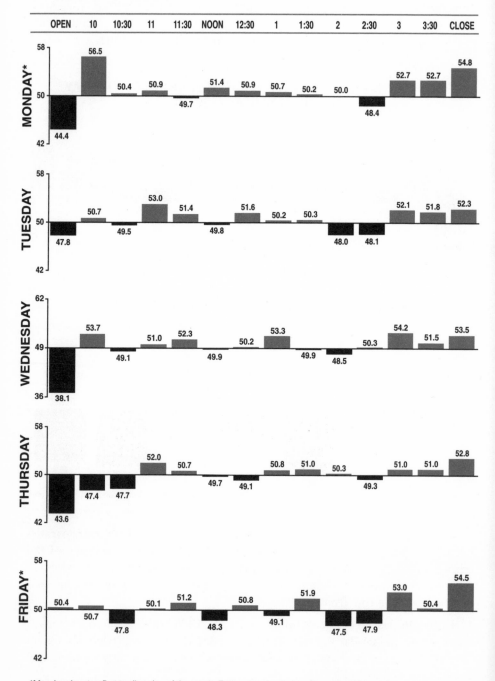

*Monday denotes first trading day of the week, Friday denotes last trading day of the week.

WEDNESDAY MOST PROFITABLE DAY OF WEEK

Between 1952 and 1989, Monday was the worst trading day of the week. The first trading day of the week (including Tuesday, when Monday is a holiday) rose only 44.3% of the time, while the other trading days closed higher 54.8% of the time. (NYSE Saturday trading discontinued June 1952.)

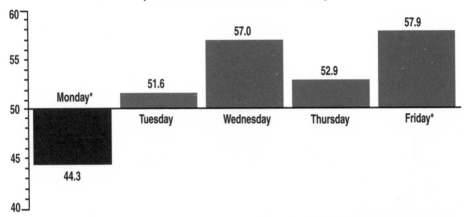

MARKET % PERFORMANCE EACH DAY OF THE WEEK
(June 1952 to December 1989)

A dramatic reversal occurred in 1990—Monday became the most powerful day of the week. However, during the last ten and a third years, Wednesday has produced the most gains. Since the top in 2000, traders have not been inclined to stay long over the weekend nor buy up equities at the outset of the week. This is not uncommon during uncertain market times. Monday was the worst day during the 2007–2009 bear, and only Tuesday was a net gainer. Since the March 2009 bottom, Monday is best. See pages 68 and 143.

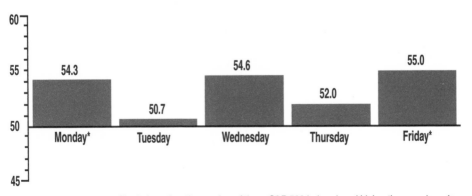

MARKET % PERFORMANCE EACH DAY OF THE WEEK
(January 1990 to May 6, 2011)

Charts based on the number of times S&P 500 index closed higher than previous day.
*Monday denotes first trading day of the week, Friday denotes last trading day of the week.

NASDAQ STRONGEST LAST 3 DAYS OF WEEK

Despite 20 years less data, daily trading patterns on NASDAQ through 1989 appear to be fairly similar to the S&P on page 141, except for more bullishness on Thursdays. During the mostly flat markets of the 1970s and early 1980s, it would appear that apprehensive investors decided to throw in the towel over weekends and sell on Mondays and Tuesdays.

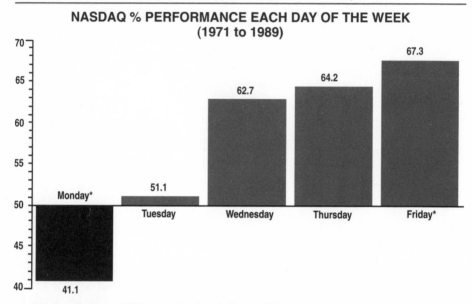

NASDAQ % PERFORMANCE EACH DAY OF THE WEEK
(1971 to 1989)

Notice the vast difference in the daily trading pattern between NASDAQ and S&P from January 1, 1990, to recent times. The reason for so much more bullishness is that NASDAQ moved up 1010%, over three times as much during the 1990 to 2000 period. The gain for the S&P was 332% and for the Dow Jones industrials, 326%. NASDAQ's weekly patterns are beginning to move in step with the rest of the market. Notice the similarities to the S&P since 2001 on pages 143 and 144—Monday and Friday weakness, midweek strength.

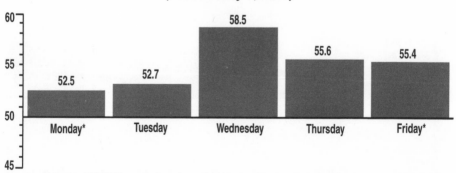

NASDAQ % PERFORMANCE EACH DAY OF THE WEEK
(1990 to May 6, 2011)

Based on NASDAQ composite, prior to February 5, 1971, based on National Quotation Bureau indices.
*Monday denotes first trading day of the week, Friday denotes last trading day of the week.

S&P DAILY PERFORMANCE EACH YEAR SINCE 1952

To determine if market trend alters performance of different days of the week, we separated 21 bear years—1953, '56, '57, '60, '62, '66, '69, '70, '73, '74, '77, '78, '81, '84, '87, '90, '94, 2000, '01, '02, and '08—from 38 bull market years. While Tuesday and Thursday did not vary much between bull and bear years, Mondays and Fridays were sharply affected. There was a swing of 10.8 percentage points in Monday's and 9.8 in Friday's performance. Wednesday is developing a reputation as the best day of the week based upon total points gained. See page 68.

PERCENTAGE OF TIMES MARKET CLOSED HIGHER THAN PREVIOUS DAY
(June 1952 to May 6, 2011)

	Monday*	Tuesday	Wednesday	Thursday	Friday*
1952	48.4%	55.6%	58.1%	51.9%	66.7%
1953	32.7	50.0	54.9	57.5	56.6
1954	50.0	57.5	63.5	59.2	73.1
1955	50.0	45.7	63.5	60.0	78.9
1956	36.5	39.6	46.9	50.0	59.6
1957	25.0	54.0	66.7	48.9	44.2
1958	59.6	52.0	59.6	68.1	72.6
1959	42.3	53.1	55.8	48.9	69.8
1960	34.6	50.0	44.2	54.0	59.6
1961	52.9	54.4	64.7	56.0	67.3
1962	28.3	52.1	54.0	51.0	50.0
1963	46.2	63.3	51.0	57.5	69.2
1964	40.4	48.0	61.5	58.7	77.4
1965	44.2	57.5	55.8	51.0	71.2
1966	36.5	47.8	53.9	42.0	57.7
1967	38.5	50.0	60.8	64.0	69.2
1968†	49.1	57.5	64.3	42.6	54.9
1969	30.8	45.8	50.0	67.4	50.0
1970	38.5	46.0	63.5	48.9	52.8
1971	44.2	64.6	57.7	55.1	51.9
1972	38.5	60.9	57.7	51.0	67.3
1973	32.1	51.1	52.9	44.9	44.2
1974	32.7	57.1	51.0	36.7	30.8
1975	53.9	38.8	61.5	56.3	55.8
1976	55.8	55.3	55.8	40.8	58.5
1977	40.4	40.4	46.2	53.1	53.9
1978	51.9	43.5	59.6	54.0	48.1
1979	54.7	53.2	58.8	66.0	44.2
1980	55.8	54.2	71.7	35.4	59.6
1981	44.2	38.8	55.8	53.2	47.2
1982	46.2	39.6	44.2	44.9	50.0
1983	55.8	46.8	61.5	52.0	55.8
1984	39.6	63.8	31.4	46.0	44.2
1985	44.2	61.2	54.9	56.3	53.9
1986	51.9	44.9	67.3	58.3	55.8
1987	51.9	57.1	63.5	61.7	49.1
1988	51.9	61.7	51.9	48.0	59.6
1989	51.9	47.8	69.2	58.0	69.2
1990	67.9	53.2	52.9	40.0	51.9
1991	44.2	46.9	52.9	49.0	51.9
1992	51.9	49.0	53.9	56.3	45.3
1993	65.4	41.7	55.8	44.9	48.1
1994	55.8	46.8	52.9	48.0	59.6
1995	63.5	56.5	63.5	62.0	63.5
1996	54.7	44.9	51.0	57.1	63.5
1997	67.3	67.4	42.3	41.7	57.7
1998	57.7	62.5	57.7	38.3	60.4
1999	46.2	29.8	67.3	53.1	57.7
2000	51.9	43.5	40.4	56.0	46.2
2001	45.3	51.1	44.0	59.2	43.1
2002	40.4	37.5	56.9	38.8	48.1
2003	59.6	62.5	42.3	58.3	50.0
2004	51.9	61.7	59.6	52.1	52.8
2005	59.6	47.8	59.6	56.0	55.8
2006	55.8	55.6	67.3	52.0	48.1
2007	47.2	50.0	64.0	50.0	61.5
2008	42.3	50.0	41.5	60.4	55.8
2009	53.9	50.0	57.7	63.8	52.8
2010	61.5	57.5	55.8	53.1	57.7
2011 ‡	50.0	50.0	61.1	52.9	77.8
Average	**47.9%**	**51.3%**	**56.0%**	**52.5%**	**56.5%**
38 Bull Years	**51.8%**	**52.8%**	**58.5%**	**53.4%**	**60.0%**
21 Bear Years	**40.9%**	**48.5%**	**51.6%**	**51.0%**	**50.1%**

Based on S&P 500

† Most Wednesdays closed last 7 months of 1968. ‡ Through 5/6/2011 only, not included in averages.
*Monday denotes first trading day of the week, Friday denotes last trading day of the week.

NASDAQ DAILY PERFORMANCE EACH YEAR SINCE 1971

After dropping a hefty 77.9% from its 2000 high (versus –37.8% on the Dow and –49.1% on the S&P 500), NASDAQ tech stocks still outpace the blue chips and big caps—but not by nearly as much as they did. From January 1, 1971 through April 29, 2011, NASDAQ moved up an impressive 3107%. The Dow (up 1427%) and the S&P (up 1379%) gained less than half as much.

Monday's performance on NASDAQ was lackluster during the three-year bear market of 2000–2002. As NASDAQ rebounded (up 50% in 2003), strength returned to Monday during 2003–2006. During the bear market from late 2007 to early 2009, weakness was most consistent on Monday and Friday.

PERCENTAGE OF TIMES NASDAQ CLOSED HIGHER THAN PREVIOUS DAY
(1971 to May 6, 2011)

	Monday*	Tuesday	Wednesday	Thursday	Friday*
1971	51.9%	52.1%	59.6%	65.3%	71.2%
1972	30.8	60.9	63.5	57.1	78.9
1973	34.0	48.9	52.9	53.1	48.1
1974	30.8	44.9	52.9	51.0	42.3
1975	44.2	42.9	63.5	64.6	63.5
1976	50.0	63.8	67.3	59.2	58.5
1977	51.9	40.4	53.9	63.3	73.1
1978	48.1	47.8	73.1	72.0	84.6
1979	45.3	53.2	64.7	86.0	82.7
1980	46.2	64.6	84.9	52.1	73.1
1981	42.3	32.7	67.3	76.6	69.8
1982	34.6	47.9	59.6	51.0	63.5
1983	42.3	44.7	67.3	68.0	73.1
1984	22.6	53.2	35.3	52.0	51.9
1985	36.5	59.2	62.8	68.8	66.0
1986	38.5	55.1	65.4	72.9	75.0
1987	42.3	49.0	65.4	68.1	66.0
1988	50.0	55.3	61.5	66.0	63.5
1989	38.5	54.4	71.2	72.0	75.0
1990	54.7	42.6	60.8	46.0	55.8
1991	51.9	59.2	66.7	65.3	51.9
1992	44.2	53.1	59.6	60.4	45.3
1993	55.8	56.3	69.2	57.1	67.3
1994	51.9	46.8	54.9	52.0	55.8
1995	50.0	52.2	63.5	64.0	63.5
1996	50.9	57.1	64.7	61.2	63.5
1997	65.4	59.2	53.9	52.1	55.8
1998	59.6	58.3	65.4	44.7	58.5
1999	61.5	40.4	63.5	57.1	65.4
2000	40.4	41.3	42.3	60.0	57.7
2001	41.5	57.8	52.0	55.1	47.1
2002	44.2	37.5	56.9	46.9	46.2
2003	57.7	60.4	40.4	60.4	46.2
2004	57.7	59.6	53.9	50.0	50.9
2005	61.5	47.8	51.9	48.0	59.6
2006	55.8	51.1	65.4	50.0	44.2
2007	47.2	63.0	66.0	56.0	57.7
2008	34.6	52.1	49.1	54.2	42.3
2009	51.9	54.2	63.5	63.8	50.9
2010	61.5	53.2	61.5	55.1	61.5
2011†	55.6	56.3	61.1	64.7	72.2
Average	**47.0%**	**51.8%**	**60.4%**	**59.5%**	**60.7%**
29 Bull Years	**49.7%**	**54.0%**	**63.0%**	**60.8%**	**63.6%**
10 Bear Years	**39.9%**	**46.1%**	**53.6%**	**55.9%**	**53.0%**

Based on NASDAQ composite; prior to February 5, 1971, based on National Quotation Bureau indices.
† Through 5/6/2011 only, not included in averages.
*Monday denotes first trading day of the week, Friday denotes last trading day of the week.

MONTHLY CASH INFLOWS INTO S&P STOCKS

For many years, the last trading day of the month, plus the first four of the following month, were the best market days of the month. This pattern is quite clear in the first chart, showing these five consecutive trading days towering above the other 16 trading days of the average month in the 1953–1981 period. The rationale was that individuals and institutions tended to operate similarly, causing a massive flow of cash into stocks near beginnings of months.

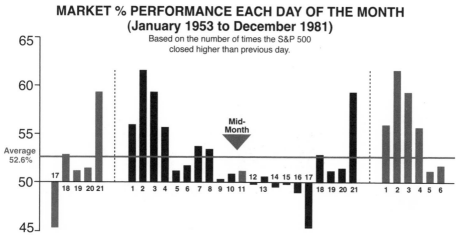

MARKET % PERFORMANCE EACH DAY OF THE MONTH
(January 1953 to December 1981)
Based on the number of times the S&P 500 closed higher than previous day.

Clearly "front-running" traders took advantage of this phenomenon, drastically altering the previous pattern. The second chart from 1982 onward shows the trading shift caused by these "anticipators" to the last three trading days of the month, plus the first two. Another astonishing development shows the ninth, tenth, and eleventh trading days rising strongly as well. Perhaps the enormous growth of 401(k) retirement plans (participants' salaries are usually paid twice monthly) is responsible for this mid-month bulge. First trading days of the month have produced the greatest gains in recent years (see page 84).

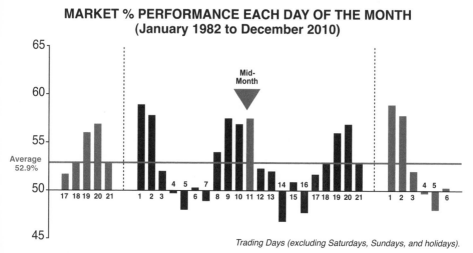

MARKET % PERFORMANCE EACH DAY OF THE MONTH
(January 1982 to December 2010)

Trading Days (excluding Saturdays, Sundays, and holidays).

145

MONTHLY CASH INFLOWS INTO NASDAQ STOCKS

NASDAQ stocks moved up 58.1% of the time through 1981 compared to 52.6% for the S&P on page 145. Ends and beginnings of the month are fairly similar, specifically the last plus the first four trading days. But notice how investors piled into NASDAQ stocks until mid-month. NASDAQ rose 118.6% from January 1, 1971, to December 31, 1981, compared to 33.0% for the S&P.

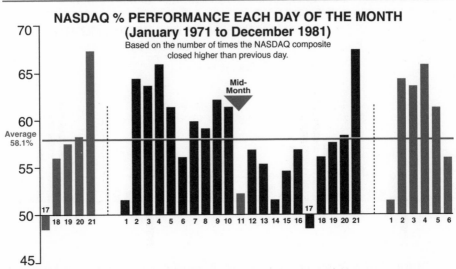

After the air was let out of the tech market 2000–2002, S&P's 926% gain over the last 29 years is more evenly matched with NASDAQ's 1255% gain. Last three, first four, and middle ninth and tenth days rose the most. Where the S&P has five days of the month that go down more often than up, NASDAQ has none. NASDAQ exhibits the most strength on the last trading day of the month; however, over the past 14 years, last days have weakened considerably, down more often then not.

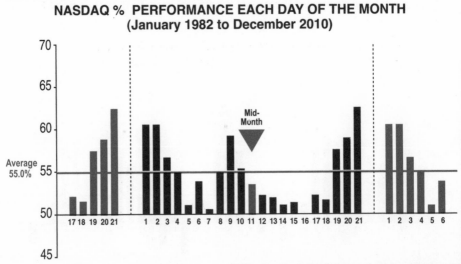

Trading Days (excluding Saturdays, Sundays, and holidays).
Based on NASDAQ composite, prior to February 5, 1971, based on National Quotation Bureau indices.

NOVEMBER, DECEMBER, AND JANUARY: YEAR'S BEST THREE-MONTH SPAN

The most important observation to be made from a chart showing the average monthly percent change in market prices since 1950 is that institutions (mutual funds, pension funds, banks, etc.) determine the trading patterns in today's market.

The "investment calendar" reflects the annual, semi-annual and quarterly operations of institutions during January, April and July. October, besides being the last campaign month before elections, is also the time when most bear markets seem to end, as in 1946, 1957, 1960, 1966, 1974, 1987, 1990, 1998 and 2002. (August and September tend to combine to make the worst consecutive two-month period.)

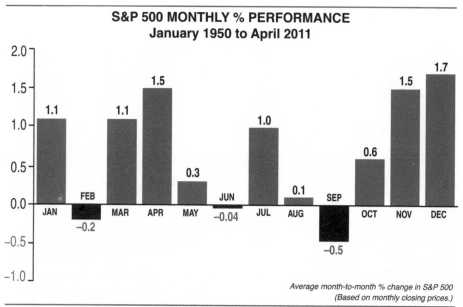

S&P 500 MONTHLY % PERFORMANCE
January 1950 to April 2011

Average month-to-month % change in S&P 500
(Based on monthly closing prices.)

Unusual year-end strength comes from corporate and private pension funds, producing a 4.3% gain on average between November 1 and January 31. In 2007–2008, these three months were all down for the fourth time since 1930; previously in 1931–1932, 1940–1941, and 1969–1970, also bear markets. September's dismal performance makes it the worst month of the year. However, in the last 16 years it has been up ten times—down five in a row 1999–2003.

In presidential election years since 1950, the best three months are November +1.4% (8–7), June +1.2% (12–3), and December +1.2% (12–3). March, May, June, July, August and November are gainers while February, September and October are losers. October is worst, −0.6% (9–6).

See page 44 for monthly performance tables for the S&P 500 and the Dow Jones industrials. See pages 48, 50, and 60 for unique switching strategies.

On page 64, you can see how the first month of the first three quarters far outperforms the second and the third months since 1950, and note the improvement in May's and October's performance since 1991.

NOVEMBER THROUGH JUNE:
NASDAQ'S EIGHT-MONTH RUN

The two-and-a-half-year plunge of 77.9% in NASDAQ stocks, between March 10, 2000, and October 9, 2002, brought several horrendous monthly losses (the two greatest were November 2000, –22.9%, and February 2001, –22.4%), which trimmed average monthly performance over the 40⅓-year period. Ample Octobers in nine of the last 13 years, including two huge turnarounds in 2001 (+12.8%) and 2002 (+13.5%), have put bear-killing October in the number two spot since 1998. January's 2.8% average gain is still awesome, and twice S&P's 1.2% January average since 1971.

NASDAQ MONTHLY PERFORMANCE
January 1971 to April 2011

Average month-to-month % change in NASDAQ composite, prior to February 5, 1971, based on National Quotation Bureau indices. (Based on monthly closing prices.)

Bear in mind, when comparing NASDAQ to the S&P on page 147, that there are 22 fewer years of data here. During this 40⅓-year (1971–April 2011) period, NASDAQ gained 3107%, while the S&P and the Dow rose only 1427% and 1380%, respectively. On page 56 is a statistical monthly comparison between NASDAQ and the Dow, and on page 58, NASDAQ's eight-month switching strategy.

Year-end strength is even more pronounced in NASDAQ, producing a 6.5% gain on average between November 1 and January 31—1.5 times greater than that of the S&P 500 on page 147. September is the worst month of the year for the over-the-counter index as well, posting an average loss of –0.5%. These extremes underscore NASDAQ's higher volatility and potential for moves of greater magnitude.

In presidential election years since 1971, the best three months are August +2.7% (6–4), February +2.6% (6–4) and January +2.0% (7–3). June and December are also solid performers. March is the worst, –2.2% (5–5). May, April, September, November, July, and October are net losers as well.

DOW JONES INDUSTRIALS ANNUAL HIGHS, LOWS, & CLOSES SINCE 1901

YEAR	HIGH DATE	HIGH CLOSE	LOW DATE	LOW CLOSE	YEAR CLOSE	YEAR	HIGH DATE	HIGH CLOSE	LOW DATE	LOW CLOSE	YEAR CLOSE
1901	6/17	57.33	12/24	45.07	47.29	1957	7/12	520.77	10/22	419.79	435.69
1902	4/24	50.14	12/15	43.64	47.10	1958	12/31	583.65	2/25	436.89	583.65
1903	2/16	49.59	11/9	30.88	35.98	1959	12/31	679.36	2/9	574.46	679.36
1904	12/5	53.65	3/12	34.00	50.99	1960	1/5	685.47	10/25	566.05	615.89
1905	12/29	70.74	1/25	50.37	70.47	1961	12/13	734.91	1/3	610.25	731.14
1906	1/19	75.45	7/13	62.40	69.12	1962	1/3	726.01	6/26	535.76	652.10
1907	1/7	70.60	11/15	38.83	43.04	1963	12/18	767.21	1/2	646.79	762.95
1908	11/13	64.74	2/13	42.94	63.11	1964	11/18	891.71	1/2	766.08	874.13
1909	11/19	73.64	2/23	58.54	72.56	1965	12/31	969.26	6/28	840.59	969.26
1910	1/3	72.04	7/26	53.93	59.60	1966	2/9	995.15	10/7	744.32	785.69
1911	6/19	63.78	9/25	53.43	59.84	1967	9/25	943.08	1/3	786.41	905.11
1912	9/30	68.97	2/10	58.72	64.37	1968	12/3	985.21	3/21	825.13	943.75
1913	1/9	64.88	6/11	52.83	57.71	1969	5/14	968.85	12/17	769.93	800.36
1914	3/20	61.12	7/30	52.32	54.58	1970	12/29	842.00	5/26	631.16	838.92
1915	12/27	99.21	2/24	54.22	99.15	1971	4/28	950.82	11/23	797.97	890.20
1916	11/21	110.15	4/22	84.96	95.00	1972	12/11	1036.27	1/26	889.15	1020.02
1917	1/3	99.18	12/19	65.95	74.38	1973	1/11	1051.70	12/5	788.31	850.86
1918	10/18	89.07	1/15	73.38	82.20	1974	3/13	891.66	12/6	577.60	616.24
1919	11/3	119.62	2/8	79.15	107.23	1975	7/15	881.81	1/2	632.04	852.41
1920	1/3	109.88	12/21	66.75	71.95	1976	9/21	1014.79	1/2	858.71	1004.65
1921	12/15	81.50	8/24	63.90	81.10	1977	1/3	999.75	11/2	800.85	831.17
1922	10/14	103.43	1/10	78.59	98.73	1978	9/8	907.74	2/28	742.12	805.01
1923	3/20	105.38	10/27	85.76	95.52	1979	10/5	897.61	11/7	796.67	838.74
1924	12/31	120.51	5/20	88.33	120.51	1980	11/20	1000.17	4/21	759.13	963.99
1925	11/6	159.39	3/30	115.00	156.66	1981	4/27	1024.05	9/25	824.01	875.00
1926	8/14	166.64	3/30	135.20	157.20	1982	12/27	1070.55	8/12	776.92	1046.54
1927	12/31	202.40	1/25	152.73	202.40	1983	11/29	1287.20	1/3	1027.04	1258.64
1928	12/31	300.00	2/20	191.33	300.00	1984	1/6	1286.64	7/24	1086.57	1211.57
1929	9/3	381.17	11/13	198.69	248.48	1985	12/16	1553.10	1/4	1184.96	1546.67
1930	4/17	294.07	12/16	157.51	164.58	1986	12/2	1955.57	1/22	1502.29	1895.95
1931	2/24	194.36	12/17	73.79	77.90	1987	8/25	2722.42	10/19	1738.74	1938.83
1932	3/8	88.78	7/8	41.22	59.93	1988	10/21	2183.50	1/20	1879.14	2168.57
1933	7/18	108.67	2/27	50.16	99.90	1989	10/9	2791.41	1/3	2144.64	2753.20
1934	2/5	110.74	7/26	85.51	104.04	1990	7/17	2999.75	10/11	2365.10	2633.66
1935	11/19	148.44	3/14	96.71	144.13	1991	12/31	3168.83	1/9	2470.30	3168.83
1936	11/17	184.90	1/6	143.11	179.90	1992	6/1	3413.21	10/9	3136.58	3301.11
1937	3/10	194.40	11/24	113.64	120.85	1993	12/29	3794.33	1/20	3241.95	3754.09
1938	11/12	158.41	3/31	98.95	154.76	1994	1/31	3978.36	4/4	3593.35	3834.44
1939	9/12	155.92	4/8	121.44	150.24	1995	12/13	5216.47	1/30	3832.08	5117.12
1940	1/3	152.80	6/10	111.84	131.13	1996	12/27	6560.91	1/10	5032.94	6448.27
1941	1/10	133.59	12/23	106.34	110.96	1997	8/6	8259.31	4/11	6391.69	7908.25
1942	12/26	119.71	4/28	92.92	119.40	1998	11/23	9374.27	8/31	7539.07	9181.43
1943	7/14	145.82	1/8	119.26	135.89	1999	12/31	11497.12	1/22	9120.67	11497.12
1944	12/16	152.53	2/7	134.22	152.32	2000	1/14	11722.98	3/7	9796.03	10786.85
1945	12/11	195.82	1/24	151.35	192.91	2001	5/21	11337.92	9/21	8235.81	10021.50
1946	5/29	212.50	10/9	163.12	177.20	2002	3/19	10635.25	10/9	7286.27	8341.63
1947	7/24	186.85	5/17	163.21	181.16	2003	12/31	10453.92	3/11	7524.06	10453.92
1948	6/15	193.16	3/16	165.39	177.30	2004	12/28	10854.54	10/25	9749.99	10783.01
1949	12/30	200.52	6/13	161.60	200.13	2005	3/4	10940.55	4/20	10012.36	10717.50
1950	11/24	235.47	1/13	196.81	235.41	2006	12/27	12510.57	1/20	10667.39	12463.15
1951	9/13	276.37	1/3	238.99	269.23	2007	10/9	14164.53	3/5	12050.41	13264.82
1952	12/30	292.00	5/1	256.35	291.90	2008	5/2	13058.20	11/20	7552.29	8776.39
1953	1/5	293.79	9/14	255.49	280.90	2009	12/30	10548.51	3/9	6547.05	10428.05
1954	12/31	404.39	1/11	279.87	404.39	2010	12/29	11585.38	7/2	9686.48	11577.51
1955	12/30	488.40	1/17	388.20	488.40	2011*	4/29	12810.54	3/16	11613.30	*At Press Time*
1956	4/6	521.05	1/23	462.35	499.47						

Through May 13, 2011

149

S&P 500 ANNUAL HIGHS, LOWS, & CLOSES SINCE 1930

YEAR	HIGH DATE	HIGH CLOSE	LOW DATE	LOW CLOSE	YEAR CLOSE	YEAR	HIGH DATE	HIGH CLOSE	LOW DATE	LOW CLOSE	YEAR CLOSE
1930	4/10	25.92	12/16	14.44	15.34	1971	4/28	104.77	11/23	90.16	102.09
1931	2/24	18.17	12/17	7.72	8.12	1972	12/11	119.12	1/3	101.67	118.05
1932	9/7	9.31	6/1	4.40	6.89	1973	1/11	120.24	12/5	92.16	97.55
1933	7/18	12.20	2/27	5.53	10.10	1974	1/3	99.80	10/3	62.28	68.56
1934	2/6	11.82	7/26	8.36	9.50	1975	7/15	95.61	1/8	70.04	90.19
1935	11/19	13.46	3/14	8.06	13.43	1976	9/21	107.83	1/2	90.90	107.46
1936	11/9	17.69	1/2	13.40	17.18	1977	1/3	107.00	11/2	90.71	95.10
1937	3/6	18.68	11/24	10.17	10.55	1978	9/12	106.99	3/6	86.90	96.11
1938	11/9	13.79	3/31	8.50	13.21	1979	10/5	111.27	2/27	96.13	107.94
1939	1/4	13.23	4/8	10.18	12.49	1980	11/28	140.52	3/27	98.22	135.76
1940	1/3	12.77	6/10	8.99	10.58	1981	1/6	138.12	9/25	112.77	122.55
1941	1/10	10.86	12/29	8.37	8.69	1982	11/9	143.02	8/12	102.42	140.64
1942	12/31	9.77	4/28	7.47	9.77	1983	10/10	172.65	1/3	138.34	164.93
1943	7/14	12.64	1/2	9.84	11.67	1984	11/6	170.41	7/24	147.82	167.24
1944	12/16	13.29	2/7	11.56	13.28	1985	12/16	212.02	1/4	163.68	211.28
1945	12/10	17.68	1/23	13.21	17.36	1986	12/2	254.00	1/22	203.49	242.17
1946	5/29	19.25	10/9	14.12	15.30	1987	8/25	336.77	12/4	223.92	247.08
1947	2/8	16.20	5/17	13.71	15.30	1988	10/21	283.66	1/20	242.63	277.72
1948	6/15	17.06	2/14	13.84	15.20	1989	10/9	359.80	1/3	275.31	353.40
1949	12/30	16.79	6/13	13.55	16.76	1990	7/16	368.95	10/11	295.46	330.22
1950	12/29	20.43	1/14	16.65	20.41	1991	12/31	417.09	1/9	311.49	417.09
1951	10/15	23.85	1/3	20.69	23.77	1992	12/18	441.28	4/8	394.50	435.71
1952	12/30	26.59	2/20	23.09	26.57	1993	12/28	470.94	1/8	429.05	466.45
1953	1/5	26.66	9/14	22.71	24.81	1994	2/2	482.00	4/4	438.92	459.27
1954	12/31	35.98	1/11	24.80	35.98	1995	12/13	621.69	1/3	459.11	615.93
1955	11/14	46.41	1/17	34.58	45.48	1996	11/25	757.03	1/10	598.48	740.74
1956	8/2	49.74	1/23	43.11	46.67	1997	12/5	983.79	1/2	737.01	970.43
1957	7/15	49.13	10/22	38.98	39.99	1998	12/29	1241.81	1/9	927.69	1229.23
1958	12/31	55.21	1/2	40.33	55.21	1999	12/31	1469.25	1/14	1212.19	1469.25
1959	8/3	60.71	2/9	53.58	59.89	2000	3/24	1527.46	12/20	1264.74	1320.28
1960	1/5	60.39	10/25	52.30	58.11	2001	2/1	1373.47	9/21	965.80	1148.08
1961	12/12	72.64	1/3	57.57	71.55	2002	1/4	1172.51	10/9	776.76	879.82
1962	1/3	71.13	6/26	52.32	63.10	2003	12/31	1111.92	3/11	800.73	1111.92
1963	12/31	75.02	1/2	62.69	75.02	2004	12/30	1213.55	8/12	1063.23	1211.92
1964	11/20	86.28	1/2	75.43	84.75	2005	12/14	1272.74	4/20	1137.50	1248.29
1965	11/15	92.63	6/28	81.60	92.43	2006	12/15	1427.09	6/13	1223.69	1418.30
1966	2/9	94.06	10/7	73.20	80.33	2007	10/9	1565.15	3/5	1374.12	1468.36
1967	9/25	97.59	1/3	80.38	96.47	2008	1/2	1447.16	11/20	752.44	903.25
1968	11/29	108.37	3/5	87.72	103.86	2009	12/28	1127.78	3/9	676.53	1115.10
1969	5/14	106.16	12/17	89.20	92.06	2010	12/29	1259.78	7/2	1022.58	1257.64
1970	1/5	93.46	5/26	69.29	92.15	2011*	4/29	1363.61	3/16	1256.88	At Press Time

*Through May 13, 2011

NASDAQ ANNUAL HIGHS, LOWS, & CLOSES SINCE 1971

YEAR	HIGH DATE	CLOSE	LOW DATE	CLOSE	YEAR CLOSE	YEAR	HIGH DATE	CLOSE	LOW DATE	CLOSE	YEAR CLOSE
1971	12/31	114.12	1/5	89.06	114.12	1992	12/31	676.95	6/26	547.84	676.95
1972	12/8	135.15	1/3	113.65	133.73	1993	10/15	787.42	4/26	645.87	776.80
1973	1/11	136.84	12/24	88.67	92.19	1994	3/18	803.93	6/24	693.79	751.96
1974	3/15	96.53	10/3	54.87	59.82	1995	12/4	1069.79	1/3	743.58	1052.13
1975	7/15	88.00	1/2	60.70	77.62	1996	12/9	1316.27	1/15	988.57	1291.03
1976	12/31	97.88	1/2	78.06	97.88	1997	10/9	1745.85	4/2	1201.00	1570.35
1977	12/30	105.05	4/5	93.66	105.05	1998	12/31	2192.69	10/8	1419.12	2192.69
1978	9/13	139.25	1/11	99.09	117.98	1999	12/31	4069.31	1/4	2208.05	4069.31
1979	10/5	152.29	1/2	117.84	151.14	2000	3/10	5048.62	12/20	2332.78	2470.52
1980	11/28	208.15	3/27	124.09	202.34	2001	1/24	2859.15	9/21	1423.19	1950.40
1981	5/29	223.47	9/28	175.03	195.84	2002	1/4	2059.38	10/9	1114.11	1335.51
1982	12/8	240.70	8/13	159.14	232.41	2003	12/30	2009.88	3/11	1271.47	2003.37
1983	6/24	328.91	1/3	230.59	278.60	2004	12/30	2178.34	8/12	1752.49	2175.44
1984	1/6	287.90	7/25	225.30	247.35	2005	12/2	2273.37	4/28	1904.18	2205.32
1985	12/16	325.16	1/2	245.91	324.93	2006	11/22	2465.98	7/21	2020.39	2415.29
1986	7/3	411.16	1/9	323.01	349.33	2007	10/31	2859.12	3/5	2340.68	2652.28
1987	8/26	455.26	10/28	291.88	330.47	2008	1/2	2609.63	11/20	1316.12	1577.03
1988	7/5	396.11	1/12	331.97	381.38	2009	12/30	2291.28	3/9	1268.64	2269.15
1989	10/9	485.73	1/3	378.56	454.82	2010	12/22	2671.48	7/2	2091.79	2652.87
1990	7/16	469.60	10/16	325.44	373.84	2011*	4/29	2873.54	3/16	2616.82	At Press Time
1991	12/31	586.34	1/14	355.75	586.34						

RUSSELL 1000 ANNUAL HIGHS, LOWS, & CLOSES SINCE 1979

YEAR	HIGH DATE	CLOSE	LOW DATE	CLOSE	YEAR CLOSE	YEAR	HIGH DATE	CLOSE	LOW DATE	CLOSE	YEAR CLOSE
1979	10/5	61.18	2/27	51.83	59.87	1996	12/2	401.21	1/10	318.24	393.75
1980	11/28	78.26	3/27	53.68	75.20	1997	12/5	519.72	4/11	389.03	513.79
1981	1/6	76.34	9/25	62.03	67.93	1998	12/29	645.36	1/9	490.26	642.87
1982	11/9	78.47	8/12	55.98	77.24	1999	12/31	767.97	2/9	632.53	767.97
1983	10/10	95.07	1/3	76.04	90.38	2000	9/1	813.71	12/20	668.75	700.09
1984	1/6	92.80	7/24	79.49	90.31	2001	1/30	727.35	9/21	507.98	604.94
1985	12/16	114.97	1/4	88.61	114.39	2002	3/19	618.74	10/9	410.52	466.18
1986	7/2	137.87	1/22	111.14	130.00	2003	12/31	594.56	3/11	425.31	594.56
1987	8/25	176.22	12/4	117.65	130.02	2004	12/30	651.76	8/13	566.06	650.99
1988	10/21	149.94	1/20	128.35	146.99	2005	12/14	692.09	4/20	613.37	679.42
1989	10/9	189.93	1/3	145.78	185.11	2006	12/15	775.08	6/13	665.81	770.08
1990	7/16	191.56	10/11	152.36	171.22	2007	10/9	852.32	3/5	749.85	799.82
1991	12/31	220.61	1/9	161.94	220.61	2008	1/2	788.62	11/20	402.91	487.77
1992	12/18	235.06	4/8	208.87	233.59	2009	12/28	619.22	3/9	367.55	612.01
1993	10/15	252.77	1/8	229.91	250.71	2010	12/29	698.11	7/2	562.58	696.90
1994	2/1	258.31	4/4	235.38	244.65	2011*	4/29	758.45	3/16	698.07	At Press Time
1995	12/13	331.18	1/3	244.41	328.89						

RUSSELL 2000 ANNUAL HIGHS, LOWS, & CLOSES SINCE 1979

YEAR	HIGH DATE	CLOSE	LOW DATE	CLOSE	YEAR CLOSE	YEAR	HIGH DATE	CLOSE	LOW DATE	CLOSE	YEAR CLOSE
1979	12/31	55.91	1/2	40.81	55.91	1996	5/22	364.61	1/16	301.75	362.61
1980	11/28	77.70	3/27	45.36	74.80	1997	10/13	465.21	4/25	335.85	437.02
1981	6/15	85.16	9/25	65.37	73.67	1998	4/21	491.41	10/8	310.28	421.96
1982	12/8	91.01	8/12	60.33	88.90	1999	12/31	504.75	3/23	383.37	504.75
1983	6/24	126.99	1/3	88.29	112.27	2000	3/9	606.05	12/20	443.80	483.53
1984	1/12	116.69	7/25	93.95	101.49	2001	5/22	517.23	9/21	378.89	488.50
1985	12/31	129.87	1/2	101.21	129.87	2002	4/16	522.95	10/9	327.04	383.09
1986	7/3	155.30	1/9	128.23	135.00	2003	12/30	565.47	3/12	345.94	556.91
1987	8/25	174.44	10/28	106.08	120.42	2004	12/28	654.57	8/12	517.10	651.57
1988	7/15	151.42	1/12	121.23	147.37	2005	12/2	690.57	4/28	575.02	673.22
1989	10/9	180.78	1/3	146.79	168.30	2006	12/27	797.73	7/21	671.94	787.66
1990	6/15	170.90	10/30	118.82	132.16	2007	7/13	855.77	11/26	735.07	766.03
1991	12/31	189.94	1/15	125.25	189.94	2008	6/5	763.27	11/20	385.31	499.45
1992	12/31	221.01	7/8	185.81	221.01	2009	12/24	634.07	3/9	343.26	625.39
1993	11/2	260.17	2/23	217.55	258.59	2010	12/27	792.35	2/8	586.49	783.65
1994	3/18	271.08	12/9	235.16	250.36	2011*	4/29	865.29	1/21	773.18	At Press Time
1995	9/14	316.12	1/30	246.56	315.97						

*Through May 13, 2011

DOW JONES INDUSTRIALS MONTHLY PERCENT CHANGE SINCE 1950

	Jan	Feb	Mar	Apr	May	Jun	Jul	Aug	Sep	Oct	Nov	Dec	Year's Change
1950	0.8	0.8	1.3	4.0	4.2	-6.4	0.1	3.6	4.4	-0.6	1.2	3.4	17.6
1951	5.7	1.3	-1.6	4.5	-3.7	-2.8	6.3	4.8	0.3	-3.2	-0.4	3.0	14.4
1952	0.5	-3.9	3.6	-4.4	2.1	4.3	1.9	-1.6	-1.6	-0.5	5.4	2.9	8.4
1953	-0.7	-1.9	-1.5	-1.8	-0.9	-1.5	2.7	-5.1	1.1	4.5	2.0	-0.2	-3.8
1954	4.1	0.7	3.0	5.2	2.6	1.8	4.3	-3.5	7.3	-2.3	9.8	4.6	44.0
1955	1.1	0.7	-0.5	3.9	-0.2	6.2	3.2	0.5	-0.3	-2.5	6.2	1.1	20.8
1956	-3.6	2.7	5.8	0.8	-7.4	3.1	5.1	-3.0	-5.3	1.0	-1.5	5.6	2.3
1957	-4.1	-3.0	2.2	4.1	2.1	-0.3	1.0	-4.8	-5.8	-3.3	2.0	-3.2	-12.8
1958	3.3	-2.2	1.6	2.0	1.5	3.3	5.2	1.1	4.6	2.1	2.6	4.7	34.0
1959	1.8	1.6	-0.3	3.7	3.2	-0.03	4.9	-1.6	-4.9	2.4	1.9	3.1	16.4
1960	-8.4	1.2	-2.1	-2.4	4.0	2.4	-3.7	1.5	-7.3	0.04	2.9	3.1	-9.3
1961	5.2	2.1	2.2	0.3	2.7	-1.8	3.1	2.1	-2.6	0.4	2.5	1.3	18.7
1962	-4.3	1.1	-0.2	-5.9	-7.8	-8.5	6.5	1.9	-5.0	1.9	10.1	0.4	-10.8
1963	4.7	-2.9	3.0	5.2	1.3	-2.8	-1.6	4.9	0.5	3.1	-0.6	1.7	17.0
1964	2.9	1.9	1.6	-0.3	1.2	1.3	1.2	-0.3	4.4	-0.3	0.3	-0.1	14.6
1965	3.3	0.1	-1.6	3.7	-0.5	-5.4	1.6	1.3	4.2	3.2	-1.5	2.4	10.9
1966	1.5	-3.2	-2.8	1.0	-5.3	-1.6	-2.6	-7.0	-1.8	4.2	-1.9	-0.7	-18.9
1967	8.2	-1.2	3.2	3.6	-5.0	0.9	5.1	-0.3	2.8	-5.1	-0.4	3.3	15.2
1968	-5.5	-1.7	0.02	8.5	-1.4	-0.1	-1.6	1.5	4.4	1.8	3.4	-4.2	4.3
1969	0.2	-4.3	3.3	1.6	-1.3	-6.9	-6.6	2.6	-2.8	5.3	-5.1	-1.5	-15.2
1970	-7.0	4.5	1.0	-6.3	-4.8	-2.4	7.4	4.1	-0.5	-0.7	5.1	5.6	4.8
1971	3.5	1.2	2.9	4.1	-3.6	-1.8	-3.7	4.6	-1.2	-5.4	-0.9	7.1	6.1
1972	1.3	2.9	1.4	1.4	0.7	-3.3	-0.5	4.2	-1.1	0.2	6.6	0.2	14.6
1973	-2.1	-4.4	-0.4	-3.1	-2.2	-1.1	3.9	-4.2	6.7	1.0	-14.0	3.5	-16.6
1974	0.6	0.6	-1.6	-1.2	-4.1	0.03	-5.6	-10.4	-10.4	9.5	-7.0	-0.4	-27.6
1975	14.2	5.0	3.9	6.9	1.3	5.6	-5.4	0.5	-5.0	5.3	2.9	-1.0	38.3
1976	14.4	-0.3	2.8	-0.3	-2.2	2.8	-1.8	-1.1	1.7	-2.6	-1.8	6.1	17.9
1977	-5.0	-1.9	-1.8	0.8	-3.0	2.0	-2.9	-3.2	-1.7	-3.4	1.4	0.2	-17.3
1978	-7.4	-3.6	2.1	10.6	0.4	-2.6	5.3	1.7	-1.3	-8.5	0.8	0.7	-3.1
1979	4.2	-3.6	6.6	-0.8	-3.8	2.4	0.5	4.9	-1.0	-7.2	0.8	2.0	4.2
1980	4.4	-1.5	-9.0	4.0	4.1	2.0	7.8	-0.3	-0.02	-0.9	7.4	-3.0	14.9
1981	-1.7	2.9	3.0	-0.6	-0.6	-1.5	-2.5	-7.4	-3.6	0.3	4.3	-1.6	-9.2
1982	-0.4	-5.4	-0.2	3.1	-3.4	-0.9	-0.4	11.5	-0.6	10.7	4.8	0.7	19.6
1983	2.8	3.4	1.6	8.5	-2.1	1.8	-1.9	1.4	1.4	-0.6	4.1	-1.4	20.3
1984	-3.0	-5.4	0.9	0.5	-5.6	2.5	-1.5	9.8	-1.4	0.1	-1.5	1.9	-3.7
1985	6.2	-0.2	-1.3	-0.7	4.6	1.5	0.9	-1.0	-0.4	3.4	7.1	5.1	27.7
1986	1.6	8.8	6.4	-1.9	5.2	0.9	-6.2	6.9	-6.9	6.2	1.9	-1.0	22.6
1987	13.8	3.1	3.6	-0.8	0.2	5.5	6.3	3.5	-2.5	-23.2	-8.0	5.7	2.3
1988	1.0	5.8	-4.0	2.2	-0.1	5.4	-0.6	-4.6	4.0	1.7	-1.6	2.6	11.8
1989	8.0	-3.6	1.6	5.5	2.5	-1.6	9.0	2.9	-1.6	-1.8	2.3	1.7	27.0
1990	-5.9	1.4	3.0	-1.9	8.3	0.1	0.9	-10.0	-6.2	-0.4	4.8	2.9	-4.3
1991	3.9	5.3	1.1	-0.9	4.8	-4.0	4.1	0.6	-0.9	1.7	-5.7	9.5	20.3
1992	1.7	1.4	-1.0	3.8	1.1	-2.3	2.3	-4.0	0.4	-1.4	2.4	-0.1	4.2
1993	0.3	1.8	1.9	-0.2	2.9	-0.3	0.7	3.2	-2.6	3.5	0.1	1.9	13.7
1994	6.0	-3.7	-5.1	1.3	2.1	-3.5	3.8	4.0	-1.8	1.7	-4.3	2.5	2.1
1995	0.2	4.3	3.7	3.9	3.3	2.0	3.3	-2.1	3.9	-0.7	6.7	0.8	33.5
1996	5.4	1.7	1.9	-0.3	1.3	0.2	-2.2	1.6	4.7	2.5	8.2	-1.1	26.0
1997	5.7	0.9	-4.3	6.5	4.6	4.7	7.2	-7.3	4.2	-6.3	5.1	1.1	22.6
1998	-0.02	8.1	3.0	3.0	-1.8	0.6	-0.8	-15.1	4.0	9.6	6.1	0.7	16.1
1999	1.9	-0.6	5.2	10.2	-2.1	3.9	-2.9	1.6	-4.5	3.8	1.4	5.7	25.2
2000	-4.8	-7.4	7.8	-1.7	-2.0	-0.7	0.7	6.6	-5.0	3.0	-5.1	3.6	-6.2
2001	0.9	-3.6	-5.9	8.7	1.6	-3.8	0.2	-5.4	-11.1	2.6	8.6	1.7	-7.1
2002	-1.0	1.9	2.9	-4.4	-0.2	-6.9	-5.5	-0.8	-12.4	10.6	5.9	-6.2	-16.8
2003	-3.5	-2.0	1.3	6.1	4.4	1.5	2.8	2.0	-1.5	5.7	-0.2	6.9	25.3
2004	0.3	0.9	-2.1	-1.3	-0.4	2.4	-2.8	0.3	-0.9	-0.5	4.0	3.4	3.1
2005	-2.7	2.6	-2.4	-3.0	2.7	-1.8	3.6	-1.5	0.8	-1.2	3.5	-0.8	-0.6
2006	1.4	1.2	1.1	2.3	-1.7	-0.2	0.3	1.7	2.6	3.4	1.2	2.0	16.3
2007	1.3	-2.8	0.7	5.7	4.3	-1.6	-1.5	1.1	4.0	0.2	-4.0	-0.8	6.4
2008	-4.6	-3.0	-0.03	4.5	-1.4	-10.2	0.2	1.5	-6.0	-14.1	-5.3	-0.6	-33.8
2009	-8.8	-11.7	7.7	7.3	4.1	-0.6	8.6	3.5	2.3	0.005	6.5	0.8	18.8
2010	-3.5	2.6	5.1	1.4	-7.9	-3.6	7.1	-4.3	7.7	3.1	-1.0	5.2	11.0
2011	2.7	2.8	0.8	4.0									
TOTALS	63.0	0.3	66.1	124.2	2.9	-21.7	74.3	-0.4	-47.1	23.0	92.5	104.5	
AVG.	1.0	0.005	1.1	2.0	0.05	-0.4	1.2	-0.01	-0.8	0.4	1.5	1.7	
# Up	40	35	40	40	31	28	38	35	24	36	40	43	
# Down	22	27	22	22	30	33	23	26	37	25	21	18	

DOW JONES INDUSTRIALS MONTHLY POINT CHANGES SINCE 1950

	Jan	Feb	Mar	Apr	May	Jun	Jul	Aug	Sep	Oct	Nov	Dec	Year's Close
1950	1.66	1.65	2.61	8.28	9.09	- 14.31	0.29	7.47	9.49	- 1.35	2.59	7.81	235.41
1951	13.42	3.22	- 4.11	11.19	- 9.48	- 7.01	15.22	12.39	0.91	- 8.81	- 1.08	7.96	269.23
1952	1.46	- 10.61	9.38	- 11.83	5.31	11.32	5.30	- 4.52	- 4.43	- 1.38	14.43	8.24	291.90
1953	- 2.13	- 5.50	- 4.40	- 5.12	- 2.47	- 4.02	7.12	- 14.16	2.82	11.77	5.56	- 0.47	280.90
1954	11.49	2.15	8.97	15.82	8.16	6.04	14.39	- 12.12	24.66	- 8.32	34.63	17.62	404.39
1955	4.44	3.04	- 2.17	15.95	- 0.79	26.52	14.47	2.33	- 1.56	- 11.75	28.39	5.14	488.40
1956	- 17.66	12.91	28.14	4.33	- 38.07	14.73	25.03	- 15.77	- 26.79	4.60	- 7.07	26.69	499.47
1957	- 20.31	- 14.54	10.19	19.55	10.57	- 1.64	5.23	- 24.17	- 28.05	- 15.26	8.83	- 14.18	435.69
1958	14.33	- 10.10	6.84	9.10	6.84	15.48	24.81	5.64	23.46	11.13	14.24	26.19	583.65
1959	10.31	9.54	- 1.79	22.04	20.04	- 0.19	31.28	- 10.47	- 32.73	14.92	12.58	20.18	679.36
1960	- 56.74	7.50	- 13.53	- 14.89	23.80	15.12	- 23.89	9.26	- 45.85	0.22	16.86	18.67	615.89
1961	32.31	13.88	14.55	2.08	18.01	- 12.76	21.41	14.57	- 18.73	2.71	17.68	9.54	731.14
1962	- 31.14	8.05	- 1.10	- 41.62	- 51.97	- 52.08	36.65	11.25	- 30.20	10.79	59.53	2.80	652.10
1963	30.75	- 19.91	19.58	35.18	9.26	- 20.08	- 11.45	33.89	3.47	22.44	- 4.71	12.43	762.95
1964	22.39	14.80	13.15	- 2.52	9.79	10.94	9.60	- 2.62	36.89	- 2.29	2.35	- 1.30	874.13
1965	28.73	0.62	- 14.43	33.26	- 4.27	- 50.01	13.71	11.36	37.48	30.24	- 14.11	22.55	969.26
1966	14.25	- 31.62	- 27.12	8.91	- 49.61	- 13.97	- 22.72	- 58.97	- 14.19	32.85	- 15.48	- 5.90	785.69
1967	64.20	- 10.52	26.61	31.07	- 44.49	7.70	43.98	- 2.95	25.37	- 46.92	- 3.93	29.30	905.11
1968	- 49.64	- 14.97	0.17	71.55	- 13.22	- 1.20	- 14.80	13.01	39.78	16.60	32.69	- 41.33	943.75
1969	2.30	- 40.84	30.27	14.70	- 12.62	- 64.37	- 57.72	21.25	- 23.63	42.90	- 43.69	- 11.94	800.36
1970	- 56.30	33.53	7.98	- 49.50	- 35.63	- 16.91	50.59	30.46	- 3.90	- 5.07	38.48	44.83	838.92
1971	29.58	10.33	25.54	37.38	- 33.94	- 16.67	- 32.71	39.64	- 10.88	- 48.19	- 7.66	58.86	890.20
1972	11.97	25.96	12.57	13.47	6.55	- 31.69	- 4.29	38.99	- 10.46	2.25	62.69	1.81	1020.02
1973	- 21.00	- 43.95	- 4.06	- 29.58	- 20.02	- 9.70	34.69	- 38.83	59.53	9.48	- 134.33	28.61	850.86
1974	4.69	4.98	- 13.85	- 9.93	- 34.58	0.24	- 44.98	- 78.85	- 70.71	57.65	- 46.86	- 2.42	616.24
1975	87.45	35.36	29.10	53.19	10.95	46.70	- 47.48	3.83	- 41.46	42.16	24.63	- 8.26	852.41
1976	122.87	- 2.67	26.84	- 2.60	- 21.62	27.55	- 18.14	- 10.90	16.45	- 25.26	- 17.71	57.43	1004.65
1977	- 50.28	- 17.95	- 17.29	7.77	- 28.24	17.64	- 26.23	- 28.58	- 14.38	- 28.76	11.35	1.47	831.17
1978	- 61.25	- 27.80	15.24	79.96	3.29	- 21.66	43.32	14.55	- 11.00	- 73.37	6.58	5.98	805.01
1979	34.21	- 30.40	53.36	- 7.28	- 32.57	19.65	4.44	41.21	- 9.05	- 62.88	6.65	16.39	838.74
1980	37.11	- 12.71	- 77.39	31.31	33.79	17.07	67.40	- 2.73	- 0.17	- 7.93	68.85	- 29.35	963.99
1981	- 16.72	27.31	29.29	- 6.12	- 6.00	- 14.87	- 24.54	- 70.87	- 31.49	2.57	36.43	- 13.98	875.00
1982	- 3.90	- 46.71	- 1.62	25.59	- 28.82	- 7.61	- 3.33	92.71	- 5.06	95.47	47.56	7.26	1046.54
1983	29.16	36.92	17.41	96.17	- 26.22	21.98	- 22.74	16.94	16.97	- 7.93	50.82	- 17.38	1258.64
1984	- 38.06	- 65.95	10.26	5.86	- 65.90	27.55	- 17.12	109.10	- 17.67	0.67	- 18.44	22.63	1211.57
1985	75.20	- 2.76	- 17.23	- 8.72	57.35	20.05	11.99	- 13.44	- 5.38	45.68	97.82	74.54	1546.67
1986	24.32	138.07	109.55	- 34.63	92.73	16.01	- 117.41	123.03	- 130.76	110.23	36.42	- 18.28	1895.95
1987	262.09	65.95	80.70	- 18.33	5.21	126.96	153.54	90.88	- 66.67	- 602.75	- 159.98	105.28	1938.83
1988	19.39	113.40	- 83.56	44.27	- 1.21	110.59	- 12.98	- 97.08	81.26	35.74	- 34.14	54.06	2168.57
1989	173.75	- 83.93	35.23	125.18	61.35	- 40.09	220.60	76.61	- 44.45	- 47.74	61.19	46.93	2753.20
1990	- 162.66	36.71	79.96	- 50.45	219.90	4.03	24.51	- 290.84	- 161.88	- 10.15	117.32	74.01	2633.66
1991	102.73	145.79	31.68	- 25.99	139.63	- 120.75	118.07	18.78	- 26.83	52.33	- 174.42	274.15	3168.83
1992	54.56	44.28	- 32.20	123.65	37.76	- 78.36	75.26	- 136.43	14.31	- 45.38	78.88	- 4.05	3301.11
1993	8.92	60.78	64.30	- 7.56	99.88	- 11.35	23.39	111.78	- 96.13	125.47	3.36	70.14	3754.09
1994	224.27	- 146.34	- 196.06	45.73	76.68	- 133.41	139.54	148.92	- 70.23	64.93	- 168.89	95.21	3834.44
1995	9.42	167.19	146.64	163.58	143.87	90.96	152.37	- 97.91	178.52	- 33.60	319.01	42.63	5117.12
1996	278.18	90.32	101.52	- 18.06	74.10	11.45	- 125.72	87.30	265.96	147.21	492.32	- 73.43	6448.27
1997	364.82	64.65	- 294.26	425.51	322.05	341.75	549.82	- 600.19	322.84	- 503.18	381.05	85.12	7908.25
1998	- 1.75	639.22	254.09	263.56	- 163.42	52.07	- 68.73	- 1344.22	303.55	749.48	524.45	64.88	9181.43
1999	177.40	- 52.25	479.58	1002.88	- 229.30	411.06	- 315.65	174.13	- 492.33	392.91	147.95	619.31	11497.12
2000	- 556.59	- 812.22	793.61	- 188.01	- 211.58	- 74.44	74.09	693.12	- 564.18	320.22	- 556.65	372.36	10786.85
2001	100.51	- 392.08	- 616.50	856.19	176.97	- 409.54	20.41	- 573.06	- 1102.19	227.58	776.42	169.94	10021.50
2002	- 101.50	186.13	297.81	- 457.72	- 20.97	- 681.99	- 506.67	- 73.09	- 1071.57	805.10	499.06	- 554.46	8341.63
2003	- 287.82	- 162.73	101.05	487.96	370.17	135.18	248.36	182.02	- 140.76	526.06	- 18.66	671.46	10453.92
2004	34.15	95.85	- 226.22	- 132.13	- 37.12	247.03	- 295.77	34.21	- 93.65	- 52.80	400.55	354.99	10783.01
2005	- 293.07	276.29	- 262.47	- 311.25	274.97	- 92.51	365.94	- 159.31	87.10	- 128.63	365.80	- 88.37	10717.50
2006	147.36	128.55	115.91	257.82	- 198.83	- 18.09	35.46	195.47	297.92	401.66	141.20	241.22	12463.15
2007	158.54	- 353.06	85.72	708.56	564.73	- 219.02	- 196.63	145.75	537.69	34.38	- 558.29	- 106.90	13264.82
2008	- 614.46	- 383.97	- 3.50	557.24	- 181.81	- 1288.31	28.01	165.53	- 692.89	- 1525.65	- 495.97	- 52.65	8776.39
2009	- 775.53	- 937.93	545.99	559.20	332.21	- 53.33	724.61	324.67	216.00	0.45	632.11	83.21	10428.05
2010	- 360.72	257.93	531.37	151.98	- 871.98	- 362.61	691.92	- 451.22	773.33	330.44	- 112.47	571.49	11577.51
2011	314.42	334.41	93.39	490.81									
TOTALS	- 440.12	- 636.75	2431.29	5483.99	748.26	- 2191.18	2115.12	- 1111.25	- 1836.33	1475.94	3084.77	3486.67	
# Up	40	35	40	40	31	28	38	35	24	36	40	43	
# Down	22	27	22	22	30	33	23	26	37	25	21	18	

DOW JONES INDUSTRIALS MONTHLY CLOSING PRICES SINCE 1950

	Jan	Feb	Mar	Apr	May	Jun	Jul	Aug	Sep	Oct	Nov	Dec
1950	201.79	203.44	206.05	214.33	223.42	209.11	209.40	216.87	226.36	225.01	227.60	235.41
1951	248.83	252.05	247.94	259.13	249.65	242.64	257.86	270.25	271.16	262.35	261.27	269.23
1952	270.69	260.08	269.46	257.63	262.94	274.26	279.56	275.04	270.61	269.23	283.66	291.90
1953	289.77	284.27	279.87	274.75	272.28	268.26	275.38	261.22	264.04	275.81	281.37	280.90
1954	292.39	294.54	303.51	319.33	327.49	333.53	347.92	335.80	360.46	352.14	386.77	404.39
1955	408.83	411.87	409.70	425.65	424.86	451.38	465.85	468.18	466.62	454.87	483.26	488.40
1956	470.74	483.65	511.79	516.12	478.05	492.78	517.81	502.04	475.25	479.85	472.78	499.47
1957	479.16	464.62	474.81	494.36	504.93	503.29	508.52	484.35	456.30	441.04	449.87	435.69
1958	450.02	439.92	446.76	455.86	462.70	478.18	502.99	508.63	532.09	543.22	557.46	583.65
1959	593.96	603.50	601.71	623.75	643.79	643.60	674.88	664.41	631.68	646.60	659.18	679.36
1960	622.62	630.12	616.59	601.70	625.50	640.62	616.73	625.99	580.14	580.36	597.22	615.89
1961	648.20	662.08	676.63	678.71	696.72	683.96	705.37	719.94	701.21	703.92	721.60	731.14
1962	700.00	708.05	706.95	665.33	613.36	561.28	597.93	609.18	578.98	589.77	649.30	652.10
1963	682.85	662.94	682.52	717.70	726.96	706.88	695.43	729.32	732.79	755.23	750.52	762.95
1964	785.34	800.14	813.29	810.77	820.56	831.50	841.10	838.48	875.37	873.08	875.43	874.13
1965	902.86	903.48	889.05	922.31	918.04	868.03	881.74	893.10	930.58	960.82	946.71	969.26
1966	983.51	951.89	924.77	933.68	884.07	870.10	847.38	788.41	774.22	807.07	791.59	785.69
1967	849.89	839.37	865.98	897.05	852.56	860.26	904.24	901.29	926.66	879.74	875.81	905.11
1968	855.47	840.50	840.67	912.22	899.00	897.80	883.00	896.01	935.79	952.39	985.08	943.75
1969	946.05	905.21	935.48	950.18	937.56	873.19	815.47	836.72	813.09	855.99	812.30	800.36
1970	744.06	777.59	785.57	736.07	700.44	683.53	734.12	764.58	760.68	755.61	794.09	838.92
1971	868.50	878.83	904.37	941.75	907.81	891.14	858.43	898.07	887.19	839.00	831.34	890.20
1972	902.17	928.13	940.70	954.17	960.72	929.03	924.74	963.73	953.27	955.52	1018.21	1020.02
1973	999.02	955.07	951.01	921.43	901.41	891.71	926.40	887.57	947.10	956.58	822.25	850.86
1974	855.55	860.53	846.68	836.75	802.17	802.41	757.43	678.58	607.87	665.52	618.66	616.24
1975	703.69	739.05	768.15	821.34	832.29	878.99	831.51	835.34	793.88	836.04	860.67	852.41
1976	975.28	972.61	999.45	996.85	975.23	1002.78	984.64	973.74	990.19	964.93	947.22	1004.65
1977	954.37	936.42	919.13	926.90	898.66	916.30	890.07	861.49	847.11	818.35	829.70	831.17
1978	769.92	742.12	757.36	837.32	840.61	818.95	862.27	876.82	865.82	792.45	799.03	805.01
1979	839.22	808.82	862.18	854.90	822.33	841.98	846.42	887.63	878.58	815.70	822.35	838.74
1980	875.85	863.14	785.75	817.06	850.85	867.92	935.32	932.59	932.42	924.49	993.34	963.99
1981	947.27	974.58	1003.87	997.75	991.75	976.88	952.34	881.47	849.98	852.55	888.98	875.00
1982	871.10	824.39	822.77	848.36	819.54	811.93	808.60	901.31	896.25	991.72	1039.28	1046.54
1983	1075.70	1112.62	1130.03	1226.20	1199.98	1221.96	1199.22	1216.16	1233.13	1225.20	1276.02	1258.64
1984	1220.58	1154.63	1164.89	1170.75	1104.85	1132.40	1115.28	1224.38	1206.71	1207.38	1188.94	1211.57
1985	1286.77	1284.01	1266.78	1258.06	1315.41	1335.46	1347.45	1334.01	1328.63	1374.31	1472.13	1546.67
1986	1570.99	1709.06	1818.61	1783.98	1876.71	1892.72	1775.31	1898.34	1767.58	1877.81	1914.23	1895.95
1987	2158.04	2223.99	2304.69	2286.36	2291.57	2418.53	2572.07	2662.95	2596.28	1993.53	1833.55	1938.83
1988	1958.22	2071.62	1988.06	2032.33	2031.12	2141.71	2128.73	2031.65	2112.91	2148.65	2114.51	2168.57
1989	2342.32	2258.39	2293.62	2418.80	2480.15	2440.06	2660.66	2737.27	2692.82	2645.08	2706.27	2753.20
1990	2590.54	2627.25	2707.21	2656.76	2876.66	2880.69	2905.20	2614.36	2452.48	2442.33	2559.65	2633.66
1991	2736.39	2882.18	2913.86	2887.87	3027.50	2906.75	3024.82	3043.60	3016.77	3069.10	2894.68	3168.83
1992	3223.39	3267.67	3235.47	3359.12	3396.88	3318.52	3393.78	3257.35	3271.66	3226.28	3305.16	3301.11
1993	3310.03	3370.81	3435.11	3427.55	3527.43	3516.08	3539.47	3651.25	3555.12	3680.59	3683.95	3754.09
1994	3978.36	3832.02	3635.96	3681.69	3758.37	3624.96	3764.50	3913.42	3843.19	3908.12	3739.23	3834.44
1995	3843.86	4011.05	4157.69	4321.27	4465.14	4556.10	4708.47	4610.56	4789.08	4755.48	5074.49	5117.12
1996	5395.30	5485.62	5587.14	5569.08	5643.18	5654.63	5528.91	5616.21	5882.17	6029.38	6521.70	6448.27
1997	6813.09	6877.74	6583.48	7008.99	7331.04	7672.79	8222.61	7622.42	7945.26	7442.08	7823.13	7908.25
1998	7906.50	8545.72	8799.81	9063.37	8899.95	8952.02	8883.29	7539.07	7842.62	8592.10	9116.55	9181.43
1999	9358.83	9306.58	9786.16	10789.04	10559.74	10970.80	10655.15	10829.28	10336.95	10729.86	10877.81	11497.12
2000	10940.53	10128.31	10921.92	10733.91	10522.33	10447.89	10521.98	11215.10	10650.92	10971.14	10414.49	10786.85
2001	10887.36	10495.28	9878.78	10734.97	10911.94	10502.40	10522.81	9949.75	8847.56	9075.14	9851.56	10021.50
2002	9920.00	10106.13	10403.94	9946.22	9925.25	9243.26	8736.59	8663.50	7591.93	8397.03	8896.09	8341.63
2003	8053.81	7891.08	7992.13	8480.09	8850.26	8985.44	9233.80	9415.82	9275.06	9801.12	9782.46	10453.92
2004	10488.07	10583.92	10357.70	10225.57	10188.45	10435.48	10139.71	10173.92	10080.27	10027.47	10428.02	10783.01
2005	10489.94	10766.23	10503.76	10192.51	10467.48	10274.97	10640.91	10481.60	10568.70	10440.07	10805.87	10717.50
2006	10864.86	10993.41	11109.32	11367.14	11168.31	11150.22	11185.68	11381.15	11679.07	12080.73	12221.93	12463.15
2007	12621.69	12268.63	12354.35	13062.91	13627.64	13408.62	13211.99	13357.74	13895.63	13930.01	13371.72	13264.82
2008	12650.36	12266.39	12262.89	12820.13	12638.32	11350.01	11378.02	11543.55	10850.66	9325.01	8829.04	8776.39
2009	8000.86	7062.93	7608.92	8168.12	8500.33	8447.00	9171.61	9496.28	9712.28	9712.73	10344.84	10428.05
2010	10067.33	10325.26	10856.63	11008.61	10136.63	9774.02	10465.94	10014.72	10788.05	11118.49	11006.02	11577.51
2011	11891.93	12226.34	12319.73	12810.54								

154

STANDARD & POOR'S 500 MONTHLY PERCENT CHANGES SINCE 1950

	Jan	Feb	Mar	Apr	May	Jun	Jul	Aug	Sep	Oct	Nov	Dec	Year's Change
1950	1.7	1.0	0.4	4.5	3.9	– 5.8	0.8	3.3	5.6	0.4	– 0.1	4.6	21.8
1951	6.1	0.6	– 1.8	4.8	– 4.1	– 2.6	6.9	3.9	– 0.1	– 1.4	– 0.3	3.9	16.5
1952	1.6	– 3.6	4.8	– 4.3	2.3	4.6	1.8	– 1.5	– 2.0	– 0.1	4.6	3.5	11.8
1953	– 0.7	– 1.8	– 2.4	– 2.6	– 0.3	– 1.6	2.5	– 5.8	0.1	5.1	0.9	0.2	– 6.6
1954	5.1	0.3	3.0	4.9	3.3	0.1	5.7	– 3.4	8.3	– 1.9	8.1	5.1	45.0
1955	1.8	0.4	– 0.5	3.8	– 0.1	8.2	6.1	– 0.8	1.1	– 3.0	7.5	– 0.1	26.4
1956	– 3.6	3.5	6.9	– 0.2	– 6.6	3.9	5.2	– 3.8	– 4.5	0.5	– 1.1	3.5	2.6
1957	– 4.2	– 3.3	2.0	3.7	3.7	– 0.1	1.1	– 5.6	– 6.2	– 3.2	1.6	– 4.1	– 14.3
1958	4.3	– 2.1	3.1	3.2	1.5	2.6	4.3	1.2	4.8	2.5	2.2	5.2	38.1
1959	0.4	– 0.02	0.1	3.9	1.9	– 0.4	3.5	– 1.5	– 4.6	1.1	1.3	2.8	8.5
1960	– 7.1	0.9	– 1.4	– 1.8	2.7	2.0	– 2.5	2.6	– 6.0	– 0.2	4.0	4.6	– 3.0
1961	6.3	2.7	2.6	0.4	1.9	– 2.9	3.3	2.0	– 2.0	2.8	3.9	0.3	23.1
1962	– 3.8	1.6	– 0.6	– 6.2	– 8.6	– 8.2	6.4	1.5	– 4.8	0.4	10.2	1.3	– 11.8
1963	4.9	– 2.9	3.5	4.9	1.4	– 2.0	– 0.3	4.9	– 1.1	3.2	– 1.1	2.4	18.9
1964	2.7	1.0	1.5	0.6	1.1	1.6	1.8	– 1.6	2.9	0.8	– 0.5	0.4	13.0
1965	3.3	– 0.1	– 1.5	3.4	– 0.8	– 4.9	1.3	2.3	3.2	2.7	– 0.9	0.9	9.1
1966	0.5	– 1.8	– 2.2	2.1	– 5.4	– 1.6	– 1.3	– 7.8	– 0.7	4.8	0.3	– 0.1	– 13.1
1967	7.8	0.2	3.9	4.2	– 5.2	1.8	4.5	– 1.2	3.3	– 2.9	0.1	2.6	20.1
1968	– 4.4	– 3.1	0.9	8.2	1.1	0.9	– 1.8	1.1	3.9	0.7	4.8	– 4.2	7.7
1969	– 0.8	– 4.7	3.4	2.1	– 0.2	– 5.6	– 6.0	4.0	– 2.5	4.4	– 3.5	– 1.9	– 11.4
1970	– 7.6	5.3	0.1	– 9.0	– 6.1	– 5.0	7.3	4.4	3.3	– 1.1	4.7	5.7	0.1
1971	4.0	0.9	3.7	3.6	– 4.2	0.1	– 4.1	3.6	– 0.7	– 4.2	– 0.3	8.6	10.8
1972	1.8	2.5	0.6	0.4	1.7	– 2.2	0.2	3.4	– 0.5	0.9	4.6	1.2	15.6
1973	– 1.7	– 3.7	– 0.1	– 4.1	– 1.9	– 0.7	3.8	– 3.7	4.0	– 0.1	–11.4	1.7	– 17.4
1974	– 1.0	– 0.4	– 2.3	– 3.9	– 3.4	– 1.5	– 7.8	– 9.0	–11.9	16.3	– 5.3	– 2.0	– 29.7
1975	12.3	6.0	2.2	4.7	4.4	4.4	– 6.8	– 2.1	– 3.5	6.2	2.5	– 1.2	31.5
1976	11.8	– 1.1	3.1	– 1.1	– 1.4	4.1	– 0.8	– 0.5	2.3	– 2.2	– 0.8	5.2	19.1
1977	– 5.1	– 2.2	– 1.4	0.02	– 2.4	4.5	– 1.6	– 2.1	– 0.2	– 4.3	2.7	0.3	– 11.5
1978	– 6.2	– 2.5	2.5	8.5	0.4	– 1.8	5.4	2.6	– 0.7	– 9.2	1.7	1.5	1.1
1979	4.0	– 3.7	5.5	0.2	– 2.6	3.9	0.9	5.3	NC	– 6.9	4.3	1.7	12.3
1980	5.8	– 0.4	–10.2	4.1	4.7	2.7	6.5	0.6	2.5	1.6	10.2	– 3.4	25.8
1981	– 4.6	1.3	3.6	– 2.3	– 0.2	– 1.0	– 0.2	– 6.2	– 5.4	4.9	3.7	– 3.0	– 9.7
1982	– 1.8	– 6.1	– 1.0	4.0	– 3.9	– 2.0	– 2.3	11.6	0.8	11.0	3.6	1.5	14.8
1983	3.3	1.9	3.3	7.5	– 1.2	3.5	– 3.3	1.1	1.0	– 1.5	1.7	– 0.9	17.3
1984	– 0.9	– 3.9	1.3	0.5	– 5.9	1.7	– 1.6	10.6	– 0.3	– 0.01	– 1.5	2.2	1.4
1985	7.4	0.9	– 0.3	– 0.5	5.4	1.2	– 0.5	– 1.2	– 3.5	4.3	6.5	4.5	26.3
1986	0.2	7.1	5.3	– 1.4	5.0	1.4	– 5.9	7.1	– 8.5	5.5	2.1	– 2.8	14.6
1987	13.2	3.7	2.6	– 1.1	0.6	4.8	4.8	3.5	– 2.4	–21.8	– 8.5	7.3	2.0
1988	4.0	4.2	– 3.3	0.9	0.3	4.3	– 0.5	– 3.9	4.0	2.6	– 1.9	1.5	12.4
1989	7.1	– 2.9	2.1	5.0	3.5	– 0.8	8.8	1.6	– 0.7	– 2.5	1.7	2.1	27.3
1990	– 6.9	0.9	2.4	– 2.7	9.2	– 0.9	– 0.5	– 9.4	– 5.1	– 0.7	6.0	2.5	– 6.6
1991	4.2	6.7	2.2	0.03	3.9	– 4.8	4.5	2.0	– 1.9	1.2	– 4.4	11.2	26.3
1992	– 2.0	1.0	– 2.2	2.8	0.1	– 1.7	3.9	– 2.4	0.9	0.2	3.0	1.0	4.5
1993	0.7	1.0	1.9	– 2.5	2.3	0.1	– 0.5	3.4	– 1.0	1.9	– 1.3	1.0	7.1
1994	3.3	– 3.0	– 4.6	1.2	1.2	– 2.7	3.1	3.8	– 2.7	2.1	– 4.0	1.2	– 1.5
1995	2.4	3.6	2.7	2.8	3.6	2.1	3.2	– 0.03	4.0	– 0.5	4.1	1.7	34.1
1996	3.3	0.7	0.8	1.3	2.3	0.2	– 4.6	1.9	5.4	2.6	7.3	– 2.2	20.3
1997	6.1	0.6	– 4.3	5.8	5.9	4.3	7.8	– 5.7	5.3	– 3.4	4.5	1.6	31.0
1998	1.0	7.0	5.0	0.9	– 1.9	3.9	– 1.2	–14.6	6.2	8.0	5.9	5.6	26.7
1999	4.1	– 3.2	3.9	3.8	– 2.5	5.4	– 3.2	– 0.6	– 2.9	6.3	1.9	5.8	19.5
2000	– 5.1	– 2.0	9.7	– 3.1	– 2.2	2.4	– 1.6	6.1	– 5.3	– 0.5	– 8.0	0.4	– 10.1
2001	3.5	– 9.2	– 6.4	7.7	0.5	– 2.5	– 1.1	– 6.4	– 8.2	1.8	7.5	0.8	– 13.0
2002	– 1.6	– 2.1	3.7	– 6.1	– 0.9	– 7.2	– 7.9	0.5	–11.0	8.6	5.7	– 6.0	– 23.4
2003	– 2.7	– 1.7	1.0	8.0	5.1	1.1	1.6	1.8	– 1.2	5.5	0.7	5.1	26.4
2004	1.7	1.2	– 1.6	– 1.7	1.2	1.8	– 3.4	0.2	0.9	1.4	3.9	3.2	9.0
2005	– 2.5	1.9	– 1.9	– 2.0	3.0	– 0.01	3.6	– 1.1	0.7	– 1.8	3.5	– 0.1	3.0
2006	2.5	0.1	1.1	1.2	– 3.1	0.01	0.5	2.1	2.5	3.2	1.6	1.3	13.6
2007	1.4	– 2.2	1.0	4.3	3.3	– 1.8	– 3.2	1.3	3.6	1.5	– 4.4	– 0.9	3.5
2008	– 6.1	– 3.5	– 0.6	4.8	1.1	– 8.6	– 1.0	1.2	– 9.1	– 16.9	– 7.5	0.8	– 38.5
2009	– 8.6	– 11.0	8.5	9.4	5.3	0.02	7.4	3.4	3.6	– 2.0	5.7	1.8	23.5
2010	– 3.7	2.9	5.9	1.5	– 8.2	– 5.4	6.9	– 4.7	8.8	3.7	– 0.2	6.5	12.8
2011	2.3	3.2	– 0.1	2.8									
TOTALS	65.2	– 11.5	71.1	95.9	15.5	– 2.7	59.9	3.3	– 28.2	38.4	93.8	104.9	
AVG.	1.1	– 0.2	1.1	1.5	0.3	– 0.04	1.0	0.1	– 0.5	0.6	1.5	1.7	
# Up	38	33	40	43	35	32	33	34	27	36	40	46	
# Down	24	29	22	19	26	29	28	27	33	25	21	15	

155

STANDARD & POOR'S 500 MONTHLY CLOSING PRICES SINCE 1950

	Jan	Feb	Mar	Apr	May	Jun	Jul	Aug	Sep	Oct	Nov	Dec
1950	17.05	17.22	17.29	18.07	18.78	17.69	17.84	18.42	19.45	19.53	19.51	20.41
1951	21.66	21.80	21.40	22.43	21.52	20.96	22.40	23.28	23.26	22.94	22.88	23.77
1952	24.14	23.26	24.37	23.32	23.86	24.96	25.40	25.03	24.54	24.52	25.66	26.57
1953	26.38	25.90	25.29	24.62	24.54	24.14	24.75	23.32	23.35	24.54	24.76	24.81
1954	26.08	26.15	26.94	28.26	29.19	29.21	30.88	29.83	32.31	31.68	34.24	35.98
1955	36.63	36.76	36.58	37.96	37.91	41.03	43.52	43.18	43.67	42.34	45.51	45.48
1956	43.82	45.34	48.48	48.38	45.20	46.97	49.39	47.51	45.35	45.58	45.08	46.67
1957	44.72	43.26	44.11	45.74	47.43	47.37	47.91	45.22	42.42	41.06	41.72	39.99
1958	41.70	40.84	42.10	43.44	44.09	45.24	47.19	47.75	50.06	51.33	52.48	55.21
1959	55.42	55.41	55.44	57.59	58.68	58.47	60.51	59.60	56.88	57.52	58.28	59.89
1960	55.61	56.12	55.34	54.37	55.83	56.92	55.51	56.96	53.52	53.39	55.54	58.11
1961	61.78	63.44	65.06	65.31	66.56	64.64	66.76	68.07	66.73	68.62	71.32	71.55
1962	68.84	69.96	69.55	65.24	59.63	54.75	58.23	59.12	56.27	56.52	62.26	63.10
1963	66.20	64.29	66.57	69.80	70.80	69.37	69.13	72.50	71.70	74.01	73.23	75.02
1964	77.04	77.80	78.98	79.46	80.37	81.69	83.18	81.83	84.18	84.86	84.42	84.75
1965	87.56	87.43	86.16	89.11	88.42	84.12	85.25	87.17	89.96	92.42	91.61	92.43
1966	92.88	91.22	89.23	91.06	86.13	84.74	83.60	77.10	76.56	80.20	80.45	80.33
1967	86.61	86.78	90.20	94.01	89.08	90.64	94.75	93.64	96.71	93.90	94.00	96.47
1968	92.24	89.36	90.20	97.59	98.68	99.58	97.74	98.86	102.67	103.41	108.37	103.86
1969	103.01	98.13	101.51	103.69	103.46	97.71	91.83	95.51	93.12	97.24	93.81	92.06
1970	85.02	89.50	89.63	81.52	76.55	72.72	78.05	81.52	84.21	83.25	87.20	92.15
1971	95.88	96.75	100.31	103.95	99.63	99.70	95.58	99.03	98.34	94.23	93.99	102.09
1972	103.94	106.57	107.20	107.67	109.53	107.14	107.39	111.09	110.55	111.58	116.67	118.05
1973	116.03	111.68	111.52	106.97	104.95	104.26	108.22	104.25	108.43	108.29	95.96	97.55
1974	96.57	96.22	93.98	90.31	87.28	86.00	79.31	72.15	63.54	73.90	69.97	68.56
1975	76.98	81.59	83.36	87.30	91.15	95.19	88.75	86.88	83.87	89.04	91.24	90.19
1976	100.86	99.71	102.77	101.64	100.18	104.28	103.44	102.91	105.24	102.90	102.10	107.46
1977	102.03	99.82	98.42	98.44	96.12	100.48	98.85	96.77	96.53	92.34	94.83	95.10
1978	89.25	87.04	89.21	96.83	97.24	95.53	100.68	103.29	102.54	93.15	94.70	96.11
1979	99.93	96.28	101.59	101.76	99.08	102.91	103.81	109.32	109.32	101.82	106.16	107.94
1980	114.16	113.66	102.09	106.29	111.24	114.24	121.67	122.38	125.46	127.47	140.52	135.76
1981	129.55	131.27	136.00	132.81	132.59	131.21	130.92	122.79	116.18	121.89	126.35	122.55
1982	120.40	113.11	111.96	116.44	111.88	109.61	107.09	119.51	120.42	133.71	138.54	140.64
1983	145.30	148.06	152.96	164.42	162.39	168.11	162.56	164.40	166.07	163.55	166.40	164.93
1984	163.41	157.06	159.18	160.05	150.55	153.18	150.66	166.68	166.10	166.09	163.58	167.24
1985	179.63	181.18	180.66	179.83	189.55	191.85	190.92	188.63	182.08	189.82	202.17	211.28
1986	211.78	226.92	238.90	235.52	247.35	250.84	236.12	252.93	231.32	243.98	249.22	242.17
1987	274.08	284.20	291.70	288.36	290.10	304.00	318.66	329.80	321.83	251.79	230.30	247.08
1988	257.07	267.82	258.89	261.33	262.16	273.50	272.02	261.52	271.91	278.97	273.70	277.72
1989	297.47	288.86	294.87	309.64	320.52	317.98	346.08	351.45	349.15	340.36	345.99	353.40
1990	329.08	331.89	339.94	330.80	361.23	358.02	356.15	322.56	306.05	304.00	322.22	330.22
1991	343.93	367.07	375.22	375.35	389.83	371.16	387.81	395.43	387.86	392.46	375.22	417.09
1992	408.79	412.70	403.69	414.95	415.35	408.14	424.21	414.03	417.80	418.68	431.35	435.71
1993	438.78	443.38	451.67	440.19	450.19	450.53	448.13	463.56	458.93	467.83	461.79	466.45
1994	481.61	467.14	445.77	450.91	456.50	444.27	458.26	475.49	462.69	472.35	453.69	459.27
1995	470.42	487.39	500.71	514.71	533.40	544.75	562.06	561.88	584.41	581.50	605.37	615.93
1996	636.02	640.43	645.50	654.17	669.12	670.63	639.95	651.99	687.31	705.27	757.02	740.74
1997	786.16	790.82	757.12	801.34	848.28	885.14	954.29	899.47	947.28	914.62	955.40	970.43
1998	980.28	1049.34	1101.75	1111.75	1090.82	1133.84	1120.67	957.28	1017.01	1098.67	1163.63	1229.23
1999	1279.64	1238.33	1286.37	1335.18	1301.84	1372.71	1328.72	1320.41	1282.71	1362.93	1388.91	1469.25
2000	1394.46	1366.42	1498.58	1452.43	1420.60	1454.60	1430.83	1517.68	1436.51	1429.40	1314.95	1320.28
2001	1366.01	1239.94	1160.33	1249.46	1255.82	1224.42	1211.23	1133.58	1040.94	1059.78	1139.45	1148.08
2002	1130.20	1106.73	1147.39	1076.92	1067.14	989.82	911.62	916.07	815.28	885.76	936.31	879.82
2003	855.70	841.15	849.18	916.92	963.59	974.50	990.31	1008.01	995.97	1050.71	1058.20	1111.92
2004	1131.13	1144.94	1126.21	1107.30	1120.68	1140.84	1101.72	1104.24	1114.58	1130.20	1173.82	1211.92
2005	1181.27	1203.60	1180.59	1156.85	1191.50	1191.33	1234.18	1220.33	1228.81	1207.01	1249.48	1248.29
2006	1280.08	1280.66	1294.83	1310.61	1270.09	1270.20	1276.66	1303.82	1335.85	1377.94	1400.63	1418.30
2007	1438.24	1406.82	1420.86	1482.37	1530.62	1503.35	1455.27	1473.99	1526.75	1549.38	1481.14	1468.36
2008	1378.55	1330.63	1322.70	1385.59	1400.38	1280.00	1267.38	1282.83	1166.36	968.75	896.24	903.25
2009	825.88	735.09	797.87	872.81	919.14	919.32	987.48	1020.62	1057.08	1036.19	1095.63	1115.10
2010	1073.87	1104.49	1169.43	1186.69	1089.41	1030.71	1101.60	1049.33	1141.20	1183.26	1180.55	1257.64
2011	1286.12	1327.22	1325.83	1363.61								

NASDAQ COMPOSITE MONTHLY PERCENT CHANGES SINCE 1971

	Jan	Feb	Mar	Apr	May	Jun	Jul	Aug	Sep	Oct	Nov	Dec	Year's Change
1971	10.2	2.6	4.6	6.0	-3.6	-0.4	-2.3	3.0	0.6	-3.6	-1.1	9.8	27.4
1972	4.2	5.5	2.2	2.5	0.9	-1.8	-1.8	1.7	-0.3	0.5	2.1	0.6	17.2
1973	-4.0	-6.2	-2.4	-8.2	-4.8	-1.6	7.6	-3.5	6.0	-0.9	-15.1	-1.4	-31.1
1974	3.0	-0.6	-2.2	-5.9	-7.7	-5.3	-7.9	-10.9	-0.7	17.2	-3.5	-5.0	-35.1
1975	16.6	4.6	3.6	3.8	5.8	4.7	-4.4	-5.0	-5.9	3.6	2.4	-1.5	29.8
1976	12.1	3.7	0.4	-0.6	-2.3	2.6	1.1	-1.7	1.7	-1.0	0.9	7.4	26.1
1977	-2.4	-1.0	-0.5	1.4	0.1	4.3	0.9	-0.5	0.7	-3.3	5.8	1.8	7.3
1978	-4.0	0.6	4.7	8.5	4.4	0.05	5.0	6.9	-1.6	-16.4	3.2	2.9	12.3
1979	6.6	-2.6	7.5	1.6	-1.8	5.1	2.3	6.4	-0.3	-9.6	6.4	4.8	28.1
1980	7.0	-2.3	-17.1	6.9	7.5	4.9	8.9	5.7	3.4	2.7	8.0	-2.8	33.9
1981	-2.2	0.1	6.1	3.1	3.1	-3.5	-1.9	-7.5	-8.0	8.4	3.1	-2.7	-3.2
1982	-3.8	-4.8	-2.1	5.2	-3.3	-4.1	-2.3	6.2	5.6	13.3	9.3	0.04	18.7
1983	6.9	5.0	3.9	8.2	5.3	3.2	-4.6	-3.8	1.4	-7.4	4.1	-2.5	19.9
1984	-3.7	-5.9	-0.7	-1.3	-5.9	2.9	-4.2	10.9	-1.8	-1.2	-1.8	2.0	-11.2
1985	12.7	2.0	-1.7	0.5	3.6	1.9	1.7	-1.2	-5.8	4.4	7.3	3.5	31.4
1986	3.3	7.1	4.2	2.3	4.4	1.3	-8.4	3.1	-8.4	2.9	-0.3	-2.8	7.5
1987	12.2	8.4	1.2	-2.8	-0.3	2.0	2.4	4.6	-2.3	-27.2	-5.6	8.3	-5.4
1988	4.3	6.5	2.1	1.2	-2.3	6.6	-1.9	-2.8	3.0	-1.4	-2.9	2.7	15.4
1989	5.2	-0.4	1.8	5.1	4.4	-2.4	4.3	3.4	0.8	-3.7	0.1	-0.3	19.3
1990	-8.6	2.4	2.3	-3.6	9.3	0.7	-5.2	-13.0	-9.6	-4.3	8.9	4.1	-17.8
1991	10.8	9.4	6.5	0.5	4.4	-6.0	5.5	4.7	0.2	3.1	-3.5	11.9	56.8
1992	5.8	2.1	-4.7	-4.2	1.1	-3.7	3.1	-3.0	3.6	3.8	7.9	3.7	15.5
1993	2.9	-3.7	2.9	-4.2	5.9	0.5	0.1	5.4	2.7	2.2	-3.2	3.0	14.7
1994	3.0	-1.0	-6.2	-1.3	0.2	-4.0	2.3	6.0	-0.2	1.7	-3.5	0.2	-3.2
1995	0.4	5.1	3.0	3.3	2.4	8.0	7.3	1.9	2.3	-0.7	2.2	-0.7	39.9
1996	0.7	3.8	0.1	8.1	4.4	-4.7	-8.8	5.6	7.5	-0.4	5.8	-0.1	22.7
1997	6.9	-5.1	-6.7	3.2	11.1	3.0	10.5	-0.4	6.2	-5.5	0.4	-1.9	21.6
1998	3.1	9.3	3.7	1.8	-4.8	6.5	-1.2	-19.9	13.0	4.6	10.1	12.5	39.6
1999	14.3	-8.7	7.6	3.3	-2.8	8.7	-1.8	3.8	0.2	8.0	12.5	22.0	85.6
2000	-3.2	19.2	-2.6	-15.6	-11.9	16.6Z	-5.0	11.7	-12.7	-8.3	-22.9	-4.9	-39.3
2001	12.2	-22.4	-14.5	15.0	-0.3	2.4	-6.2	-10.9	-17.0	12.8	14.2	1.0	-21.1
2002	-0.8	-10.5	6.6	-8.5	-4.3	-9.4	-9.2	-1.0	-10.9	13.5	11.2	-9.7	-31.5
2003	-1.1	1.3	0.3	9.2	9.0	1.7	6.9	4.3	-1.3	8.1	1.5	2.2	50.0
2004	3.1	-1.8	-1.8	-3.7	3.5	3.1	-7.8	-2.6	3.2	4.1	6.2	3.7	8.6
2005	-5.2	-0.5	-2.6	-3.9	7.6	-0.5	6.2	-1.5	-0.02	-1.5	5.3	-1.2	1.4
2006	4.6	-1.1	2.6	-0.7	-6.2	-0.3	-3.7	4.4	3.4	4.8	2.7	-0.7	9.5
2007	2.0	-1.9	0.2	4.3	3.1	-0.05	-2.2	2.0	4.0	5.8	-6.9	-0.3	9.8
2008	-9.9	-5.0	0.3	5.9	4.6	-9.1	1.4	1.8	-11.6	-17.7	-10.8	2.7	-40.5
2009	-6.4	-6.7	10.9	12.3	3.3	3.4	7.8	1.5	5.6	-3.6	4.9	5.8	43.9
2010	-5.4	4.2	7.1	2.6	-8.3	-6.5	6.9	-6.2	12.0	5.9	-0.4	6.2	16.9
2011	1.8	3.0	-0.04	3.3									
TOTALS	115.2	13.7	30.6	64.6	38.8	30.8	1.4	9.6	-21.3	13.7	65.0	84.3	
AVG.	2.8	0.3	0.7	1.6	1.0	0.8	0.04	0.2	-0.5	0.3	1.6	2.1	
# Up	27	21	26	27	24	23	20	22	22	21	26	24	
# Down	14	20	15	14	16	17	20	18	18	19	14	16	

Based on NASDAQ composite; prior to February 5, 1971, based on National Quotation Bureau indices.

NASDAQ COMPOSITE MONTHLY CLOSING PRICES SINCE 1971

	Jan	Feb	Mar	Apr	May	Jun	Jul	Aug	Sep	Oct	Nov	Dec
1971	98.77	101.34	105.97	112.30	108.25	107.80	105.27	108.42	109.03	105.10	103.97	114.12
1972	118.87	125.38	128.14	131.33	132.53	130.08	127.75	129.95	129.61	130.24	132.96	133.73
1973	128.40	120.41	117.46	107.85	102.64	100.98	108.64	104.87	111.20	110.17	93.51	92.19
1974	94.93	94.35	92.27	86.86	80.20	75.96	69.99	62.37	55.67	65.23	62.95	59.82
1975	69.78	73.00	75.66	78.54	83.10	87.02	83.19	79.01	74.33	76.99	78.80	77.62
1976	87.05	90.26	90.62	90.08	88.04	90.32	91.29	89.70	91.26	90.35	91.12	97.88
1977	95.54	94.57	94.13	95.48	95.59	99.73	100.65	100.10	100.85	97.52	103.15	105.05
1978	100.84	101.47	106.20	115.18	120.24	120.30	126.32	135.01	132.89	111.12	114.69	117.98
1979	125.82	122.56	131.76	133.82	131.42	138.13	141.33	150.44	149.98	135.53	144.26	151.14
1980	161.75	158.03	131.00	139.99	150.45	157.78	171.81	181.52	187.76	192.78	208.15	202.34
1981	197.81	198.01	210.18	216.74	223.47	215.75	211.63	195.75	180.03	195.24	201.37	195.84
1982	188.39	179.43	175.65	184.70	178.54	171.30	167.35	177.71	187.65	212.63	232.31	232.41
1983	248.35	260.67	270.80	293.06	308.73	318.70	303.96	292.42	296.65	274.55	285.67	278.60
1984	268.43	252.57	250.78	247.44	232.82	239.65	229.70	254.64	249.94	247.03	242.53	247.35
1985	278.70	284.17	279.20	280.56	290.80	296.20	301.29	297.71	280.33	292.54	313.95	324.93
1986	335.77	359.53	374.72	383.24	400.16	405.51	371.37	382.86	350.67	360.77	359.57	349.33
1987	392.06	424.97	430.05	417.81	416.54	424.67	434.93	454.97	444.29	323.30	305.16	330.47
1988	344.66	366.95	374.64	379.23	370.34	394.66	387.33	376.55	387.71	382.46	371.45	381.38
1989	401.30	399.71	406.73	427.55	446.17	435.29	453.84	469.33	472.92	455.63	456.09	454.82
1990	415.81	425.83	435.54	420.07	458.97	462.29	438.24	381.21	344.51	329.84	359.06	373.84
1991	414.20	453.05	482.30	484.72	506.11	475.92	502.04	525.68	526.88	542.98	523.90	586.34
1992	620.21	633.47	603.77	578.68	585.31	563.60	580.83	563.12	583.27	605.17	652.73	676.95
1993	696.34	670.77	690.13	661.42	700.53	703.95	704.70	742.84	762.78	779.26	754.39	776.80
1994	800.47	792.50	743.46	733.84	735.19	705.96	722.16	765.62	764.29	777.49	750.32	751.96
1995	755.20	793.73	817.21	843.98	864.58	933.45	1001.21	1020.11	1043.54	1036.06	1059.20	1052.13
1996	1059.79	1100.05	1101.40	1190.52	1243.43	1185.02	1080.59	1141.50	1226.92	1221.51	1292.61	1291.03
1997	1379.85	1309.00	1221.70	1260.76	1400.32	1442.07	1593.81	1587.32	1685.69	1593.61	1600.55	1570.35
1998	1619.36	1770.51	1835.68	1868.41	1778.87	1894.74	1872.39	1499.25	1693.84	1771.39	1949.54	2192.69
1999	2505.89	2288.03	2461.40	2542.85	2470.52	2686.12	2638.49	2739.35	2746.16	2966.43	3336.16	4069.31
2000	3940.35	4696.69	4572.83	3860.66	3400.91	3966.11	3766.99	4206.35	3672.82	3369.63	2597.93	2470.52
2001	2772.73	2151.83	1840.26	2116.24	2110.49	2160.54	2027.13	1805.43	1498.80	1690.20	1930.58	1950.40
2002	1934.03	1731.49	1845.35	1688.23	1615.73	1463.21	1328.26	1314.85	1172.06	1329.75	1478.78	1335.51
2003	1320.91	1337.52	1341.17	1464.31	1595.91	1622.80	1735.02	1810.45	1786.94	1932.21	1960.26	2003.37
2004	2066.15	2029.82	1994.22	1920.15	1986.74	2047.79	1887.36	1838.10	1896.84	1974.99	2096.81	2175.44
2005	2062.41	2051.72	1999.23	1921.65	2068.22	2056.96	2184.83	2152.09	2151.69	2120.30	2232.82	2205.32
2006	2305.82	2281.39	2339.79	2322.57	2178.88	2172.09	2091.47	2183.75	2258.43	2366.71	2431.77	2415.29
2007	2463.93	2416.15	2421.64	2525.09	2604.52	2603.23	2545.57	2596.36	2701.50	2859.12	2660.96	2652.28
2008	2389.86	2271.48	2279.10	2412.80	2522.66	2292.98	2325.55	2367.52	2091.88	1720.95	1535.57	1577.03
2009	1476.42	1377.84	1528.59	1717.30	1774.33	1835.04	1978.50	2009.06	2122.42	2045.11	2144.60	2269.15
2010	2147.35	2238.26	2397.96	2461.19	2257.04	2109.24	2254.70	2114.03	2368.62	2507.41	2498.23	2652.87
2011	2700.08	2782.27	2781.07	2873.54								

Based on NASDAQ composite; prior to February 5, 1971, based on National Quotation Bureau indices.

RUSSELL 1000 INDEX MONTHLY PERCENT CHANGES SINCE 1979

	Jan	Feb	Mar	Apr	May	Jun	Jul	Aug	Sep	Oct	Nov	Dec	Year's Change
1979	4.2	-3.5	6.0	0.3	-2.2	4.3	1.1	5.6	0.02	-7.1	5.1	2.1	16.1
1980	5.9	-0.5	-11.5	4.6	5.0	3.2	6.4	1.1	2.6	1.8	10.1	-3.9	25.6
1981	-4.6	1.0	3.8	-1.9	0.2	-1.2	-0.1	-6.2	-6.4	5.4	4.0	-3.3	-9.7
1982	-2.7	-5.9	-1.3	3.9	-3.6	-2.6	-2.3	11.3	1.2	11.3	4.0	1.3	13.7
1983	3.2	2.1	3.2	7.1	-0.2	3.7	-3.2	0.5	1.3	-2.4	2.0	-1.2	17.0
1984	-1.9	-4.4	1.1	0.3	-5.9	2.1	-1.8	10.8	-0.2	-0.1	-1.4	2.2	-0.1
1985	7.8	1.1	-0.4	-0.3	5.4	1.6	-0.8	-1.0	-3.9	4.5	6.5	4.1	26.7
1986	0.9	7.2	5.1	-1.3	5.0	1.4	-5.9	6.8	-8.5	5.1	1.4	-3.0	13.6
1987	12.7	4.0	1.9	-1.8	0.4	4.5	4.2	3.8	-2.4	-21.9	-8.0	7.2	0.02
1988	4.3	4.4	-2.9	0.7	0.2	4.8	-0.9	-3.3	3.9	2.0	-2.0	1.7	13.1
1989	6.8	-2.5	2.0	4.9	3.8	-0.8	8.2	1.7	-0.5	-2.8	1.5	1.8	25.9
1990	-7.4	1.2	2.2	-2.8	8.9	-0.7	-1.1	-9.6	-5.3	-0.8	6.4	2.7	-7.5
1991	4.5	6.9	2.5	-0.1	3.8	-4.7	4.6	2.2	-1.5	1.4	-4.1	11.2	28.8
1992	-1.4	0.9	-2.4	2.3	0.3	-1.9	4.1	-2.5	1.0	0.7	3.5	1.4	5.9
1993	0.7	0.6	2.2	-2.8	2.4	0.4	-0.4	3.5	-0.5	1.2	-1.7	1.6	7.3
1994	2.9	-2.9	-4.5	1.1	1.0	-2.9	3.1	3.9	-2.6	1.7	-3.9	1.2	-2.4
1995	2.4	3.8	2.3	2.5	3.5	2.4	3.7	0.5	3.9	-0.6	4.2	1.4	34.4
1996	3.1	1.1	0.7	1.4	2.1	-0.1	-4.9	2.5	5.5	2.1	7.1	-1.8	19.7
1997	5.8	0.2	-4.6	5.3	6.2	4.0	8.0	-4.9	5.4	-3.4	4.2	1.9	30.5
1998	0.6	7.0	4.9	0.9	-2.3	3.6	-1.3	-15.1	6.5	7.8	6.1	6.2	25.1
1999	3.5	-3.3	3.7	4.2	-2.3	5.1	-3.2	-1.0	-2.8	6.5	2.5	6.0	19.5
2000	-4.2	-0.4	8.9	-3.3	-2.7	2.5	-1.8	7.4	-4.8	-1.2	-9.3	1.1	-8.8
2001	3.2	-9.5	-6.7	8.0	0.5	-2.4	-1.4	-6.2	-8.6	2.0	7.5	0.9	-13.6
2002	-1.4	-2.1	4.0	-5.8	-1.0	-7.5	-7.5	0.3	-10.9	8.1	5.7	-5.8	-22.9
2003	-2.5	-1.7	0.9	7.9	5.5	1.2	1.8	1.9	-1.2	5.7	1.0	4.6	27.5
2004	1.8	1.2	-1.5	-1.9	1.3	1.7	-3.6	0.3	1.1	1.5	4.1	3.5	9.5
2005	-2.6	2.0	-1.7	-2.0	3.4	0.3	3.8	-1.1	0.8	-1.9	3.5	0.01	4.4
2006	2.7	0.01	1.3	1.1	-3.2	0.003	0.1	2.2	2.3	3.3	1.9	1.1	13.3
2007	1.8	-1.9	0.9	4.1	3.4	-2.0	-3.2	1.2	3.7	1.6	-4.5	-0.8	3.9
2008	-6.1	-3.3	-0.8	5.0	1.6	-8.5	-1.3	1.2	-9.7	-17.6	-7.9	1.3	-39.0
2009	-8.3	-10.7	8.5	10.0	5.3	0.1	7.5	3.4	3.9	-2.3	5.6	2.3	25.5
2010	-3.7	3.1	6.0	1.8	-8.1	-5.7	6.8	-4.7	9.0	3.8	0.1	6.5	13.9
2011	2.3	3.3	0.1	2.9									
TOTALS	34.3	-1.5	33.9	56.3	37.7	5.9	18.7	16.5	-17.7	15.4	55.2	55.5	
AVG.	1.0	-0.05	1.0	1.7	1.2	0.2	0.6	0.5	-0.6	0.5	1.7	1.7	
# Up	21	19	22	22	22	19	14	21	16	20	23	25	
# Down	12	14	11	11	10	13	18	11	16	12	9	7	

RUSSELL 1000 INDEX MONTHLY CLOSING PRICES SINCE 1979

	Jan	Feb	Mar	Apr	May	Jun	Jul	Aug	Sep	Oct	Nov	Dec
1979	53.76	51.88	54.97	55.15	53.92	56.25	56.86	60.04	60.05	55.78	58.65	59.87
1980	63.40	63.07	55.79	58.38	61.31	63.27	67.30	68.05	69.84	71.08	78.26	75.20
1981	71.75	72.49	75.21	73.77	73.90	73.01	72.92	68.42	64.06	67.54	70.23	67.93
1982	66.12	62.21	61.43	63.85	61.53	59.92	58.54	65.14	65.89	73.34	76.28	77.24
1983	79.75	81.45	84.06	90.04	89.89	93.18	90.18	90.65	91.85	89.69	91.50	90.38
1984	88.69	84.76	85.73	86.00	80.94	82.61	81.13	89.87	89.67	89.62	88.36	90.31
1985	97.31	98.38	98.03	97.72	103.02	104.65	103.78	102.76	98.75	103.16	109.91	114.39
1986	115.39	123.71	130.07	128.44	134.82	136.75	128.74	137.43	125.70	132.11	133.97	130.00
1987	146.48	152.29	155.20	152.39	152.94	159.84	166.57	172.95	168.83	131.89	121.28	130.02
1988	135.55	141.54	137.45	138.37	138.66	145.31	143.99	139.26	144.68	147.55	144.59	146.99
1989	156.93	152.98	155.99	163.63	169.85	168.49	182.27	185.33	184.40	179.17	181.85	185.11
1990	171.44	173.43	177.28	172.32	187.66	186.29	184.32	166.69	157.83	156.62	166.69	171.22
1991	179.00	191.34	196.15	195.94	203.32	193.78	202.67	207.18	204.02	206.96	198.46	220.61
1992	217.52	219.50	214.29	219.13	219.71	215.60	224.37	218.86	221.15	222.65	230.44	233.59
1993	235.25	236.67	241.80	235.13	240.80	241.78	240.78	249.20	247.95	250.97	246.70	250.71
1994	258.08	250.52	239.19	241.71	244.13	237.11	244.44	254.04	247.49	251.62	241.82	244.65
1995	250.52	260.08	266.11	272.81	282.48	289.29	299.98	301.40	313.28	311.37	324.36	328.89
1996	338.97	342.56	345.01	349.84	357.35	357.10	339.44	347.79	366.77	374.38	401.05	393.75
1997	416.77	417.46	398.19	419.15	445.06	462.95	499.89	475.33	500.78	483.86	504.25	513.79
1998	517.02	553.14	580.31	585.46	572.16	592.57	584.97	496.66	529.11	570.63	605.31	642.87
1999	665.64	643.67	667.49	695.25	679.10	713.61	690.51	683.27	663.83	707.19	724.66	767.97
2000	736.08	733.04	797.99	771.58	750.98	769.68	755.57	811.17	772.60	763.06	692.40	700.09
2001	722.55	654.25	610.36	658.90	662.39	646.64	637.43	597.67	546.46	557.29	599.32	604.94
2002	596.66	583.88	607.35	572.04	566.18	523.72	484.39	486.08	433.22	468.51	495.00	466.18
2003	454.30	446.37	450.35	486.09	512.92	518.94	528.53	538.40	532.15	562.51	568.32	594.56
2004	605.21	612.58	603.42	591.83	599.40	609.31	587.21	589.09	595.66	604.51	629.26	650.99
2005	633.99	646.93	635.78	623.32	644.28	645.92	670.26	663.13	668.53	656.09	679.35	679.42
2006	697.79	697.83	706.74	714.37	691.78	691.80	692.59	707.55	723.48	747.30	761.43	770.08
2007	784.11	768.92	775.97	807.82	835.14	818.17	792.11	801.22	830.59	844.20	806.44	799.82
2008	750.97	726.42	720.32	756.03	768.28	703.22	694.07	702.17	634.08	522.47	481.43	487.77
2009	447.32	399.61	433.67	476.84	501.95	502.27	539.88	558.21	579.97	566.50	598.41	612.01
2010	589.41	607.45	643.79	655.06	601.79	567.37	606.09	577.68	629.78	653.57	654.24	696.90
2011	712.97	736.24	737.07	758.45								

RUSSELL 2000 INDEX MONTHLY PERCENT CHANGES SINCE 1979

	Jan	Feb	Mar	Apr	May	Jun	Jul	Aug	Sep	Oct	Nov	Dec	Year's Change
1979	9.0	-3.2	9.7	2.3	-1.8	5.3	2.9	7.8	-0.7	-11.3	8.1	6.6	38.0
1980	8.2	-2.1	-18.5	6.0	8.0	4.0	11.0	6.5	2.9	3.9	7.0	-3.7	33.8
1981	-0.6	0.3	7.7	2.5	3.0	-2.5	-2.6	-8.0	-8.6	8.2	2.8	-2.0	-1.5
1982	-3.7	-5.3	-1.5	5.1	-3.2	-4.0	-1.7	7.5	3.6	14.1	8.8	1.1	20.7
1983	7.5	6.0	2.5	7.2	7.0	4.4	-3.0	-4.0	1.6	-7.0	5.0	-2.1	26.3
1984	-1.8	-5.9	0.4	-0.7	-5.4	2.6	-5.0	11.5	-1.0	-2.0	-2.9	1.4	-9.6
1985	13.1	2.4	-2.2	-1.4	3.4	1.0	2.7	-1.2	-6.2	3.6	6.8	4.2	28.0
1986	1.5	7.0	4.7	1.4	3.3	-0.2	-9.5	3.0	-6.3	3.9	-0.5	-3.1	4.0
1987	11.5	8.2	2.4	-3.0	-0.5	2.3	2.8	2.9	-2.0	-30.8	-5.5	7.8	-10.8
1988	4.0	8.7	4.4	2.0	-2.5	7.0	-0.9	-2.8	2.3	-1.2	-3.6	3.8	22.4
1989	4.4	0.5	2.2	4.3	4.2	-2.4	4.2	2.1	0.01	-6.0	0.4	0.1	14.2
1990	-8.9	2.9	3.7	-3.4	6.8	0.1	-4.5	-13.6	-9.2	-6.2	7.3	3.7	-21.5
1991	9.1	11.0	6.9	-0.2	4.5	-6.0	3.1	3.7	0.6	2.7	-4.7	7.7	43.7
1992	8.0	2.9	-3.5	-3.7	1.2	-5.0	3.2	-3.1	2.2	3.1	7.5	3.4	16.4
1993	3.2	-2.5	3.1	-2.8	4.3	0.5	1.3	4.1	2.7	2.5	-3.4	3.3	17.0
1994	3.1	-0.4	-5.4	0.6	-1.3	-3.6	1.6	5.4	-0.5	-0.4	-4.2	2.5	-3.2
1995	-1.4	3.9	1.6	2.1	1.5	5.0	5.7	1.9	1.7	-4.6	4.2	2.4	26.2
1996	-0.2	3.0	1.8	5.3	3.9	-4.2	-8.8	5.7	3.7	-1.7	4.0	2.4	14.8
1997	1.9	-2.5	-4.9	0.1	11.0	4.1	4.6	2.2	7.2	-4.5	-0.8	1.7	20.5
1998	-1.6	7.4	4.1	0.5	-5.4	0.2	-8.2	-19.5	7.6	4.0	5.2	6.1	-3.4
1999	1.2	-8.2	1.4	8.8	1.4	4.3	-2.8	-3.8	-0.1	0.3	5.9	11.2	19.6
2000	-1.7	16.4	-6.7	-6.1	-5.9	8.6	-3.2	7.4	-3.1	-4.5	-10.4	8.4	-4.2
2001	5.1	-6.7	-5.0	7.7	2.3	3.3	-5.4	-3.3	-13.6	5.8	7.6	6.0	1.0
2002	-1.1	-2.8	7.9	0.8	-4.5	-5.1	-15.2	-0.4	-7.3	3.1	8.8	-5.7	-21.6
2003	-2.9	-3.1	1.1	9.4	10.6	1.7	6.2	4.5	-2.0	8.3	3.5	1.9	45.4
2004	4.3	0.8	0.8	-5.2	1.5	4.1	-6.8	-0.6	4.6	1.9	8.6	2.8	17.0
2005	-4.2	1.6	-3.0	-5.8	6.4	3.7	6.3	-1.9	0.2	-3.2	4.7	-0.6	3.3
2006	8.9	-0.3	4.7	-0.1	-5.7	0.5	-3.3	2.9	0.7	5.7	2.5	0.2	17.0
2007	1.6	-0.9	0.9	1.7	4.0	-1.6	-6.9	2.2	1.6	2.8	-7.3	-0.2	-2.7
2008	-6.9	-3.8	0.3	4.1	4.5	-7.8	3.6	3.5	-8.1	-20.9	-12.0	5.6	-34.8
2009	-11.2	-12.3	8.7	15.3	2.9	1.3	9.5	2.8	5.6	-6.9	3.0	7.9	25.2
2010	-3.7	4.4	8.0	5.6	-7.7	-7.9	6.8	-7.5	12.3	4.0	3.4	7.8	25.3
2011	-0.3	5.4	2.4	2.6									
TOTALS	55.4	32.8	40.7	63.0	51.8	13.7	-12.3	17.9	-7.6	-33.3	59.8	92.6	
AVG.	1.7	1.0	1.2	1.9	1.6	0.4	-0.4	0.6	-0.2	-1.0	1.9	2.9	
# Up	18	18	24	22	21	20	16	19	18	17	21	25	
# Down	15	15	9	11	11	12	16	13	14	15	11	7	

RUSSELL 2000 INDEX MONTHLY CLOSING PRICES SINCE 1979

	Jan	Feb	Mar	Apr	May	Jun	Jul	Aug	Sep	Oct	Nov	Dec
1979	44.18	42.78	46.94	48.00	47.13	49.62	51.08	55.05	54.68	48.51	52.43	55.91
1980	60.50	59.22	48.27	51.18	55.26	57.47	63.81	67.97	69.94	72.64	77.70	74.80
1981	74.33	74.52	80.25	82.25	84.72	82.56	80.41	73.94	67.55	73.06	75.14	73.67
1982	70.96	67.21	66.21	69.59	67.39	64.67	63.59	68.38	70.84	80.86	87.96	88.90
1983	95.53	101.23	103.77	111.20	118.94	124.17	120.43	115.60	117.43	109.17	114.66	112.27
1984	110.21	103.72	104.10	103.34	97.75	100.30	95.25	106.21	105.17	103.07	100.11	101.49
1985	114.77	117.54	114.92	113.35	117.26	118.38	121.56	120.10	112.65	116.73	124.62	129.87
1986	131.78	141.00	147.63	149.66	154.61	154.23	139.65	143.83	134.73	139.95	139.26	135.00
1987	150.48	162.84	166.79	161.82	161.02	164.75	169.42	174.25	170.81	118.26	111.70	120.42
1988	125.24	136.10	142.15	145.01	141.37	151.30	149.89	145.74	149.08	147.25	142.01	147.37
1989	153.84	154.56	157.89	164.68	171.53	167.42	174.50	178.20	178.21	167.47	168.17	168.30
1990	153.27	157.72	163.63	158.09	168.91	169.04	161.51	139.52	126.70	118.83	127.50	132.16
1991	144.17	160.00	171.01	170.61	178.34	167.61	172.76	179.11	180.16	185.00	176.37	189.94
1992	205.16	211.15	203.69	196.25	198.52	188.64	194.74	188.79	192.92	198.90	213.81	221.01
1993	228.10	222.41	229.21	222.68	232.19	233.35	236.46	246.19	252.95	259.18	250.41	258.59
1994	266.52	265.53	251.06	252.55	249.28	240.29	244.06	257.32	256.12	255.02	244.25	250.36
1995	246.85	256.57	260.77	266.17	270.25	283.63	299.72	305.31	310.38	296.25	308.58	315.97
1996	315.38	324.93	330.77	348.28	361.85	346.61	316.00	333.88	346.39	340.57	354.11	362.61
1997	369.45	360.05	342.56	343.00	380.76	396.37	414.48	423.43	453.82	433.26	429.92	437.02
1998	430.05	461.83	480.68	482.89	456.62	457.39	419.75	337.95	363.59	378.16	397.75	421.96
1999	427.22	392.26	397.63	432.81	438.68	457.68	444.77	427.83	427.30	428.64	454.08	504.75
2000	496.23	577.71	539.09	506.25	476.18	517.23	500.64	537.89	521.37	497.68	445.94	483.53
2001	508.34	474.37	450.53	485.32	496.50	512.64	484.78	468.56	404.87	428.17	460.78	488.50
2002	483.10	469.36	506.46	510.67	487.47	462.64	392.42	390.96	362.27	373.50	406.35	383.09
2003	372.17	360.52	364.54	398.68	441.00	448.37	476.02	497.42	487.68	528.22	546.51	556.91
2004	580.76	585.56	590.31	559.80	568.28	591.52	551.29	547.93	572.94	583.79	633.77	651.57
2005	624.02	634.06	615.07	579.38	616.71	639.66	679.75	666.51	667.80	646.61	677.29	673.22
2006	733.20	730.64	765.14	764.54	721.01	724.67	700.56	720.53	725.59	766.84	786.12	787.66
2007	800.34	793.30	800.71	814.57	847.19	833.69	776.13	792.86	805.45	828.02	767.77	766.03
2008	713.30	686.18	687.97	716.18	748.28	689.66	714.52	739.50	679.58	537.52	473.14	499.45
2009	443.53	389.02	422.75	487.56	501.58	508.28	556.71	572.07	604.28	562.77	579.73	625.39
2010	602.04	628.56	678.64	716.60	661.61	609.49	650.89	602.06	676.14	703.35	727.01	783.65
2011	781.25	823.45	843.55	865.29								

10 <u>BEST</u> DAYS BY PERCENT AND POINT

DAY	CLOSE	PNT CHANGE	% CHANGE	DAY	CLOSE	PNT CHANGE	% CHANGE
			DJIA 1901 to 1949				
3/15/33	62.10	8.26	15.3	10/30/29	258.47	28.40	12.3
10/6/31	99.34	12.86	14.9	11/14/29	217.28	18.59	9.4
10/30/29	258.47	28.40	12.3	10/5/29	341.36	16.19	5.0
9/21/32	75.16	7.67	11.4	10/31/29	273.51	15.04	5.8
8/3/32	58.22	5.06	9.5	10/6/31	99.34	12.86	14.9
2/11/32	78.60	6.80	9.5	11/15/29	228.73	11.45	5.3
11/14/29	217.28	18.59	9.4	6/19/30	228.97	10.13	4.6
12/18/31	80.69	6.90	9.4	9/5/39	148.12	10.03	7.3
2/13/32	85.82	7.22	9.2	11/22/28	290.34	9.81	3.5
5/6/32	59.01	4.91	9.1	10/1/30	214.14	9.24	4.5
			DJIA 1950 to APRIL 2011				
10/13/08	9387.61	936.42	11.1	10/13/08	9387.61	936.42	11.1
10/28/08	9065.12	889.35	10.9	10/28/08	9065.12	889.35	10.9
10/21/87	2027.85	186.84	10.2	11/13/08	8835.25	552.59	6.7
3/23/09	7775.86	497.48	6.8	3/16/00	10630.60	499.19	4.9
11/13/08	8835.25	552.59	6.7	3/23/09	7775.86	497.48	6.8
11/21/08	8046.42	494.13	6.5	11/21/08	8046.42	494.13	6.5
7/24/02	8191.29	488.95	6.4	7/24/02	8191.29	488.95	6.4
10/20/87	1841.01	102.27	5.9	9/30/08	10850.66	485.21	4.7
3/10/09	6926.49	379.44	5.8	7/29/02	8711.88	447.49	5.4
7/29/02	8711.88	447.49	5.4	3/18/08	12392.66	420.41	3.0
			S&P 500 1930 to APRIL 2011				
3/15/33	6.81	0.97	16.6	10/13/08	1003.35	104.13	11.6
10/6/31	9.91	1.09	12.4	10/28/08	940.51	91.59	10.8
9/21/32	8.52	0.90	11.8	3/16/00	1458.47	66.32	4.8
10/13/08	1003.35	104.13	11.6	1/3/01	1347.56	64.29	5.0
10/28/08	940.51	91.59	10.8	9/30/08	1166.36	59.97	5.4
2/16/35	10.00	0.94	10.4	11/13/08	911.29	58.99	6.9
8/17/35	11.70	1.08	10.2	3/23/09	822.92	54.38	7.1
3/16/35	9.05	0.82	10.0	3/18/08	1330.74	54.14	4.2
9/12/38	12.06	1.06	9.6	11/24/08	851.81	51.78	6.5
9/5/39	12.64	1.11	9.6	12/5/00	1376.54	51.57	3.9
			NASDAQ 1971 to APRIL 2011				
1/3/01	2616.69	324.83	14.2	1/3/01	2616.69	324.83	14.2
10/13/08	1844.25	194.74	11.8	12/5/00	2889.80	274.05	10.5
12/5/00	2889.80	274.05	10.5	4/18/00	3793.57	254.41	7.2
10/28/08	1649.47	143.57	9.5	5/30/00	3459.48	254.37	7.9
4/5/01	1785.00	146.20	8.9	10/19/00	3418.60	247.04	7.8
4/18/01	2079.44	156.22	8.1	10/13/08	3316.77	242.09	7.9
5/30/00	3459.48	254.37	7.9	6/2/00	3813.38	230.88	6.4
10/13/00	3316.77	242.09	7.9	4/25/00	3711.23	228.75	6.6
10/19/00	3418.60	247.04	7.8	4/17/00	3539.16	217.87	6.6
5/8/02	1696.29	122.47	7.8	10/13/08	1844.25	194.74	11.8
			RUSSELL 1000 1979 to APRIL 2011				
10/13/08	542.98	56.75	11.7	10/13/08	542.98	56.75	11.7
10/28/08	503.74	47.68	10.5	10/28/08	503.74	47.68	10.5
10/21/87	135.85	11.15	8.9	3/16/00	777.86	36.60	4.9
3/23/09	446.90	29.36	7.0	1/3/01	712.63	35.74	5.3
11/13/08	489.83	31.99	7.0	11/13/08	489.83	31.99	7.0
11/24/08	456.14	28.26	6.6	9/30/08	634.08	31.74	5.3
3/10/09	391.01	23.46	6.4	12/5/00	728.44	30.36	4.4
11/21/08	427.88	24.97	6.2	3/23/09	446.90	29.36	7.0
7/24/02	448.05	23.87	5.6	3/18/08	723.59	29.05	4.2
7/29/02	477.61	24.69	5.5	11/24/08	456.14	28.26	6.6
			RUSSELL 2000 1979 to APRIL 2011				
10/13/08	570.89	48.41	9.3	10/13/08	570.89	48.41	9.3
11/13/08	491.23	38.43	8.5	9/18/08	723.68	47.30	7.0
3/23/09	433.72	33.61	8.4	11/13/08	491.23	38.43	8.5
10/21/87	130.65	9.26	7.6	5/10/10	689.61	36.61	5.6
10/28/08	482.55	34.15	7.6	10/16/08	536.57	34.46	6.9
11/24/08	436.80	30.26	7.4	10/28/08	482.55	34.15	7.6
3/10/09	367.75	24.49	7.1	3/23/09	433.72	33.61	8.4
9/18/08	723.68	47.30	7.0	3/18/08	681.93	31.45	4.8
10/16/08	536.57	34.46	6.9	9/18/07	806.63	30.82	4.0
10/30/87	118.26	7.46	6.7	12/16/08	482.85	30.28	6.7

161

10 <u>WORST</u> DAYS BY PERCENT AND POINT

	BY PERCENT CHANGE				BY POINT CHANGE		
DAY	CLOSE	PNT CHANGE	% CHANGE	DAY	CLOSE	PNT CHANGE	% CHANGE
DJIA 1901 to 1949							
10/28/29	260.64	−38.33	−12.8	10/28/29	260.64	−38.33	−12.8
10/29/29	230.07	−30.57	−11.7	10/29/29	230.07	−30.57	−11.7
11/6/29	232.13	−25.55	−9.9	11/6/29	232.13	−25.55	−9.9
8/12/32	63.11	−5.79	−8.4	10/23/29	305.85	−20.66	−6.3
3/14/07	55.84	−5.05	−8.3	11/11/29	220.39	−16.14	−6.8
7/21/33	88.71	−7.55	−7.8	11/4/29	257.68	−15.83	−5.8
10/18/37	125.73	−10.57	−7.8	12/12/29	243.14	−15.30	−5.9
2/1/17	88.52	−6.91	−7.2	10/3/29	329.95	−14.55	−4.2
10/5/32	66.07	−5.09	−7.2	6/16/30	230.05	−14.20	−5.8
9/24/31	107.79	−8.20	−7.1	8/9/29	337.99	−14.11	−4.0
DJIA 1950 to APRIL 2011							
10/19/87	1738.74	−508.00	−22.6	9/29/08	10365.45	−777.68	−7.0
10/26/87	1793.93	−156.83	−8.0	10/15/08	8577.91	−733.08	−7.9
10/15/08	8577.91	−733.08	−7.9	9/17/01	8920.70	−684.81	−7.1
12/1/08	8149.09	−679.95	−7.7	12/1/08	8149.09	−679.95	−7.7
10/9/08	8579.19	−678.91	−7.3	10/9/08	8579.19	−678.91	−7.3
10/27/97	7161.15	−554.26	−7.2	4/14/00	10305.77	−617.78	−5.7
9/17/01	8920.70	−684.81	−7.1	10/27/97	7161.15	−554.26	−7.2
9/29/08	10365.45	−777.68	−7.0	10/22/08	8519.21	−514.45	−5.7
10/13/89	2569.26	−190.58	−6.9	8/31/98	7539.07	−512.61	−6.4
1/8/88	1911.31	−140.58	−6.9	10/16/87	9447.11	−508.39	−5.1
S&P 500 1930 to APRIL 2011							
10/19/87	224.84	−57.86	−20.5	9/29/08	1106.39	−106.62	−8.8
3/18/35	8.14	−0.91	−10.1	10/15/08	907.84	−90.17	−9.0
4/16/35	8.22	−0.91	−10.0	4/14/00	1356.56	−83.95	−5.8
9/3/46	15.00	−1.65	−9.9	12/1/08	816.21	−80.03	−8.9
10/18/37	10.76	−1.10	−9.3	10/9/08	909.92	−75.02	−7.6
10/15/08	907.84	−90.17	−9.0	8/31/98	957.28	−69.86	−6.8
12/1/08	816.21	−80.03	−8.9	10/27/97	876.99	−64.65	−6.9
7/20/33	10.57	−1.03	−8.9	10/7/08	996.23	−60.66	−5.7
9/29/08	1106.39	−106.62	−8.8	9/15/08	1192.70	−59.00	−4.7
7/21/33	9.65	−0.92	−8.7	10/22/08	896.78	−58.27	−6.1
NASDAQ 1971 to APRIL 2011							
10/19/87	360.21	−46.12	−11.4	4/14/00	3321.29	−355.49	−9.7
4/14/00	3321.29	−355.49	−9.7	4/3/00	4223.68	−349.15	−7.6
9/29/08	1983.73	−199.61	−9.1	4/12/00	3769.63	−286.27	−7.1
10/26/87	298.90	−29.55	−9.0	4/10/00	4188.20	−258.25	−5.8
10/20/87	327.79	−32.42	−9.0	1/4/00	3901.69	−229.46	−5.6
12/1/08	1398.07	−137.50	−9.0	3/14/00	4706.63	−200.61	−4.1
8/31/98	1499.25	−140.43	−8.6	5/10/00	3384.73	−200.28	−5.6
10/15/08	1628.33	−150.68	−8.5	5/23/00	3164.55	−199.66	−5.9
4/3/00	4223.68	−349.15	−7.6	9/29/08	1983.73	−199.61	−9.1
1/2/01	2291.86	−178.66	−7.2	10/25/00	3229.57	−190.22	−5.6
RUSSELL 1000 1979 to APRIL 2011							
10/19/87	121.04	−28.40	−19.0	9/29/08	602.34	−57.35	−8.7
10/15/08	489.71	−49.11	−9.1	10/15/08	489.71	−49.11	−9.1
12/1/08	437.75	−43.68	−9.1	4/14/00	715.20	−45.74	−6.0
9/29/08	602.34	−57.35	−8.7	12/1/08	437.75	−43.68	−9.1
10/26/87	119.45	−10.74	−8.3	10/9/08	492.13	−40.05	−7.5
10/9/08	492.13	−40.05	−7.5	8/31/98	496.66	−35.77	−6.7
11/20/08	402.91	−29.62	−6.9	10/27/97	465.44	−32.96	−6.6
8/31/98	496.66	−35.77	−6.7	10/7/08	538.15	−32.64	−5.7
10/27/97	465.44	−32.96	−6.6	9/15/08	650.57	−32.15	−4.7
11/19/08	432.53	−28.80	−6.2	10/22/08	484.08	−31.56	−6.1
RUSSELL 2000 1979 to APRIL 2011							
10/19/87	133.60	−19.14	−12.5	12/1/08	417.07	−56.07	−11.9
12/1/08	417.07	−56.07	−11.9	10/15/08	502.11	−52.54	−9.5
10/15/08	502.11	−52.54	−9.5	10/9/08	499.20	−47.37	−8.7
10/26/87	110.33	−11.26	−9.3	9/29/08	657.72	−47.07	−6.7
10/20/87	121.39	−12.21	−9.1	10/7/08	558.95	−36.96	−6.2
10/9/08	499.20	−47.37	−8.7	4/14/00	453.72	−35.50	−7.3
11/19/08	412.38	−35.13	−7.9	11/19/08	412.38	−35.13	−7.9
4/14/00	453.72	−35.50	−7.3	11/14/08	456.52	−34.71	−7.1
11/14/08	456.52	−34.71	−7.1	5/20/10	640.04	−34.36	−5.1
1/20/09	433.65	−32.80	−7.0	9/17/08	676.38	−34.27	−4.8

10 **BEST** WEEKS BY PERCENT AND POINT

	BY PERCENT CHANGE				BY POINT CHANGE		
WEEK ENDS	CLOSE	PNT CHANGE	% CHANGE	WEEK ENDS	CLOSE	PNT CHANGE	% CHANGE
			DJIA 1901 to 1949				
8/6/32	66.56	12.30	22.7	12/7/29	263.46	24.51	10.3
6/25/38	131.94	18.71	16.5	6/25/38	131.94	18.71	16.5
2/13/32	85.82	11.37	15.3	6/27/31	156.93	17.97	12.9
4/22/33	72.24	9.36	14.9	11/22/29	245.74	17.01	7.4
10/10/31	105.61	12.84	13.8	8/17/29	360.70	15.86	4.6
7/30/32	54.26	6.42	13.4	12/22/28	285.94	15.22	5.6
6/27/31	156.93	17.97	12.9	8/24/29	375.44	14.74	4.1
9/24/32	74.83	8.39	12.6	2/21/29	310.06	14.21	4.8
8/27/32	75.61	8.43	12.6	5/10/30	272.01	13.70	5.3
3/18/33	60.56	6.72	12.5	11/15/30	186.68	13.54	7.8
			DJIA 1950 to APRIL 2011				
10/11/74	658.17	73.61	12.6	10/31/08	9325.01	946.06	11.3
10/31/08	9325.01	946.06	11.3	11/28/08	8829.04	782.62	9.7
8/20/82	869.29	81.24	10.3	3/17/00	10595.23	666.41	6.7
11/28/08	8829.04	782.62	9.7	3/21/03	8521.97	662.26	8.4
3/13/09	7223.98	597.04	9.0	9/28/01	8847.56	611.75	7.4
10/8/82	986.85	79.11	8.7	7/17/09	8743.94	597.42	7.3
3/21/03	8521.97	662.26	8.4	3/13/09	7223.98	597.04	9.0
8/3/84	1202.08	87.46	7.9	7/2/99	11139.24	586.68	5.6
9/28/01	8847.56	611.75	7.4	4/20/00	10844.05	538.28	5.2
7/17/09	8743.94	597.42	7.3	2/1/08	12743.19	536.02	4.4
			S&P 500 1930 to APRIL 2011				
8/6/32	7.22	1.12	18.4	6/2/00	1477.26	99.24	7.2
6/25/38	11.39	1.72	17.8	11/28/08	896.24	96.21	12.0
7/30/32	6.10	0.89	17.1	10/31/08	968.75	91.98	10.5
4/22/33	7.75	1.09	16.4	4/20/00	1434.54	77.98	5.8
10/11/74	71.14	8.80	14.1	7/2/99	1391.22	75.91	5.8
2/13/32	8.80	1.08	14.0	3/3/00	1409.17	75.81	5.7
9/24/32	8.52	1.02	13.6	9/28/01	1040.94	75.14	7.8
10/10/31	10.64	1.27	13.6	3/13/09	756.55	73.17	10.7
8/27/32	8.57	1.01	13.4	10/16/98	1056.42	72.10	7.3
3/18/33	6.61	0.77	13.2	3/17/00	1464.47	69.40	5.0
			NASDAQ 1971 to APRIL 2011				
6/2/00	3813.38	608.27	19.0	6/2/00	3813.38	608.27	19.0
4/12/01	1961.43	241.07	14.0	2/4/00	4244.14	357.07	9.2
11/28/08	1535.57	151.22	10.9	3/3/00	4914.79	324.29	7.1
10/31/08	1720.95	168.92	10.9	4/20/00	3643.88	322.59	9.7
3/13/09	1431.50	137.65	10.6	12/8/00	2917.43	272.14	10.3
4/20/01	2163.41	201.98	10.3	4/12/01	1961.43	241.07	14.0
12/8/00	2917.43	272.14	10.3	7/14/00	4246.18	222.98	5.5
4/20/00	3643.88	322.59	9.7	1/12/01	2626.50	218.85	9.1
10/11/74	60.42	5.26	9.5	4/28/00	3860.66	216.78	6.0
2/4/00	4244.14	357.07	9.0	12/23/99	3969.44	216.38	5.8
			RUSSELL 1000 1979 to APRIL 2011				
11/28/08	481.43	53.55	12.5	6/2/00	785.02	57.93	8.0
10/31/08	522.47	50.94	10.8	11/28/08	481.43	53.55	12.5
3/13/09	411.10	39.88	10.7	10/31/08	522.47	50.94	10.8
8/20/82	61.51	4.83	8.5	4/20/00	757.32	42.12	5.9
6/2/00	785.02	57.93	8.0	3/3/00	756.41	41.55	5.8
9/28/01	546.46	38.48	7.6	3/13/09	411.10	39.88	10.7
10/16/98	546.09	38.45	7.6	7/2/99	723.25	38.80	5.7
8/3/84	87.43	6.13	7.5	9/28/01	546.46	38.48	7.6
3/21/03	474.58	32.69	7.4	10/16/98	546.09	38.45	7.6
10/8/82	71.55	4.90	7.4	2/1/08	761.15	36.97	5.1
			RUSSELL 2000 1979 to APRIL 2011				
11/28/08	473.14	66.60	16.4	11/28/08	473.14	66.60	16.4
10/31/08	537.52	66.40	14.1	10/31/08	537.52	66.40	14.1
6/2/00	513.03	55.66	12.2	6/2/00	513.03	55.66	12.2
3/13/09	393.09	42.04	12.0	3/13/09	393.09	42.04	12.0
7/17/09	519.22	38.24	8.0	2/1/08	730.50	41.90	6.1
10/16/98	342.87	24.47	7.7	3/3/00	597.88	41.14	7.4
12/18/87	116.94	8.31	7.7	5/14/10	693.98	40.98	6.3
3/3/00	597.88	41.14	7.4	7/23/10	650.65	40.26	6.6
3/27/09	429.00	28.89	7.2	10/5/07	844.87	39.42	4.9
10/23/98	367.05	24.18	7.1	7/17/09	519.22	38.24	8.0

10 <u>WORST</u> WEEKS BY PERCENT AND POINT

	BY PERCENT CHANGE				BY POINT CHANGE		
WEEK ENDS	**CLOSE**	**PNT CHANGE**	**% CHANGE**	**WEEK ENDS**	**CLOSE**	**PNT CHANGE**	**% CHANGE**
DJIA 1901 to 1949							
7/22/33	88.42	−17.68	−16.7	11/8/29	236.53	−36.98	−13.5
5/18/40	122.43	−22.42	−15.5	12/8/28	257.33	−33.47	−11.5
10/8/32	61.17	−10.92	−15.2	6/21/30	215.30	−28.95	−11.9
10/3/31	92.77	−14.59	−13.6	10/19/29	323.87	−28.82	−8.2
11/8/29	236.53	−36.98	−13.5	5/3/30	258.31	−27.15	−9.5
9/17/32	66.44	−10.10	−13.2	10/31/29	273.51	−25.46	−8.5
10/21/33	83.64	−11.95	−12.5	10/26/29	298.97	−24.90	−7.7
12/12/31	78.93	−11.21	−12.4	5/18/40	122.43	−22.42	−15.5
5/8/15	62.77	−8.74	−12.2	2/8/29	301.53	−18.23	−5.7
6/21/30	215.30	−28.95	−11.9	10/11/30	193.05	−18.05	−8.6
DJIA 1950 to APRIL 2011							
10/10/08	8451.19	−1874.19	−18.2	10/10/08	8451.19	−1874.19	−18.2
9/21/01	8235.81	−1369.70	−14.3	9/21/01	8235.81	−1369.70	−14.3
10/23/87	1950.76	−295.98	−13.2	3/16/01	9823.41	−821.21	−7.7
10/16/87	2246.74	−235.47	−9.5	10/3/08	10325.38	−817.75	−7.3
10/13/89	2569.26	−216.26	−7.8	4/14/00	10305.77	−805.71	−7.3
3/16/01	9823.41	−821.21	−7.7	7/12/02	8684.53	−694.97	−7.4
7/19/02	8019.26	−665.27	−7.7	7/19/02	8019.26	−665.27	−7.7
12/4/87	1766.74	−143.74	−7.5	10/15/99	10019.71	−630.05	−5.9
9/13/74	627.19	−50.69	−7.5	5/7/10	10380.43	−628.18	−5.7
9/12/86	1758.72	−141.03	−7.4	7/27/07	13265.47	−585.61	−4.2
S&P 500 1930 to APRIL 2011							
7/22/33	9.71	−2.20	−18.5	10/10/08	899.22	−200.01	−18.2
10/10/08	899.22	−200.01	−18.2	4/14/00	1356.56	−159.79	−10.5
5/18/40	9.75	−2.05	−17.4	9/21/01	965.80	−126.74	−11.6
10/8/32	6.77	−1.38	−16.9	10/3/08	1099.23	−113.78	−9.4
9/17/32	7.50	−1.28	−14.6	10/15/99	1247.41	−88.61	−6.6
10/21/33	8.57	−1.31	−13.3	3/16/01	1150.53	−82.89	−6.7
10/3/31	9.37	−1.36	−12.7	1/28/00	1360.16	−81.20	−5.6
10/23/87	248.22	−34.48	−12.2	1/18/08	1325.19	−75.83	−5.4
12/12/31	8.20	−1.13	−12.1	5/7/10	1110.88	−75.81	−6.4
3/26/38	9.20	−1.21	−11.6	7/27/07	1458.95	−75.15	−4.9
NASDAQ 1971 to APRIL 2011							
4/14/00	3321.29	−1125.16	−25.3	4/14/00	3321.29	−1125.16	−25.3
10/23/87	328.45	−77.88	−19.2	7/28/00	3663.00	−431.45	−10.5
9/21/01	1423.19	−272.19	−16.1	11/10/00	3028.99	−422.59	−12.2
10/10/08	1649.51	−297.88	−15.3	3/31/00	4572.83	−390.20	−7.9
11/10/00	3028.99	−422.59	−12.2	1/28/00	3887.07	−348.33	−8.2
10/3/08	1947.39	−235.95	−10.8	10/6/00	3361.01	−311.81	−8.5
7/28/00	3663.00	−431.45	−10.5	10/10/08	1649.51	−297.88	−15.3
10/24/08	1552.03	−159.26	−9.3	5/12/00	3529.06	−287.76	−7.5
12/15/00	2653.27	−264.16	−9.1	9/21/01	1423.19	−272.19	−16.1
12/1/00	2645.29	−259.09	−8.9	12/15/00	2653.27	−264.16	−9.1
RUSSELL 1000 1979 to APRIL 2011							
10/10/08	486.23	−108.31	−18.2	10/10/08	486.23	−108.31	−18.2
10/23/87	130.19	−19.25	−12.9	4/14/00	715.20	−90.39	−11.2
9/21/01	507.98	−67.59	−11.7	9/21/01	507.98	−67.59	−11.7
4/14/00	715.20	−90.39	−11.2	10/3/08	594.54	−65.15	−9.9
10/3/08	594.54	−65.15	−9.9	10/15/99	646.79	−43.89	−6.4
10/16/87	149.44	−14.42	−8.8	3/16/01	605.71	−43.88	−6.8
11/21/08	427.88	−41.15	−8.8	5/7/10	611.63	−43.43	−6.6
9/12/86	124.95	−10.87	−8.0	7/27/07	793.72	−41.97	−5.0
7/19/02	450.64	−36.13	−7.4	1/28/00	719.67	−41.85	−5.5
10/24/08	471.53	−36.29	−7.2	11/21/08	427.88	−41.15	−8.0
RUSSELL 2000 1979 to APRIL 2011							
10/23/87	121.59	−31.15	−20.4	10/10/08	522.48	−96.92	−15.7
4/14/00	453.72	−89.27	−16.4	4/14/00	453.72	−89.27	−16.4
10/10/08	522.48	−96.92	−15.7	10/3/08	619.40	−85.39	−12.1
9/21/01	378.89	−61.84	−14.0	5/7/10	653.00	−63.60	−8.9
10/3/08	619.40	−85.39	−12.1	9/21/01	378.89	−61.84	−14.0
11/21/08	406.54	−49.98	−11.0	7/27/07	777.83	−58.61	−7.0
10/24/08	471.12	−55.31	−10.5	10/24/08	471.12	−55.31	−10.5
3/6/09	351.05	−37.97	−9.8	3/2/07	775.44	−51.20	−6.2
11/14/08	456.52	−49.27	−9.7	1/4/08	721.60	−50.16	−6.5
8/28/98	358.54	−37.10	−9.4	11/21/08	406.54	−49.98	−11.0

10 **BEST** MONTHS BY PERCENT AND POINT

	BY PERCENT CHANGE				BY POINT CHANGE		
MONTH	CLOSE	PNT CHANGE	% CHANGE	MONTH	CLOSE	PNT CHANGE	% CHANGE
DJIA 1901 to 1949							
APR-1933	77.66	22.26	40.2	NOV-1928	293.38	41.22	16.3
AUG-1932	73.16	18.90	34.8	JUN-1929	333.79	36.38	12.2
JUL-1932	54.26	11.42	26.7	AUG-1929	380.33	32.63	9.4
JUN-1938	133.88	26.14	24.3	JUN-1938	133.88	26.14	24.3
APR-1915	71.78	10.95	18.0	AUG-1928	240.41	24.41	11.3
JUN-1931	150.18	21.72	16.9	APR-1933	77.66	22.26	40.2
NOV-1928	293.38	41.22	16.3	FEB-1931	189.66	22.11	13.2
NOV-1904	52.76	6.59	14.3	JUN-1931	150.18	21.72	16.9
MAY-1919	105.50	12.62	13.6	AUG-1932	73.16	18.90	34.8
SEP-1939	152.54	18.13	13.5	JAN-1930	267.14	18.66	7.5
DJIA 1950 to APRIL 2011							
JAN-1976	975.28	122.87	14.4	APR-1999	10789.04	1002.88	10.2
JAN-1975	703.69	87.45	14.2	APR-2001	10734.97	856.19	8.7
JAN-1987	2158.04	262.09	13.8	OCT-2002	8397.03	805.10	10.6
AUG-1982	901.31	92.71	11.5	MAR-2000	10921.92	793.61	7.8
OCT-1982	991.72	95.47	10.7	NOV-2001	9851.56	776.42	8.6
OCT-2002	8397.03	805.10	10.6	SEP-2010	10788.05	773.33	7.7
APR-1978	837.32	79.96	10.6	OCT-1998	8592.10	749.48	9.6
APR-1999	10789.04	1002.88	10.2	JUL-2009	9171.61	724.61	8.6
NOV-1962	649.30	59.53	10.1	APR-2007	13062.91	708.56	5.7
NOV-1954	386.77	34.63	9.8	AUG-2000	11215.10	693.12	6.6
S&P 500 1930 to APRIL 2011							
APR-1933	8.32	2.47	42.2	MAR-2000	1498.58	132.16	9.7
JUL-1932	6.10	1.67	37.7	SEP-2010	1141.20	91.87	8.8
AUG-1932	8.39	2.29	37.5	APR-2001	1249.46	89.13	7.7
JUN-1938	11.56	2.29	24.7	AUG-2000	1517.68	86.85	6.1
SEP-1939	13.02	1.84	16.5	OCT-1998	1098.67	81.66	8.0
OCT-1974	73.90	10.36	16.3	DEC-1999	1469.25	80.34	5.8
MAY-1933	9.64	1.32	15.9	OCT-1999	1362.93	80.22	6.3
APR-1938	9.70	1.20	14.1	NOV-2001	1139.45	79.67	7.5
JUN-1931	14.83	1.81	13.9	DEC-2010	1257.64	77.09	6.5
JAN-1987	274.08	31.91	13.2	APR-2009	872.81	74.94	9.4
NASDAQ 1971 to APRIL 2011							
DEC-1999	4069.31	733.15	22.0	FEB-2000	4696.69	756.34	19.2
FEB-2000	4696.69	756.34	19.2	DEC-1999	4069.31	733.15	22.0
OCT-1974	65.23	9.56	17.2	JUN-2000	3966.11	565.20	16.6
JAN-1975	69.78	9.96	16.6	AUG-2000	4206.35	439.36	11.7
JUN-2000	3966.11	565.20	16.6	NOV-1999	3336.16	369.73	12.5
APR-2001	2116.24	275.98	15.0	JAN-1999	2505.89	313.20	14.3
JAN-1999	2505.89	313.20	14.3	JAN-2001	2772.73	302.21	12.2
NOV-2001	1930.58	240.38	14.2	APR-2001	2116.24	275.98	15.0
OCT-2002	1329.75	157.69	13.5	SEP-2010	2368.62	254.59	12.0
OCT-1982	212.63	24.98	13.3	DEC-1998	2192.69	243.15	12.5
RUSSELL 1000 1979 to APRIL 2011							
JAN-1987	146.48	16.48	12.7	MAR-2000	797.99	64.95	8.9
OCT-1982	73.34	7.45	11.3	AUG-2000	811.17	55.60	7.4
AUG-1982	65.14	6.60	11.3	SEP-2010	629.78	52.10	9.0
DEC-1991	220.61	22.15	11.2	APR-2001	658.90	48.54	8.0
AUG-1984	89.87	8.74	10.8	OCT-1999	707.19	43.36	6.5
NOV-1980	78.26	7.18	10.1	DEC-1999	767.97	43.31	6.0
APR-2009	476.84	43.17	10.0	APR-2009	476.84	43.17	10.0
SEP-2010	629.78	52.10	9.0	DEC-2010	696.90	42.66	6.5
MAY-1990	187.66	15.34	8.9	NOV-2001	599.32	42.03	7.5
MAR-2000	797.99	64.95	8.9	OCT-1998	570.63	41.52	7.8
RUSSELL 2000 1979 to APRIL 2011							
FEB-2000	577.71	81.48	16.4	FEB-2000	577.71	81.48	16.4
APR-2009	487.56	64.81	15.3	SEP-2010	676.14	74.08	12.3
OCT-1982	80.86	10.02	14.1	APR-2009	487.56	64.81	15.3
JAN-1985	114.77	13.28	13.1	JAN-2006	733.20	59.98	8.9
SEP-2010	676.14	74.08	12.3	DEC-2010	783.65	56.64	7.8
AUG-1984	106.21	10.96	11.5	DEC-1999	504.75	50.67	11.2
JAN-1987	150.48	15.48	11.5	MAR-2010	678.64	50.08	8.0
DEC-1999	504.75	50.67	11.2	NOV-2004	633.77	49.98	8.6
JUL-1980	63.81	6.34	11.0	JUL-2009	556.71	48.43	9.5
MAY-1997	380.76	37.76	11.0	DEC-2009	625.39	45.66	7.9

10 <u>WORST</u> MONTHS BY PERCENT AND POINT

	BY PERCENT CHANGE				BY POINT CHANGE		
MONTH	CLOSE	PNT CHANGE	% CHANGE	MONTH	CLOSE	PNT CHANGE	% CHANGE
DJIA 1901 to 1949							
SEP-1931	96.61	-42.80	-30.7	OCT-1929	273.51	-69.94	-20.4
MAR-1938	98.95	-30.69	-23.7	JUN-1930	226.34	-48.73	-17.7
APR-1932	56.11	-17.17	-23.4	SEP-1931	96.61	-42.80	-30.7
MAY-1940	116.22	-32.21	-21.7	SEP-1929	343.45	-36.88	-9.7
OCT-1929	273.51	-69.94	-20.4	SEP-1930	204.90	-35.52	-14.8
MAY-1932	44.74	-11.37	-20.3	NOV-1929	238.95	-34.56	-12.6
JUN-1930	226.34	-48.73	-17.7	MAY-1940	116.22	-32.21	-21.7
DEC-1931	77.90	-15.97	-17.0	MAR-1938	98.95	-30.69	-23.7
FEB-1933	51.51	-9.51	-15.6	SEP-1937	154.57	-22.84	-12.9
MAY-1931	128.46	-22.73	-15.0	MAY-1931	128.46	-22.73	-15.0
DJIA 1950 to APRIL 2011							
OCT-1987	1993.53	-602.75	-23.2	OCT-2008	9325.01	-1525.65	-14.1
AUG-1998	7539.07	-1344.22	-15.1	AUG-1998	7539.07	-1344.22	-15.1
OCT-2008	9325.01	-1525.65	-14.1	JUN-2008	11350.01	-1288.31	-10.2
NOV-1973	822.25	-134.33	-14.0	SEP-2001	8847.56	-1102.19	-11.1
SEP-2002	7591.93	-1071.57	-12.4	SEP-2002	7591.93	-1071.57	-12.4
FEB-2009	7062.93	-937.93	-11.7	FEB-2009	7062.93	-937.93	-11.7
SEP-2001	8847.56	-1102.19	-11.1	MAY-2010	10136.63	-871.98	-7.9
SEP-1974	607.87	-70.71	-10.4	FEB-2000	10128.31	-812.22	-7.4
AUG-1974	678.58	-78.85	-10.4	JAN-2009	8000.86	-775.53	-8.8
JUN-2008	11350.01	-1288.31	-10.2	SEP-2008	10850.66	-692.89	-6.0
S&P 500 1930 to APRIL 2011							
SEP-1931	9.71	-4.15	-29.9	OCT-2008	968.75	-197.61	-16.9
MAR-1938	8.50	-2.84	-25.0	AUG-1998	957.28	-163.39	-14.6
MAY-1940	9.27	-2.92	-24.0	FEB-2001	1239.94	-126.07	-9.2
MAY-1932	4.47	-1.36	-23.3	JUN-2008	1280.00	-120.38	-8.6
OCT-1987	251.79	-70.04	-21.8	SEP-2008	1166.36	-116.47	-9.1
APR-1932	5.83	-1.48	-20.2	NOV-2000	1314.95	-114.45	-8.0
FEB-1933	5.66	-1.28	-18.4	SEP-2002	815.28	-100.79	-11.0
OCT-2008	968.75	-197.61	-16.9	MAY-2010	1089.41	-97.28	-8.2
JUN-1930	20.46	-4.03	-16.5	SEP-2001	1040.94	-92.64	-8.2
AUG-1998	957.28	-163.39	-14.6	FEB-2009	735.09	-90.79	-11.0
NASDAQ 1971 to APRIL 2011							
OCT-1987	323.30	-120.99	-27.2	NOV-2000	2597.93	-771.70	-22.9
NOV-2000	2597.93	-771.70	-22.9	APR-2000	3860.66	-712.17	-15.6
FEB-2001	2151.83	-620.90	-22.4	FEB-2001	2151.83	-620.90	-22.4
AUG-1998	1499.25	-373.14	-19.9	SEP-2001	3672.82	-533.53	-12.7
OCT-2008	1720.95	-370.93	-17.7	MAY-2000	3400.91	-459.75	-11.9
MAR-1980	131.00	-27.03	-17.1	AUG-1998	1499.25	-373.14	-19.9
SEP-2001	1498.80	-306.63	-17.0	OCT-2008	1720.95	-370.93	-17.7
OCT-1978	111.12	-21.77	-16.4	MAR-2001	1840.26	-311.57	-14.5
APR-2000	3860.66	-712.17	-15.6	SEP-2001	1498.80	-306.63	-17.0
NOV-1973	93.51	-16.66	-15.1	OCT-2000	3369.63	-303.19	-8.3
RUSSELL 1000 1979 to APRIL 2011							
OCT-1987	131.89	-36.94	-21.9	OCT-2008	522.47	-111.61	-17.6
OCT-2008	522.47	-111.61	-17.6	AUG-1998	496.66	-88.31	-15.1
AUG-1998	496.66	-88.31	-15.1	NOV-2000	692.40	-70.66	-9.3
MAR-1980	55.79	-7.28	-11.5	FEB-2001	654.25	-68.30	-9.5
SEP-2002	433.22	-52.86	-10.9	SEP-2008	634.08	-68.09	-9.7
FEB-2009	399.61	-47.71	-10.7	JUN-2008	703.22	-65.06	-8.5
SEP-2008	634.08	-68.09	-9.7	MAY-2010	601.79	-53.27	-8.1
AUG-1990	166.69	-17.63	-9.6	SEP-2002	433.22	-52.86	-10.9
FEB-2001	654.25	-68.30	-9.5	SEP-2001	546.46	-51.21	-8.6
NOV-2000	692.40	-70.66	-9.3	JAN-2008	750.97	-48.85	-6.1
RUSSELL 2000 1979 to APRIL 2011							
OCT-1987	118.26	-52.55	-30.8	OCT-2008	537.52	-142.06	-20.9
OCT-2008	537.52	-142.06	-20.9	AUG-1998	337.95	-81.80	-19.5
AUG-1998	337.95	-81.80	-19.5	JUL-2002	392.42	-70.22	-15.2
MAR-1980	48.27	-10.95	-18.5	NOV-2008	473.14	-64.38	-12.0
JUL-2002	392.42	-70.22	-15.2	SEP-2001	404.87	-63.69	-13.6
AUG-1990	139.52	-21.99	-13.6	NOV-2007	767.77	-60.25	-7.3
SEP-2001	404.87	-63.69	-13.6	SEP-2008	679.58	-59.92	-8.1
FEB-2009	389.02	-54.51	-12.3	JUN-2008	689.66	-58.62	-7.8
NOV-2008	473.14	-64.38	-12.0	JUL-2007	776.13	-57.56	-6.9
OCT-1979	48.51	-6.17	-11.3	JAN-2009	443.53	-55.92	-11.2

10 **BEST** QUARTERS BY PERCENT AND POINT

	BY PERCENT CHANGE				BY POINT CHANGE		
QUARTER	CLOSE	PNT CHANGE	% CHANGE	QUARTER	CLOSE	PNT CHANGE	% CHANGE
DJIA 1901 to 1949							
JUN-1933	98.14	42.74	77.1	DEC-1928	300.00	60.57	25.3
SEP-1932	71.56	28.72	67.0	JUN-1933	98.14	42.74	77.1
JUN-1938	133.88	34.93	35.3	MAR-1930	286.10	37.62	15.1
SEP-1915	90.58	20.52	29.3	JUN-1938	133.88	34.93	35.3
DEC-1928	300.00	60.57	25.3	SEP-1927	197.59	31.36	18.9
DEC-1904	50.99	8.80	20.9	SEP-1928	239.43	28.88	13.7
JUN-1919	106.98	18.13	20.4	SEP-1932	71.56	28.72	67.0
SEP-1927	197.59	31.36	18.9	JUN-1929	333.79	24.94	8.1
DEC-1905	70.47	10.47	17.4	SEP-1939	152.54	21.91	16.8
JUN-1935	118.21	17.40	17.3	SEP-1915	90.58	20.52	29.3
DJIA 1950 to APRIL 2011							
MAR-1975	768.15	151.91	24.7	DEC-1998	9181.43	1338.81	17.1
MAR-1987	2304.69	408.74	21.6	SEP-2009	9712.28	1265.28	15.0
MAR-1986	1818.61	271.94	17.6	JUN-1999	10970.80	1184.64	12.1
MAR-1976	999.45	147.04	17.2	DEC-2003	10453.92	1178.86	12.7
DEC-1998	9181.43	1338.81	17.1	DEC-2001	10021.50	1173.94	13.3
DEC-1982	1046.54	150.29	16.8	DEC-1999	11497.12	1160.17	11.2
JUN-1997	7672.79	1089.31	16.5	JUN-1997	7672.79	1089.31	16.5
DEC-1985	1546.67	218.04	16.4	JUN-2007	13408.62	1054.27	8.5
SEP-2009	9712.28	1265.28	15.0	SEP-2010	10788.05	1014.03	10.4
JUN-1975	878.99	110.84	14.4	JUN-2003	8985.44	993.31	12.4
S&P 500 1930 to APRIL 2011							
JUN-1933	10.91	5.06	86.5	DEC-1998	1229.23	212.22	20.9
SEP-1932	8.08	3.65	82.4	DEC-1999	1469.25	186.54	14.5
JUN-1938	11.56	3.06	36.0	SEP-2009	1057.08	137.76	15.0
MAR-1975	83.36	14.80	21.6	MAR-1998	1101.75	131.32	13.5
DEC-1998	1229.23	212.22	20.9	JUN-1997	885.14	128.02	16.9
JUN-1935	10.23	1.76	20.8	JUN-2003	974.50	125.32	14.8
MAR-1987	291.70	49.53	20.5	JUN-2009	919.32	121.45	15.2
SEP-1939	13.02	2.16	19.9	DEC-2010	1257.64	116.44	10.2
MAR-1943	11.58	1.81	18.5	DEC-2003	1111.92	115.95	11.6
MAR-1930	25.14	3.69	17.2	SEP-2010	1141.20	110.49	10.7
NASDAQ 1971 to APRIL 2011							
DEC-1999	4069.31	1323.15	48.2	DEC-1999	4069.31	1323.15	48.2
DEC-2001	1950.40	451.60	30.1	MAR-2000	4572.83	503.52	12.4
DEC-1998	2192.69	498.85	29.5	DEC-1998	2192.69	498.85	29.5
MAR-1991	482.30	108.46	29.0	DEC-2001	1950.40	451.60	30.1
MAR-1975	75.66	15.84	26.5	JUN-2001	2160.54	320.28	17.4
DEC-1982	232.41	44.76	23.9	JUN-2009	1835.04	306.45	20.0
MAR-1987	430.05	80.72	23.1	SEP-2009	2122.42	287.38	15.7
JUN-2003	1622.80	281.63	21.0	DEC-2010	2652.87	284.25	12.0
JUN-1980	157.78	26.78	20.4	JUN-2003	1622.80	281.63	21.0
JUN-2009	1835.04	306.45	20.0	DEC-2004	2175.44	278.60	14.7
RUSSELL 1000 1979 to APRIL 2011							
DEC-1998	642.87	113.76	21.5	DEC-1998	642.87	113.76	21.5
MAR-1987	155.20	25.20	19.4	DEC-1999	767.97	104.14	15.7
DEC-1982	77.24	11.35	17.2	SEP-2009	579.97	77.70	15.5
JUN-1997	462.95	64.76	16.3	JUN-2009	502.27	68.60	15.8
DEC-1985	114.39	15.64	15.8	JUN-2003	518.94	68.59	15.2
JUN-2009	502.27	68.60	15.8	DEC-2010	696.90	67.12	10.7
DEC-1999	767.97	104.14	15.7	MAR-1998	580.31	66.52	12.9
SEP-2009	579.97	77.70	15.5	JUN-1997	462.95	64.76	16.3
JUN-2003	518.94	68.59	15.2	DEC-2003	594.56	62.41	11.7
MAR-1991	196.15	24.93	14.6	SEP-2010	629.78	62.41	11.0
RUSSELL 2000 1979 to APRIL 2011							
MAR-1991	171.01	38.85	29.4	DEC-2010	783.65	107.51	15.9
DEC-1982	88.90	18.06	25.5	SEP-2009	604.28	96.00	18.9
MAR-1987	166.79	31.79	23.5	MAR-2006	765.14	91.92	13.7
JUN-2003	448.37	83.83	23.0	JUN-2009	508.28	85.53	20.2
SEP-1980	69.94	12.47	21.7	JUN-2003	448.37	83.83	23.0
DEC-2001	488.50	83.63	20.7	DEC-2001	488.50	83.63	20.7
JUN-1983	124.17	20.40	19.7	DEC-2004	651.57	78.63	13.7
JUN-1980	57.47	9.20	19.1	DEC-1999	504.75	77.45	18.1
DEC-1999	504.75	77.45	18.1	DEC-2003	556.91	69.23	14.2
SEP-2009	604.28	96.00	18.9	SEP-2010	676.14	66.65	10.9

167

10 <u>WORST</u> QUARTERS BY PERCENT AND POINT

	BY PERCENT CHANGE				BY POINT CHANGE		
QUARTER	CLOSE	PNT CHANGE	% CHANGE	QUARTER	CLOSE	PNT CHANGE	% CHANGE
DJIA 1901 to 1949							
JUN-1932	42.84	−30.44	−41.5	DEC-1929	248.48	−94.97	−27.7
SEP-1931	96.61	−53.57	−35.7	JUN-1930	226.34	−59.76	−20.9
DEC-1929	248.48	−94.97	−27.7	SEP-1931	96.61	−53.57	−35.7
SEP-1903	33.55	−9.73	−22.5	DEC-1930	164.58	−40.32	−19.7
DEC-1937	120.85	−33.72	−21.8	DEC-1937	120.85	−33.72	−21.8
JUN-1930	226.34	−59.76	−20.9	SEP-1946	172.42	−33.20	−16.1
DEC-1930	164.58	−40.32	−19.7	JUN-1932	42.84	−30.44	−41.5
DEC-1931	77.90	−18.71	−19.4	JUN-1940	121.87	−26.08	−17.6
MAR-1938	98.95	−21.90	−18.1	MAR-1939	131.84	−22.92	−14.8
JUN-1940	121.87	−26.08	−17.6	JUN-1931	150.18	−22.18	−12.9
DJIA 1950 to APRIL 2011							
DEC-1987	1938.83	−657.45	−25.3	DEC-2008	8776.39	−2074.27	−19.1
SEP-1974	607.87	−194.54	−24.2	SEP-2001	8847.56	−1654.84	−15.8
JUN-1962	561.28	−145.67	−20.6	SEP-2002	7591.93	−1651.33	−17.9
DEC-2008	8776.39	−2074.27	−19.1	MAR-2009	7608.92	−1167.47	−13.3
SEP-2002	7591.93	−1651.33	−17.9	JUN-2002	9243.26	−1160.68	−11.2
SEP-2001	8847.56	−1654.84	−15.8	SEP-1998	7842.62	−1109.40	−12.4
SEP-1990	2452.48	−428.21	−14.9	JUN-2010	9774.02	−1082.61	−10.0
MAR-2009	7608.92	−1167.47	−13.3	MAR-2008	12262.89	−1001.93	−7.6
SEP-1981	849.98	−126.90	−13.0	JUN-2008	11350.01	−912.88	−7.4
JUN-1970	683.53	−102.04	−13.0	MAR-2001	9878.78	−908.07	−8.4
S&P 500 1930 to APRIL 2011							
JUN-1932	4.43	−2.88	−39.4	DEC-2008	903.25	−263.11	−22.6
SEP-1931	9.71	−5.12	−34.5	SEP-2001	1040.94	−183.48	−15.0
SEP-1974	63.54	−22.46	−26.1	SEP-2002	815.28	−174.54	−17.6
DEC-1937	10.55	−3.21	−23.3	MAR-2001	1160.33	−159.95	−12.1
DEC-1987	247.08	−74.75	−23.2	JUN-2002	989.82	−157.57	−13.7
DEC-2008	903.25	−263.11	−22.6	MAR-2008	1322.70	−145.66	−9.9
JUN-1962	54.75	−14.80	−21.3	JUN-2010	1030.71	−138.72	−11.9
MAR-1938	8.50	−2.05	−19.4	SEP-1998	1017.01	−116.83	−10.3
JUN-1970	72.72	−16.91	−18.9	DEC-2000	1320.28	−116.23	−8.1
SEP-1946	14.96	−3.47	−18.8	SEP-2008	1166.36	−113.64	−8.9
NASDAQ 1971 to APRIL 2011							
DEC-2000	2470.52	−1202.30	−32.7	DEC-2000	2470.52	−1202.30	−32.7
SEP-2001	1498.80	−661.74	−30.6	SEP-2001	1498.80	−661.74	−30.6
SEP-1974	55.67	−20.29	−26.7	MAR-2001	1840.26	−630.26	−25.5
DEC-1987	330.47	−113.82	−25.6	JUN-2000	3966.11	−606.72	−13.3
MAR-2001	1840.26	−630.26	−25.5	DEC-2008	1577.03	−514.85	−24.6
SEP-1990	344.51	−117.78	−25.5	JUN-2002	1463.21	−382.14	−20.7
DEC-2008	1577.03	−514.85	−24.6	MAR-2008	2279.10	−373.18	−14.1
JUN-2002	1463.21	−382.14	−20.7	SEP-2000	3672.82	−293.29	−7.4
SEP-2002	1172.06	−291.15	−19.9	SEP-2002	1172.06	−291.15	−19.9
JUN-1974	75.96	−16.31	−17.7	JUN-2010	2109.24	−288.72	−12.0
RUSSELL 1000 1979 to APRIL 2011							
DEC-2008	487.77	−146.31	−23.1	DEC-2008	487.77	−146.31	−23.1
DEC-1987	130.02	−38.81	−23.0	SEP-2001	546.46	−100.18	−15.5
SEP-2002	433.22	−90.50	−17.3	SEP-2002	433.22	−90.50	−17.3
SEP-2001	546.46	−100.18	−15.5	MAR-2001	610.36	−89.73	−12.8
SEP-1990	157.83	−28.46	−15.3	JUN-2002	523.72	−83.63	−13.8
JUN-2002	523.72	−83.63	−13.8	MAR-2008	720.32	−79.50	−9.9
MAR-2001	610.36	−89.73	−12.8	JUN-2010	567.37	−76.42	−11.9
SEP-1981	64.06	−8.95	−12.3	DEC-2000	700.09	−72.51	−9.4
JUN-2010	567.37	−76.42	−11.9	SEP-2008	634.08	−69.14	−9.8
MAR-2009	433.67	−54.10	−11.1	SEP-1998	529.11	−63.46	−10.7
RUSSELL 2000 1979 to APRIL 2011							
DEC-1987	120.42	−50.39	−29.5	DEC-2008	499.45	−180.13	−26.5
DEC-2008	499.45	−180.13	−26.5	SEP-2001	404.87	−107.77	−21.0
SEP-1990	126.70	−42.34	−25.0	SEP-2002	362.27	−100.37	−21.7
SEP-2002	362.27	−100.37	−21.7	SEP-1998	363.59	−93.80	−20.5
SEP-2001	404.87	−107.77	−21.0	MAR-2008	687.97	−78.06	−10.2
SEP-1998	363.59	−93.80	−20.5	MAR-2009	422.75	−76.70	−15.4
SEP-1981	67.55	−15.01	−18.2	JUN-2010	609.49	−69.15	−10.2
MAR-2009	422.75	−76.70	−15.4	DEC-1987	120.42	−50.39	−29.5
MAR-1980	48.27	−7.64	−13.7	JUN-2002	462.64	−43.82	−8.7
SEP-1986	134.73	−19.50	−12.6	SEP-1990	126.70	−42.34	−25.0

10 <u>BEST</u> YEARS BY PERCENT AND POINT

	BY PERCENT CHANGE				BY POINT CHANGE		
YEAR	CLOSE	PNT CHANGE	% CHANGE	YEAR	CLOSE	PNT CHANGE	% CHANGE
			DJIA 1901 to 1949				
1915	99.15	44.57	81.7	1928	300.00	97.60	48.2
1933	99.90	39.97	66.7	1927	202.40	45.20	28.8
1928	300.00	97.60	48.2	1915	99.15	44.57	81.7
1908	63.11	20.07	46.6	1945	192.91	40.59	26.6
1904	50.99	15.01	41.7	1935	144.13	40.09	38.5
1935	144.13	40.09	38.5	1933	99.90	39.97	66.7
1905	70.47	19.48	38.2	1925	156.66	36.15	30.0
1919	107.23	25.03	30.5	1936	179.90	35.77	24.8
1925	156.66	36.15	30.0	1938	154.76	33.91	28.1
1927	202.40	45.20	28.8	1919	107.23	25.03	30.5
			DJIA 1950 to APRIL 2011				
1954	404.39	123.49	44.0	1999	11497.12	2315.69	25.2
1975	852.41	236.17	38.3	2003	10453.92	2112.29	25.3
1958	583.65	147.96	34.0	2006	12463.15	1745.65	16.3
1995	5117.12	1282.68	33.5	2009	10428.05	1651.66	18.8
1985	1546.67	335.10	27.7	1997	7908.25	1459.98	22.6
1989	2753.20	584.63	27.0	1996	6448.27	1331.15	26.0
1996	6448.27	1331.15	26.0	1995	5117.12	1282.68	33.5
2003	10453.92	2112.29	25.3	1998	9181.43	1273.18	16.1
1999	11497.12	2315.69	25.2	2010	11577.51	1149.46	11.0
1997	7908.25	1459.98	22.6	2007	13264.82	801.67	6.4
			S&P 500 1930 to APRIL 2011				
1933	10.10	3.21	46.6	1998	1229.23	258.80	26.7
1954	35.98	11.17	45.0	1999	1469.25	240.02	19.5
1935	13.43	3.93	41.4	2003	1111.92	232.10	26.4
1958	55.21	15.22	38.1	1997	970.43	229.69	31.0
1995	615.93	156.66	34.1	2009	1115.10	211.85	23.5
1975	90.19	21.63	31.5	2006	1418.30	170.01	13.6
1997	970.43	229.69	31.0	1995	615.93	156.66	34.1
1945	17.36	4.08	30.7	2010	1257.64	142.54	12.8
1936	17.18	3.75	27.9	1996	740.74	124.81	20.3
1989	353.40	75.68	27.3	2004	1211.92	100.00	9.0
			NASDAQ 1971 to APRIL 2011				
1999	4069.31	1876.62	85.6	1999	4069.31	1876.62	85.6
1991	586.34	212.50	56.8	2009	2269.15	692.12	43.9
2003	2003.37	667.86	50.0	2003	2003.37	667.86	50.0
2009	2269.15	692.12	43.9	1998	2192.69	622.34	39.6
1995	1052.13	300.17	39.9	2010	2652.87	383.72	16.9
1998	2192.69	622.34	39.6	1995	1052.13	300.17	39.9
1980	202.34	51.20	33.9	1997	1570.35	279.32	21.6
1985	324.93	77.58	31.4	1996	1291.03	238.90	22.7
1975	77.62	17.80	29.8	2007	2652.28	236.99	9.8
1979	151.14	33.16	28.1	1991	586.34	212.50	56.8
			RUSSELL 1000 1979 to APRIL 2011				
1995	328.89	84.24	34.4	1998	642.87	129.08	25.1
1997	513.79	120.04	30.5	2003	594.56	128.38	27.5
1991	220.61	49.39	28.8	1999	767.97	125.10	19.5
2003	594.56	128.38	27.5	2009	612.01	124.24	25.5
1985	114.39	24.08	26.7	1997	513.79	120.04	30.5
1989	185.11	38.12	25.9	2006	770.08	90.66	13.3
1980	75.20	15.33	25.6	2010	696.90	84.89	13.9
2009	612.01	124.24	25.5	1995	328.89	84.24	34.4
1998	642.87	129.08	25.1	1996	393.75	64.86	19.7
1996	393.75	64.86	19.7	2004	650.99	56.43	9.5
			RUSSELL 2000 1979 to APRIL 2011				
2003	556.91	173.82	45.4	2003	556.91	173.82	45.4
1991	189.94	57.78	43.7	2010	783.65	158.26	25.3
1979	55.91	15.39	38.0	2009	625.39	125.94	25.2
1980	74.80	18.89	33.8	2006	787.66	114.44	17.0
1985	129.87	28.38	28.0	2004	651.57	94.66	17.0
1983	112.27	23.37	26.3	1999	504.75	82.79	19.6
1995	315.97	65.61	26.2	1997	437.02	74.41	20.5
2010	783.65	158.26	25.3	1995	315.97	65.61	26.2
2009	625.39	125.94	25.2	1991	189.94	57.78	43.7
1988	147.37	26.95	22.4	1996	362.61	46.64	14.8

10 <u>WORST</u> YEARS BY PERCENT AND POINT

	BY PERCENT CHANGE				BY POINT CHANGE		
YEAR	CLOSE	PNT CHANGE	% CHANGE	YEAR	CLOSE	PNT CHANGE	% CHANGE
DJIA 1901 to 1949							
1931	77.90	−86.68	−52.7	1931	77.90	−86.68	−52.7
1907	43.04	−26.08	−37.7	1930	164.58	−83.90	−33.8
1930	164.58	−83.90	−33.8	1937	120.85	−59.05	−32.8
1920	71.95	−35.28	−32.9	1929	248.48	−51.52	−17.2
1937	120.85	−59.05	−32.8	1920	71.95	−35.28	−32.9
1903	35.98	−11.12	−23.6	1907	43.04	−26.08	−37.7
1932	59.93	−17.97	−23.1	1917	74.38	−20.62	−21.7
1917	74.38	−20.62	−21.7	1941	110.96	−20.17	−15.4
1910	59.60	−12.96	−17.9	1940	131.13	−19.11	−12.7
1929	248.48	−51.52	−17.2	1932	59.93	−17.97	−23.1
DJIA 1950 to APRIL 2011							
2008	8776.39	−4488.43	−33.8	2008	8776.39	−4488.43	−33.8
1974	616.24	−234.62	−27.6	2002	8341.63	−1679.87	−16.8
1966	785.69	−183.57	−18.9	2001	10021.50	−765.35	−7.1
1977	831.17	−173.48	−17.3	2000	10786.85	−710.27	−6.2
2002	8341.63	−1679.87	−16.8	1974	616.24	−234.62	−27.6
1973	850.86	−169.16	−16.6	1966	785.69	−183.57	−18.9
1969	800.36	−143.39	−15.2	1977	831.17	−173.48	−17.3
1957	435.69	−63.78	−12.8	1973	850.86	−169.16	−16.6
1962	652.10	−79.04	−10.8	1969	800.36	−143.39	−15.2
1960	615.89	−63.47	−9.3	1990	2633.66	−119.54	−4.3
S&P 500 1930 to APRIL 2011							
1931	8.12	−7.22	−47.1	2008	903.25	−565.11	−38.5
1937	10.55	−6.63	−38.6	2002	879.82	−268.26	−23.4
2008	903.25	−565.11	−38.5	2001	1148.08	−172.20	−13.0
1974	68.56	−28.99	−29.7	2000	1320.28	−148.97	−10.1
1930	15.34	−6.11	−28.5	1974	68.56	−28.99	−29.7
2002	879.82	−268.26	−23.4	1990	330.22	−23.18	−6.6
1941	8.69	−1.89	−17.9	1973	97.55	−20.50	−17.4
1973	97.55	−20.50	−17.4	1981	122.55	−13.21	−9.7
1940	10.58	−1.91	−15.3	1977	95.10	−12.36	−11.5
1932	6.89	−1.23	−15.1	1966	80.33	−12.10	−13.1
NASDAQ 1971 to APRIL 2011							
2008	1577.03	−1075.25	−40.5	2000	2470.52	−1598.79	−39.3
2000	2470.52	−1598.79	−39.3	2008	1577.03	−1075.25	−40.5
1974	59.82	−32.37	−35.1	2002	1335.51	−614.89	−31.5
2002	1335.51	−614.89	−31.5	2001	1950.40	−520.12	−21.1
1973	92.19	−41.54	−31.1	1990	373.84	−80.98	−17.8
2001	1950.40	−520.12	−21.1	1973	92.19	−41.54	−31.1
1990	373.84	−80.98	−17.8	1974	59.82	−32.37	−35.1
1984	247.35	−31.25	−11.2	1984	247.35	−31.25	−11.2
1987	330.47	−18.86	−5.4	1994	751.96	−24.84	−3.2
1981	195.84	−6.50	−3.2	1987	330.47	−18.86	−5.4
RUSSELL 1000 1979 to APRIL 2011							
2008	487.77	−312.05	−39.0	2008	487.77	−312.05	−39.0
2002	466.18	−138.76	−22.9	2002	466.18	−138.76	−22.9
2001	604.94	−95.15	−13.6	2001	604.94	−95.15	−13.6
1981	67.93	−7.27	−9.7	2000	700.09	−67.88	−8.8
2000	700.09	−67.88	−8.8	1990	171.22	−13.89	−7.5
1990	171.22	−13.89	−7.5	1981	67.93	−7.27	−9.7
1994	244.65	−6.06	−2.4	1994	244.65	−6.06	−2.4
1984	90.31	−0.07	−0.1	1984	90.31	−0.07	−0.1
1987	130.02	0.02	0.02	1987	130.02	0.02	0.02
2007	799.82	29.74	3.9	1979	59.87	8.29	16.0
RUSSELL 2000 1979 to APRIL 2011							
2008	499.45	−266.58	−34.8	2008	499.45	−266.58	−34.8
2002	383.09	−105.41	−21.6	2002	383.09	−105.41	−21.6
1990	132.16	−36.14	−21.5	1990	132.16	−36.14	−21.5
1987	120.42	−14.58	−10.8	2007	766.03	−21.63	−2.7
1984	101.49	−10.78	−9.6	2000	483.53	−21.22	−4.2
2000	483.53	−21.22	−4.2	1998	421.96	−15.06	−3.4
1998	421.96	−15.06	−3.4	1987	120.42	−14.58	−10.8
1994	250.36	−8.23	−3.2	1984	101.49	−10.78	−9.6
2007	766.03	−21.63	−2.7	1994	250.36	−8.23	−3.2
1981	73.67	−1.13	−1.5	1981	73.67	−1.13	−1.5

STRATEGY PLANNING AND RECORD SECTION

CONTENTS

These forms are available at our website www.stocktradersalmanac.com.

PORTFOLIO AT START OF 2012

DATE ACQUIRED	NO. OF SHARES	SECURITY	PRICE	TOTAL COST	PAPER PROFITS	PAPER LOSSES

ADDITIONAL PURCHASES

DATE ACQUIRED	NO. OF SHARES	SECURITY	PRICE	TOTAL COST	REASON FOR PURCHASE PRIME OBJECTIVE, ETC.

ADDITIONAL PURCHASES

DATE ACQUIRED	NO. OF SHARES	SECURITY	PRICE	TOTAL COST	REASON FOR PURCHASE PRIME OBJECTIVE, ETC.

SHORT-TERM TRANSACTIONS

Pages 175–178 can accompany next year's income tax return (Schedule D). Enter transactions as completed to avoid last-minute pressures.

NO. OF SHARES	SECURITY	DATE ACQUIRED	DATE SOLD	SALE PRICE	COST	LOSS	GAIN

TOTALS: Carry over to next page

SHORT-TERM TRANSACTIONS *(continued)*

NO. OF SHARES	SECURITY	DATE ACQUIRED	DATE SOLD	SALE PRICE	COST	LOSS	GAIN

TOTALS:

LONG-TERM TRANSACTIONS

Pages 175–178 can accompany next year's income tax return (Schedule D). Enter transactions as completed to avoid last-minute pressures.

NO. OF SHARES	SECURITY	DATE ACQUIRED	DATE SOLD	SALE PRICE	COST	LOSS	GAIN

TOTALS:
Carry over to next page

177

LONG-TERM TRANSACTIONS *(continued)*

NO. OF SHARES	SECURITY	DATE ACQUIRED	DATE SOLD	SALE PRICE	COST	LOSS	GAIN

TOTALS:

INTEREST/DIVIDENDS RECEIVED DURING 2012

SHARES	STOCK / BOND	FIRST QUARTER		SECOND QUARTER		THIRD QUARTER		FOURTH QUARTER	
		$		$		$		$	

BROKERAGE ACCOUNT DATA 2012

	MARGIN INTEREST	TRANSFER TAXES	CAPITAL ADDED	CAPITAL WITHDRAWN
JAN				
FEB				
MAR				
APR				
MAY				
JUN				
JUL				
AUG				
SEP				
OCT				
NOV				
DEC				

PORTFOLIO PRICE RECORD 2012 (FIRST HALF)

Place purchase price above stock name and weekly closes below.

STOCKS										
Week Ending	1	2	3	4	5	6	7	8	9	10
JANUARY 6										
13										
20										
27										
FEBRUARY 3										
10										
17										
24										
MARCH 2										
9										
16										
23										
30										
APRIL 6										
13										
20										
27										
MAY 4										
11										
18										
25										
JUNE 1										
8										
15										
22										
29										

PORTFOLIO PRICE RECORD 2012 (SECOND HALF)

Place purchase price above stock name and weekly closes below.

STOCKS Week Ending	1	2	3	4	5	6	7	8	9	10
JULY 6										
13										
20										
27										
AUGUST 3										
10										
17										
24										
31										
SEPTEMBER 7										
14										
21										
28										
OCTOBER 5										
12										
19										
26										
NOVEMBER 2										
9										
16										
23										
30										
DECEMBER 7										
14										
21										
28										
4										

WEEKLY INDICATOR DATA 2012 (FIRST HALF)

	Week Ending	Dow Jones Industrial Average	Net Change for Week	Net Change on Friday	Net Change Next Monday	S&P or NASDAQ	NYSE Advances	NYSE Declines	New Highs	New Lows	CBOE Put/Call Ratio	90-Day Treas. Rate	Moody's AAA Rate
JANUARY	6												
	13												
	20												
	27												
FEBRUARY	3												
	10												
	17												
	24												
MARCH	2												
	9												
	16												
	23												
	30												
APRIL	6												
	13												
	20												
	27												
MAY	4												
	11												
	18												
	25												
JUNE	1												
	8												
	15												
	22												
	29												

WEEKLY INDICATOR DATA 2012 (SECOND HALF)

Week Ending		Dow Jones Industrial Average	Net Change for Week	Net Change on Friday	Net Change Next Monday	S&P or NASDAQ	NYSE Ad-vances	NYSE De-clines	New Highs	New Lows	CBOE Put/Call Ratio	90-Day Treas. Rate	Moody's AAA Rate
JULY	6												
	13												
	20												
	27												
AUGUST	3												
	10												
	17												
	24												
	31												
SEPTEMBER	7												
	14												
	21												
	28												
OCTOBER	5												
	12												
	19												
	26												
NOVEMBER	2												
	9												
	16												
	23												
	30												
DECEMBER	7												
	14												
	21												
	28												
	4												

MONTHLY INDICATOR DATA 2012

	DJIA% Last 3 + 1st 2 Days	DJIA% 9th to 11th Trading Days	DJIA% Change Rest of Month	DJIA% Change Whole Month	% Change Your Stocks	Gross Domestic Product	Prime Rate	Trade Deficit $ Billion	CPI % Change	% Unem- ployment Rate
JAN										
FEB										
MAR										
APR										
MAY										
JUN										
JUL										
AUG										
SEP										
OCT										
NOV										
DEC										

INSTRUCTIONS:

Weekly Indicator Data (pages 182–183). Keeping data on several indicators may give you a better feel of the market. In addition to the closing DJIA and its net change for the week, post the net change for Friday's Dow and also the following Monday's. A series of "down Fridays" followed by "down Mondays" often precedes a downswing. Tracking either the S&P or NASDAQ composite, and advances and declines, will help prevent the Dow from misleading you. New highs and lows and put/call ratios (www.cboe.com) are also useful indicators. All these weekly figures appear in weekend papers or *Barron's*. Data for 90-day Treasury Rate and Moody's AAA Bond Rate are quite important for tracking short- and long-term interest rates. These figures are available from:

Weekly U.S. Financial Data
Federal Reserve Bank of St. Louis
P.O. Box 442
St. Louis MO 63166
http://research.stlouisfed.org

Monthly Indicator Data. The purpose of the first three columns is to enable you to track the market's bullish bias near the end, beginning, and middle of the month, which has been shifting lately (see pages 88, 145, and 146). Market direction, performance of your stocks, gross domestic product, prime rate, trade deficit, Consumer Price Index, and unemployment rate are worthwhile indicators to follow. Or, readers may wish to gauge other data.

PORTFOLIO AT END OF 2012

DATE ACQUIRED	NO. OF SHARES	SECURITY	PRICE	TOTAL COST	PAPER PROFITS	PAPER LOSSES

IF YOU DON'T PROFIT FROM YOUR INVESTMENT MISTAKES, SOMEONE ELSE WILL

No matter how much we may deny it, almost every successful person in Wall Street pays a great deal of attention to trading suggestions—especially when they come from "the right sources."

One of the hardest things to learn is to distinguish between good tips and bad ones. Usually, the best tips have a logical reason in back of them, which accompanies the tip. Poor tips usually have no reason to support them.

The important thing to remember is that the market discounts. It does not review, it does not reflect. The Street's real interest in "tips," inside information, buying and selling suggestions, and everything else of this kind emanates from a desire to find out just what the market has on hand to discount. The process of finding out involves separating the wheat from the chaff—and there is plenty of chaff.

HOW TO MAKE USE OF STOCK "TIPS"

- The source should be **reliable**. (By listing all "tips" and suggestions on a Performance Record of Recommendations, such as the form below, and then periodically evaluating the outcomes, you will soon know the "batting average" of your sources.)

- The story should make sense. Would the merger violate antitrust laws? Are there too many computers on the market already? How many years will it take to become profitable?

- The stock should not have had a recent sharp run-up. Otherwise, the story may already be discounted, and confirmation or denial in the press would most likely be accompanied by a sell-off in the stock.

PERFORMANCE RECORD OF RECOMMENDATIONS

STOCK RECOMMENDED	BY WHOM	DATE	PRICE	REASON FOR RECOMMENDATION	SUBSEQUENT ACTION OF STOCK

INDIVIDUAL RETIREMENT ACCOUNTS: MOST AWESOME INVESTMENT INCENTIVE EVER DEVISED

MAX IRA INVESTMENTS OF $5,000* A YEAR COMPOUNDED AT VARIOUS INTEREST RATES OF RETURN FOR DIFFERENT PERIODS

Annual Rate	5 Yrs	10 Yrs	15 Yrs	20 Yrs	25 Yrs	30 Yrs	35 Yrs	40 Yrs	45 Yrs	50 Yrs
1%	$25,760	$52,834	$81,289	$111,196	$142,628	$175,664	$210,384	$246,876	$285,229	$325,539
2%	26,541	55,844	88,196	123,917	163,355	206,897	254,972	308,050	366,653	431,355
3%	27,342	59,039	95,784	138,382	187,765	245,013	311,380	388,316	477,507	580,904
4%	28,165	62,432	104,123	154,846	216,559	291,642	382,992	494,133	629,353	793,869
5%	29,010	66,034	113,287	173,596	250,567	348,804	474,182	634,199	838,426	1,099,077
6%	29,877	69,858	123,363	194,964	290,782	419,008	590,604	820,238	1,127,541	1,538,780
7%	30,766	73,918	134,440	219,326	338,382	505,365	739,567	1,068,048	1,528,759	2,174,930
8%	31,680	78,227	146,621	247,115	394,772	611,729	930,511	1,398,905	2,087,130	3,098,359
9%	32,617	82,801	160,017	278,823	461,620	742,876	1,175,624	1,841,459	2,865,930	4,442,205
10%	33,578	87,656	174,749	315,012	540,909	904,717	1,490,634	2,434,259	3,953,977	6,401,497
11%	34,564	92,807	190,950	356,326	634,994	1,104,566	1,895,822	3,229,135	5,475,844	9,261,680
12%	35,576	98,273	208,766	403,494	746,670	1,351,463	2,417,316	4,295,712	7,606,088	13,440,102
13%	36,614	104,072	228,359	457,350	879,250	1,656,576	3,088,747	5,727,429	10,589,030	19,546,215
14%	37,678	110,223	249,902	518,842	1,036,664	2,033,685	3,953,364	7,649,543	14,766,219	28,468,772
15%	38,769	116,746	273,587	589,051	1,223,560	2,499,785	5,066,728	10,229,769	20,614,489	41,501,869
16%	39,887	123,665	299,625	669,203	1,445,441	3,075,808	6,500,135	13,692,392	28,798,589	60,526,763
17%	41,034	131,000	328,244	760,693	1,708,813	3,787,519	8,344,972	18,336,953	40,243,850	88,273,585
18%	42,210	138,776	359,695	865,105	2,021,361	4,666,593	10,718,245	24,562,957	56,236,305	128,697,253
19%	43,415	147,018	394,251	984,237	2,392,153	5,751,937	13,769,572	32,902,482	78,560,374	187,516,251
20%	44,650	155,752	432,211	1,120,128	2,831,886	7,091,289	17,690,047	44,063,147	109,687,860	272,983,145

* At press time, 2012 Contribution Limit will be indexed to inflation.

By Average Daily Volume. See pages 92, 94, and 96, Almanac Investor, and stocktradersalmanac.com for more.

Symbol	Name	Symbol	Name
SPY	SPDR S&P 500	IYF	iShares DJ US Financial
XLF	SPDR Financial	IYM	iShares DJ US Basic Materials
FAS	Direxion Financial Bull 3x	TYH	Direxion Technology Bull 3x
QQQ	PowerShares QQQ	JNK	SPDR Barclays High Yield Bond
EEM	iShares Emerging Market Income	RTH	Retail HOLDRs
IWM	iShares Russell 2000	IWN	iShares Russell 2000 Value
SDS	ProShares UltraShort S&P 500	IWD	iShares Russell 1000 Value
FXI	iShares FTSE/Xinhua China 25	EDZ	Direxion Emerging Markets Bear 3x
EWJ	iShares Japan	VTI	Vanguard Total Market
XLE	SPDR Energy	TWM	ProShares UltraShort R2K
EWZ	iShares Brazil	TZA	Direxion Small Cap Bear 3x
EFA	iShares EAFE	IWB	iShares Russell 1000
SSO	ProShares Ultra S&P 500	GDXJ	Market Vectors Jr Gold Miners
GLD	SPDR Gold	DBA	PowerShares DB Agriculture
IYR	iShares DJ US Real Estate	EWM	iShares Malaysia
SMH	Semiconductor HOLDRs	IJR	iShares S&P Small Cap 600
FAZ	Direxion Financial Bear 3x	EPP	iShares Pacific Ex-Japan
XLB	SPDR Materials	FXP	ProShares UltraShort FTSE/Xinhua China 25
EWT	iShares Taiwan	EWU	iShares United Kingdom
GDX	Market Vectors Gold Miners	EWG	iShares Germany
UNG	United States Natural Gas	BGZ	Direxion Large Cap Bear 3x
XRT	SPDR Retail	VEA	Vanguard Europe Pacific
VWO	Vanguard Emerging Markets	IWS	iShares Russell Mid Cap Val
XLI	SPDR Industrial	DUG	ProShares UltraShort Oil&Gas
USO	United States Oil Fund	UCO	ProShares Ultra DJ-AIG Crude Oil
SLV	iShares Silver Trust	ICF	iShares Cohen & Steers Realty
XLK	SPDR Tech	TIP	iShares Barclays TIPS Bond
DIA	SPDR DJIA	EPI	WisdomTree India Earnings Fund
TNA	Direxion Small Cap Bull 3x	VEU	Vanguard FTSE All-World ex-US
TBT	ProShares UltraShort Barclays 20+ Yr	IJH	iShares S&P Mid Cap 400
QLD	ProShares Ultra QQQ	SMN	ProShares UltraShort Materials
XLV	SPDR Healthcare	PFF	iShares S&P US Preferred
XLY	SPDR Consumer Discretionary	HYG	iShares iBoxx $ HY Corp Bond
XME	SPDR Metals & Mining	SHY	iShares Barclays 1-3Yr Trsry Bnd
XHB	SPDR Homebuilders	RSP	Rydex S&P Equal Weight
EWH	iShares Hong Kong	LQD	iShares GS Corporate Bond
OIH	Oil Service HOLDRs	IVW	iShares S&P 500 BARRA Growth
XLU	SPDR Utilities	IYT	iShares DJ Transports
XLP	SPDR Consumer Staples	IWR	iShares Russell Mid Cap
KBE	KBW Bank	KIE	KBW Insurance
DXD	ProShares UltraShort Dow 30	FCG	First Trust ISE-Revere Natural Gas
SPXU	ProShares UltraPro Short S&P 500	VGK	Vanguard European
UUP	PowerShares DB US Dollar-Bull	EUO	ProShares UltraShort Euro
EWA	iShares Australia	EEV	ProShares UltraShort MSCI Emrgng Mrkts
UYM	ProShares Ultra Materials	FXE	CurrencyShares Euro
BGU	Direxion Large Cap Bull 3x	PGF	PowerShares Fin Preferred
XOP	SPDR Oil & Gas Explore & Prod	RKH	Regional Bank HOLDRs
EDC	Direxion Emerging Markets Bull 3x	AGG	iShares Barclays Aggregate Bond
SRS	ProShares UltraShort Rl Estate	IBB	iShares NASDAQ Biotech
UPRO	ProShares UltraPro S&P 500	IWP	iShares Russell Mid Cap Gr
TLT	iShares Barclays 20+yr Bond	MOO	Market Vectors Agribusiness
KRE	KBW Regional Bank	DRV	Direxion Daily Real Estate Bear 3X
IVV	iShares S&P 100	OEF	iShares S&P 100
DIG	ProShares Ultra Oil & Gas	VB	Vanguard Small Cap
EWY	iShares South Korea	IWV	iShares Russell 3000
ERX	Direxion Energy Bull 3x	BND	Vanguard Total Bond Market
EWC	iShares Canada	ITB	iShares DJ US Home Const
QID	ProShares UltraShort QQQ	SHV	iShares Barclays Shrt-Term Trsry
RSX	Market Vectors Russia Trust	SCO	ProShares UltraShort DJ-UBS Crude Oil
EWW	iShares Mexico	BSV	Vanguard Short-Term Bond
SKF	ProShares UltraShort Financial	ERY	Direxion Energy Bear 3x
MDY	S&P Mid Cap 400 SPDR	AGQ	ProShares Ultra Silver
EWS	iShares Singapore	PHYS	Sprott Physical Gold
URE	ProShares Ultra Real Estate	PBW	PowerShares Wilder Hill Energy
VNQ	Vanguard REIT	PGX	PowerShares Preferred
IWF	iShares Russell 1000 Growth	IYZ	iShares DJ US Telecom
UWM	ProShares Ultra Russell 2000	CYB	WisdomTree Dreyfus Chinese Yuan
ILF	iShares S&P Latin America 40	CSJ	iShares Barclays 1-3Yr Crdt Bond
DRN	Direxion Daily Real Estate Bull 3X	VIG	Vanguard Dividend Appreciation
UYG	ProShares Ultra Financials	KOL	Market Vectors Coal
DDM	ProShares Ultra Dow 30	IEO	iShares DJ US Oil&Gas Exp&Prod
IWO	iShares Russell 2000 Growth	BIL	SPDR Barclays 1-3 Month T-Bill
IAU	iShares Comex Gold	TAN	Guggenheim Global Solar
DBC	PowerShares DB Commodity	RWR	SPDR DJ REIT
SH	ProShares Short S&P 500	IVE	iShares S&P 500/BARRA Value

TOP 300 EXCHANGE TRADED FUNDS (As of 4/29/2011)

By Average Daily Volume. See pages 92, 94, and 96, Almanac Investor, and stocktradersalmanac.com for more.

Ticker	Name	Ticker	Name
SHM	SPDR Barclays Short Term Muni Bond	SCHF	Schwab International Equity
DBB	PowerShares DB Base Metals	EFV	iShares MSCI EAFE Value
BRF	Market Vectors Brazil Small-Cap	IJT	iShares S&P Sm Cp 600/BARRA Gr
SLX	Market Vectors Steel	GUR	SPDR S&P Emerging Europe
IJS	iShares S&P Sm Cp 600/BARRA Va	FXZ	First Trust Materials
PPH	Pharmaceutical HOLDRs	QTEC	First Trust NASDAQ-100-Tech
IGE	iShares Natural Resources	PZA	PowerShares Insrd Ntnl Muni Bond
VUG	Vanguard Growth	VT	Vanguard Total World
DVY	iShares DJ Select Dvnd Index	FXO	First Trust Financials
IEF	iShares Barclays 7-10 Year	PSP	PowerShares Listed Private Eq
SDY	SPDR Dividend	CVY	Guggenheim Multi-Asset Income
PVI	PowerShares VRDO Tax-Free	ECH	iShares MSCI Chile
IYW	iShares DJ US Tech	FXD	First Trust Consumer Discr
IEV	iShares S&P Europe 350	DGS	WisdomTree Emrgng Mrkts Sm Cp Dvdnd
IDX	Market Vectors Indonesia	VPL	Vanguard MSCI Pacific
GSG	iShares GSCI Commodity	FXY	CurrencyShares Japanese Yen
RWM	ProShares Short Russell 2000	PIO	PowerShares Global Water
EWQ	iShares France	VBR	Vanguard Small Cap Val
EEB	Guggenheim BRIC	VO	Vanguard Mid Cap
PIN	PowerShares India	EWO	iShares Austria
USD	ProShares Ultra Semiconductors	VDE	Vanguard Energy
DOG	ProShares Short Dow 30	GWX	SPDR S&P International SmCp
VTV	Vanguard Value	MVV	ProShares Ultra Mid Cap 400
PCY	PowerShares Emrgng Mrkts Svrgn Debt	FBT	First Trust Amex Biotech
EZU	iShares EMU	BIK	SPDR S&P BRIC 40
IJK	iShares S&P Md Cp 400/BARRA Gr	IXC	iShares S&P Global Energy
ACWI	iShares MSCI ACWI	ACWX	iShares MSCI ACWI ex US
HAO	Guggenheim China Sm Cp	VBK	Vanguard Small Cap Growth
EZA	iShares S Africa Index	EWX	SPDR S&P Emerging Markets Sm Cp
EWK	iShares Belgium	CUT	Guggenheim Global Timber
AAXJ	iShares MSCI Asia ex Japan	EWN	iShares Netherlands
PHO	PowerShares Water Resource	SIVR	ETFS Silver
YCS	ProShares UltraShort Yen	PGJ	PowerShares Golden Dragon
IAI	iShares DJ US Broker-Dealers	EWI	iShares Italy
IYG	iShares DJ US Financial Serv	DBV	PowerShares DB G10 Currency
THD	iShares MSCI Thailand Investable	STPZ	PIMCO 1-5 Year US TIPS
XBI	SPDR Biotech	WIP	SPDR DB Int Govt Inflation-Protected
MWJ	Direxion Mid Cap Bull 3X	VAW	Vanguard Materials
BKF	iShares MSCI BRIC	RPV	Rydex S&P 500 Va
IYE	iShares DJ US Energy	EFG	iShares MSCI EAFE Growth
TUR	iShares MSCI Turkey Investable	FDN	First Trust DJ Internet
URTY	ProShares UltraPro Russell 2000	MXI	iShares S&P Global Materials
BWX	SPDR Barclays Intl Treasury Bond	PEY	PowerShares High Yield
SCZ	iShares MSCI EAFE Small Cap	TMV	Direxion 30-Yr Treasury Bear 3X
PSQ	ProShares Short QQQ	ADRE	BLDRS Emerging Market 50
EWP	iShares Spain	PST	ProShares UltraShort Barclays 7-10 Yr
IWC	iShares Russell Microcap	EUM	ProShares Short MSCI Emrgng Mrkts
CEW	WisdomTree Dreyfus Emerging Currency	BIV	Vanguard Intermed-Term Bond
DBO	PowerShares DB Oil	DEM	WisdomTree Emerging Markets HY
XES	SPDR Oil & Gas Equip & Service	SCHE	Schwab Emerging Markets
IJJ	iShares S&P Md Cp 400/BARRA Va	RZV	Rydex S&P Smallcap 600 Va
TFI	SPDR Barclays Municipal Bond	IGN	iShares Multimedia Networking
IEZ	iShares DJ US Oil Equip & Serv	KCE	KBW Capital Mkts
EWD	iShares Sweden	GLL	ProShares UltraShort Gold
UDN	PowerShares DB US Dollar-Bear	PHB	PowerShares Hgh Yld Corp Bond
TBF	ProShares Short 20+ Year Treasury	VOE	Vanguard Mid-Cap Value
SCHX	Schwab U.S. Large-Cap	VNM	Market Vectors Vietnam
FXC	CurrencyShares Canadian Dollar	DBP	PowerShares DB Precious Metals
SCHA	Schwab U.S. Small-Cap	BZQ	ProShares UltraShort MSCI Brazil
PALL	ETFS Physical Palladium	MBB	iShares Barclays MBS Fixed-Rate
UGL	ProShares Ultra Gold	PIE	PowerShares DWA EM Tchncl Ldrs
RWX	SPDR DJ Wilshire Int Real Estate	IYH	iShares DJ US Healthcare
XSD	SPDR Semiconductors	PWV	PowerShares Dynamic Lg Cap Val
EWL	iShares Switzerland	IWX	iShares Russell Top 200 Val
SCHB	Schwab U.S. Broad Market	ROM	ProShares Ultra Technology
VV	Vanguard Large Cap	RSW	Rydex Inverse 2x S&P 500
PXH	PowerShares FTSE RAFI Emrgng Mrkt	VYM	Vanguard High Dividend Yield
PID	PowerShares Int' Dvnd	IOO	iShares S&P Global 100
EMB	iShares JPMorgan USD EM Bond	IGF	iShares S&P Global Infrastructure
IAT	iShares DJ US Regional Banks	EPU	iShares MSCI All Peru Capped
CIU	iShares Barclays Intrm Crdt Bond	PBS	PowerShares Dyn Media
VFH	Vanguard Financial	IWY	iShares Russell Top 200 Gr
VGT	Vanguard IT	GMF	SPDR S&P Emerging Asia Pacific
TYP	Direxion Technology Bear 3x	SRTY	ProShares UltraPro Short Russell 2000
FXA	CurrencyShares Aussie Dollar	IHF	iShares DJ US Healthcare Prov

OPTION TRADING CODES

Expanding equity, exchange traded fund (ETF), and derivative markets have mushroomed in recent years, creating problems for single letter strike price and expiration codes, underlying option symbols, and the entire option contract coding system. With the proliferation of Long-term Equity AnticiPation Securities (LEAPS®), flexible (FLEX) options contracts, and other non-standard options, the old three- to five-letter option coding convention has been rendered obsolete. Letters will no longer be used to indicate strike (exercise) prices and expiration dates.

To ensure we covered all the essential information as we distilled these sweeping changes onto one page, we consulted with two of our most trusted colleagues in this arena: options guru, Larry McMillan at *www.optionstrategist.com* and professional trader, John Person, our *Commodity Trader's Almanac* coauthor, at *www.nationalfutures.com*.

On May 14, 2010, the total overhaul of option trading codes was completed. This process began in July 2005 when the Options Clearing Corporation (OCC) put together an industry consortium to address the inherent and growing problem with option trading codes. Over the next several years, the Symbology Committee of broker dealers, exchanges, vendors, and the OCC developed the Options Symbology Initiative (OSI).

Options Symbology Initiative (OSI)

OSI was a comprehensive, industry-wide conversion to the new method of identifying exchange-listed options. New option trading codes are more transparent, easy to understand, and can accommodate newer types of options. New option root symbols match underlying security symbols; eliminate the need for wrap, LEAP, and the plethora of other symbols created by the 5-letter code limitations; and reduce corporate action symbol conversions and back-office errors. For the most part, each security will have one root symbol instead of the myriad of root symbols the old system created. Thousands of symbols have been freed up, and all symbols have become much more intuitive.

The new coding method is robust though long, up to 21 characters: six characters for option symbols; two each for expiration year, month, and day; one for call or put ("C" or "P"), five characters for strike dollar amount, and 3 characters for strike decimal amount. Fractions have also been eliminated, and all options have been converted to 3 decimals. For example, the old symbol for the Microsoft May 2012 25 Call was MSQEE. It is now MSFT120518C00025000.

OLD OPTION CODES

Option Root Symbol	Expiration Date Code	Strike Price Code
XXX	X	X
3 Characters	1 Characters	1 Characters

NEW OPTION CODES

Symbol	Year	Month	Day	Call/Put (C/P)	Strike Dollar	Strike Decimal
XXXXXX	XX	XX	XX	X	XXXXX	XXX
6 Characters	2 Characters	2 Characters	2 Characters	1 Characters	5 Characters	3 Characters

In some instances, the option trading code could be as long as 24 characters. FLEX option symbols begin with a numeric value. Adjusted symbols will be appended with a numeric value as the last character of the symbol. But a few exceptions will remain. Non-standard symbols that do not equal the primary underlying security will consolidate to a unique root symbol. We need to be familiar with this new symbology that the OCC, Chicago Board Options Exchange (CBOE), and other exchanges use. But many data vendors, brokerage firms, and other data providers have made minor adjustments, creating their own version. However, in addition to the symbol, the full name of the option is usually displayed: MSFT May 2012 25.000 call (MSFT120518C00025000).

Details of the "old way" can be found on page 190 of the *2010 Stock Trader's Almanac*.

Sources: Larry McMillan, John Person, cboe.com, and theocc.com

G. M. LOEB'S "BATTLE PLAN" FOR INVESTMENT SURVIVAL

LIFE IS CHANGE: Nothing can ever be the same a minute from now as it was a minute ago. Everything you own is changing in price and value. You can find that last price of an active security on the stock ticker, but you cannot find the next price anywhere. The value of your money is changing. Even the value of your home is changing, though no one walks in front of it with a sandwich board consistently posting the changes.

RECOGNIZE CHANGE: Your basic objective should be to profit from change. The art of investing is being able to recognize change and to adjust investment goals accordingly.

WRITE THINGS DOWN: You will score more investment success and avoid more investment failures if you write things down. Very few investors have the drive and inclination to do this.

KEEP A CHECKLIST: If you aim to improve your investment results, get into the habit of keeping a checklist on every issue you consider buying. Before making a commitment, it will pay you to write down the answers to at least some of the basic questions—How much am I investing in this company? How much do I think I can make? How much do I have to risk? How long do I expect to take to reach my goal?

HAVE A SINGLE RULING REASON: Above all, writing things down is the best way to find "the ruling reason." When all is said and done, there is invariably a single reason that stands out above all others, why a particular security transaction can be expected to show a profit. All too often, many relatively unimportant statistics are allowed to obscure this single important point.

Any one of a dozen factors may be the point of a particular purchase or sale. It could be a technical reason—an increase in earnings or dividend not yet discounted in the market price—a change of management—a promising new product—an expected improvement in the market's valuation of earnings—or many others. But, in any given case, one of these factors will almost certainly be more important than all the rest put together.

CLOSING OUT A COMMITMENT: If you have a loss, the solution is automatic, provided you decide what to do at the time you buy. Otherwise, the question divides itself into two parts. Are we in a bull or bear market? Few of us really know until it is too late. For the sake of the record, if you think it is a bear market, just put that consideration first and sell as much as your conviction suggests and your nature allows.

If you think it is a bull market, or at least a market where some stocks move up, some mark time, and only a few decline, do not sell unless:

✓ You see a bear market ahead.

✓ You see trouble for a particular company in which you own shares.

✓ Time and circumstances have turned up a new and seemingly far better buy than the issue you like least in your list.

✓ Your shares stop going up and start going down.

A subsidiary question is, which stock to sell first? Two further observations may help:

✓ Do not sell solely because you think a stock is "overvalued."

✓ If you want to sell some of your stocks and not all, in most cases it is better to go against your emotional inclinations and sell first the issues with losses, small profits, or none at all, the weakest, the most disappointing, etc.

Mr. Loeb is the author of *The Battle for Investment Survival*, John Wiley & Sons.

G. M. LOEB'S INVESTMENT SURVIVAL CHECKLIST

OBJECTIVES AND RISKS

Security		Price	Shares	Date

"Ruling reason" for commitment	Amount of commitment
	$ _____
	% of my investment capital
	_____ %

Price objective	Est. time to achieve it	I will risk _____ points	Which would be $ _____

TECHNICAL POSITION

Price action of stock:		Dow Jones Industrial Average
❏ Hitting new highs	❏ In a trading range	
❏ Pausing in an uptrend	❏ Moving up from low ground	Trend of market
❏ Acting stronger than market	❏ _____	

SELECTED YARDSTICKS

	Price Range		Earnings Per Share Actual or Projected	Price/Earnings Ratio Actual or Projected
	High	Low		
Current year				
Previous year				
Merger possibilities			Years for earnings to double in past	
Comment on future			Years for market price to double in past	

PERIODIC RE-CHECKS

Date	Stock Price	DJIA	Comment	Action taken, if any

COMPLETED TRANSACTIONS

Date closed	Period of time held	Profit or loss

Reason for profit or loss